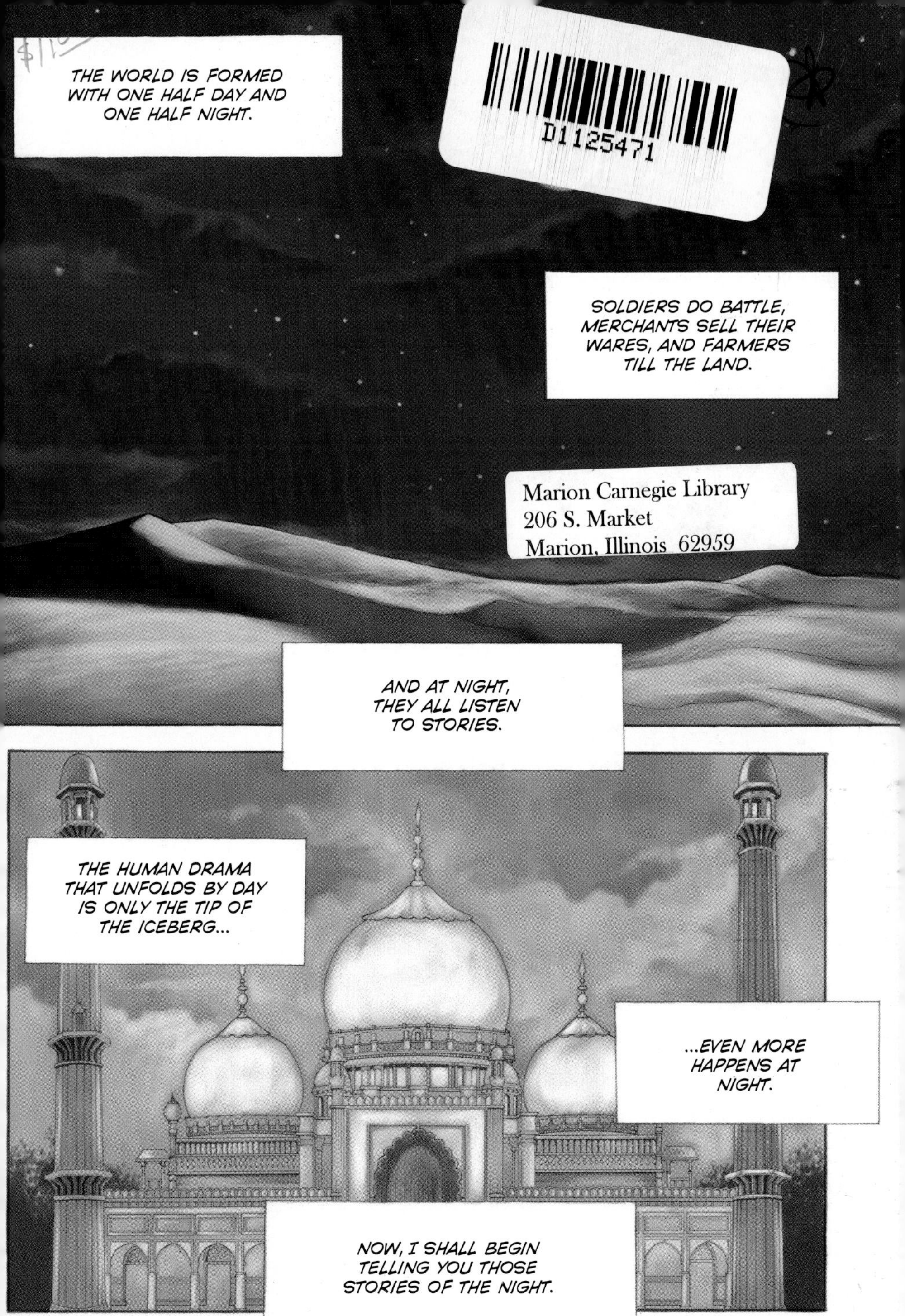
THE WORLD IS FORMED WITH ONE HALF DAY AND ONE HALF NIGHT.
SOLDIERS DO BATTLE, MERCHANTS SELL THEIR WARES, AND FARMERS TILL THE LAND.
AND AT NIGHT, THEY ALL LISTEN TO STORIES.
THE HUMAN DRAMA THAT UNFOLDS BY DAY IS ONLY THE TIP OF THE ICEBERG...
...EVEN MORE HAPPENS AT NIGHT.
NOW, I SHALL BEGIN TELLING YOU THOSE STORIES OF THE NIGHT.

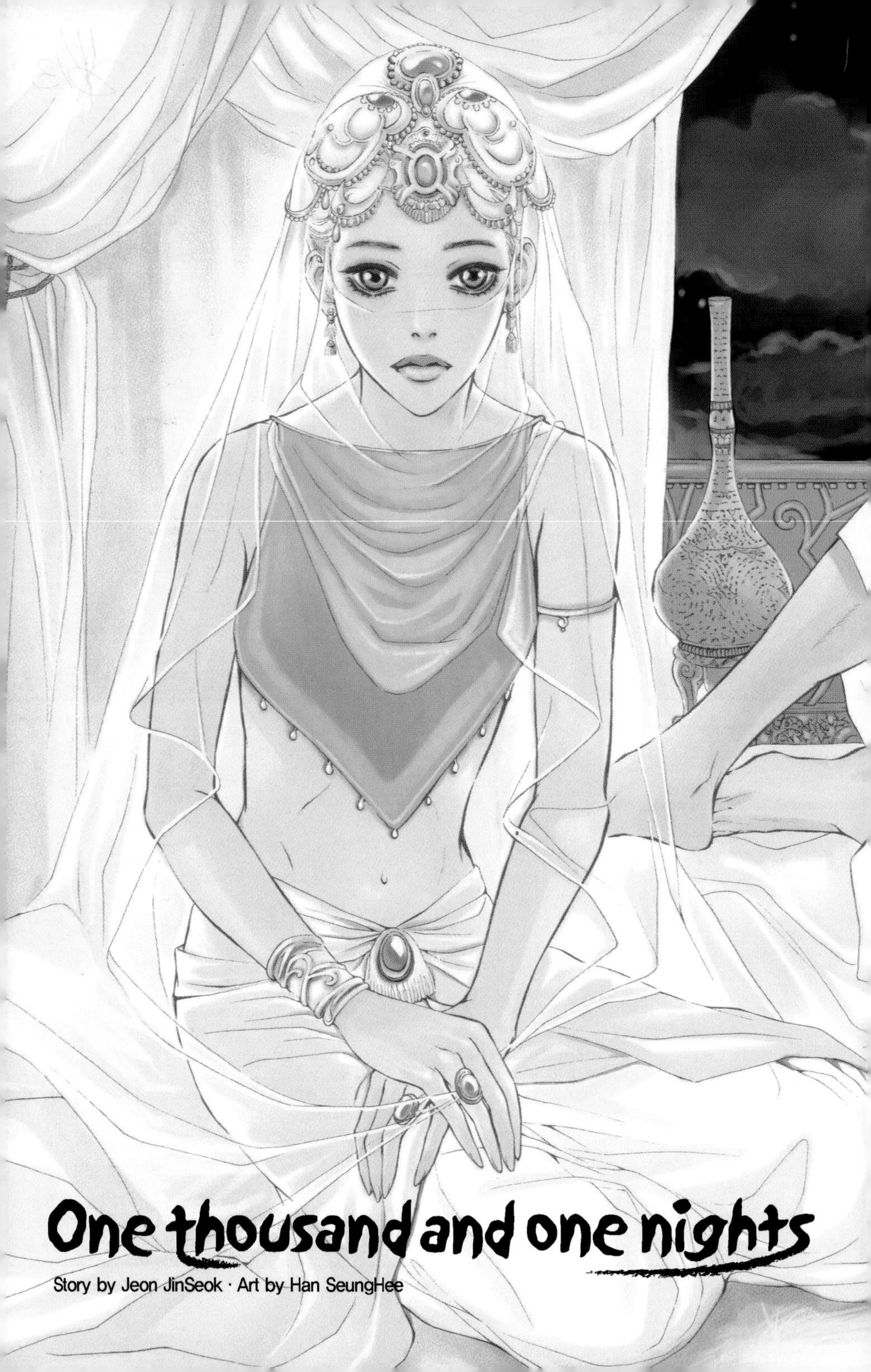
One thousand and one nights
Story by Jeon JinSeok · Art by Han SeungHee

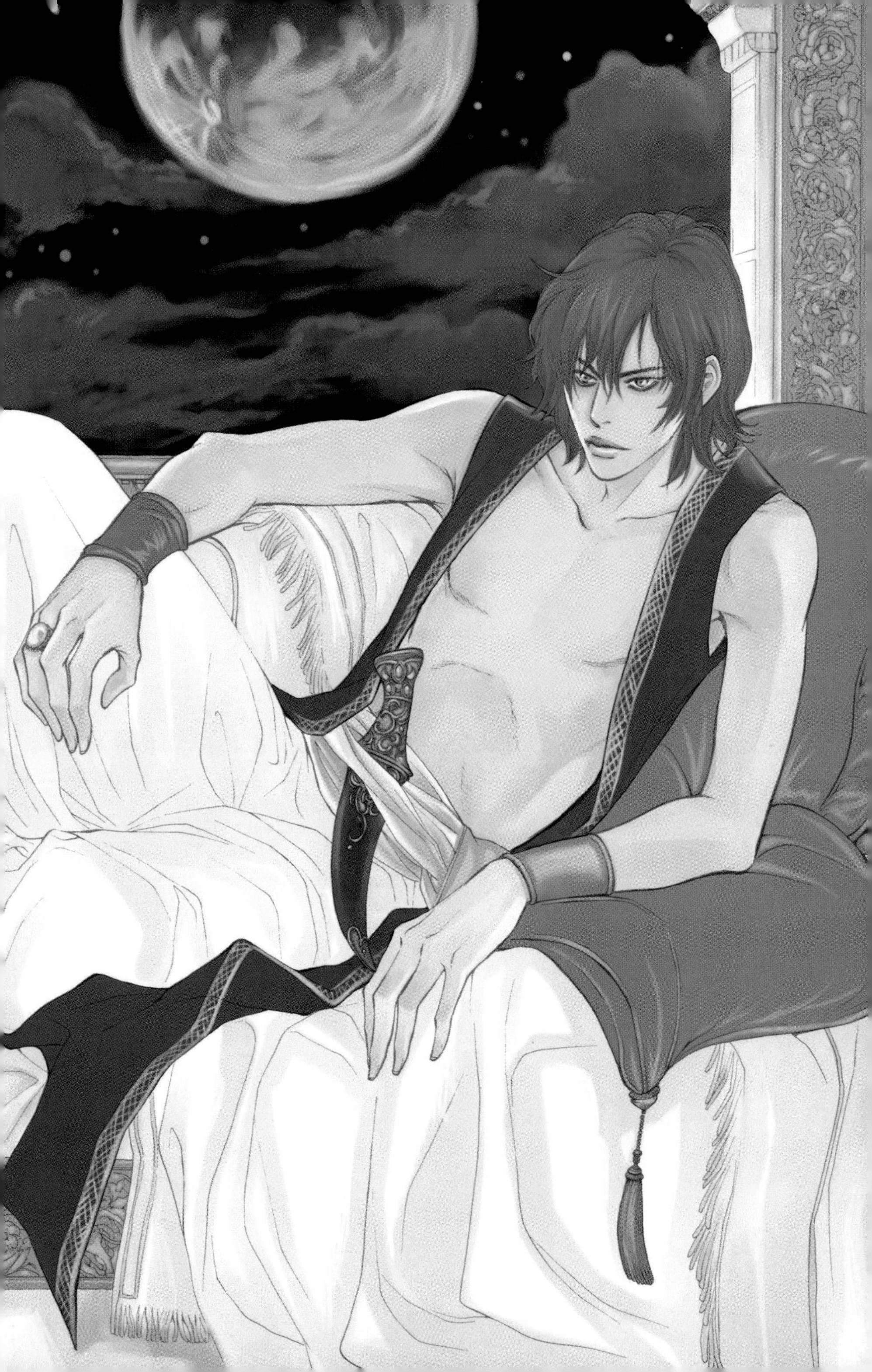

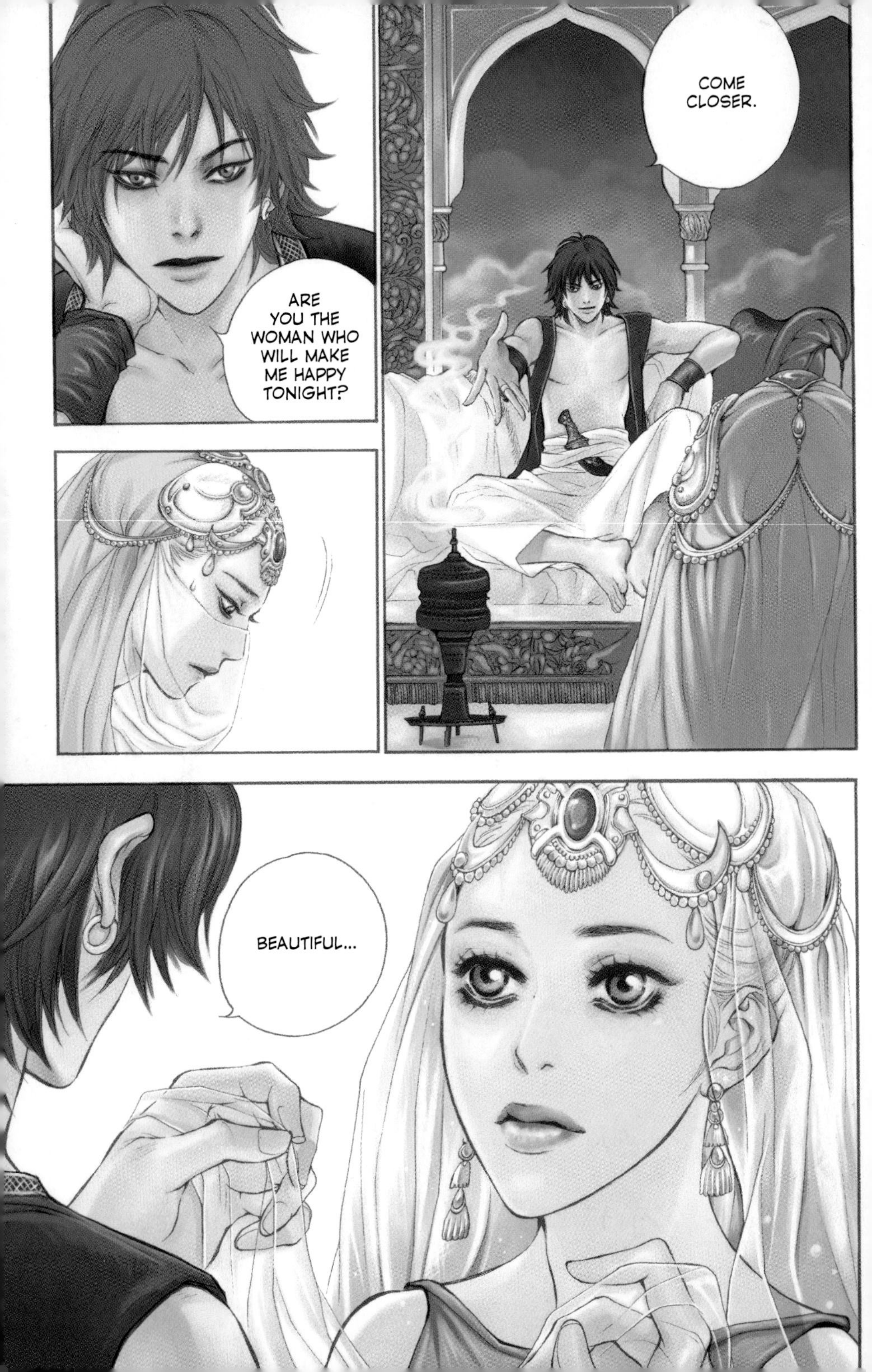
ARE YOU THE WOMAN WHO WILL MAKE ME HAPPY TONIGHT?
COME CLOSER.
BEAUTIFUL...

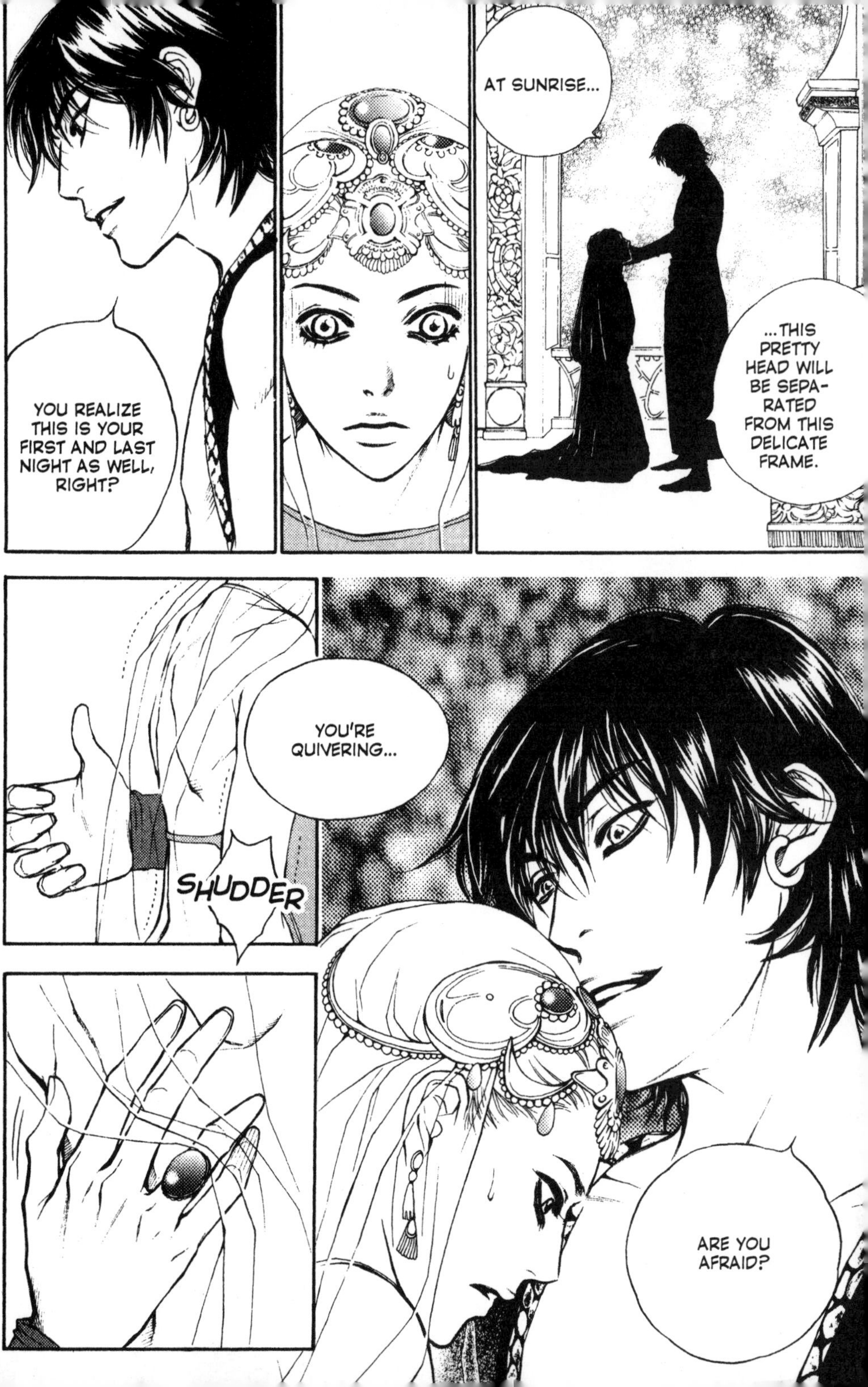
YOU REALIZE THIS IS YOUR FIRST AND LAST NIGHT AS WELL, RIGHT?
AT SUNRISE...
...THIS PRETTY HEAD WILL BE SEPA-RATED FROM THIS DELICATE FRAME.
YOU'RE QUIVERING...
SHUDDER
ARE YOU AFRAID?

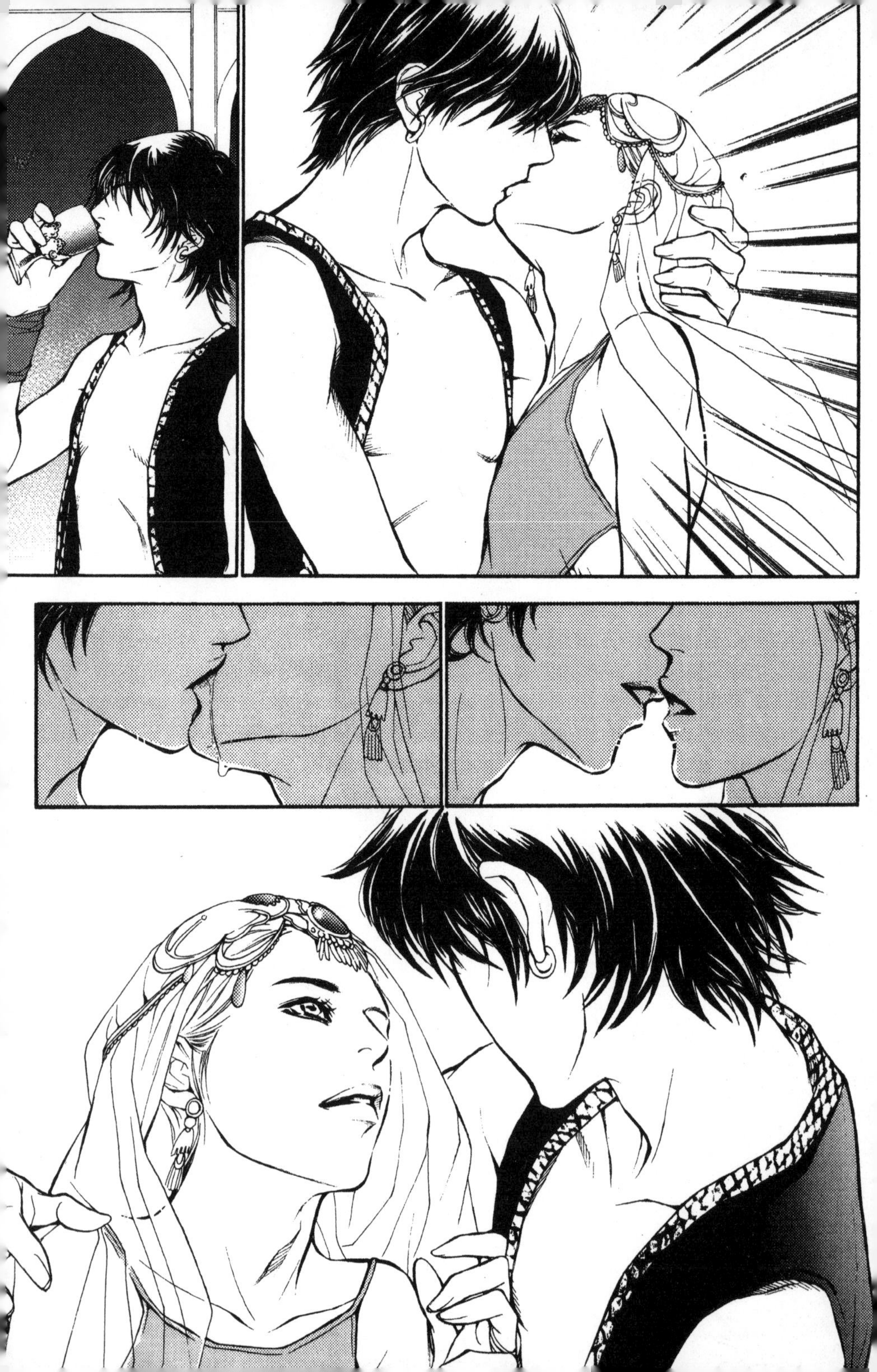

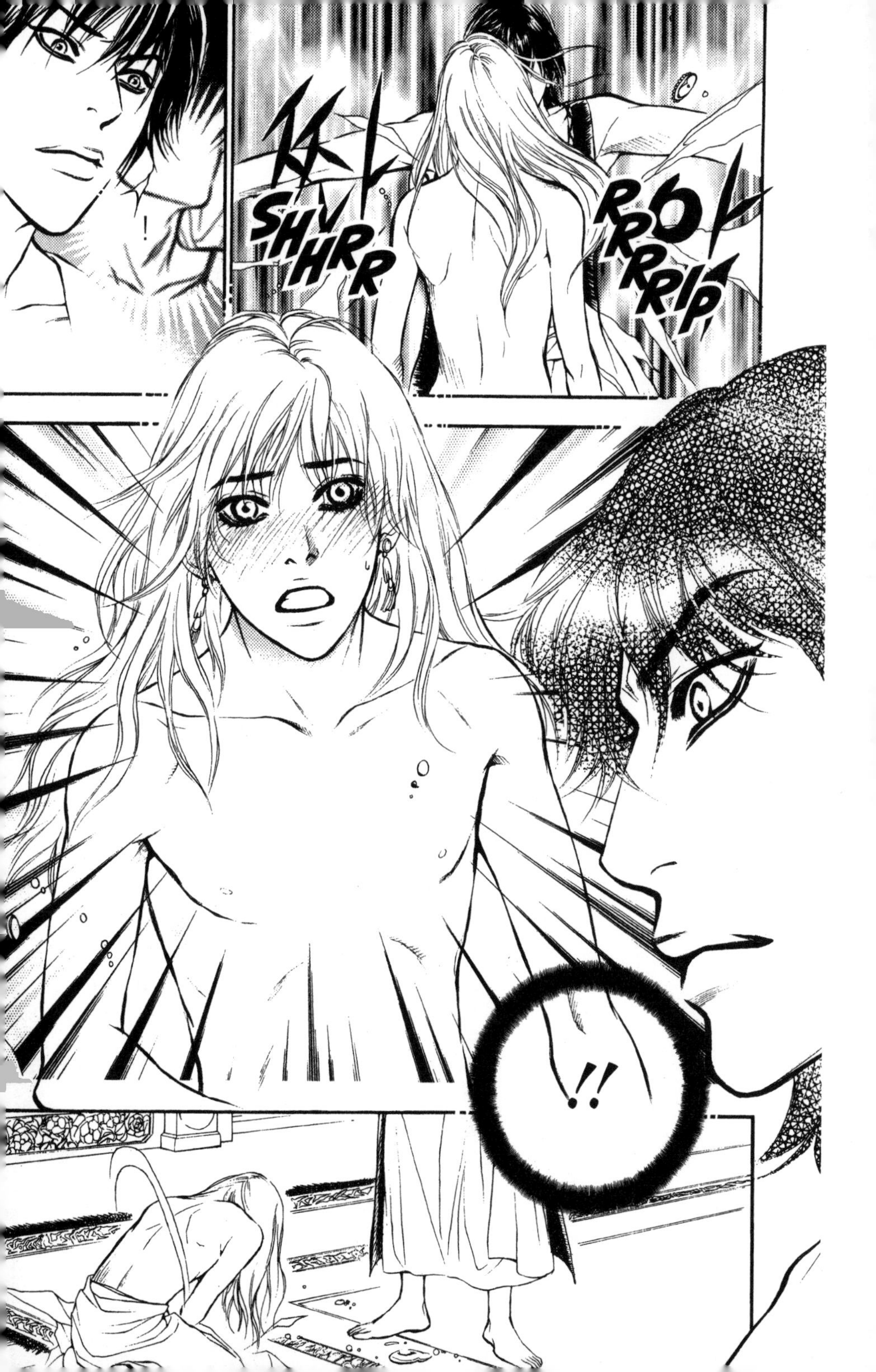
!
SHHRR
RRRRIP
!!

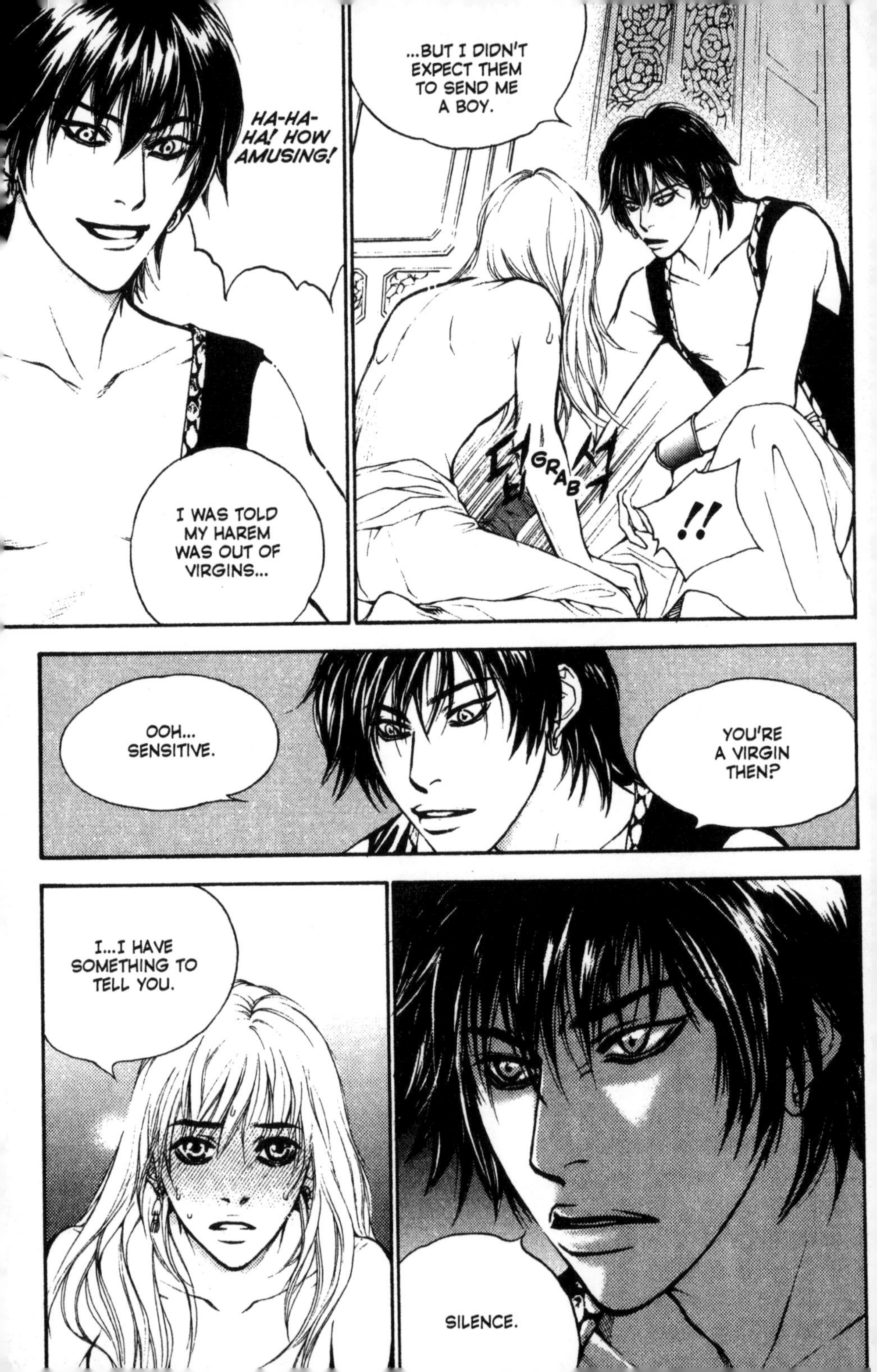
HA-HA-HA! HOW AMUSING!
I WAS TOLD MY HAREM WAS OUT OF VIRGINS...
...BUT I DIDN'T EXPECT THEM TO SEND ME A BOY.
GRAB
!!
OOH... SENSITIVE.
YOU'RE A VIRGIN THEN?
I...I HAVE SOMETHING TO TELL YOU.
SILENCE.

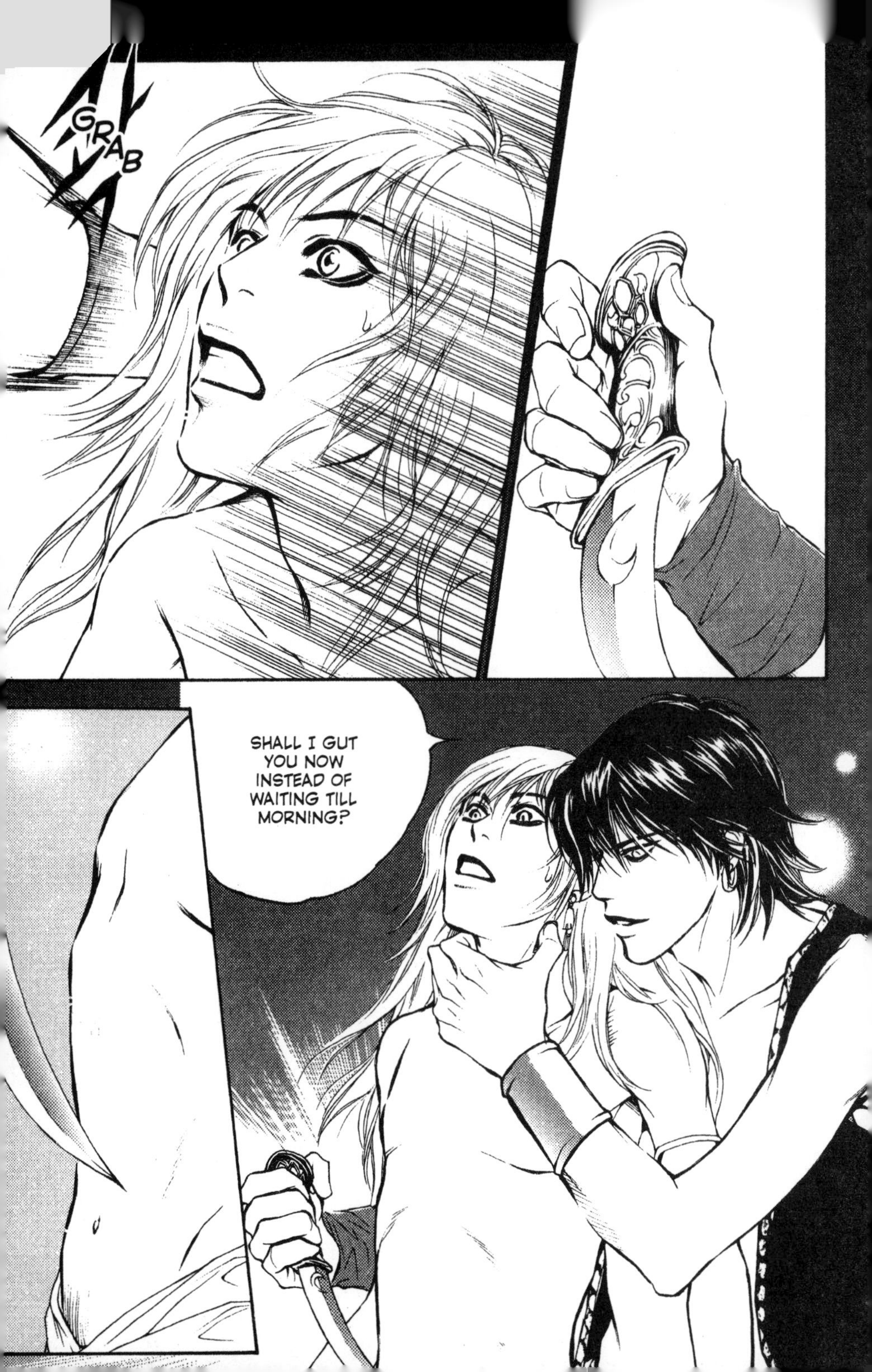
GRAB
SHALL I GUT YOU NOW INSTEAD OF WAITING TILL MORNING?

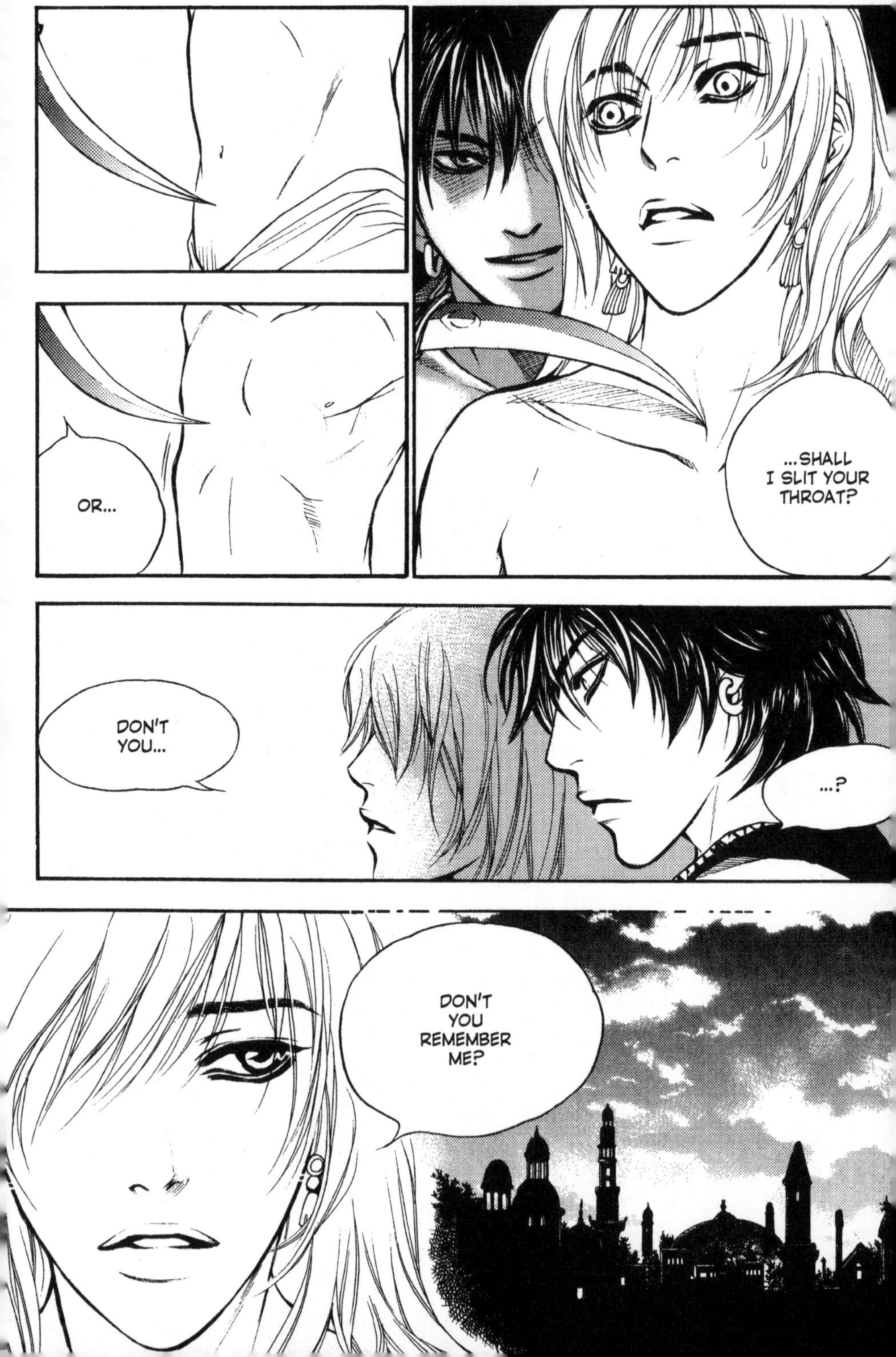
OR...
...SHALL I SLIT YOUR THROAT?
DON'T YOU...
...?
DON'T YOU REMEMBER ME?

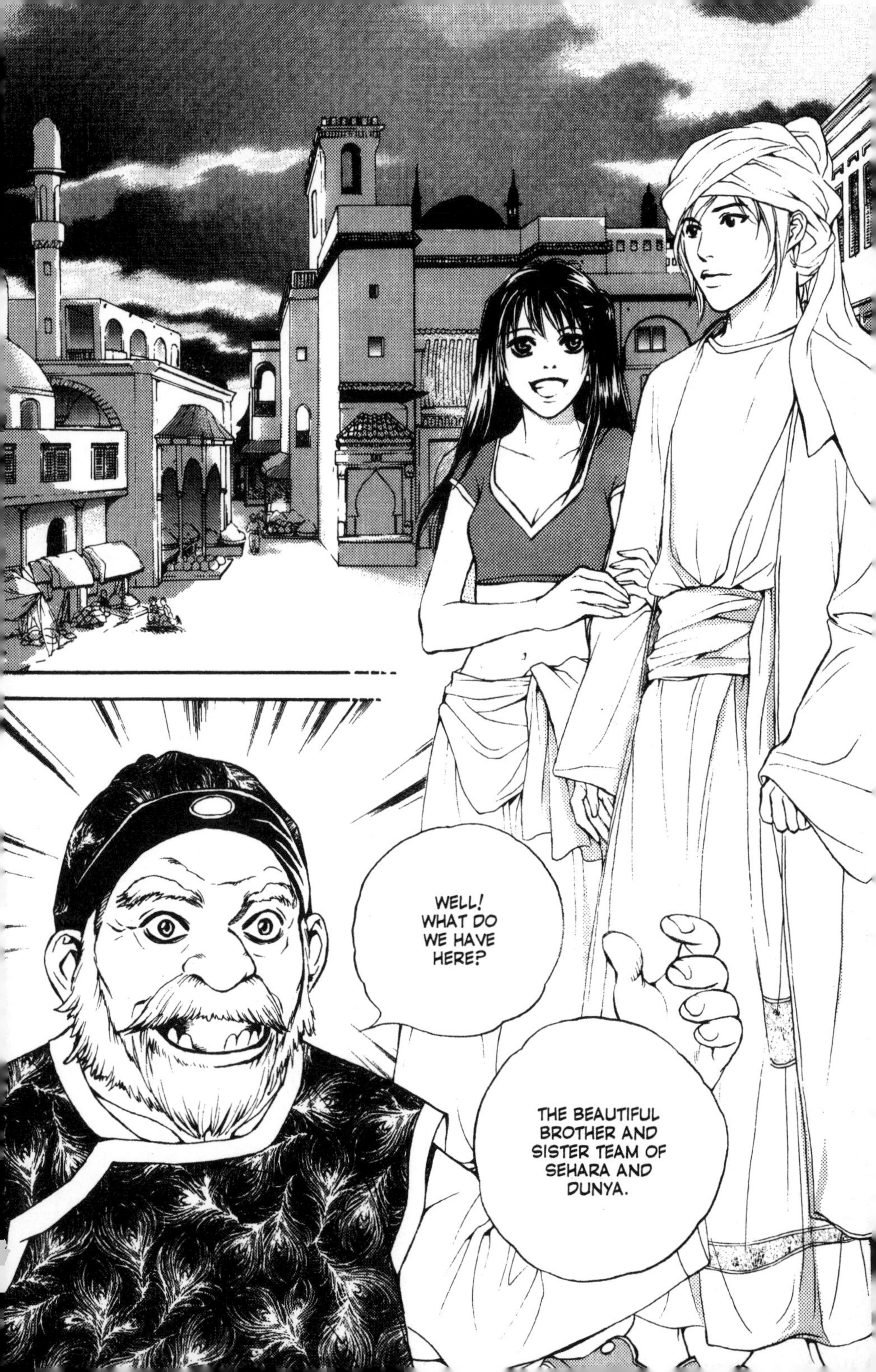
WELL! WHAT DO WE HAVE HERE?
THE BEAUTIFUL BROTHER AND SISTER TEAM OF SEHARA AND DUNYA.

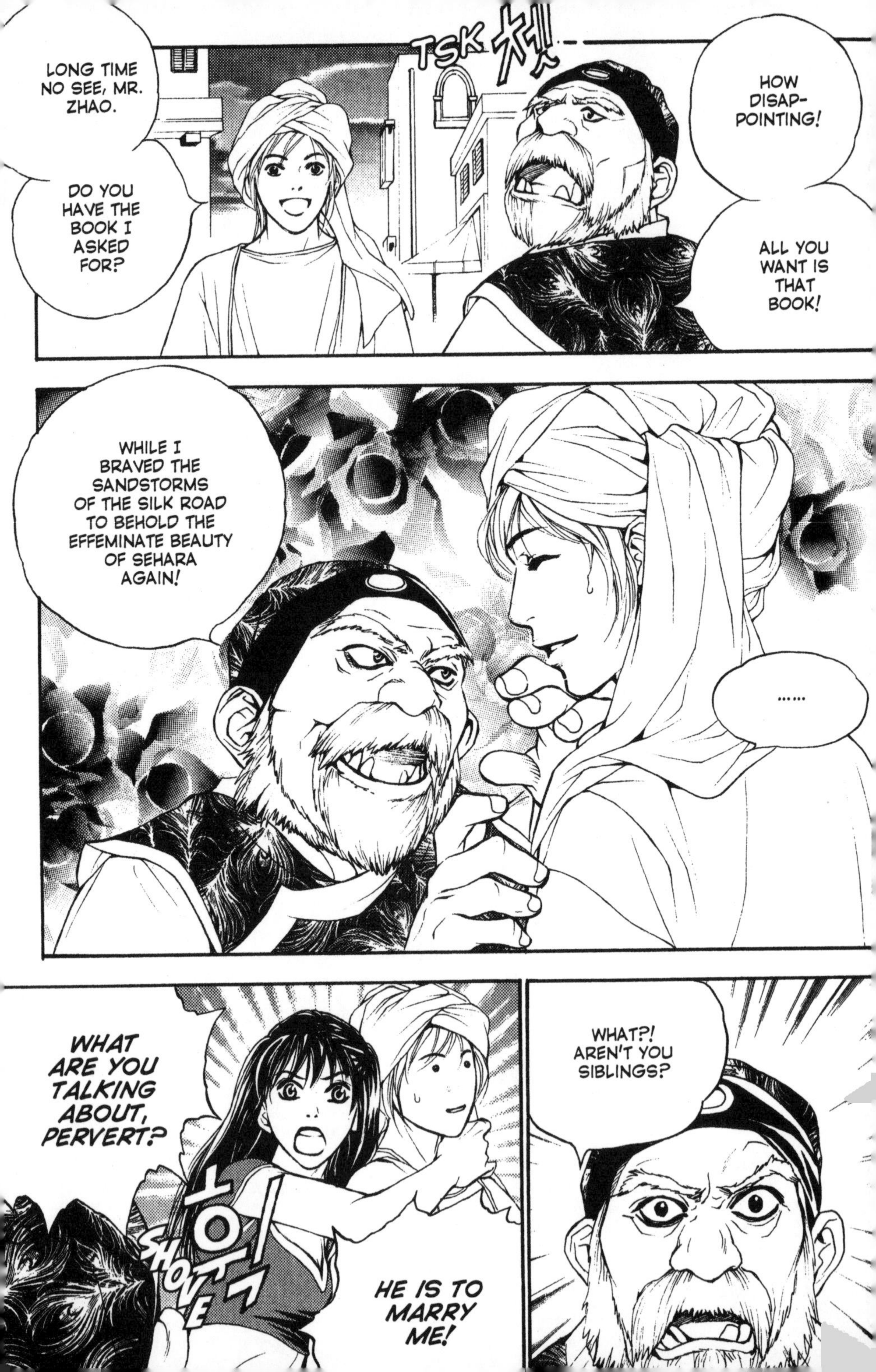
LONG TIME NO SEE, MR. ZHAO.
DO YOU HAVE THE BOOK I ASKED FOR?
TSK
HOW DISAP-POINTING!
ALL YOU WANT IS THAT BOOK!
WHILE I BRAVED THE SANDSTORMS OF THE SILK ROAD TO BEHOLD THE EFFEMINATE BEAUTY OF SEHARA AGAIN!
......
WHAT ARE YOU TALKING ABOUT, PERVERT?
SHOVE
HE IS TO MARRY ME!
WHAT?! AREN'T YOU SIBLINGS?

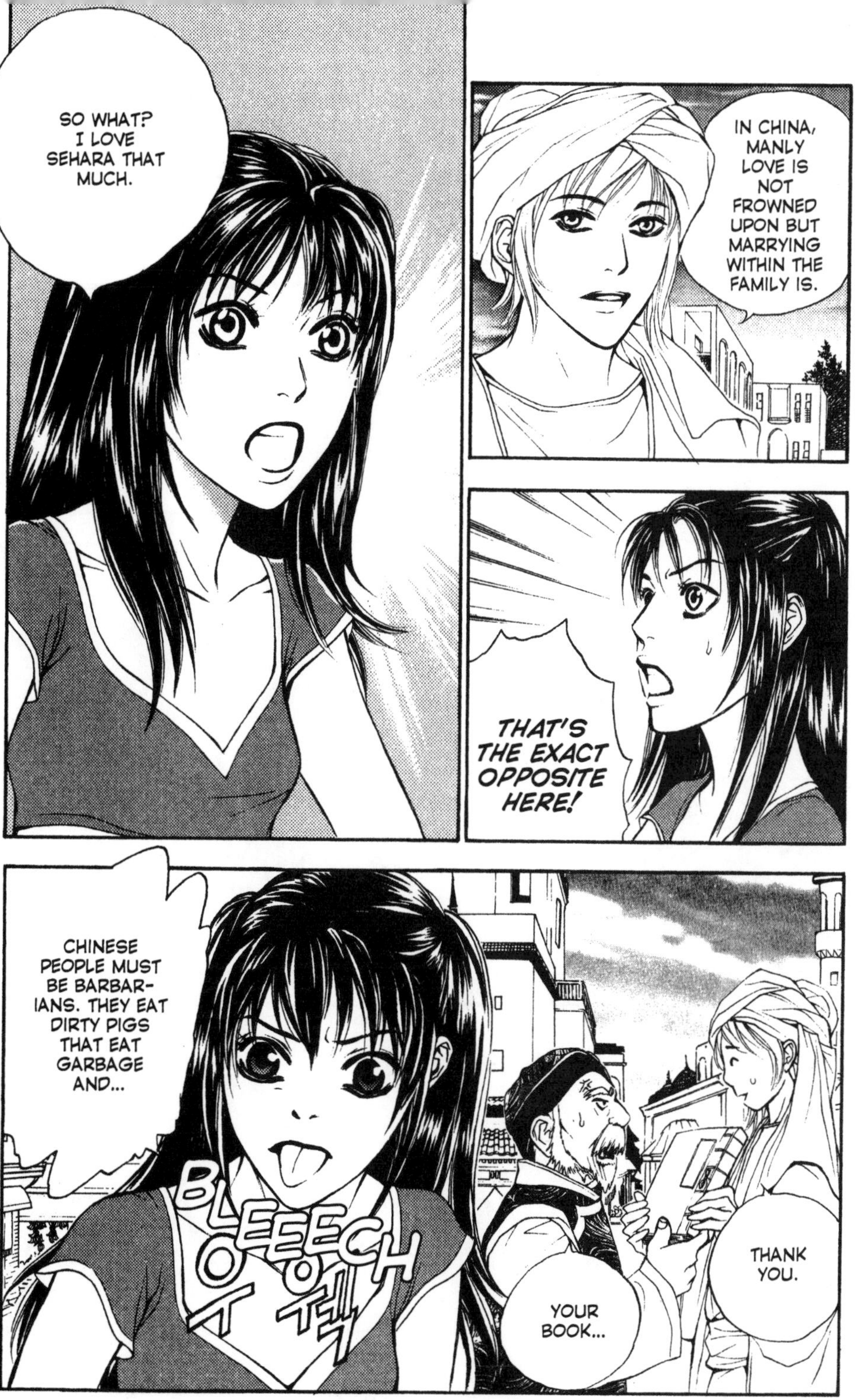
SO WHAT? I LOVE SEHARA THAT MUCH.
IN CHINA, MANLY LOVE IS NOT FROWNED UPON BUT MARRYING WITHIN THE FAMILY IS.
THAT'S THE EXACT OPPOSITE HERE!
CHINESE PEOPLE MUST BE BARBAR-IANS. THEY EAT DIRTY PIGS THAT EAT GARBAGE AND...
BLEEECH
YOUR BOOK...
THANK YOU.

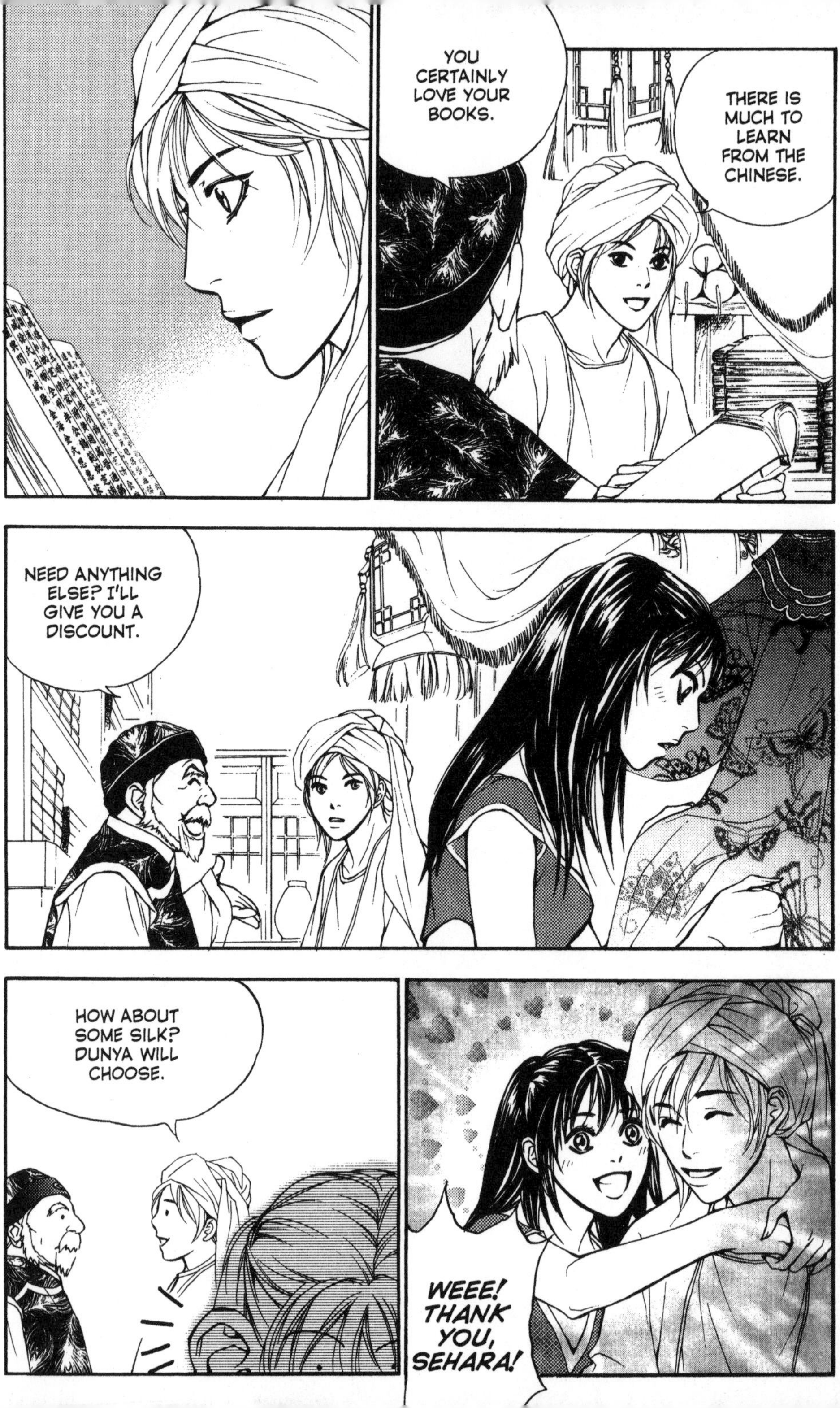
YOU CERTAINLY LOVE YOUR BOOKS.
THERE IS MUCH TO LEARN FROM THE CHINESE.
NEED ANYTHING ELSE? I'LL GIVE YOU A DISCOUNT.
HOW ABOUT SOME SILK? DUNYA WILL CHOOSE.
WEEE! THANK YOU, SEHARA!

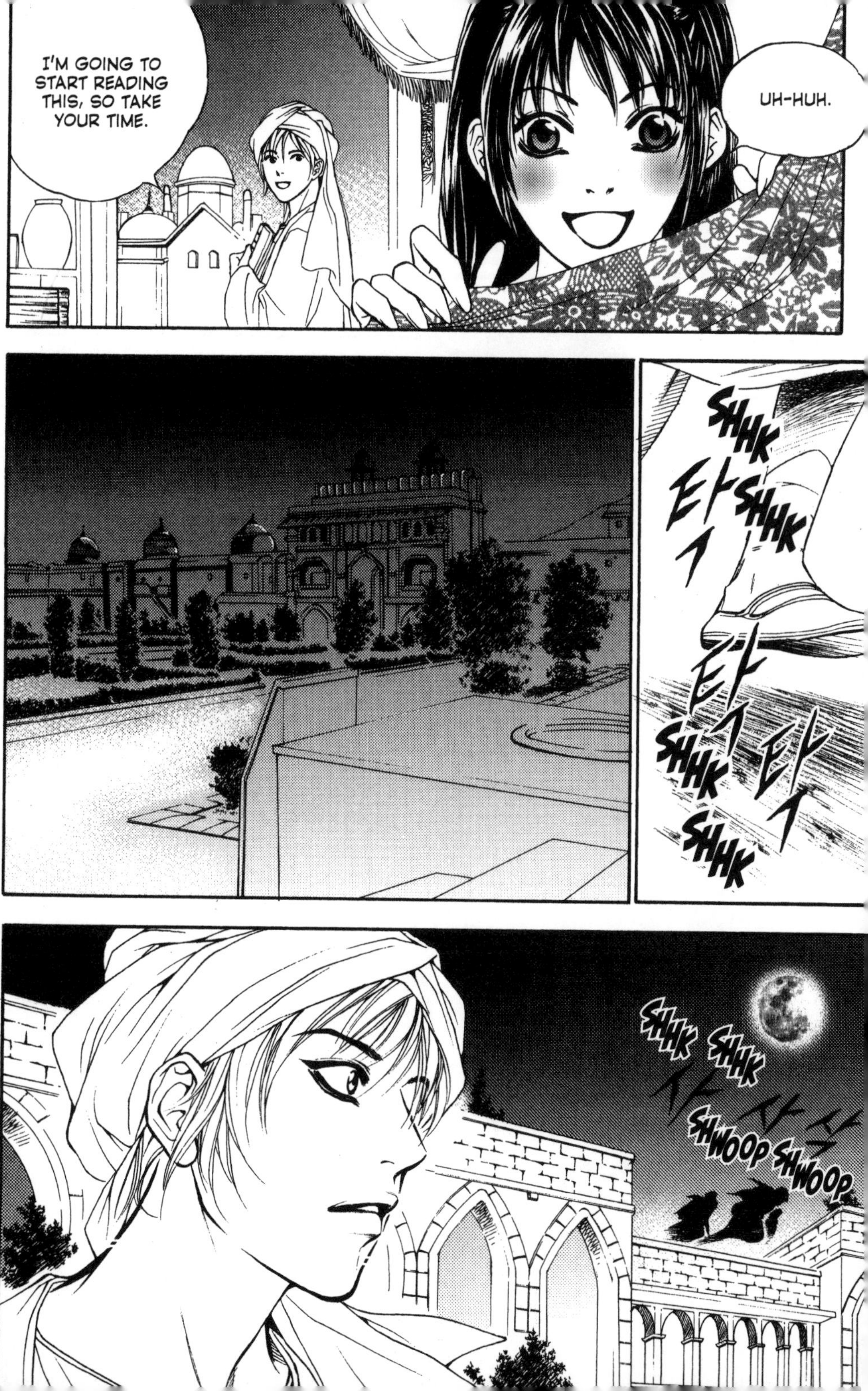
I'M GOING TO START READING THIS, SO TAKE YOUR TIME.
UH-HUH.
SHHK
SHHK
SHHK
SHHK
SHHK
SHHK
SHWOOP
SHWOOP

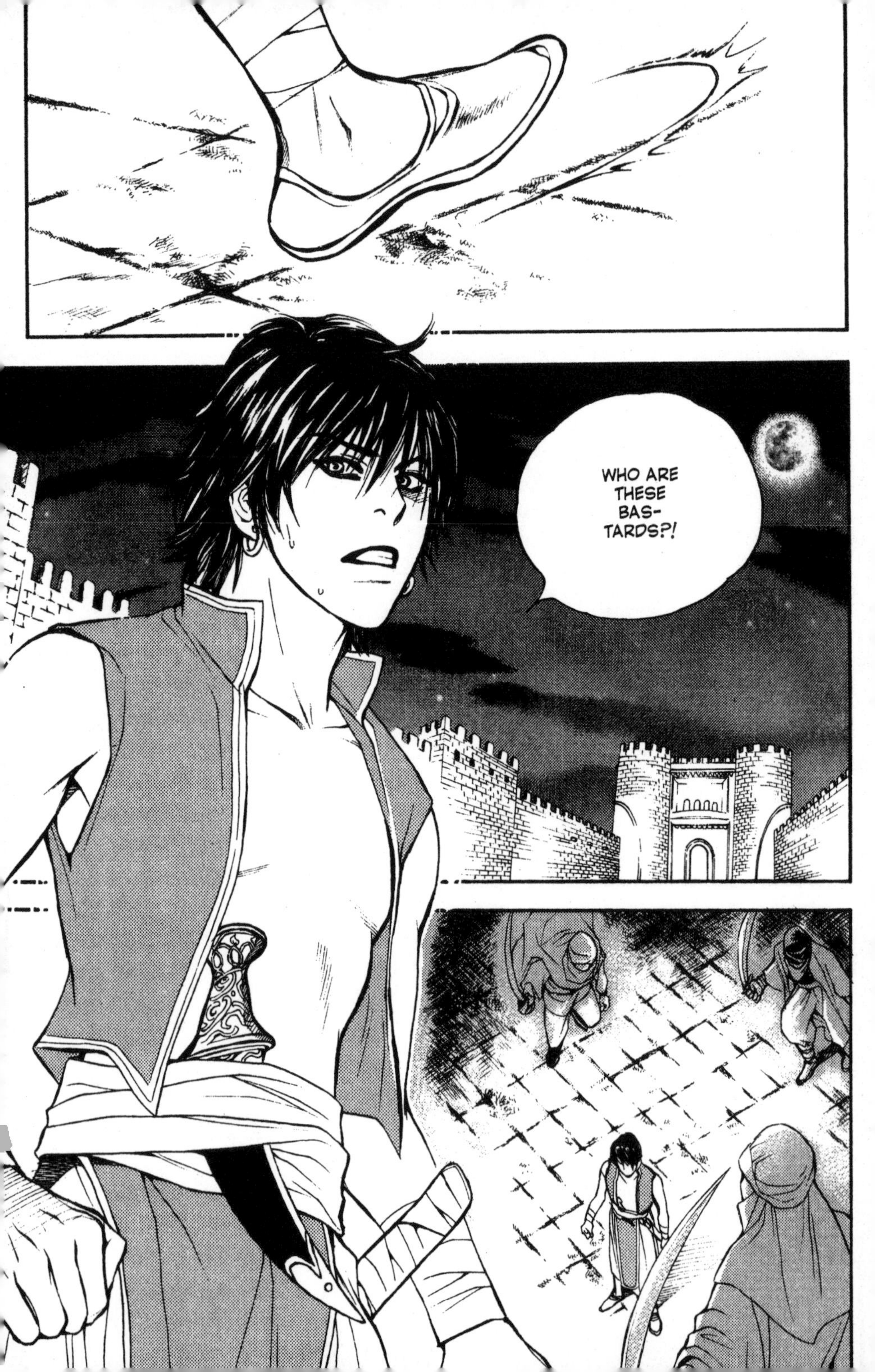
WHO ARE THESE BAS-TARDS?!

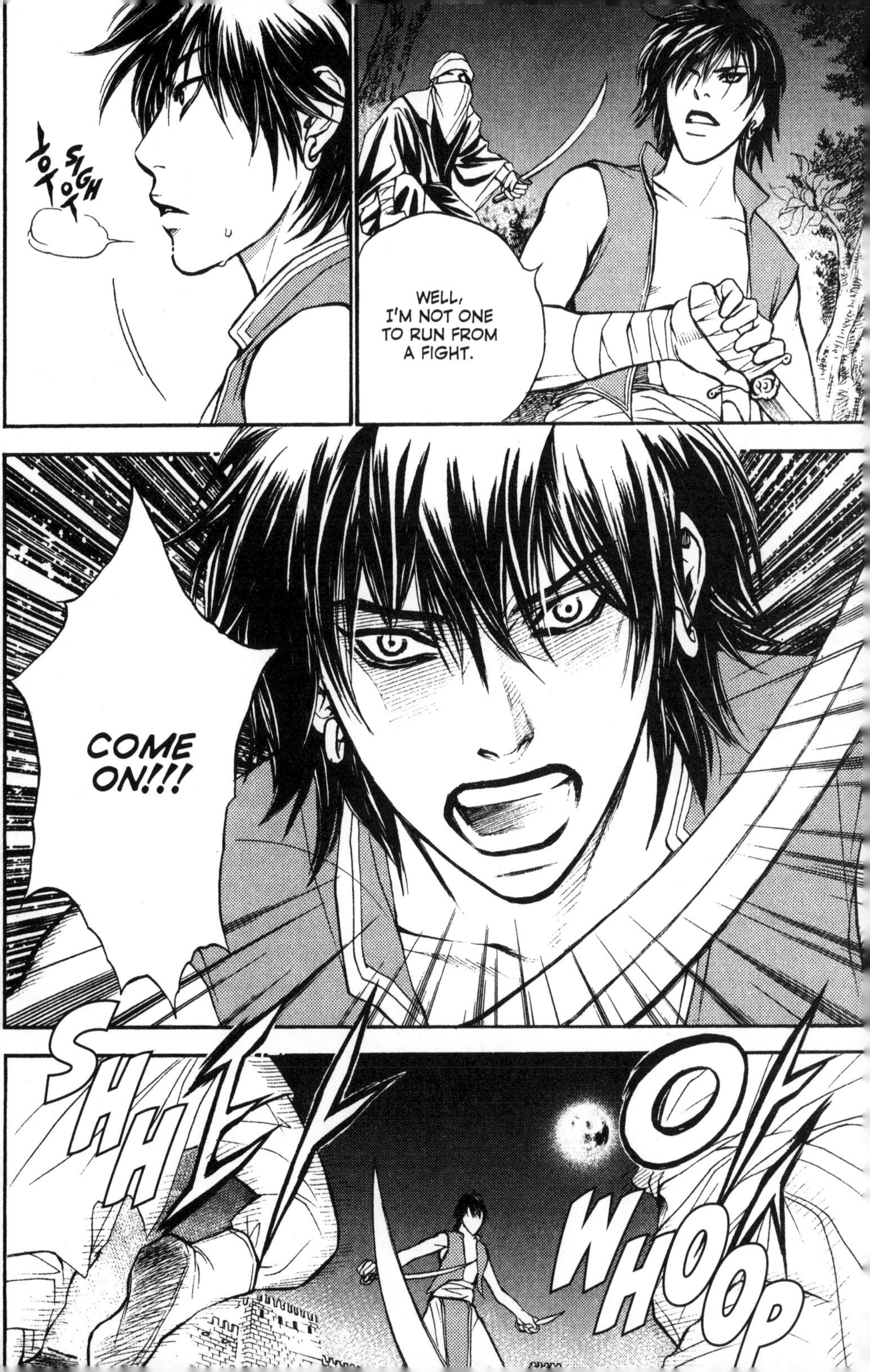
SIGH
WELL, I'M NOT ONE TO RUN FROM A FIGHT.
COME ON!!!
WHOOP

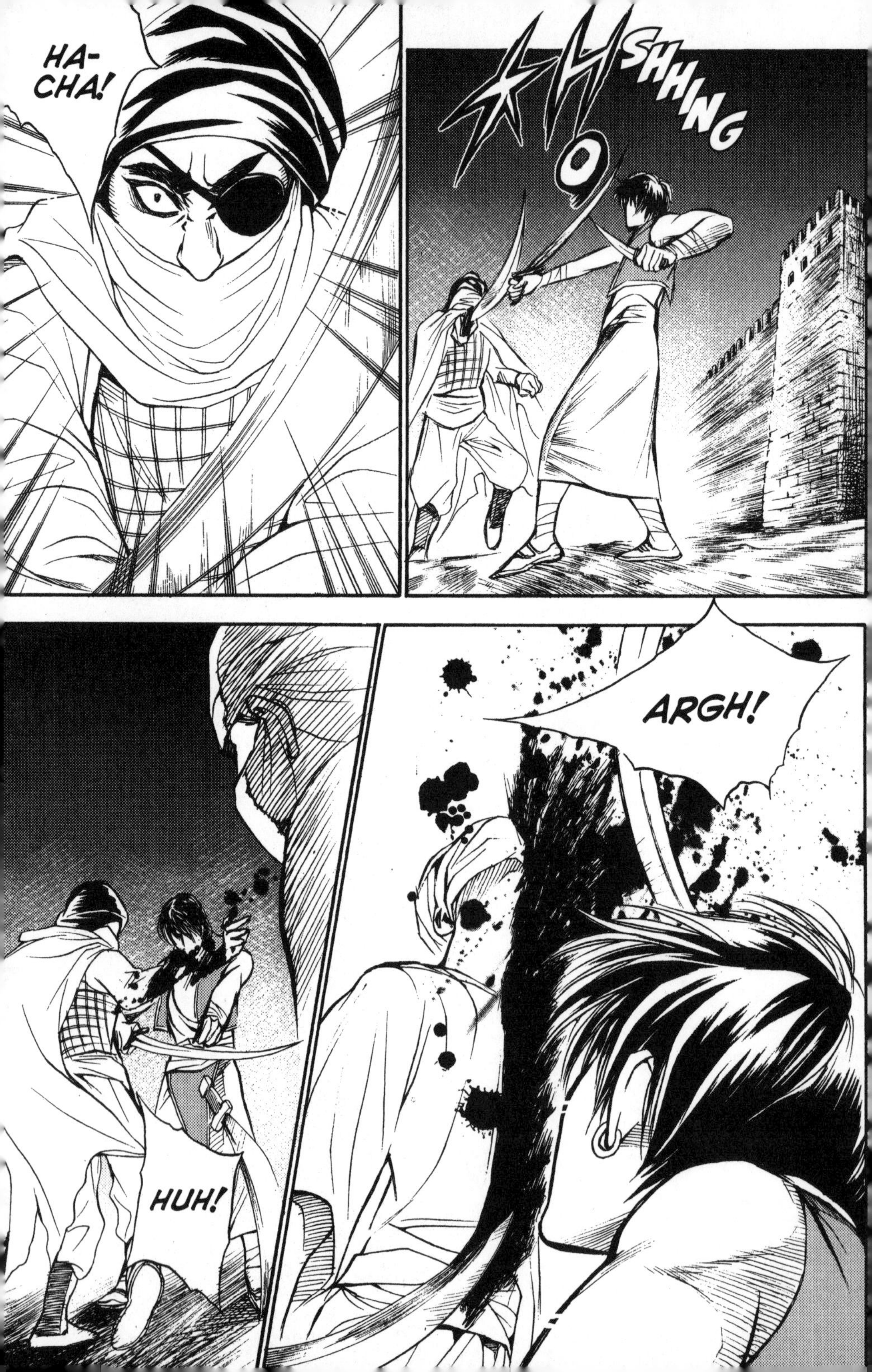
HA-CHA!
SHHING
HUH!
ARGH!

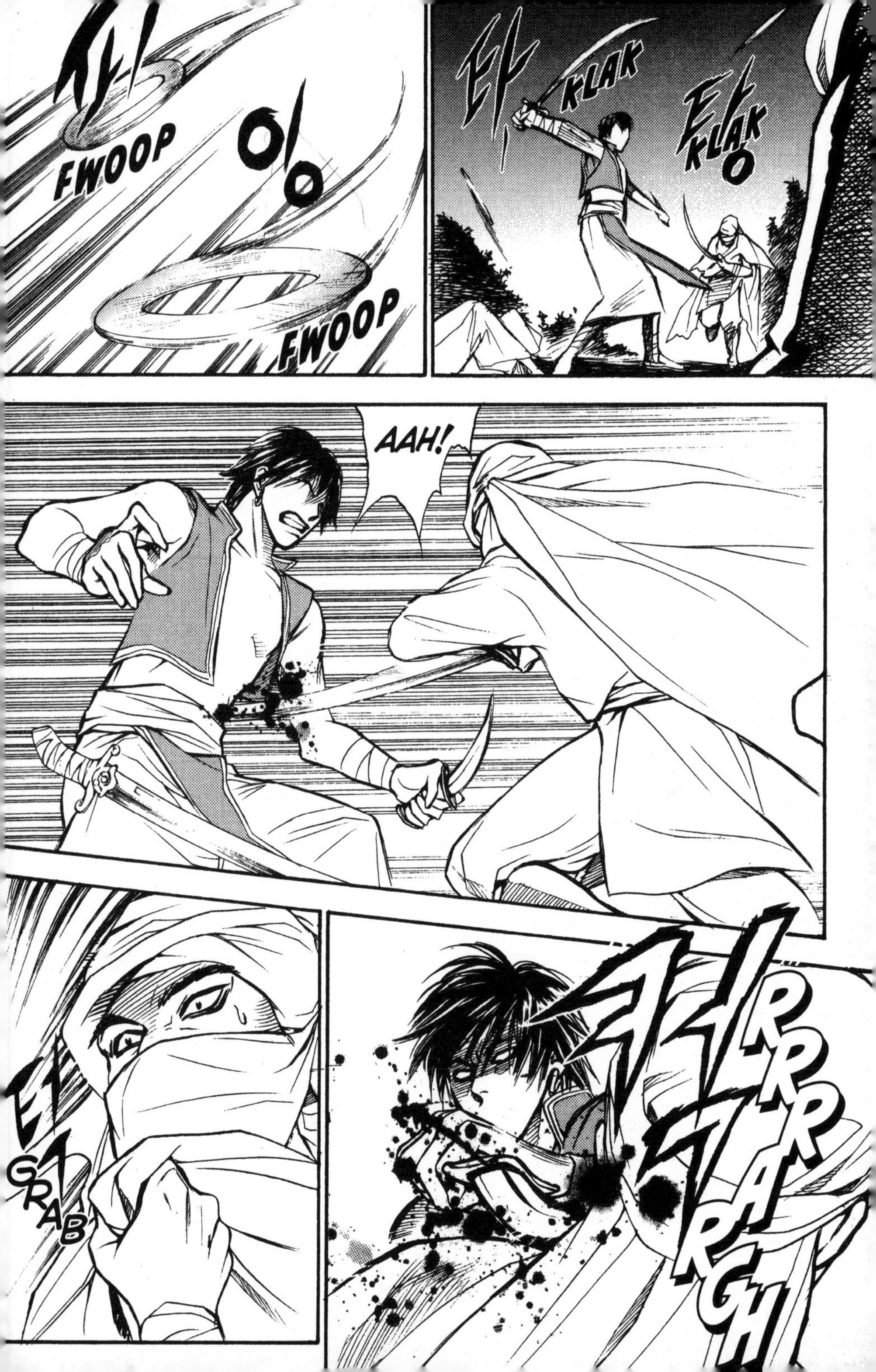
FWOOP
FWOOP
KLAK
KLAK
AAH!
GRAB
RRRRARGH

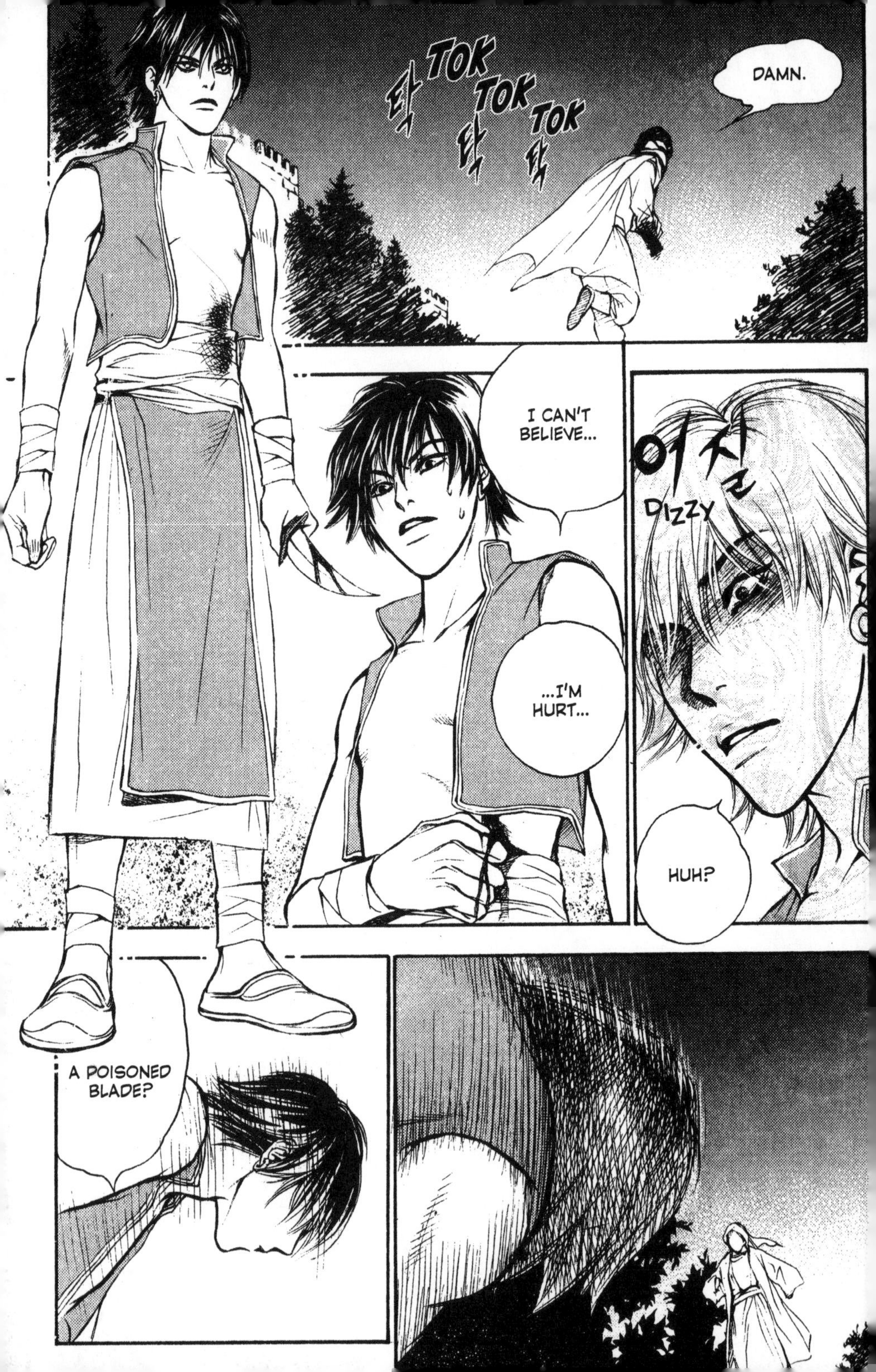
탁 TOK
TOK 탁
TOK 탁
DAMN.
I CAN'T BELIEVE...
...I'M HURT...
어질 DIZZY
HUH?
A POISONED BLADE?

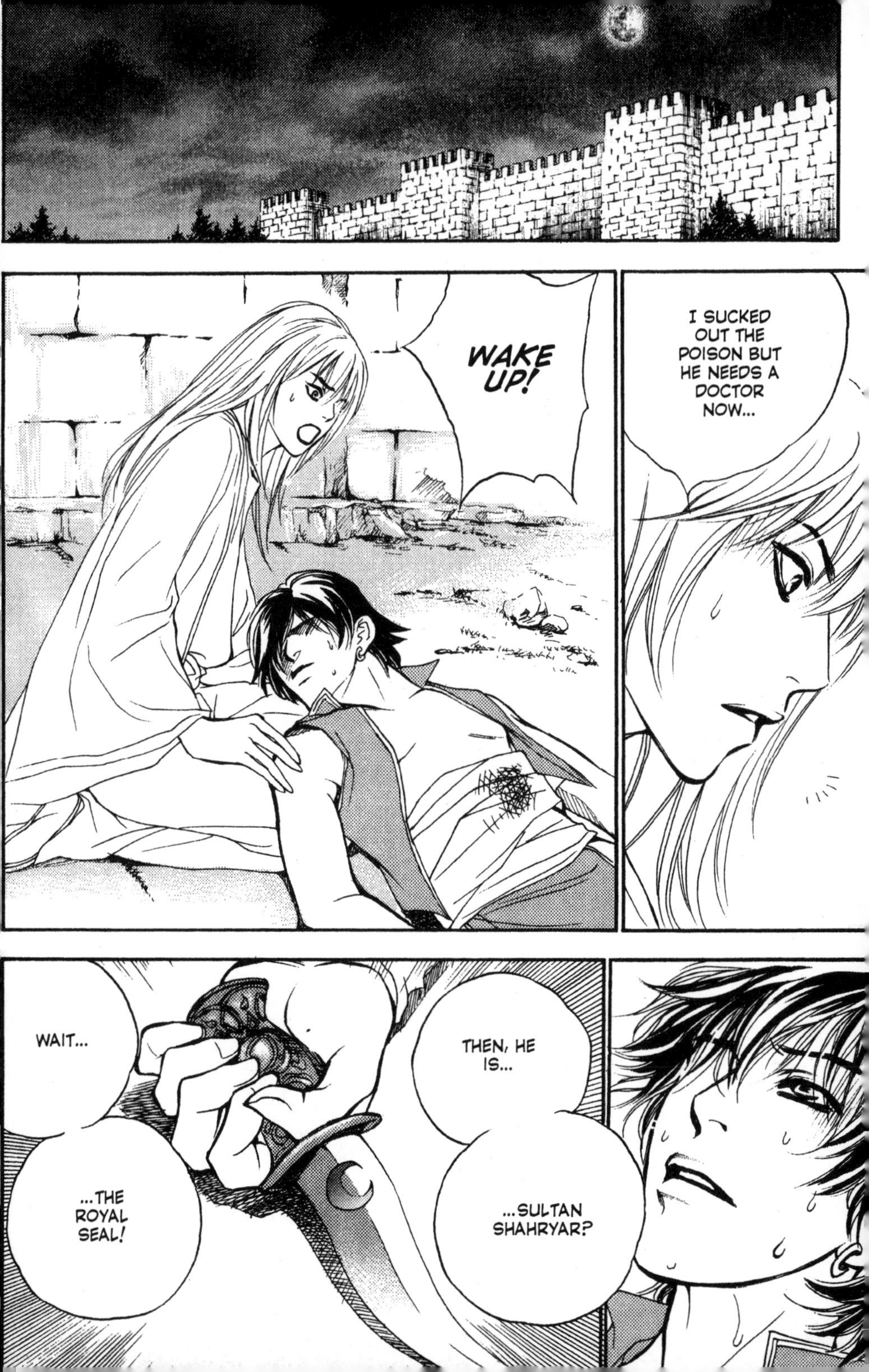
WAKE UP!
I SUCKED OUT THE POISON BUT HE NEEDS A DOCTOR NOW...
WAIT...
...THE ROYAL SEAL!
THEN, HE IS...
...SULTAN SHAHRYAR?

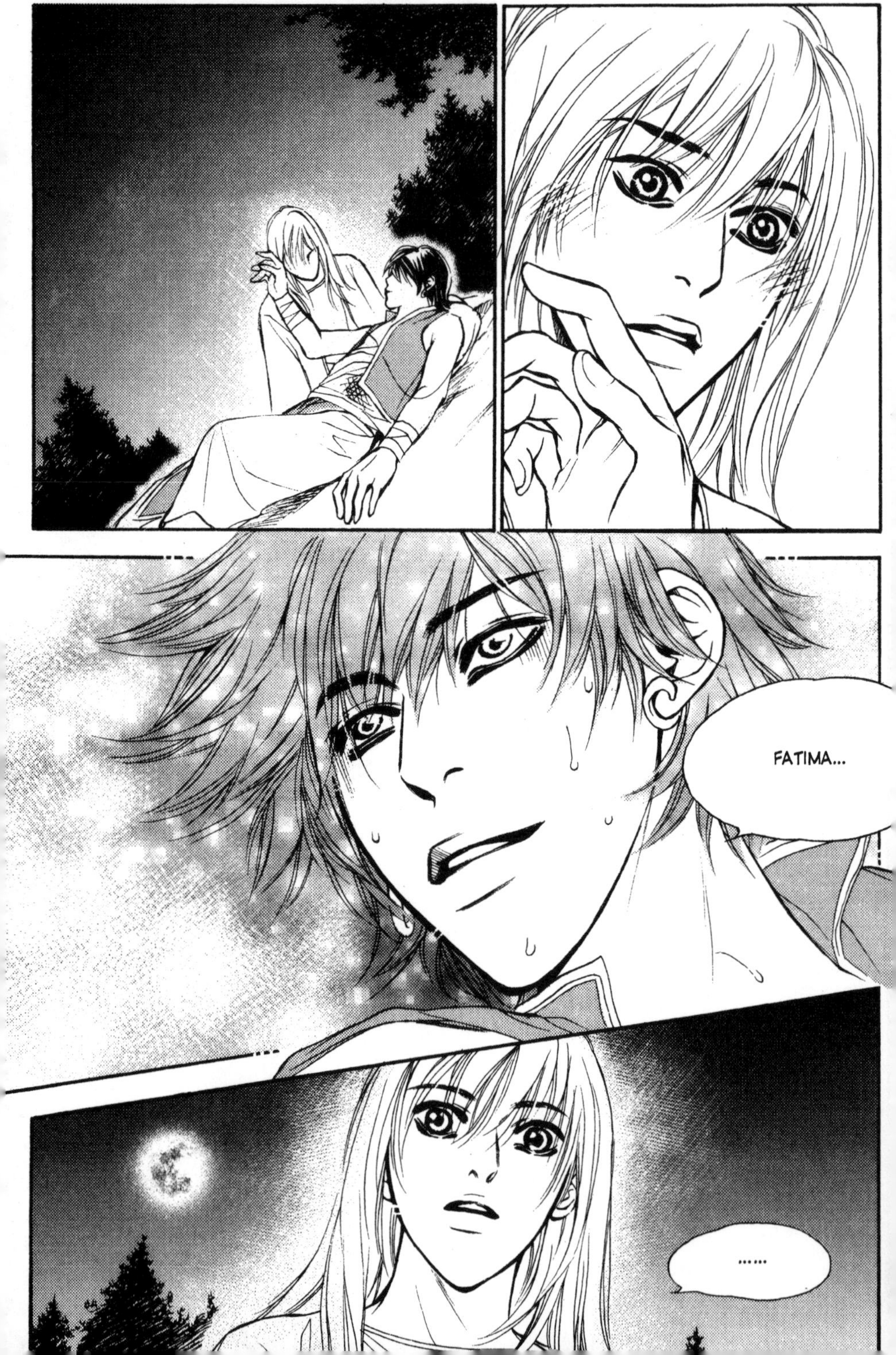
FATIMA...
......

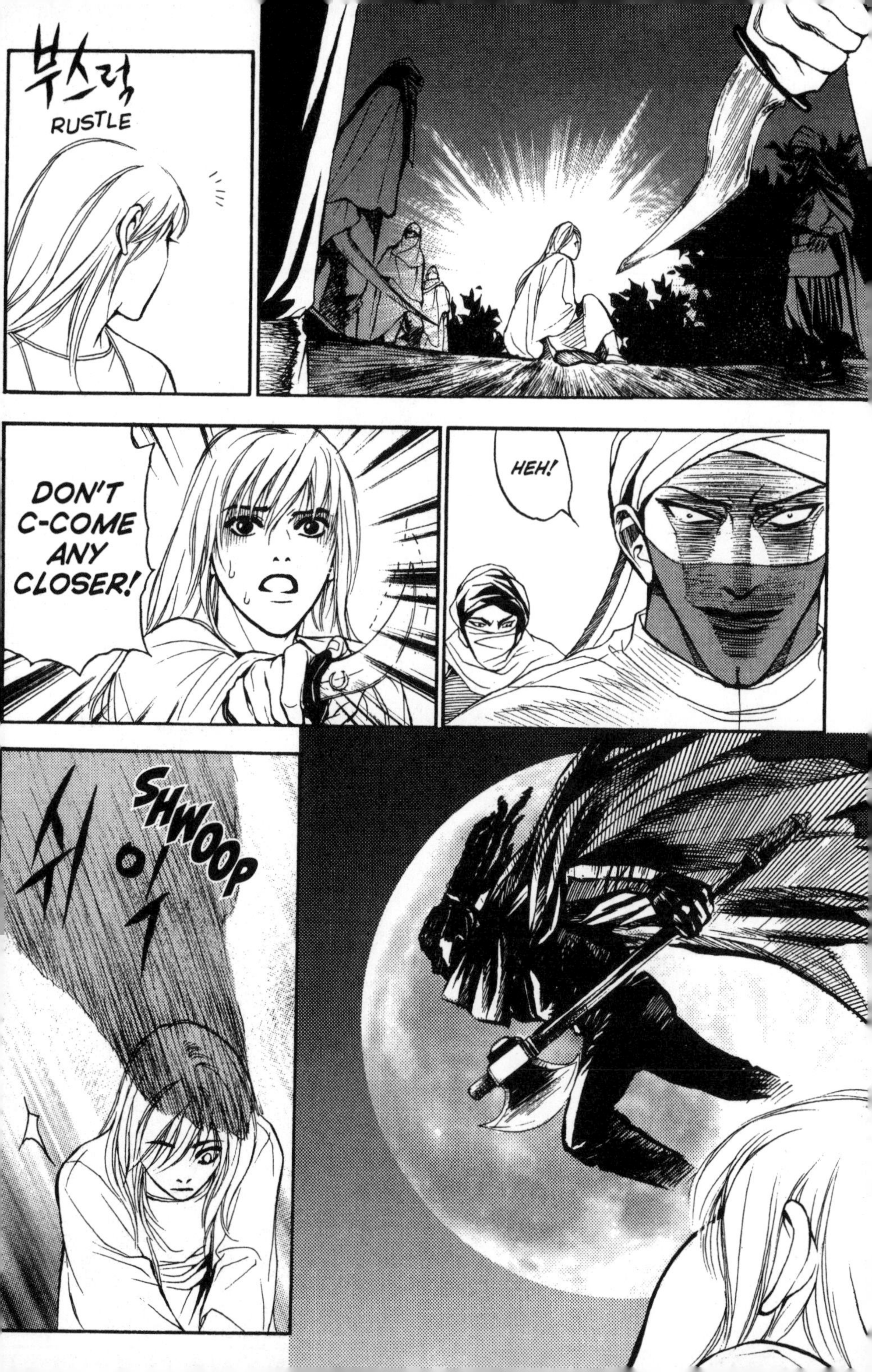

부스럭
RUSTLE
DON'T C-COME ANY CLOSER!
HEH!
쉬익
SHWOOP

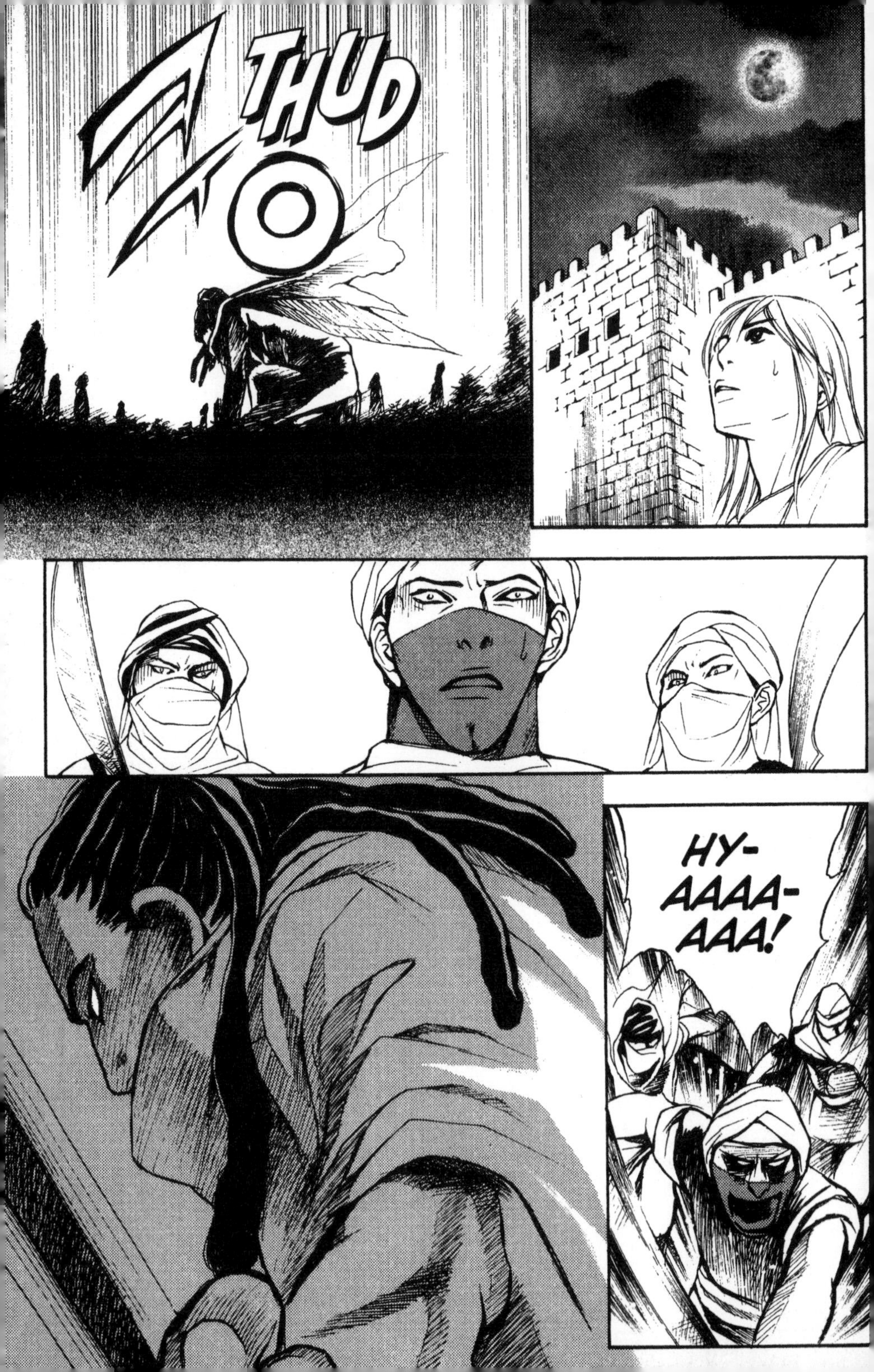
THUD
HY-AAAA-AAA!

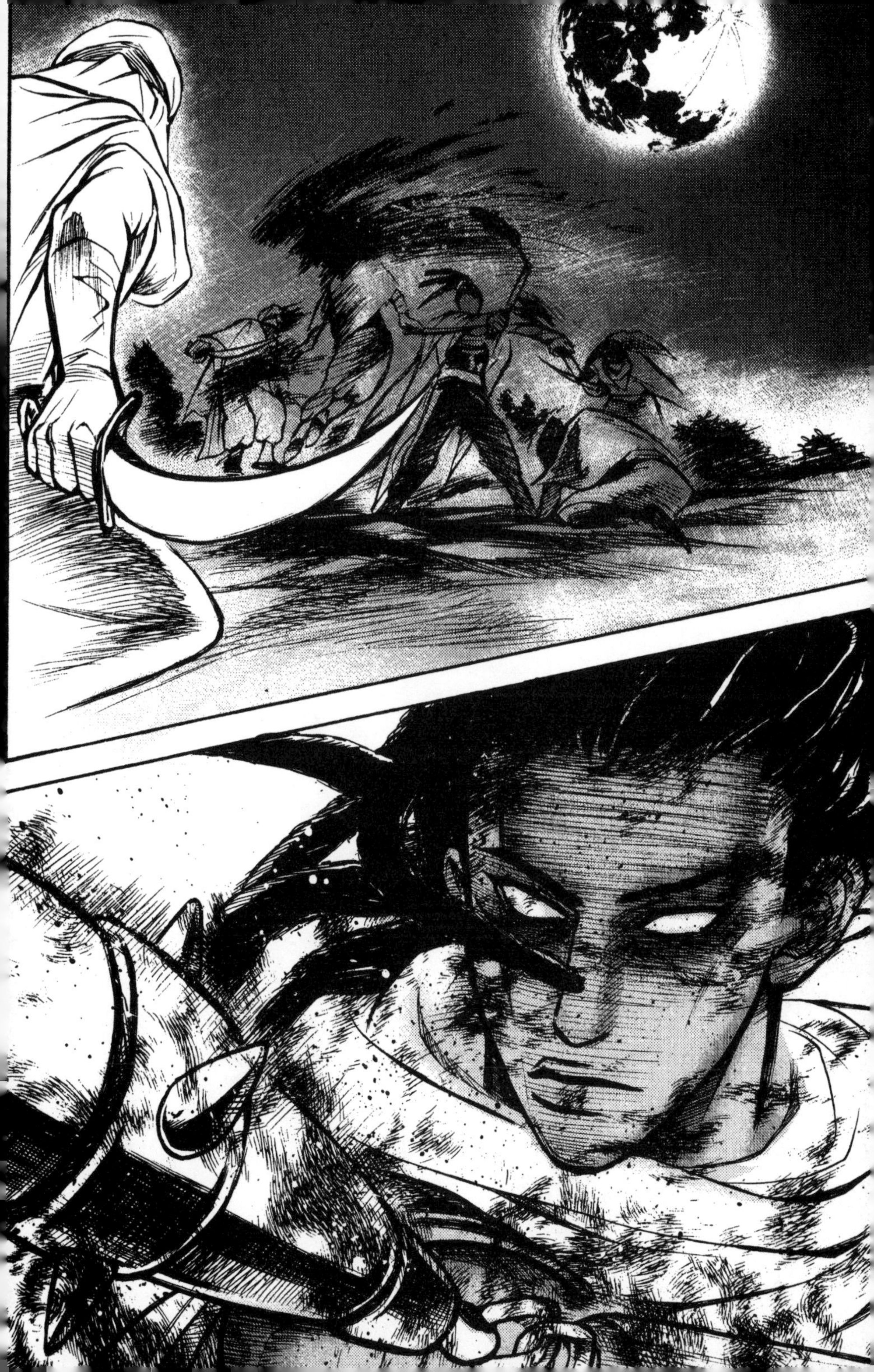

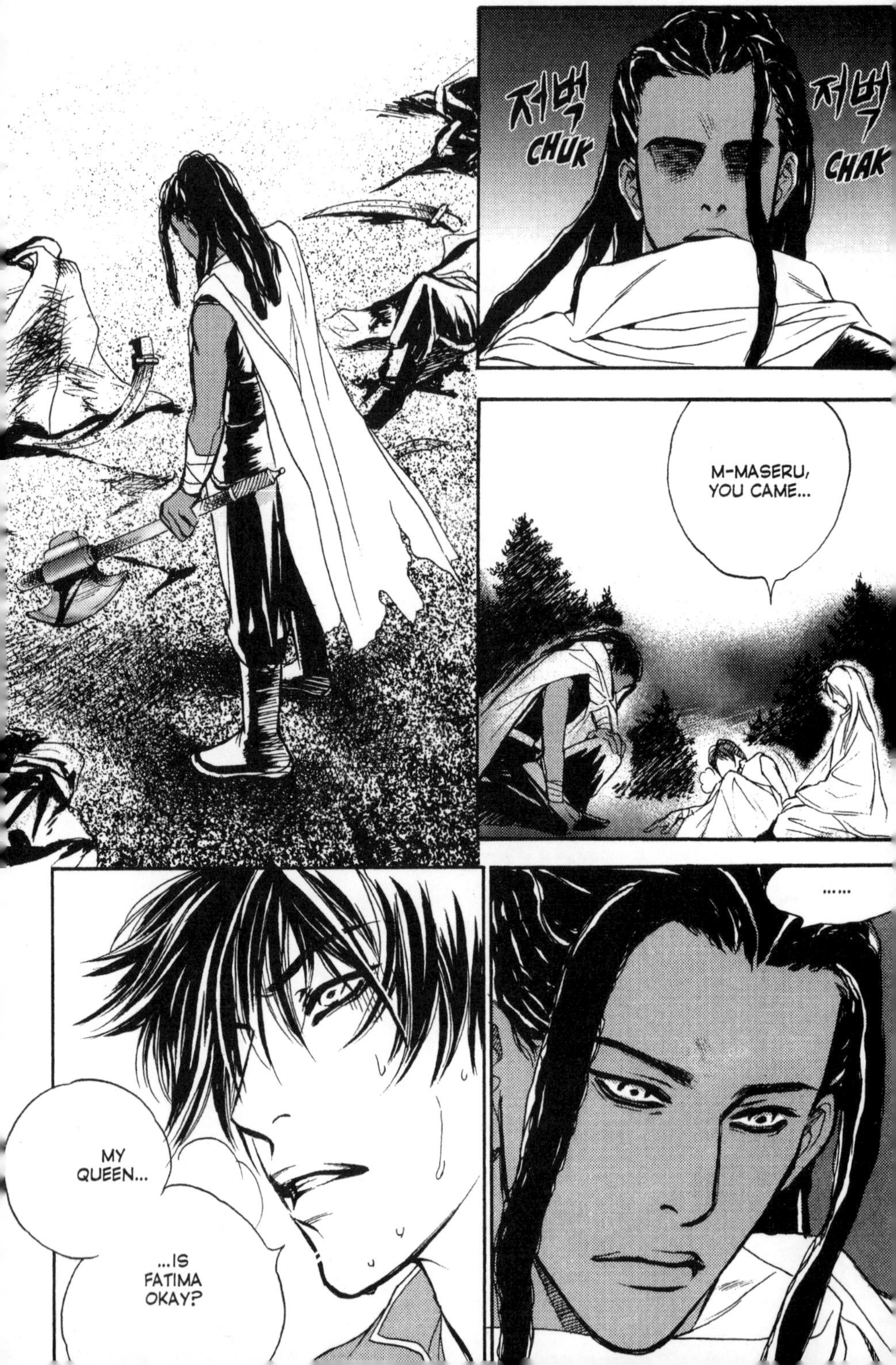

저벅
CHUK
저벅
CHAK
M-MASERU, YOU CAME...
MY QUEEN...
...IS FATIMA OKAY?
......

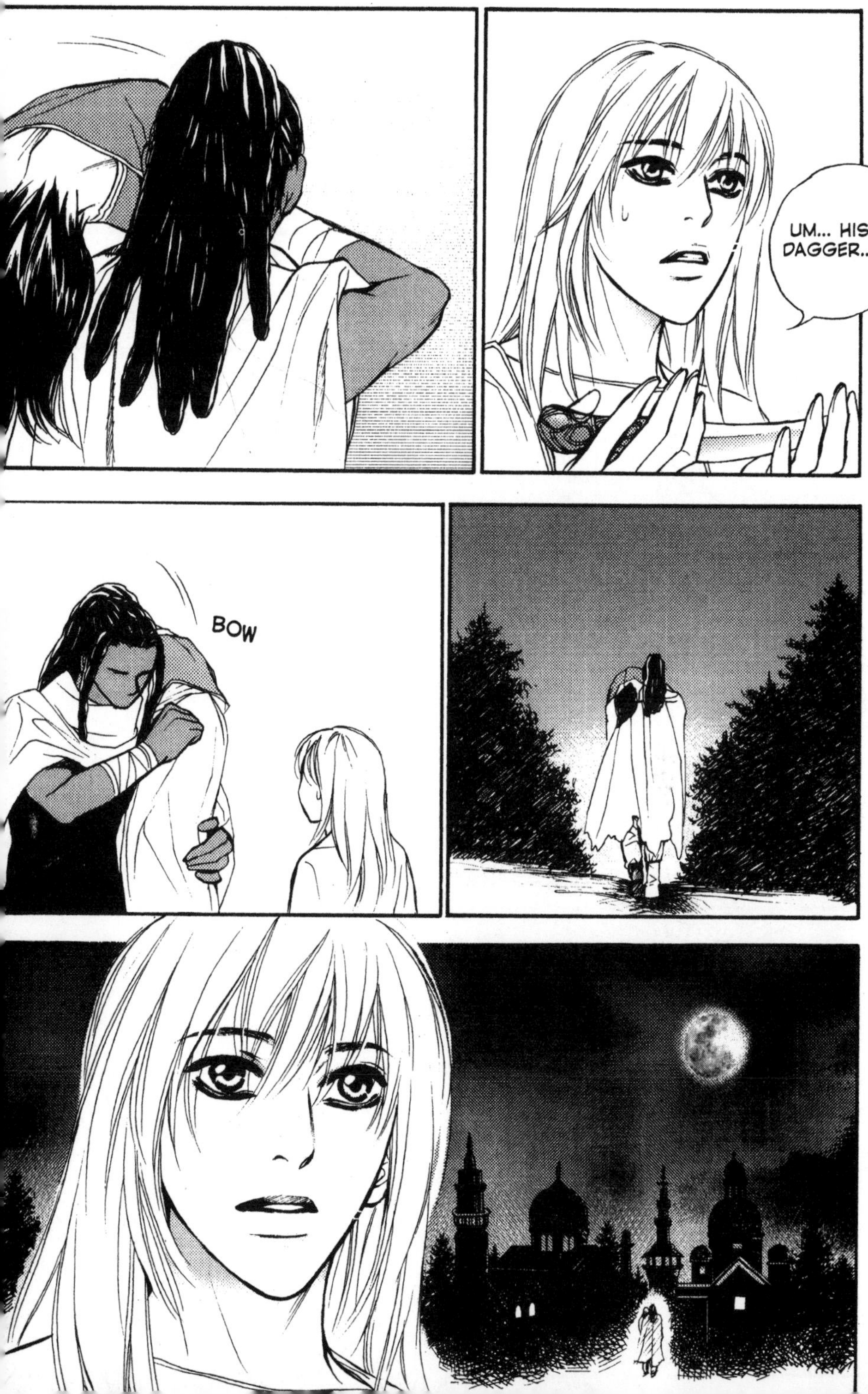
UM... HIS DAGGER...
BOW

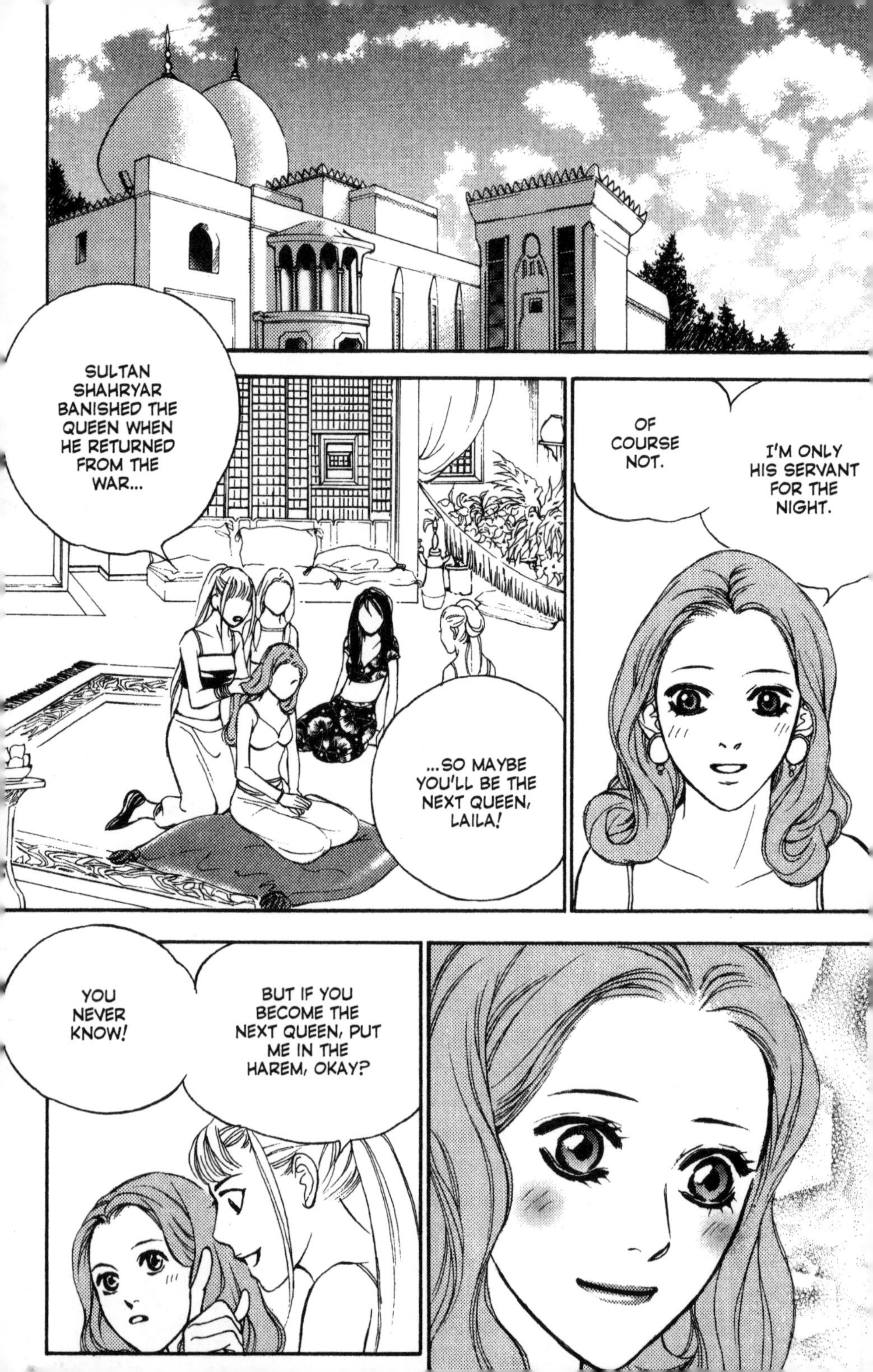
SULTAN SHAHRYAR BANISHED THE QUEEN WHEN HE RETURNED FROM THE WAR...
...SO MAYBE YOU'LL BE THE NEXT QUEEN, LAILA!
OF COURSE NOT.
I'M ONLY HIS SERVANT FOR THE NIGHT.
YOU NEVER KNOW!
BUT IF YOU BECOME THE NEXT QUEEN, PUT ME IN THE HAREM, OKAY?

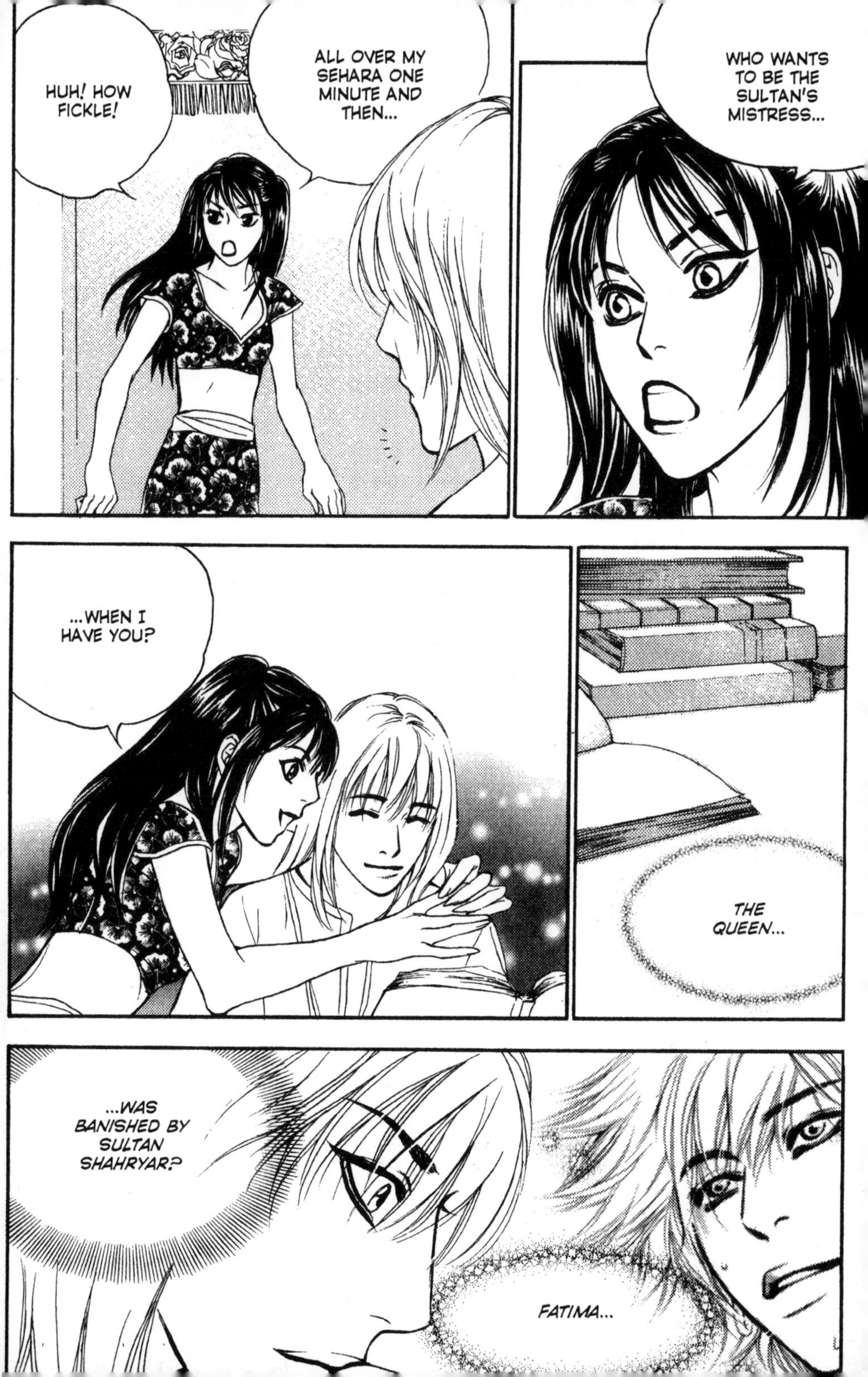
HUH! HOW FICKLE!
ALL OVER MY SEHARA ONE MINUTE AND THEN...
WHO WANTS TO BE THE SULTAN'S MISTRESS...
...WHEN I HAVE YOU?
THE QUEEN...
...WAS BANISHED BY SULTAN SHAHRYAR?
FATIMA...

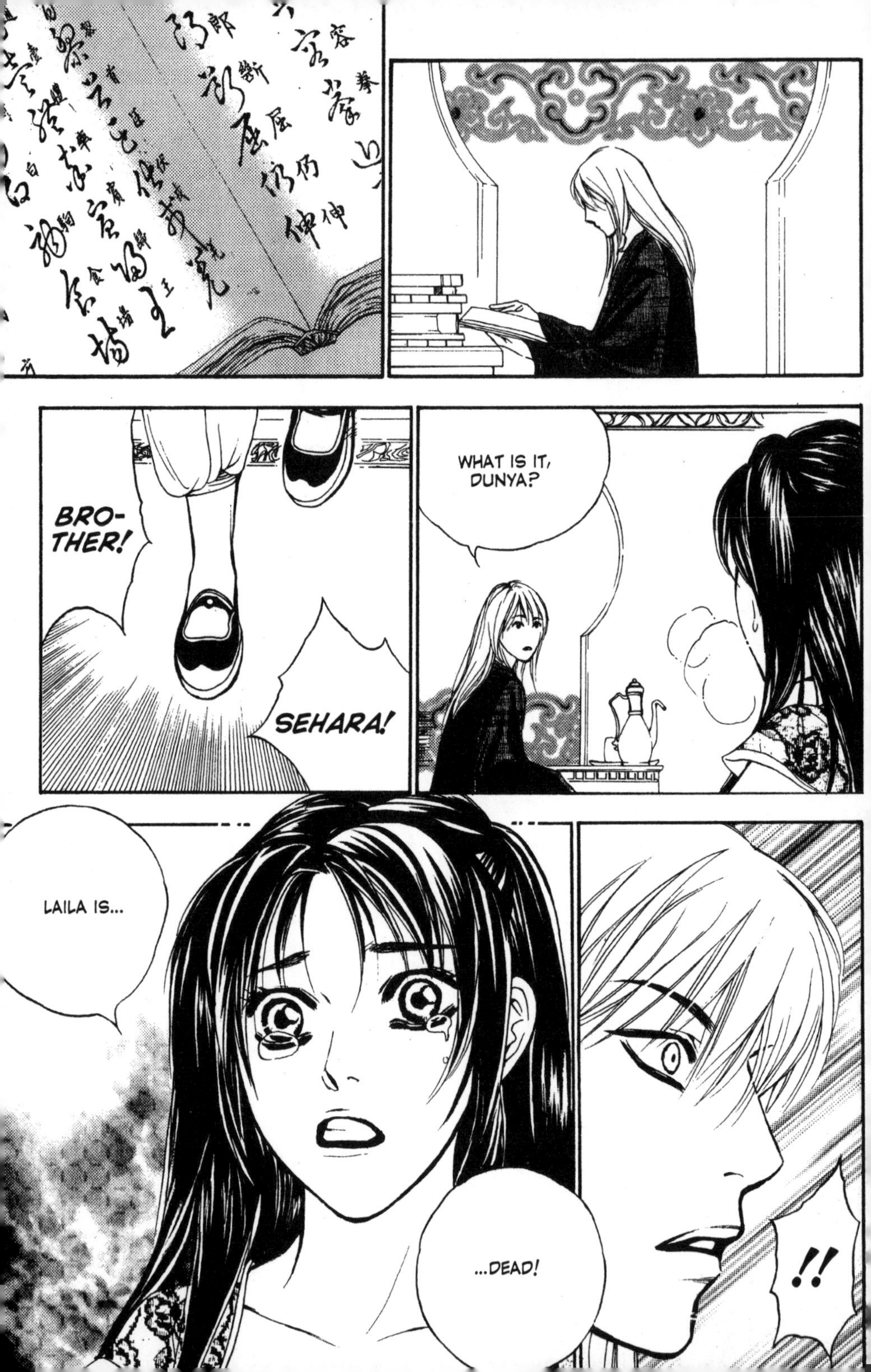
BRO-THER!
SEHARA!
WHAT IS IT, DUNYA?
LAILA IS...
...DEAD!
!!

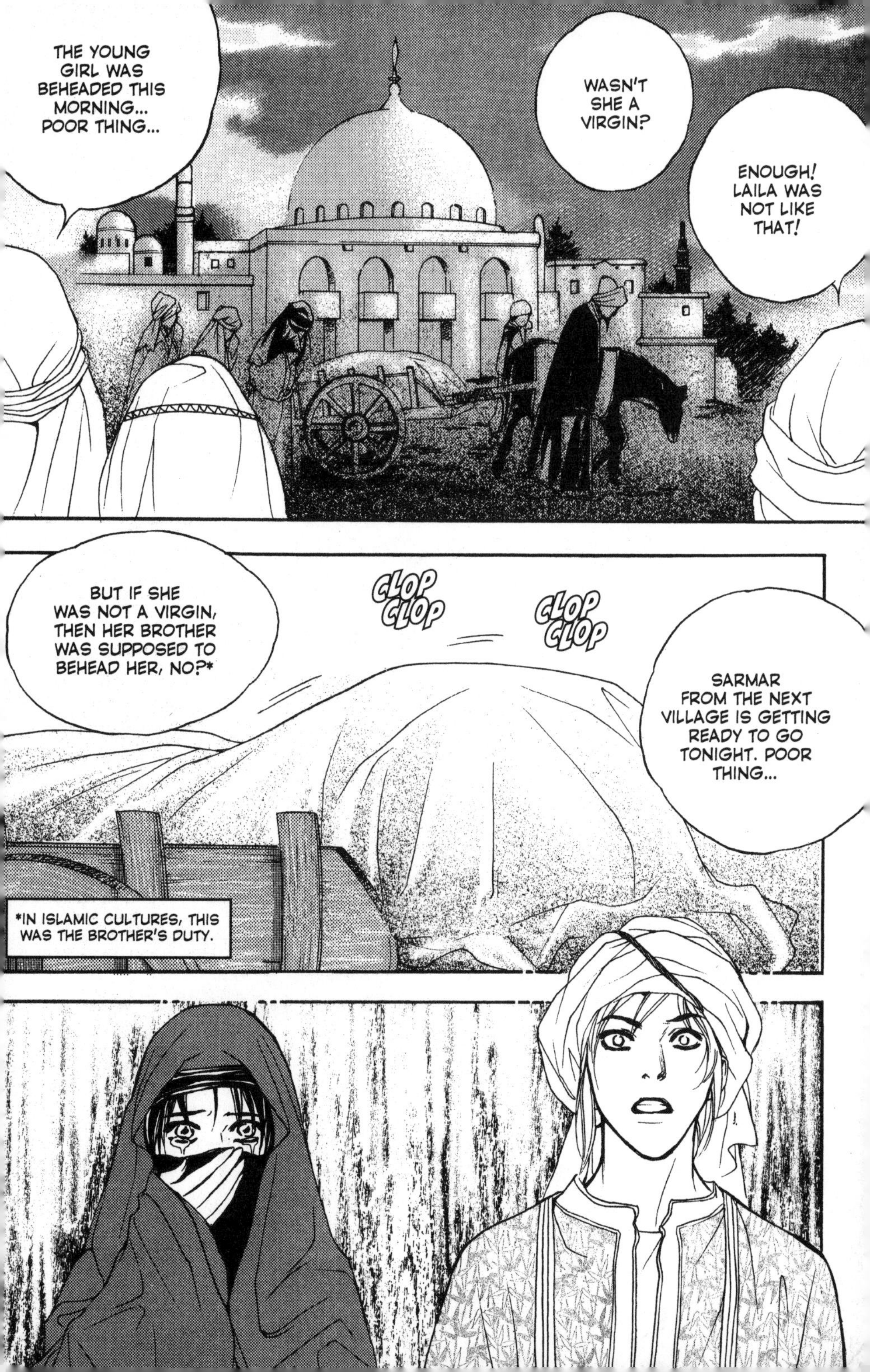
THE YOUNG GIRL WAS BEHEADED THIS MORNING... POOR THING...
WASN'T SHE A VIRGIN?
ENOUGH! LAILA WAS NOT LIKE THAT!
BUT IF SHE WAS NOT A VIRGIN, THEN HER BROTHER WAS SUPPOSED TO BEHEAD HER, NO?*
CLOP CLOP
CLOP CLOP
SARMAR FROM THE NEXT VILLAGE IS GETTING READY TO GO TONIGHT. POOR THING...
*IN ISLAMIC CULTURES, THIS WAS THE BROTHER'S DUTY.

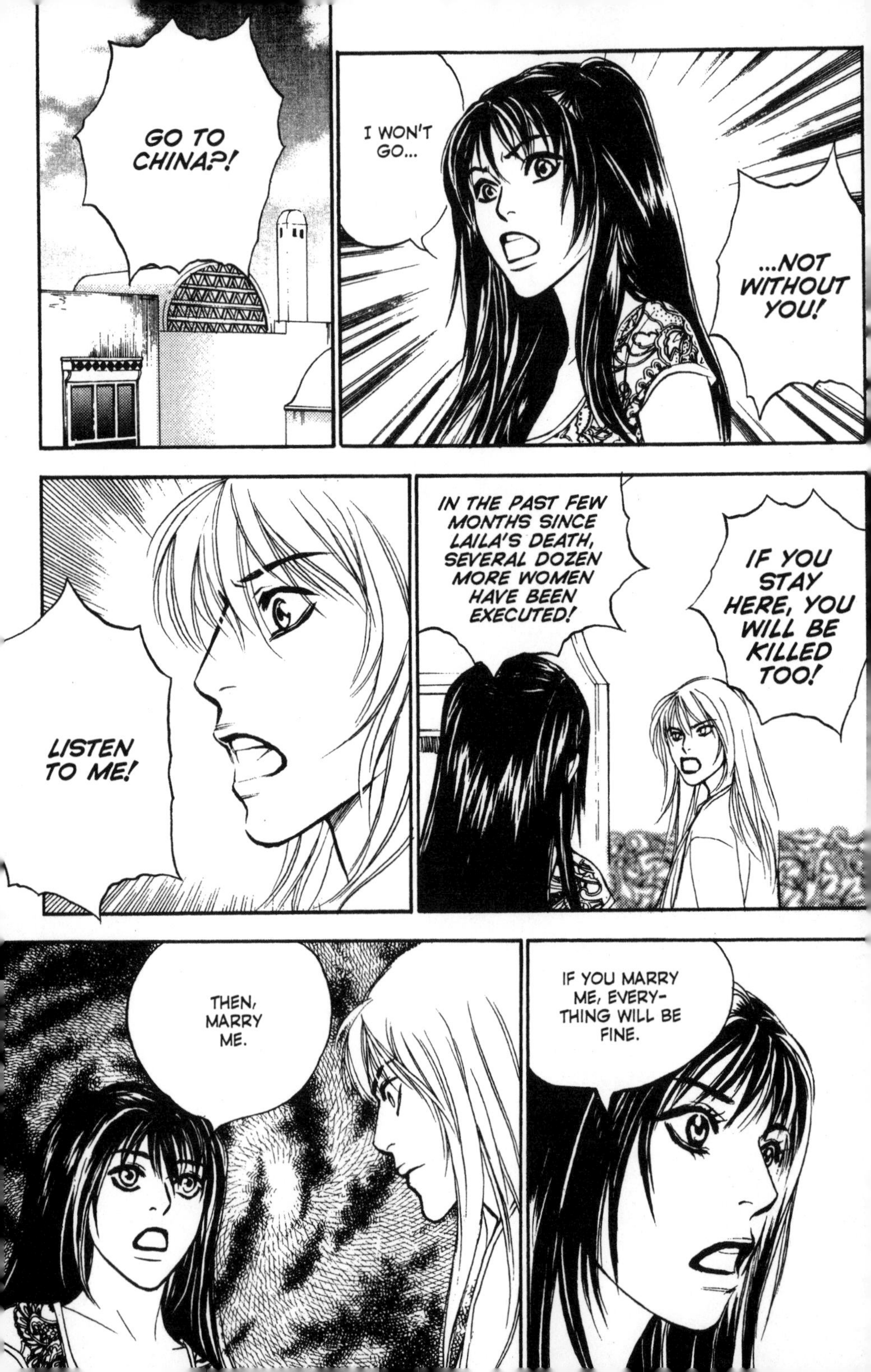
GO TO CHINA?!
I WON'T GO...
...NOT WITHOUT YOU!
LISTEN TO ME!
IN THE PAST FEW MONTHS SINCE LAILA'S DEATH, SEVERAL DOZEN MORE WOMEN HAVE BEEN EXECUTED!
IF YOU STAY HERE, YOU WILL BE KILLED TOO!
THEN, MARRY ME.
IF YOU MARRY ME, EVERY-THING WILL BE FINE.

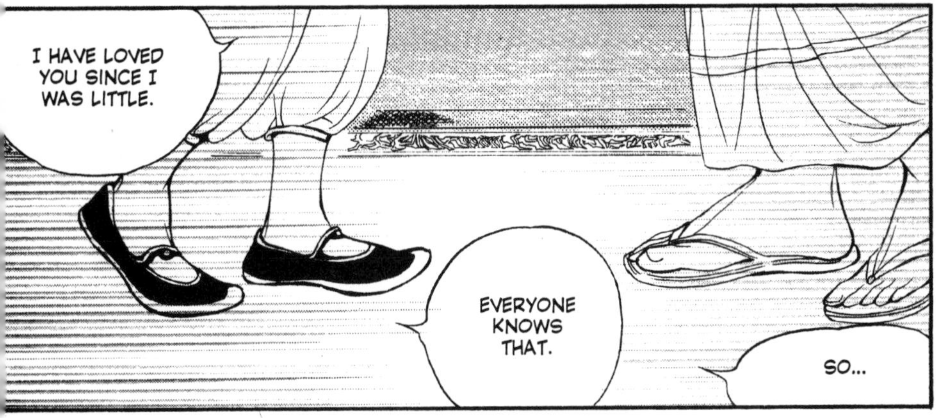
I HAVE LOVED YOU SINCE I WAS LITTLE.
EVERYONE KNOWS THAT.
SO...
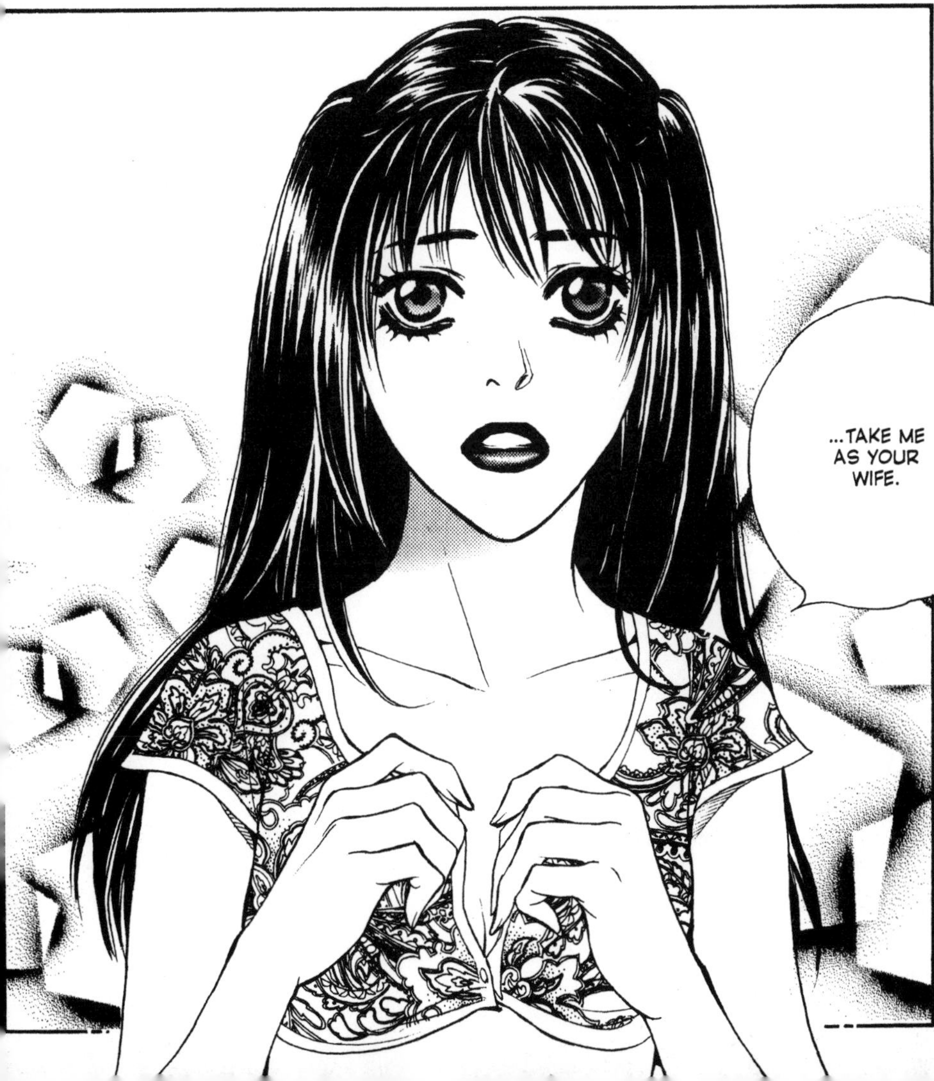
...TAKE ME AS YOUR WIFE.

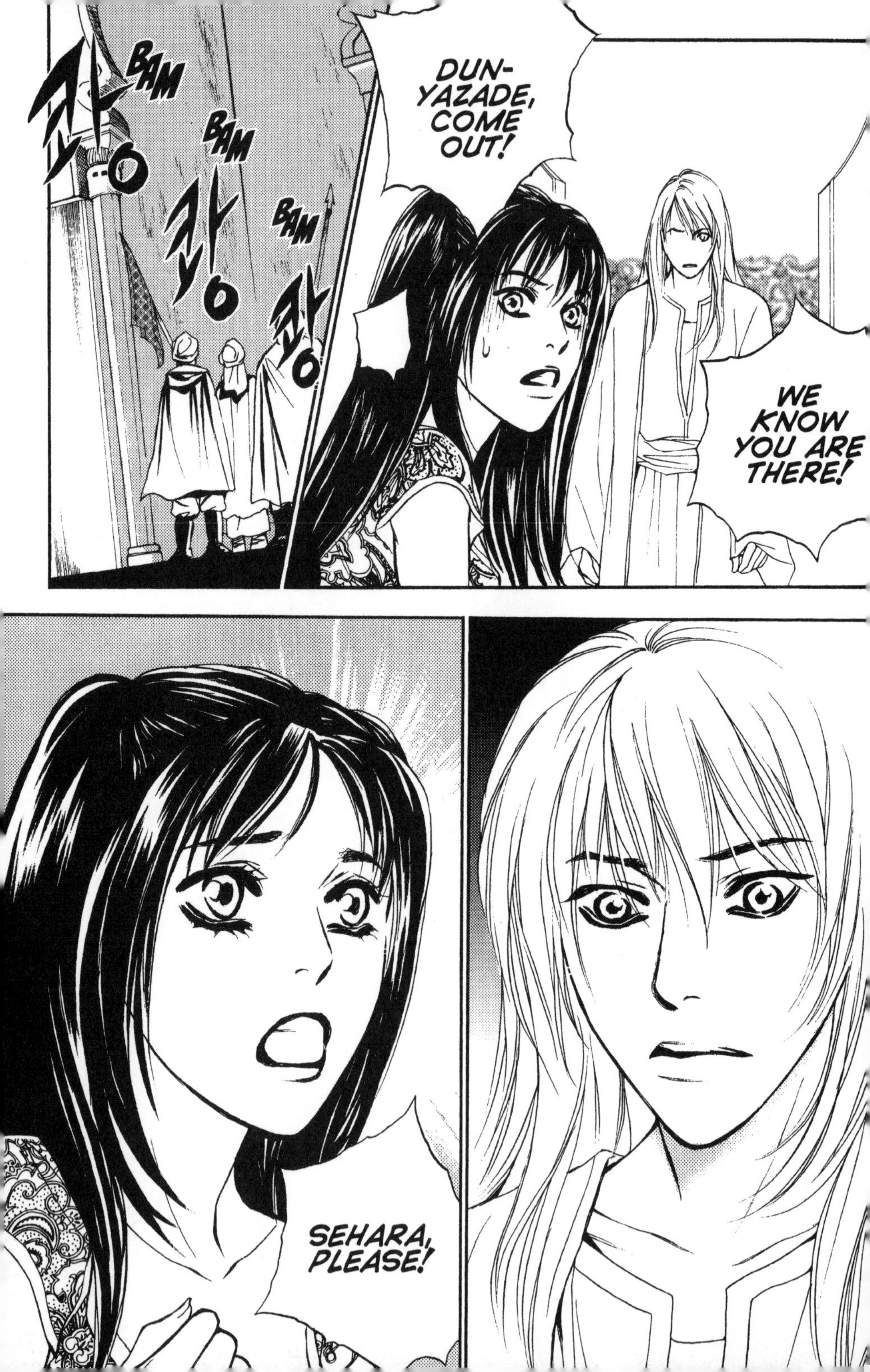
쾅
BAM
쾅
BAM
쾅
BAM
DUN-YAZADE, COME OUT!
WE KNOW YOU ARE THERE!
SEHARA, PLEASE!

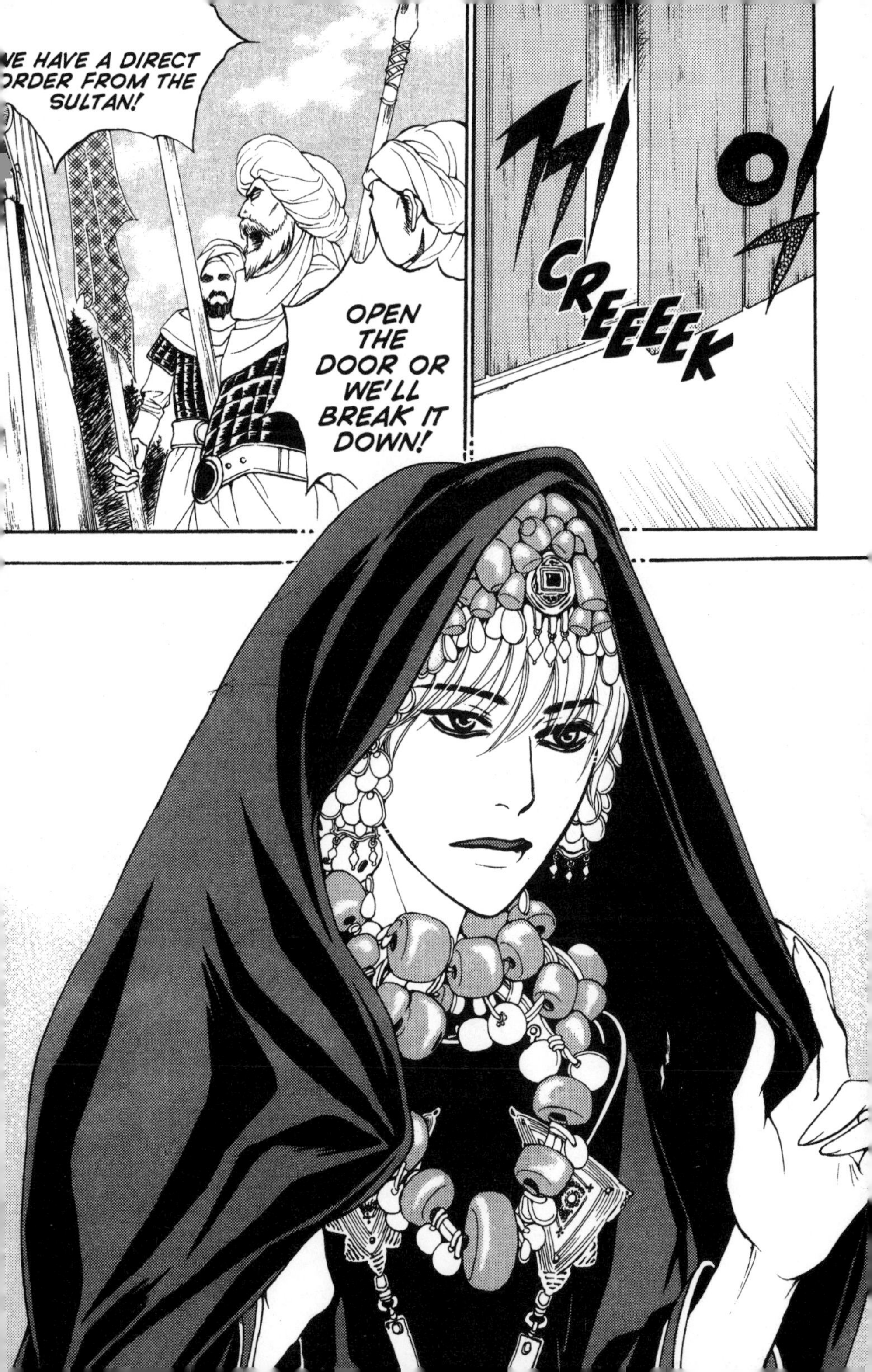

WE HAVE A DIRECT ORDER FROM THE SULTAN!
OPEN THE DOOR OR WE'LL BREAK IT DOWN!
CREEEEK

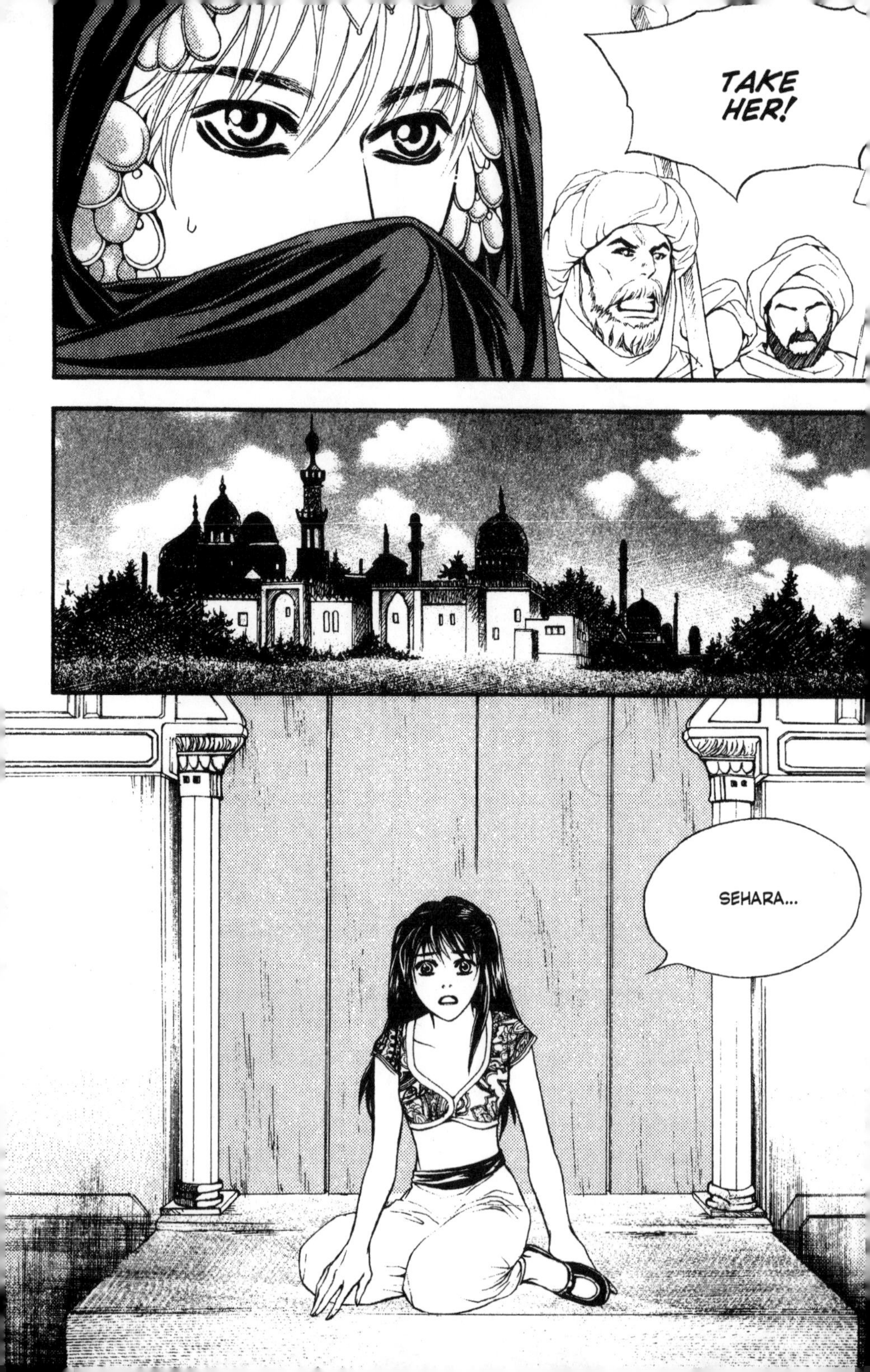
TAKE HER!
SEHARA...

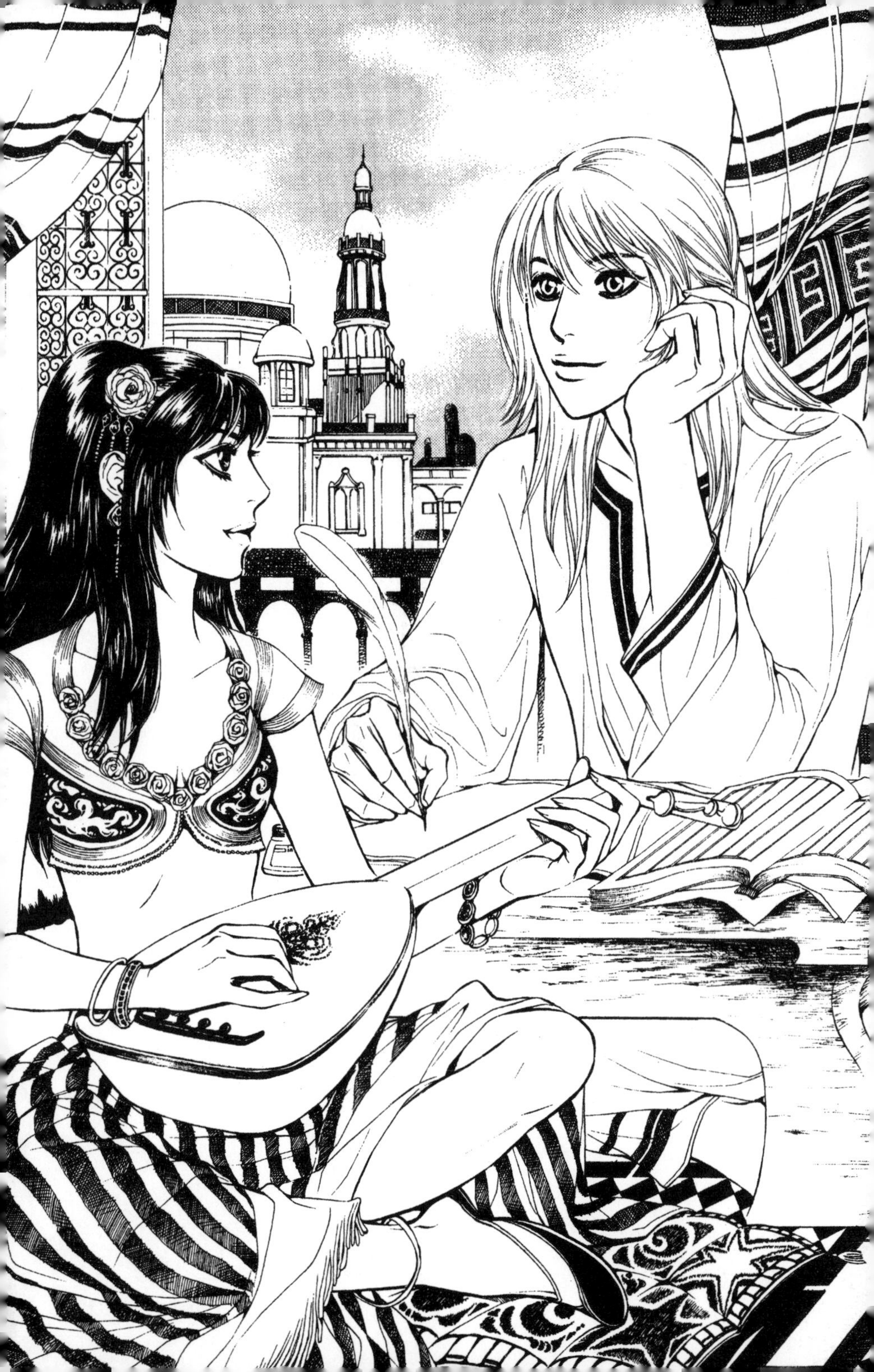

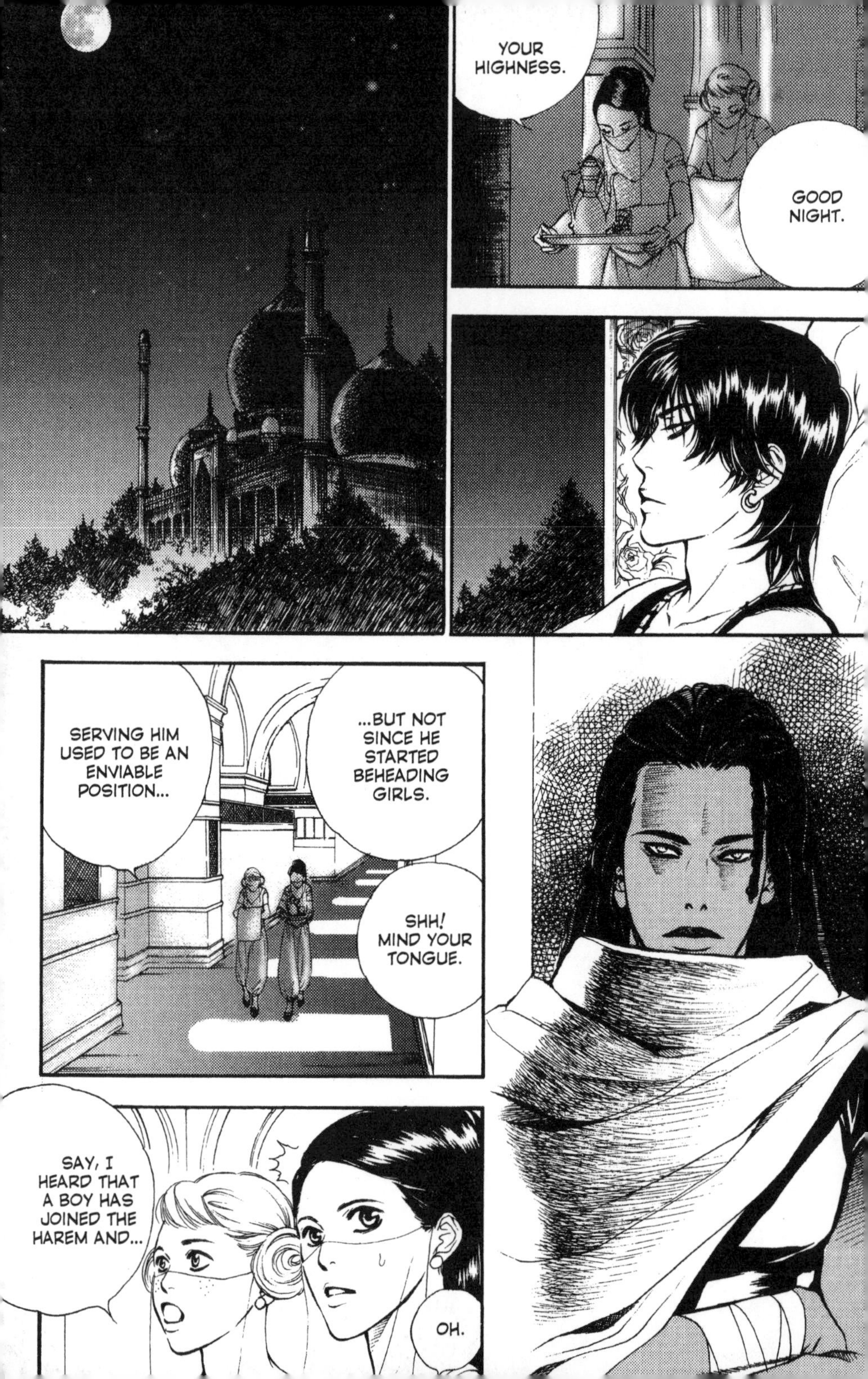
YOUR HIGHNESS.
GOOD NIGHT.
SERVING HIM USED TO BE AN ENVIABLE POSITION...
...BUT NOT SINCE HE STARTED BEHEADING GIRLS.
SHH! MIND YOUR TONGUE.
SAY, I HEARD THAT A BOY HAS JOINED THE HAREM AND...
OH.

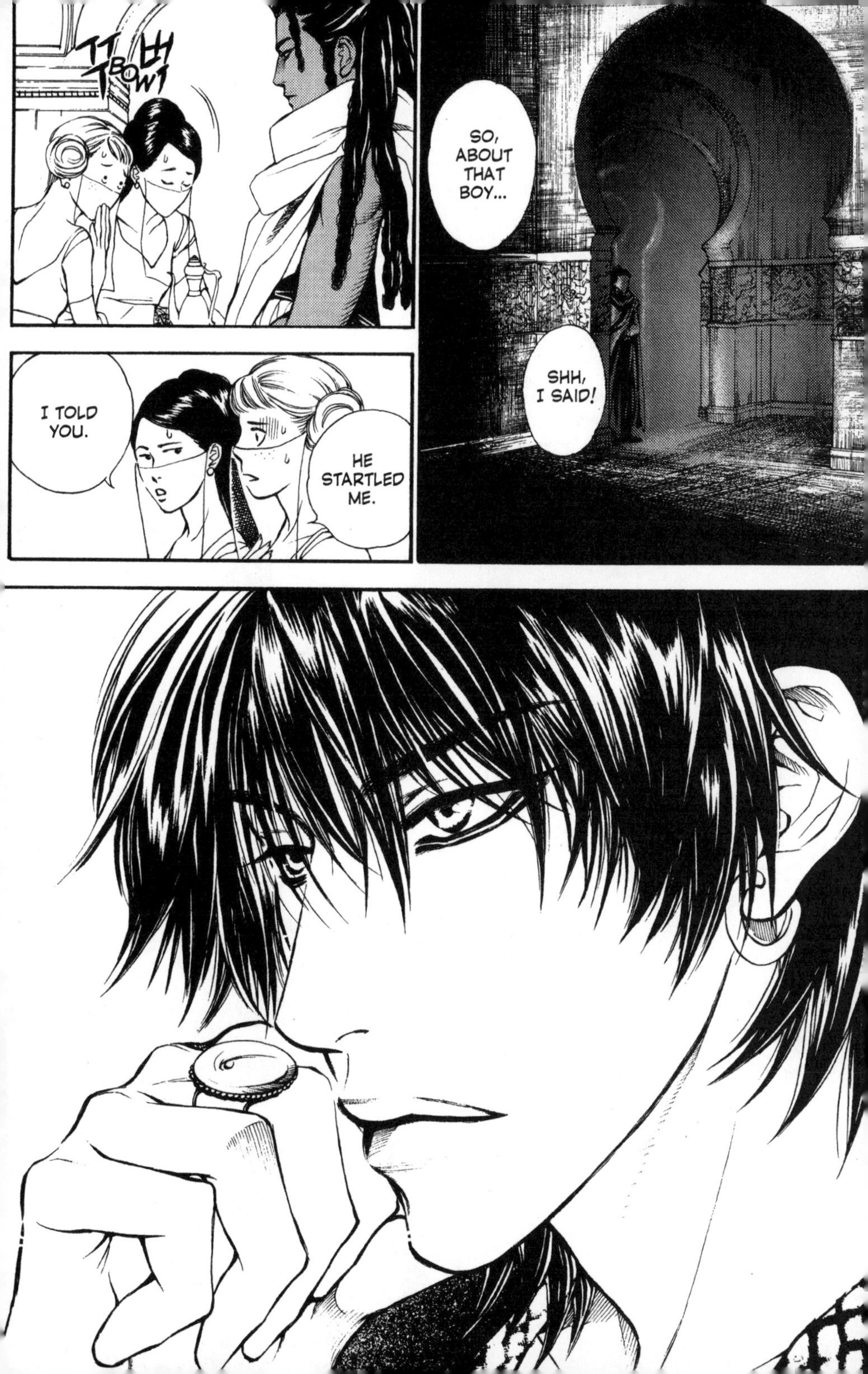
BOW
I TOLD YOU.
HE STARTLED ME.
SO, ABOUT THAT BOY...
SHH, I SAID!

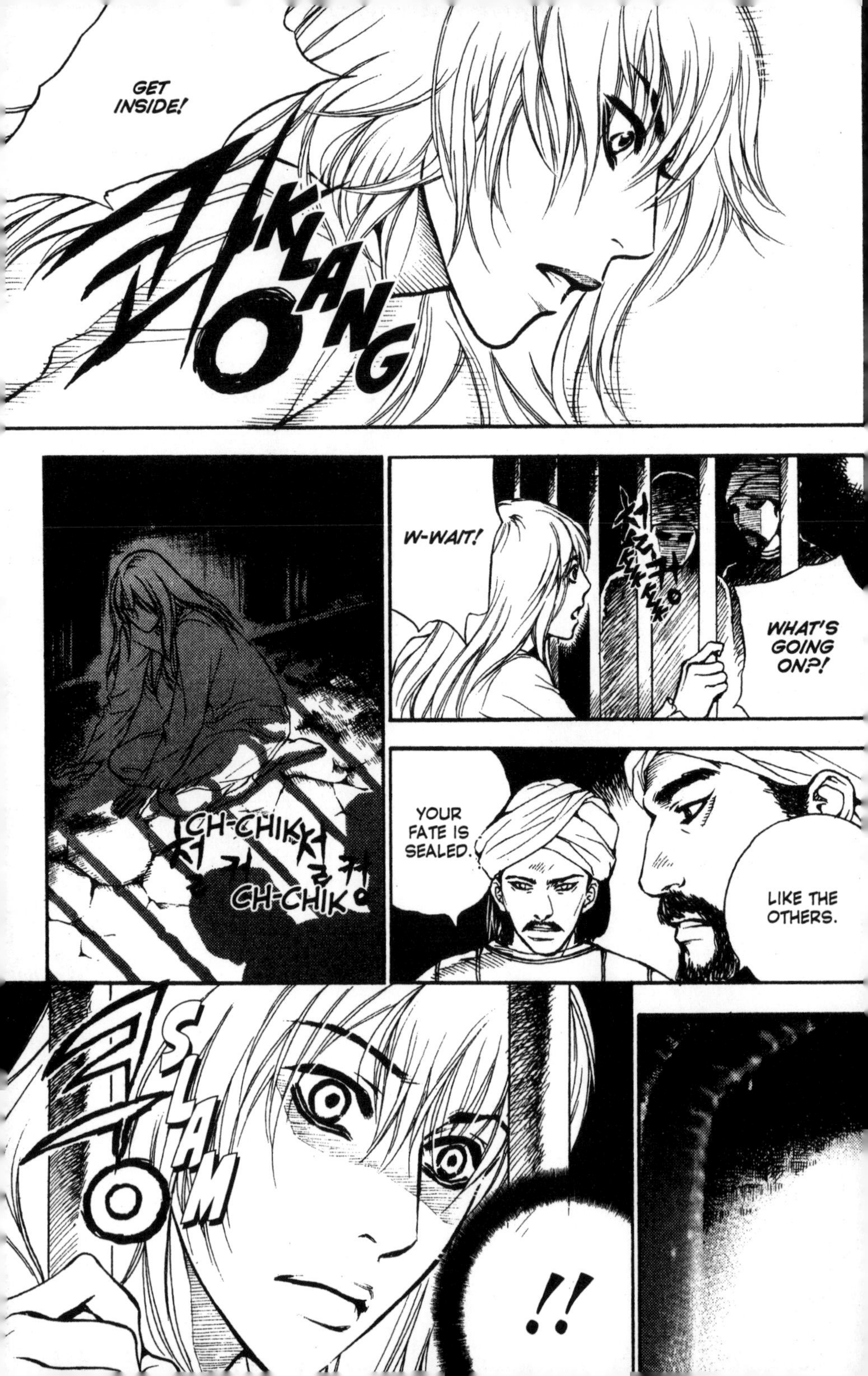
GET INSIDE!
KLANG
CH-CHIK
CH-CHIK
W-WAIT!
WHAT'S GOING ON?!
YOUR FATE IS SEALED.
LIKE THE OTHERS.
SLAM
!!

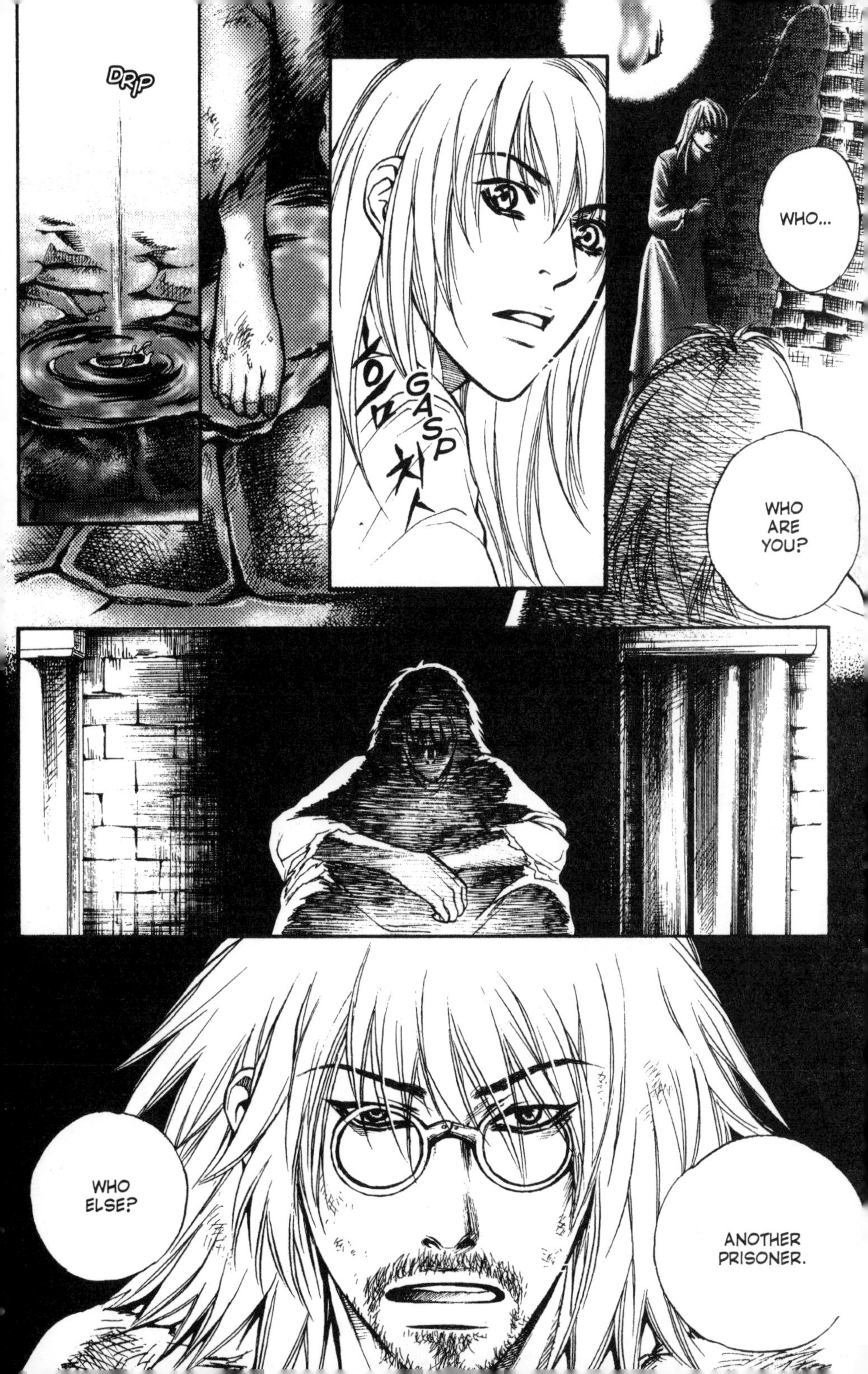
DRIP
GASP
WHO...
WHO ARE YOU?
WHO ELSE?
ANOTHER PRISONER.

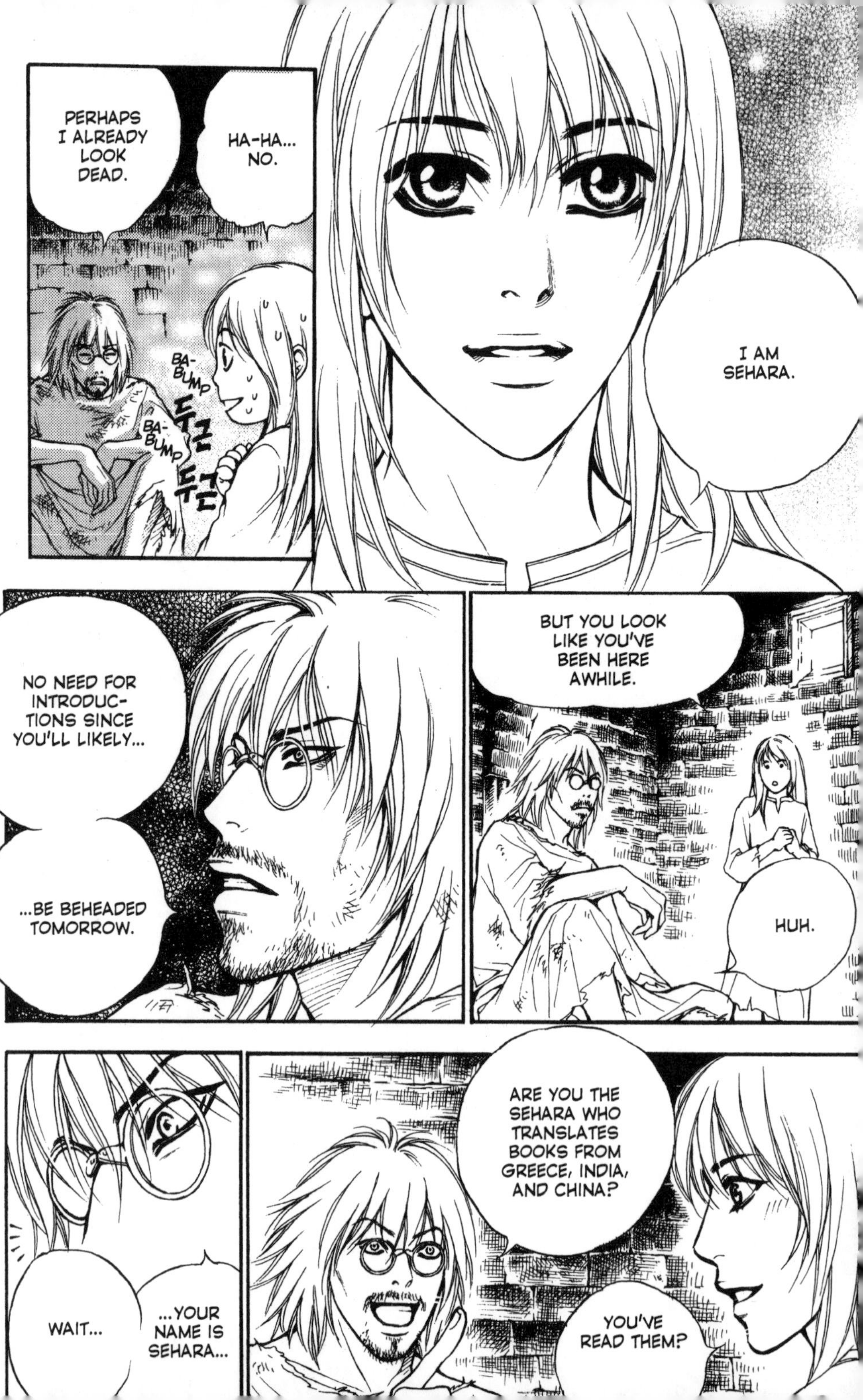
PERHAPS I ALREADY LOOK DEAD.
HA-HA... NO.
BA-BUMP
BA-BUMP
I AM SEHARA.
NO NEED FOR INTRODUC-TIONS SINCE YOU'LL LIKELY...
...BE BEHEADED TOMORROW.
BUT YOU LOOK LIKE YOU'VE BEEN HERE AWHILE.
HUH.
WAIT...
...YOUR NAME IS SEHARA...
ARE YOU THE SEHARA WHO TRANSLATES BOOKS FROM GREECE, INDIA, AND CHINA?
YOU'VE READ THEM?

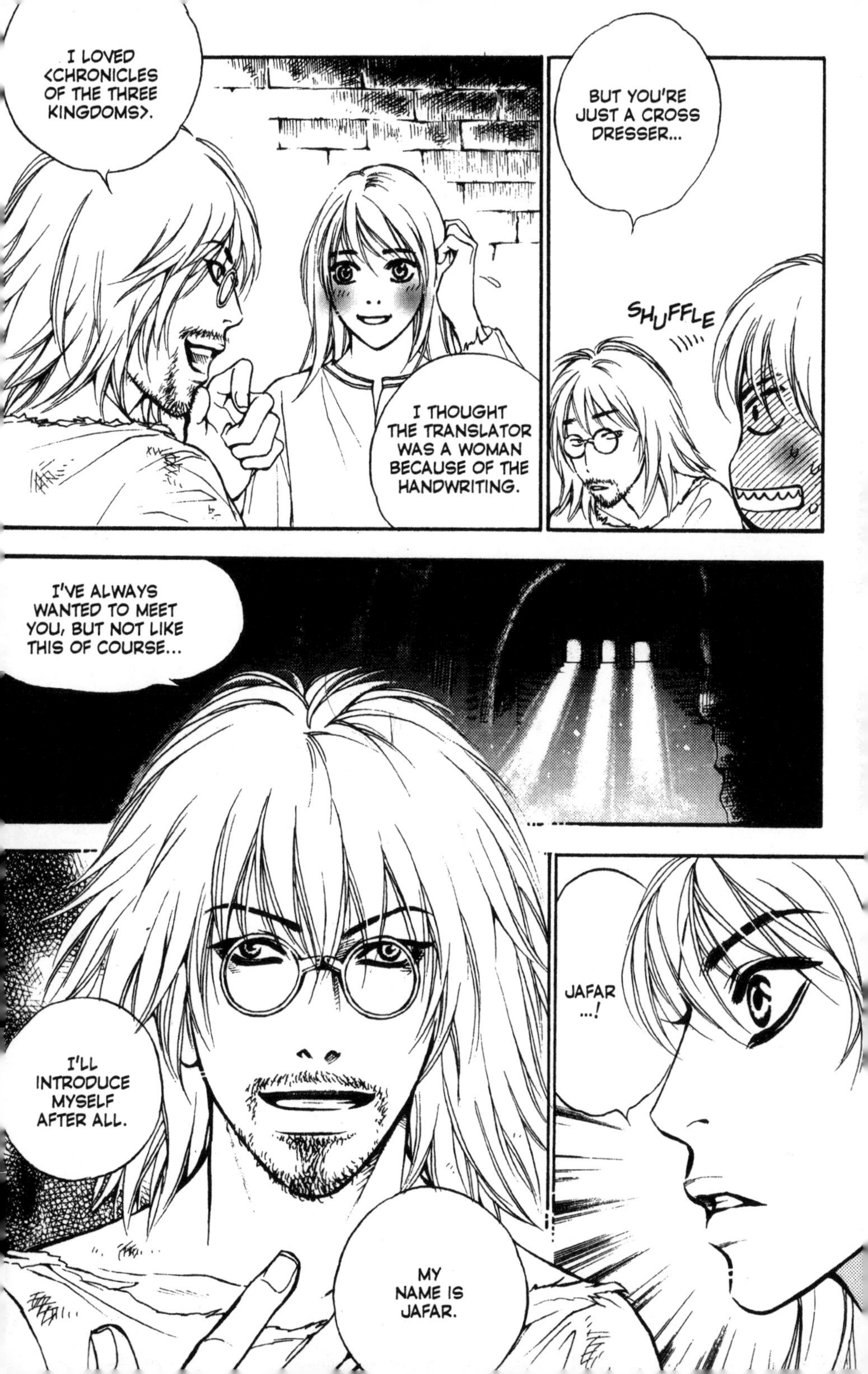

I LOVED <CHRONICLES OF THE THREE KINGDOMS>.
I THOUGHT THE TRANSLATOR WAS A WOMAN BECAUSE OF THE HANDWRITING.
BUT YOU'RE JUST A CROSS DRESSER...
SHUFFLE
I'VE ALWAYS WANTED TO MEET YOU, BUT NOT LIKE THIS OF COURSE...
I'LL INTRODUCE MYSELF AFTER ALL.
MY NAME IS JAFAR.
JAFAR ...!

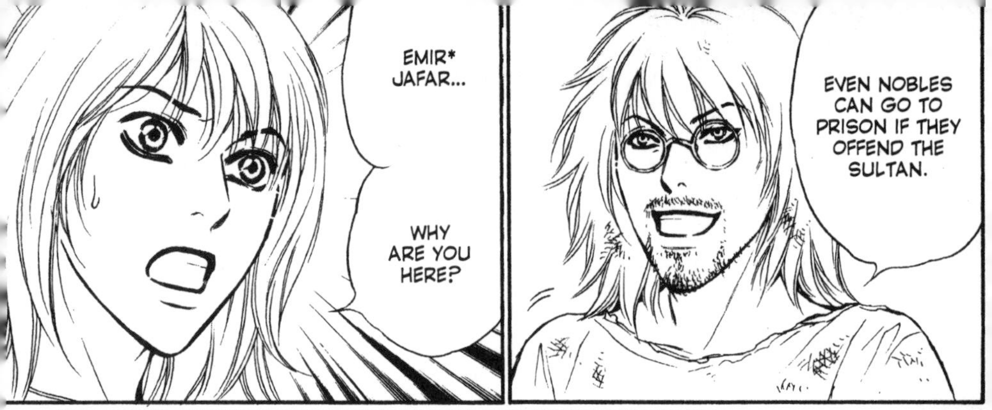
EMIR* JAFAR...
WHY ARE YOU HERE?
EVEN NOBLES CAN GO TO PRISON IF THEY OFFEND THE SULTAN.

* EMIR: A TITLE OF NOBILITY HISTORICALLY USED IN ISLAMIC NATIONS OF THE MIDDLE EAST AND NORTH AFRICA

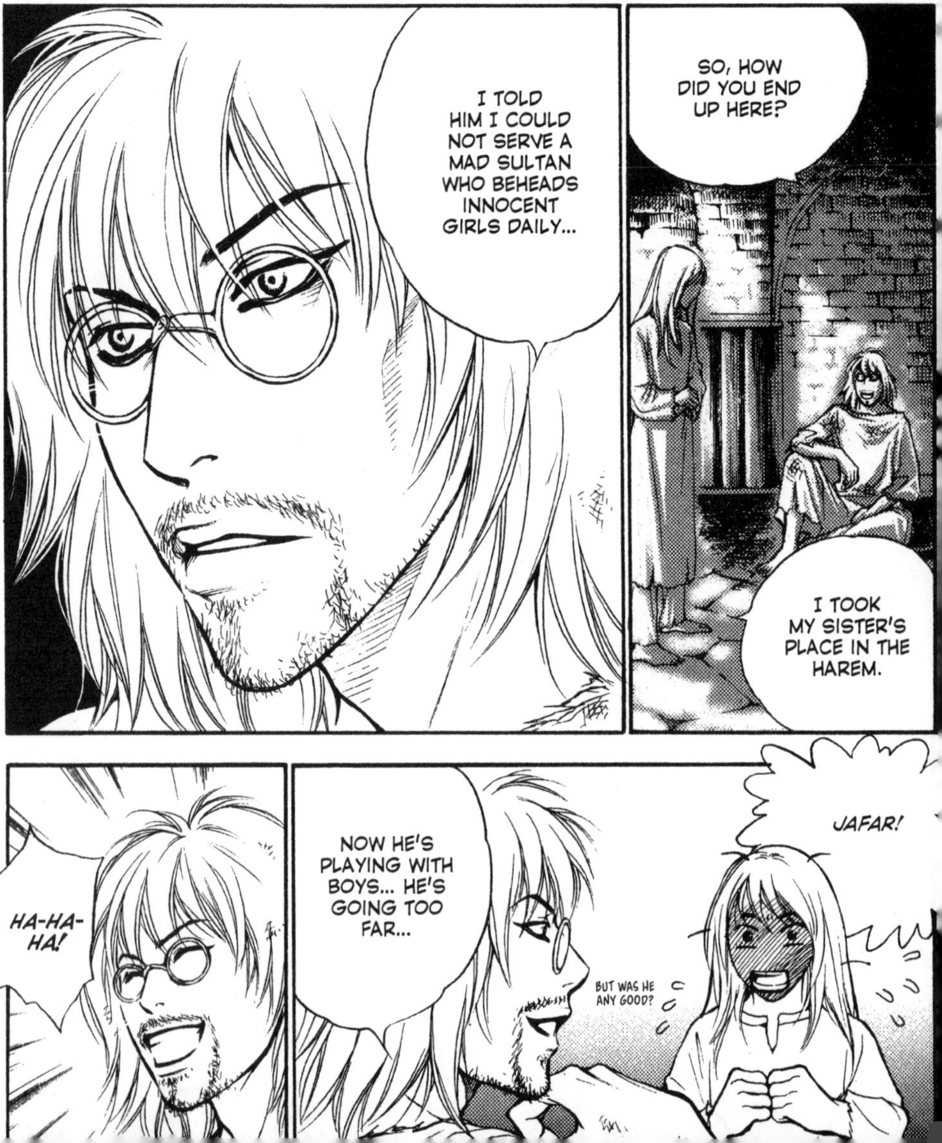
I TOLD HIM I COULD NOT SERVE A MAD SULTAN WHO BEHEADS INNOCENT GIRLS DAILY...
SO, HOW DID YOU END UP HERE?
I TOOK MY SISTER'S PLACE IN THE HAREM.
HA-HA-HA!
NOW HE'S PLAYING WITH BOYS... HE'S GOING TOO FAR...
BUT WAS HE ANY GOOD?
JAFAR!

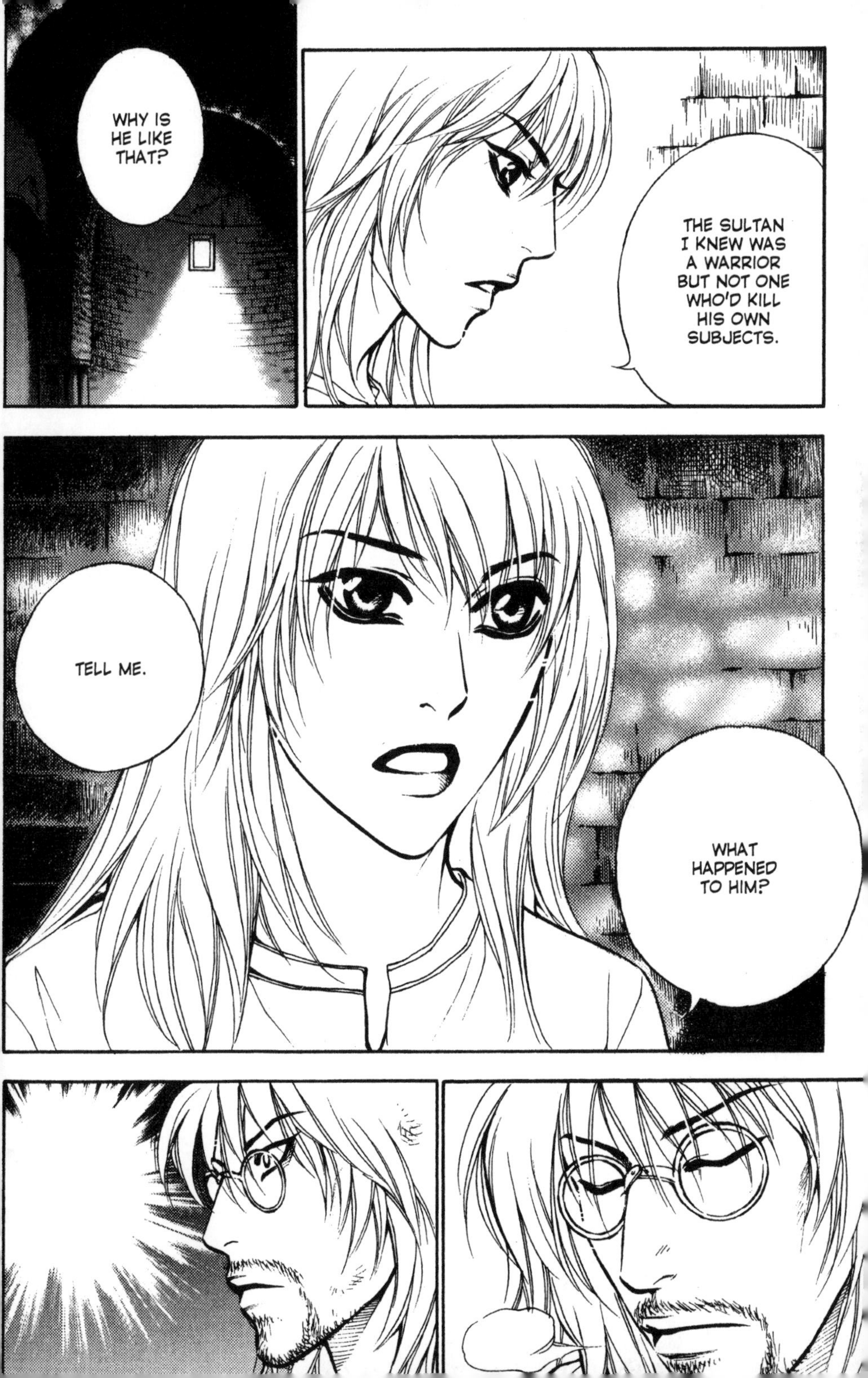
WHY IS HE LIKE THAT?
THE SULTAN I KNEW WAS A WARRIOR BUT NOT ONE WHO'D KILL HIS OWN SUBJECTS.
TELL ME.
WHAT HAPPENED TO HIM?

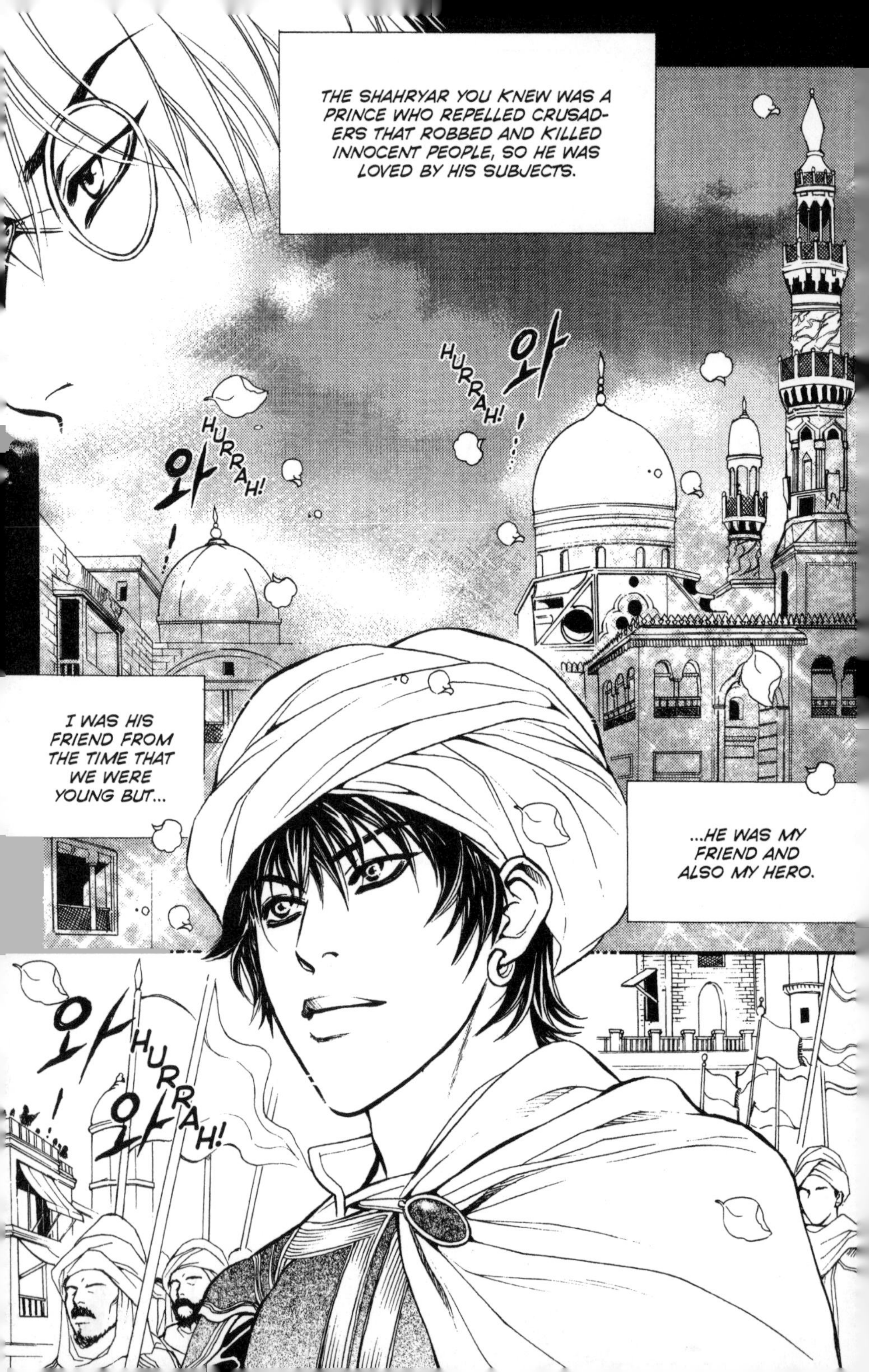
THE SHAHRYAR YOU KNEW WAS A PRINCE WHO REPELLED CRUSADERS THAT ROBBED AND KILLED INNOCENT PEOPLE, SO HE WAS LOVED BY HIS SUBJECTS.
와 HURRAH!
와 HURRAH!
I WAS HIS FRIEND FROM THE TIME THAT WE WERE YOUNG BUT...
...HE WAS MY FRIEND AND ALSO MY HERO.
와아 HURRAH!
와아

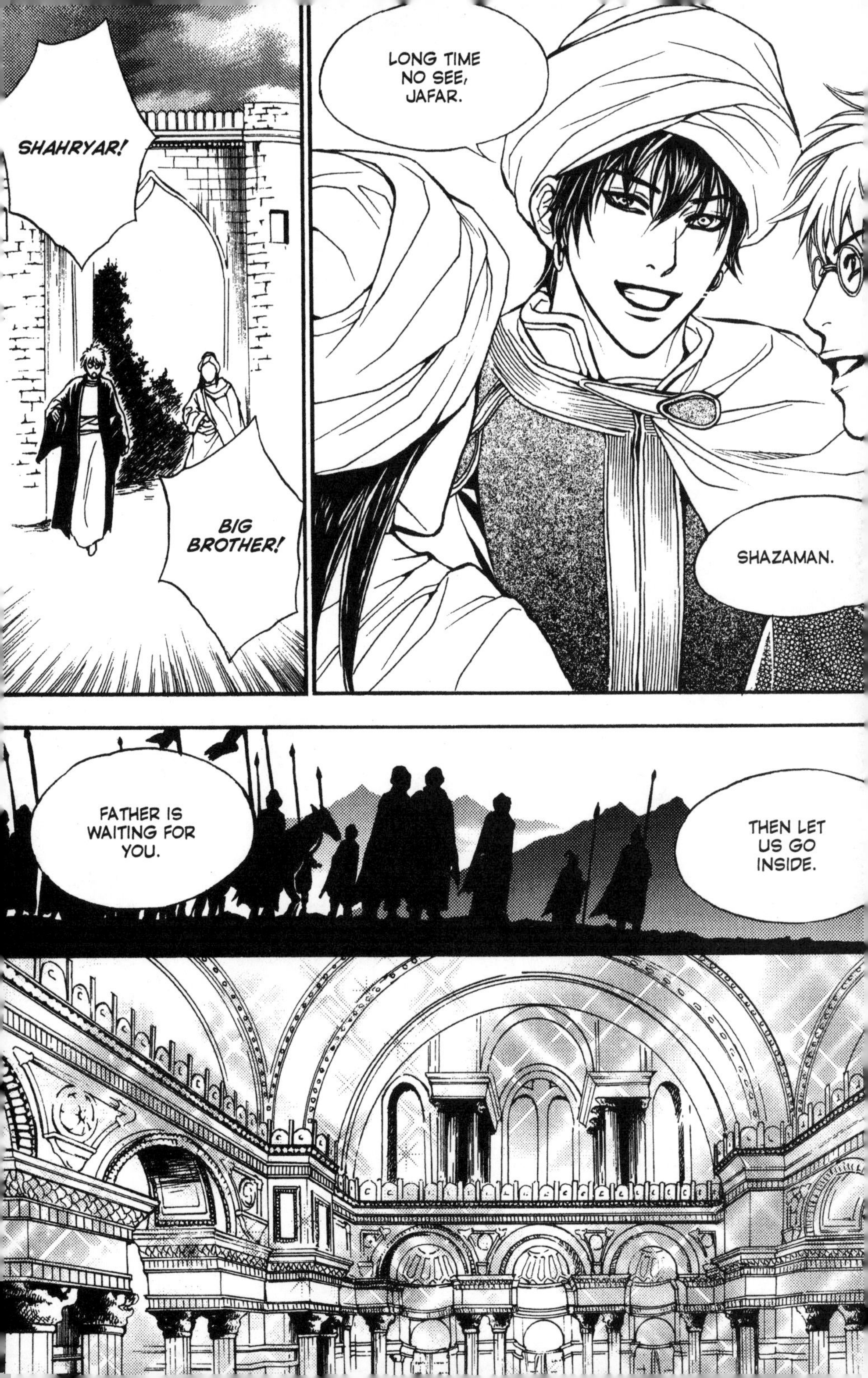
SHAHRYAR!
BIG BROTHER!
LONG TIME NO SEE, JAFAR.
SHAZAMAN.
FATHER IS WAITING FOR YOU.
THEN LET US GO INSIDE.

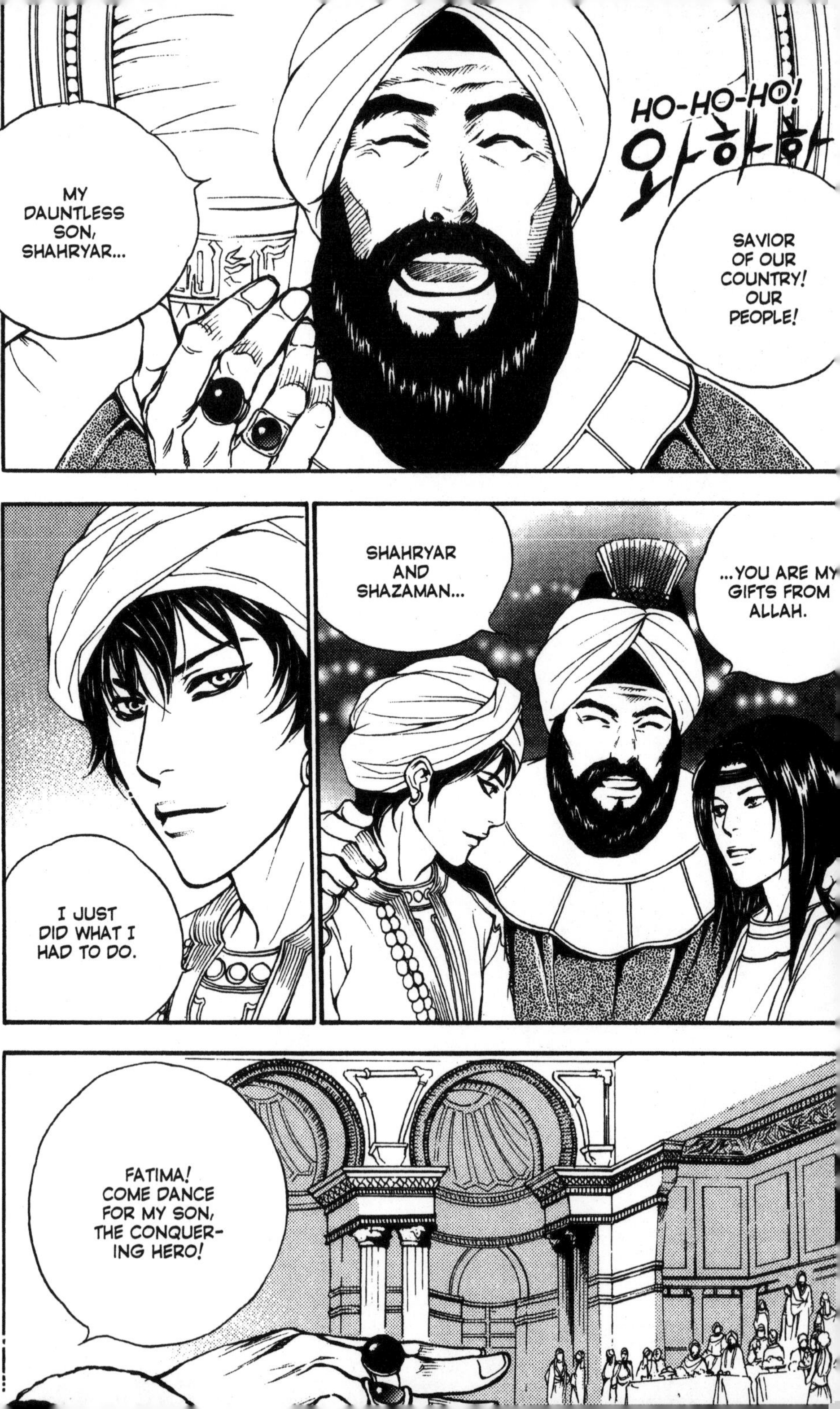
MY DAUNTLESS SON, SHAHRYAR...
HO-HO-HO!
와하하
SAVIOR OF OUR COUNTRY! OUR PEOPLE!
I JUST DID WHAT I HAD TO DO.
SHAHRYAR AND SHAZAMAN...
...YOU ARE MY GIFTS FROM ALLAH.
FATIMA! COME DANCE FOR MY SON, THE CONQUER-ING HERO!

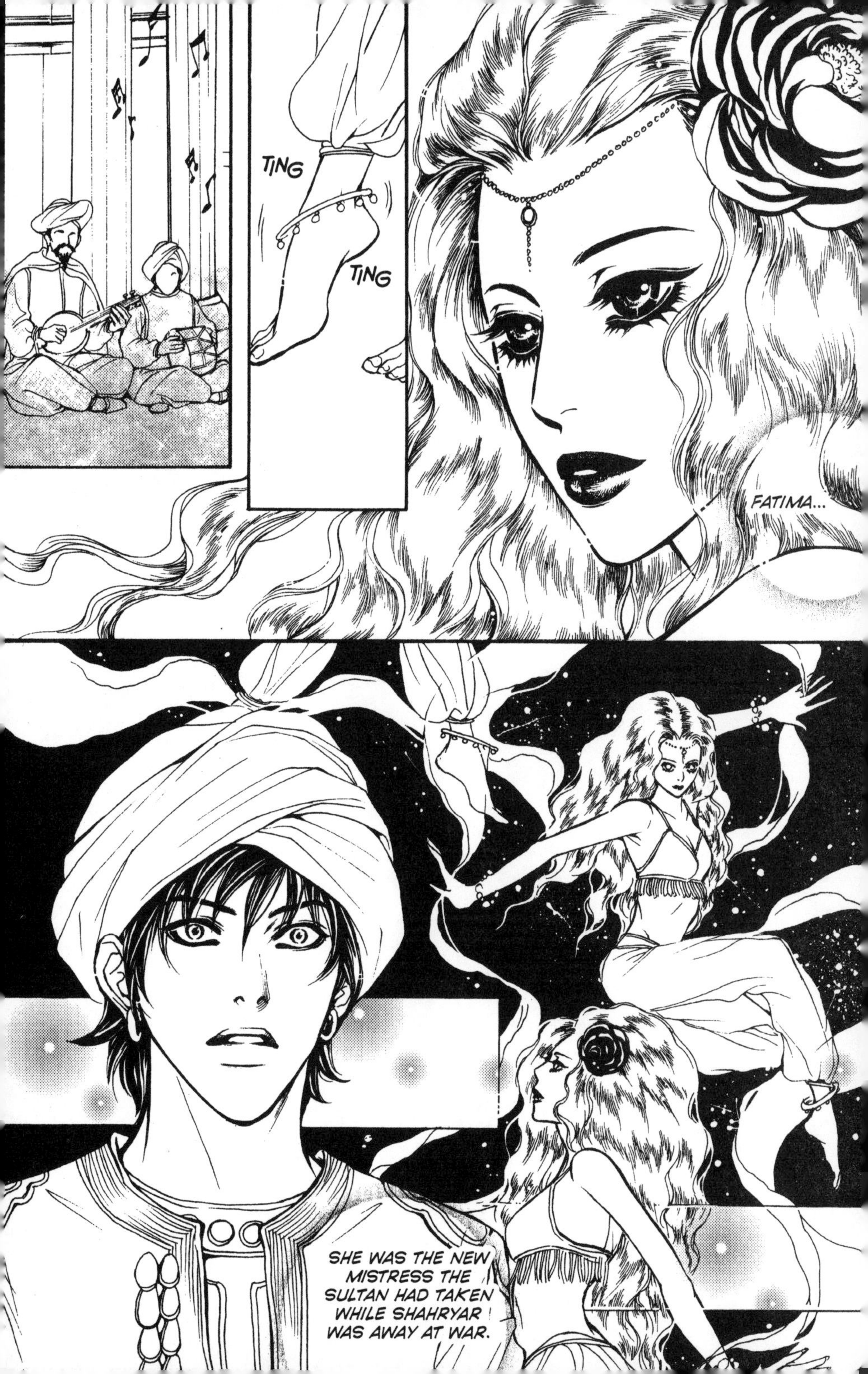
TING
TING
FATIMA...
SHE WAS THE NEW MISTRESS THE SULTAN HAD TAKEN WHILE SHAHRYAR WAS AWAY AT WAR.

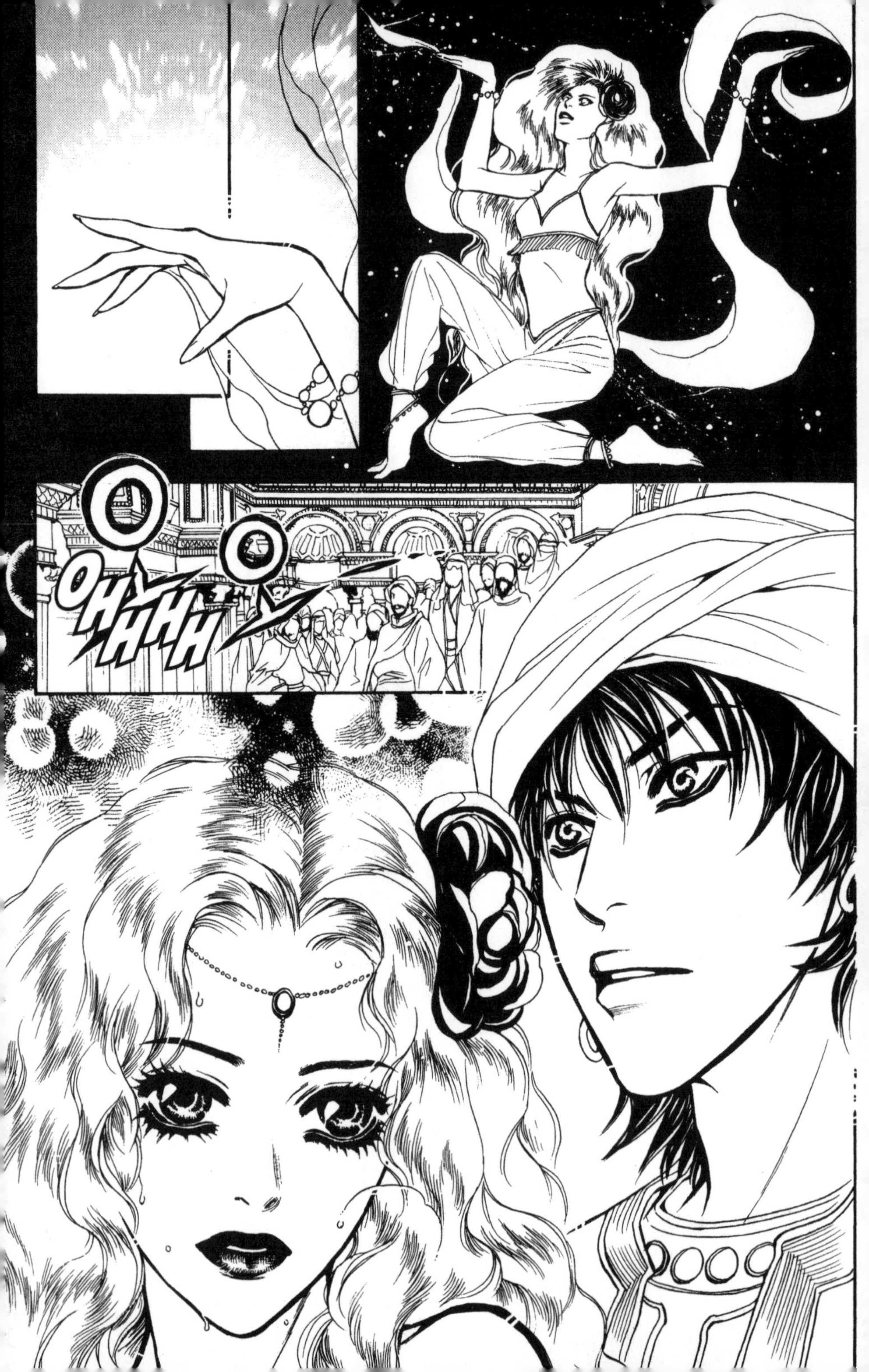
OHHHH

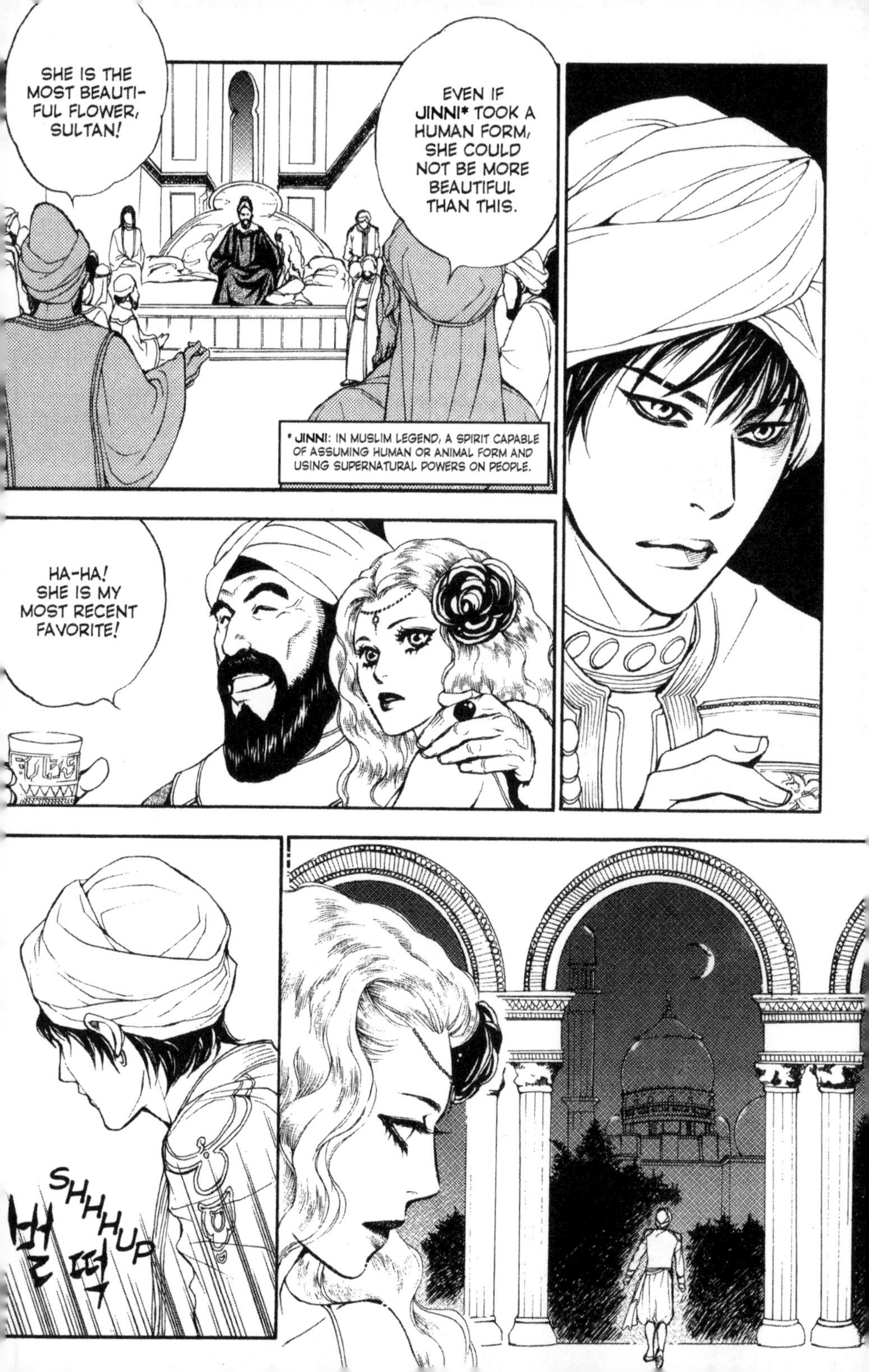
SHE IS THE MOST BEAUTI-FUL FLOWER, SULTAN!
EVEN IF JINNI* TOOK A HUMAN FORM, SHE COULD NOT BE MORE BEAUTIFUL THAN THIS.
* JINNI: IN MUSLIM LEGEND, A SPIRIT CAPABLE OF ASSUMING HUMAN OR ANIMAL FORM AND USING SUPERNATURAL POWERS ON PEOPLE.
HA-HA! SHE IS MY MOST RECENT FAVORITE!
SHHHUP
벌떡

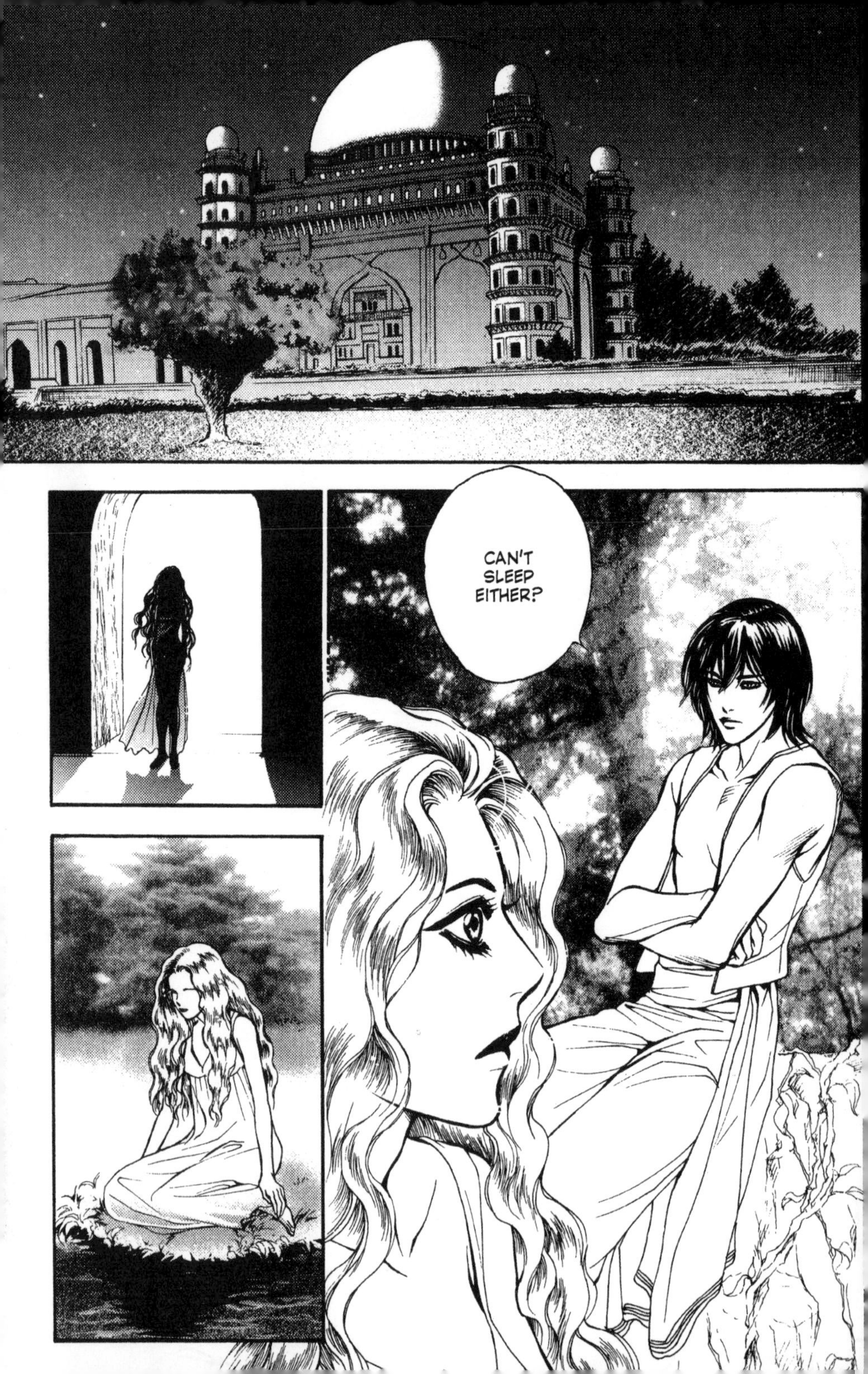
CAN'T SLEEP EITHER?

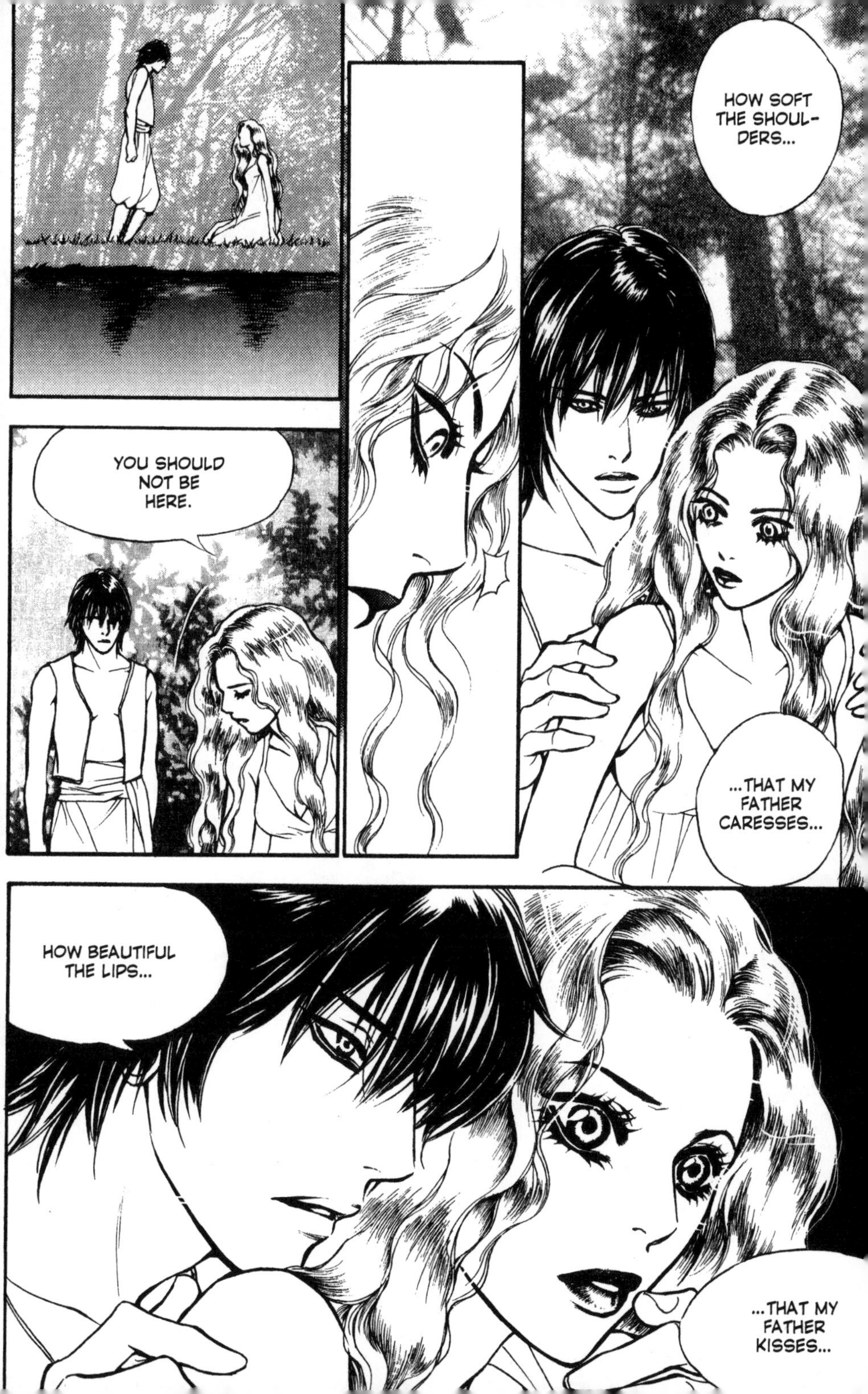
YOU SHOULD NOT BE HERE.
HOW SOFT THE SHOUL-DERS...
...THAT MY FATHER CARESSES...
HOW BEAUTIFUL THE LIPS...
...THAT MY FATHER KISSES...

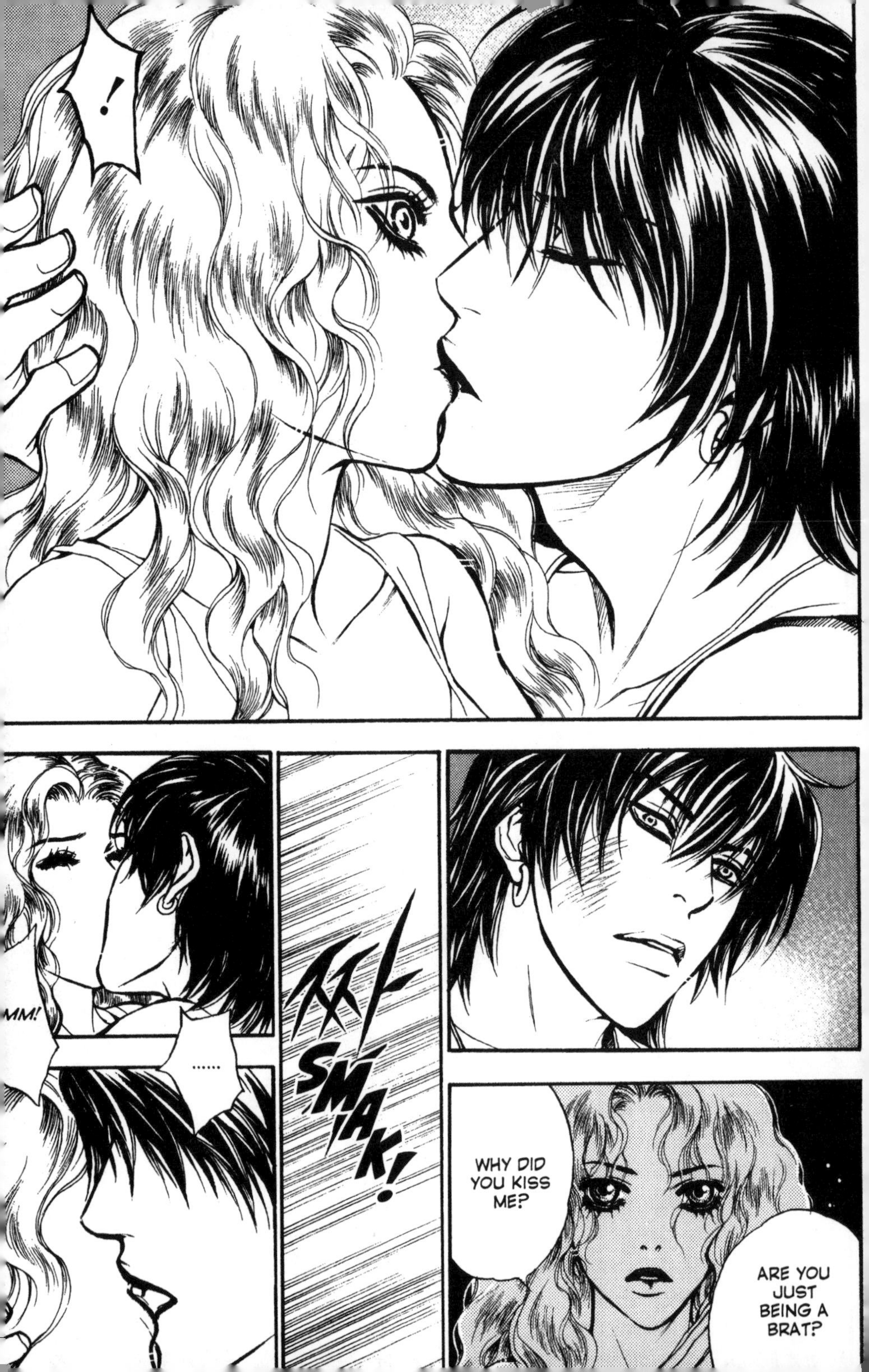
!
MM!
......
SMAK!
WHY DID YOU KISS ME?
ARE YOU JUST BEING A BRAT?

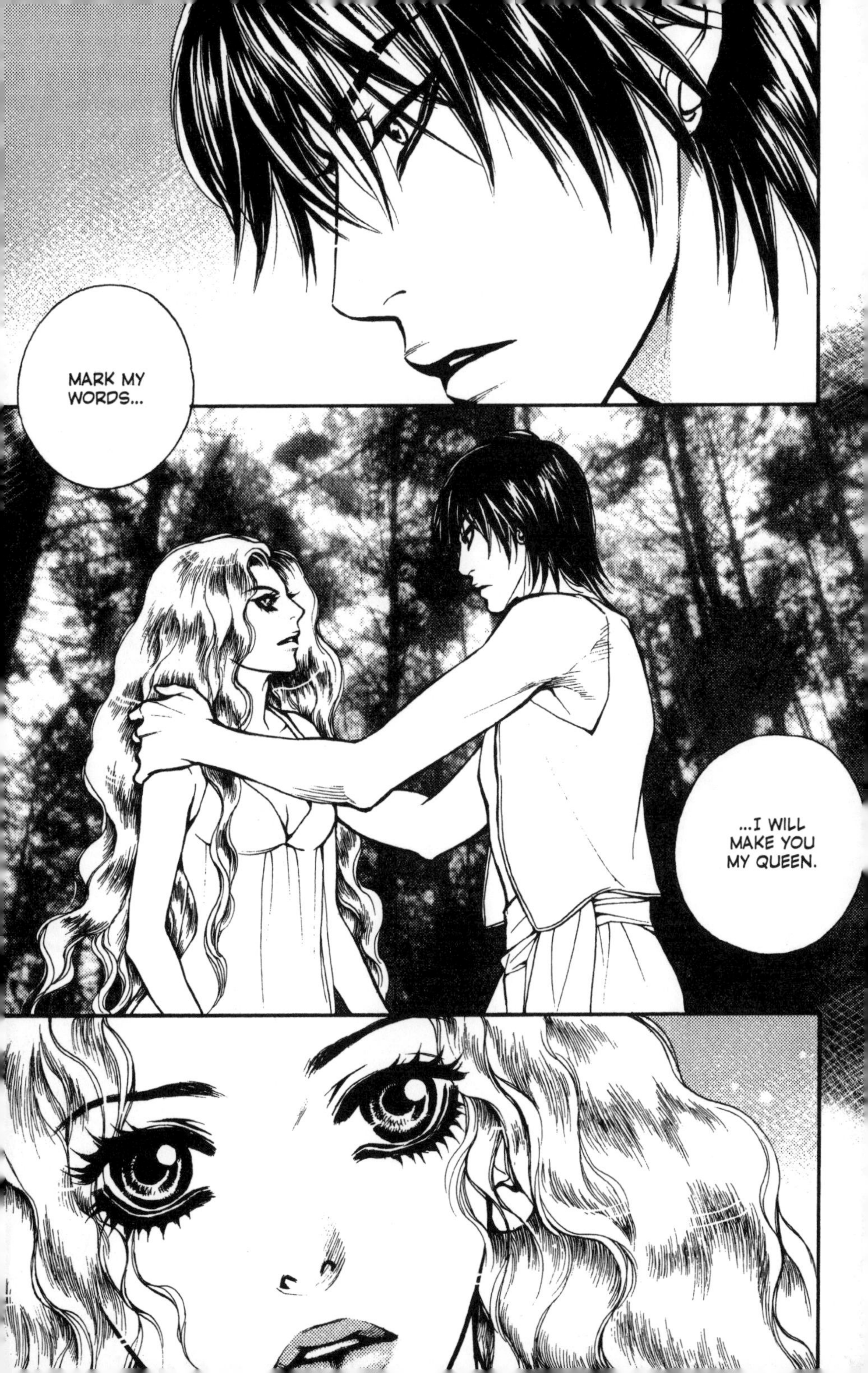
MARK MY WORDS...
...I WILL MAKE YOU MY QUEEN.

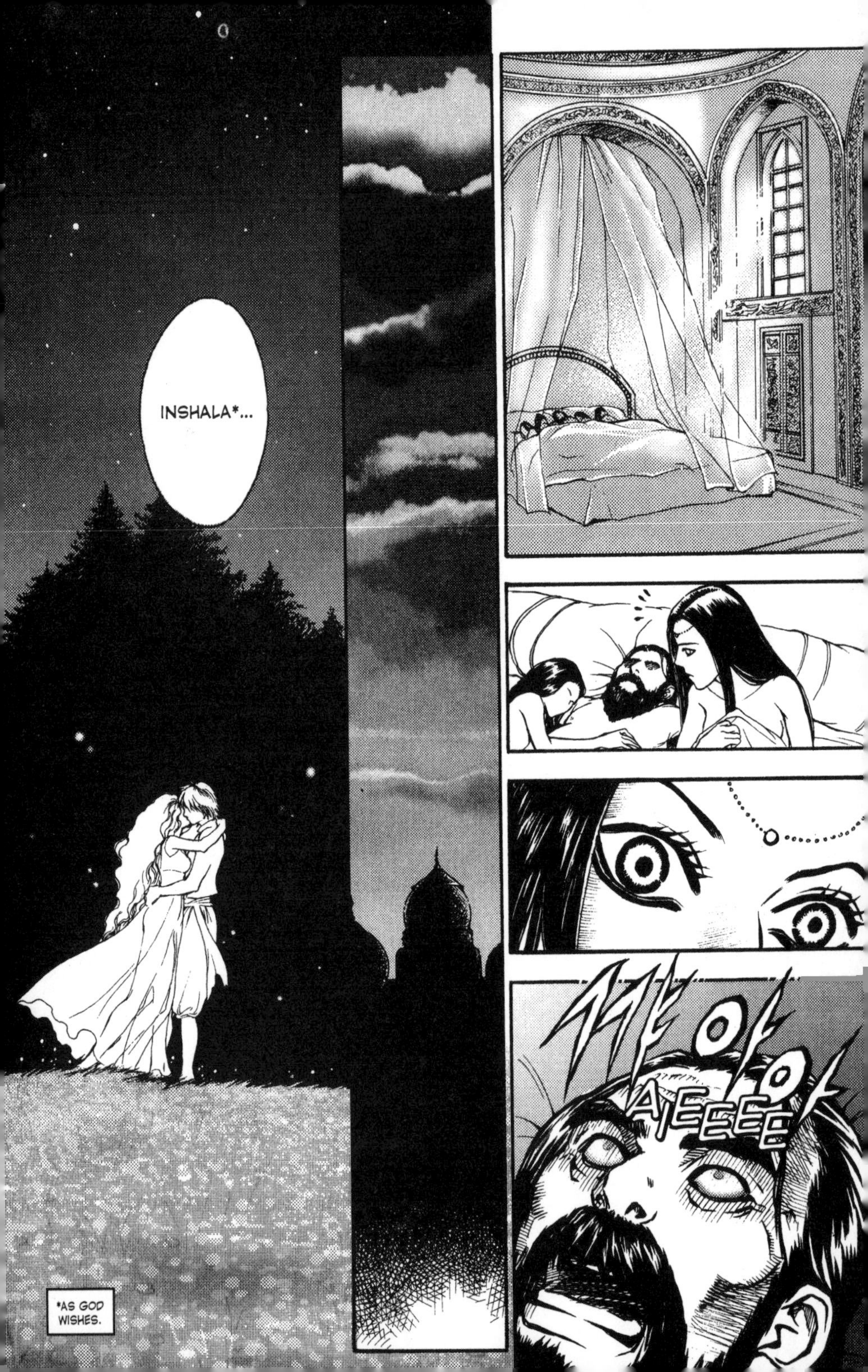
INSHALA*...
*AS GOD WISHES.
AIEEEEE

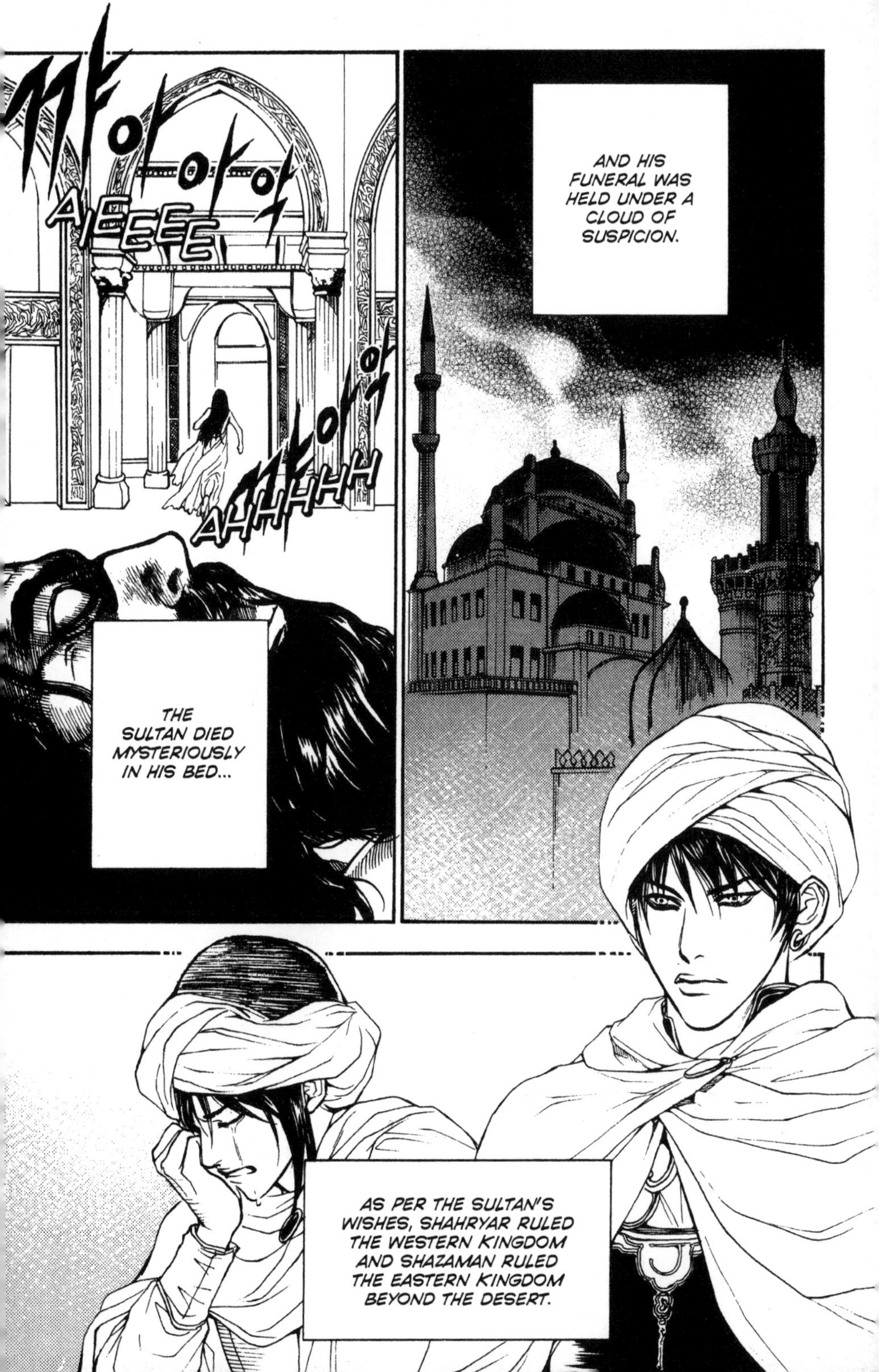
꺄아아아악
AIEEEE
꺄아악
AHHHHHH
THE SULTAN DIED MYSTERIOUSLY IN HIS BED...
AND HIS FUNERAL WAS HELD UNDER A CLOUD OF SUSPICION.
AS PER THE SULTAN'S WISHES, SHAHRYAR RULED THE WESTERN KINGDOM AND SHAZAMAN RULED THE EASTERN KINGDOM BEYOND THE DESERT.

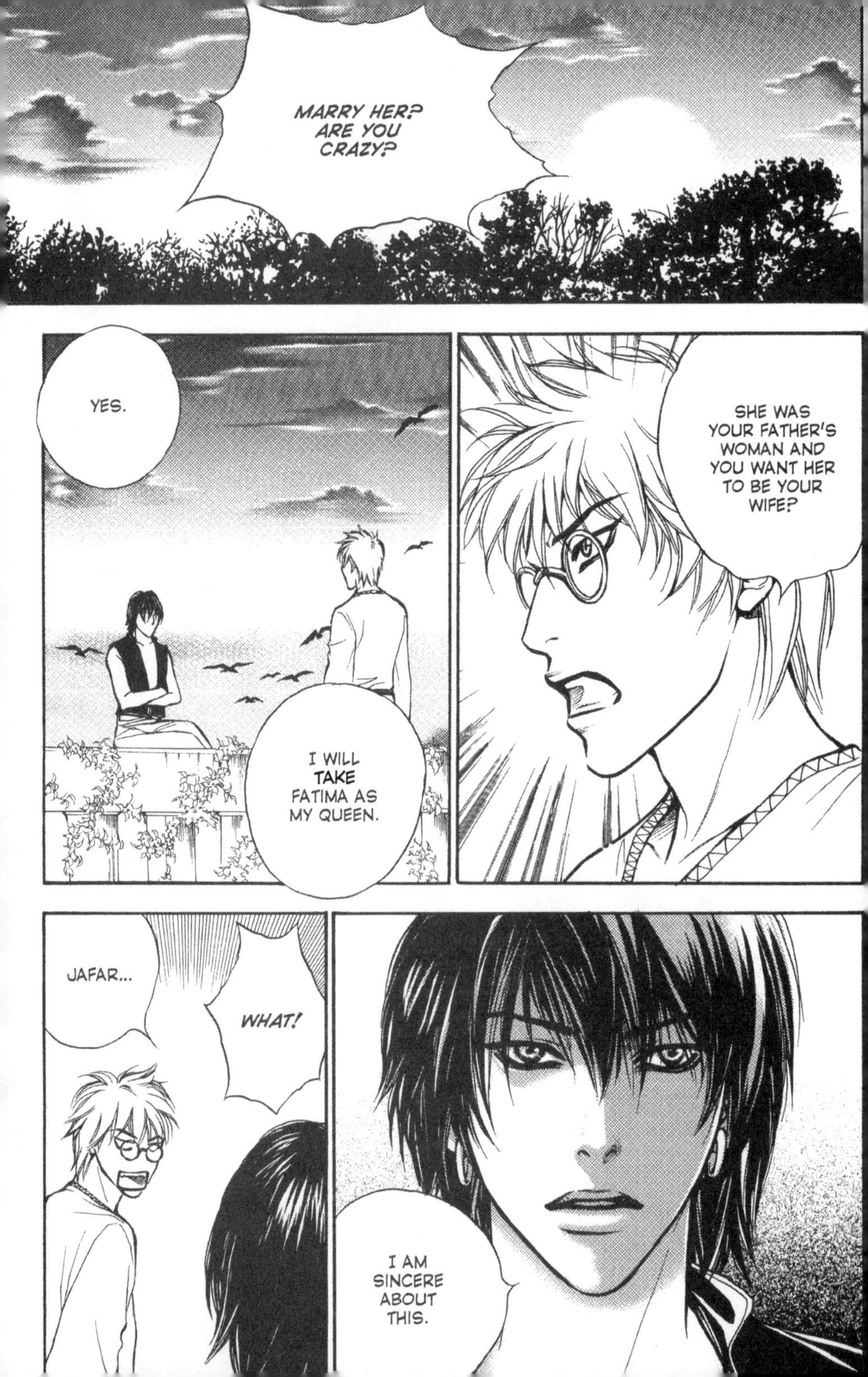
MARRY HER? ARE YOU CRAZY?
YES.
I WILL TAKE FATIMA AS MY QUEEN.
SHE WAS YOUR FATHER'S WOMAN AND YOU WANT HER TO BE YOUR WIFE?
JAFAR...
WHAT!
I AM SINCERE ABOUT THIS.

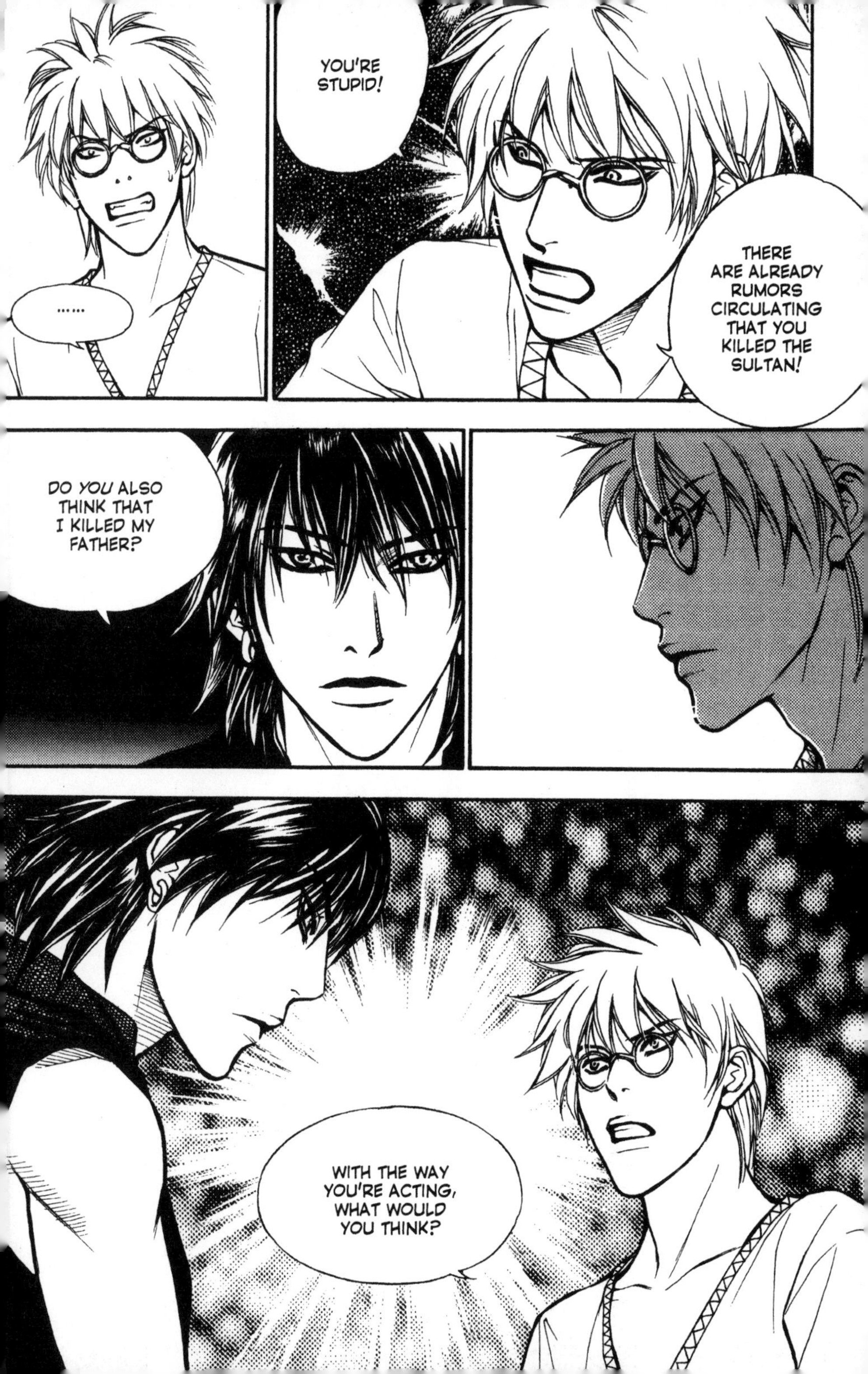
......
YOU'RE STUPID!
THERE ARE ALREADY RUMORS CIRCULATING THAT YOU KILLED THE SULTAN!
DO *YOU* ALSO THINK THAT I KILLED MY FATHER?
WITH THE WAY YOU'RE ACTING, WHAT WOULD YOU THINK?

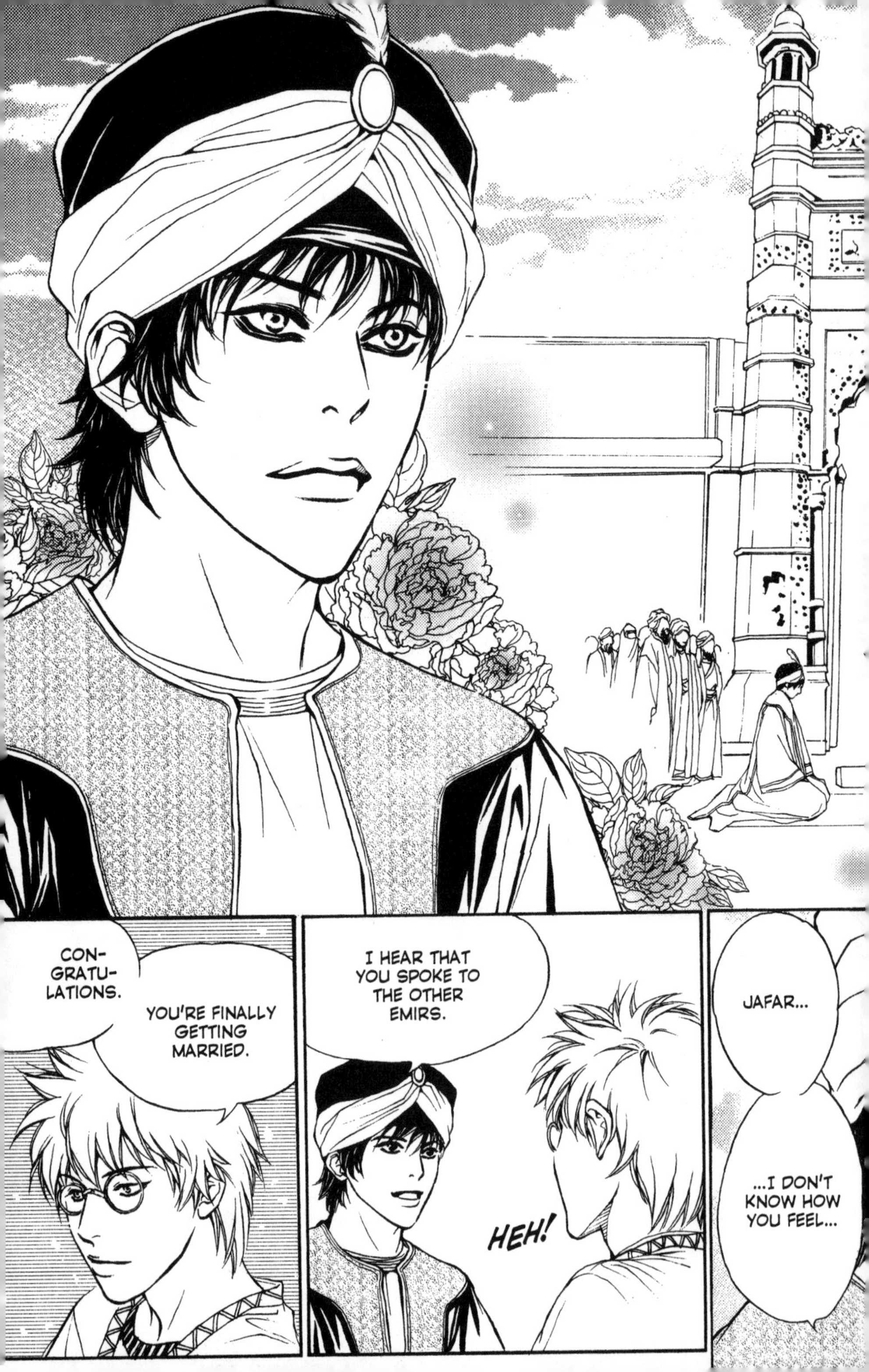
CON-GRATU-LATIONS.
YOU'RE FINALLY GETTING MARRIED.
I HEAR THAT YOU SPOKE TO THE OTHER EMIRS.
HEH!
JAFAR...
...I DON'T KNOW HOW YOU FEEL...

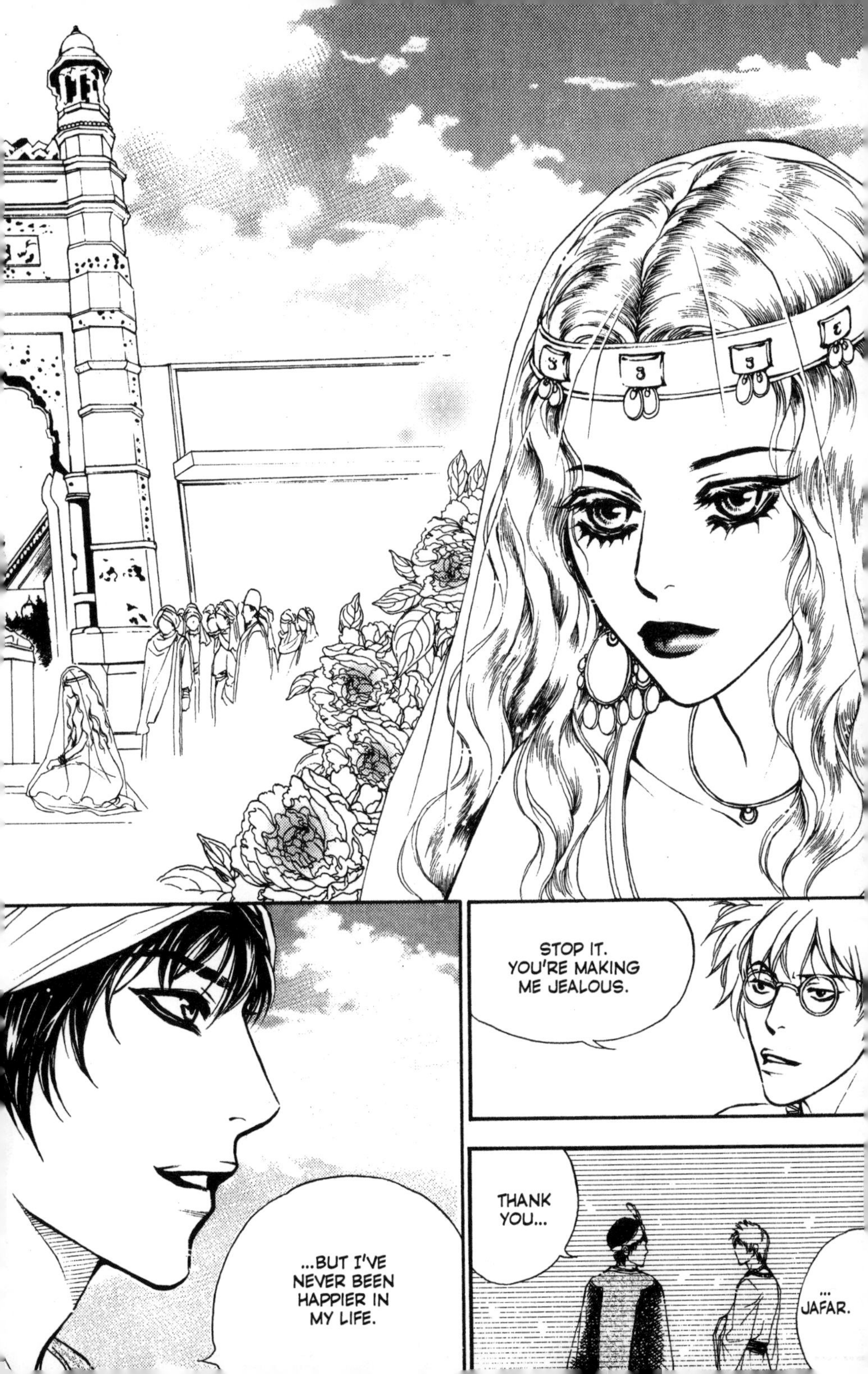
...BUT I'VE NEVER BEEN HAPPIER IN MY LIFE.
STOP IT. YOU'RE MAKING ME JEALOUS.
THANK YOU...
... JAFAR.

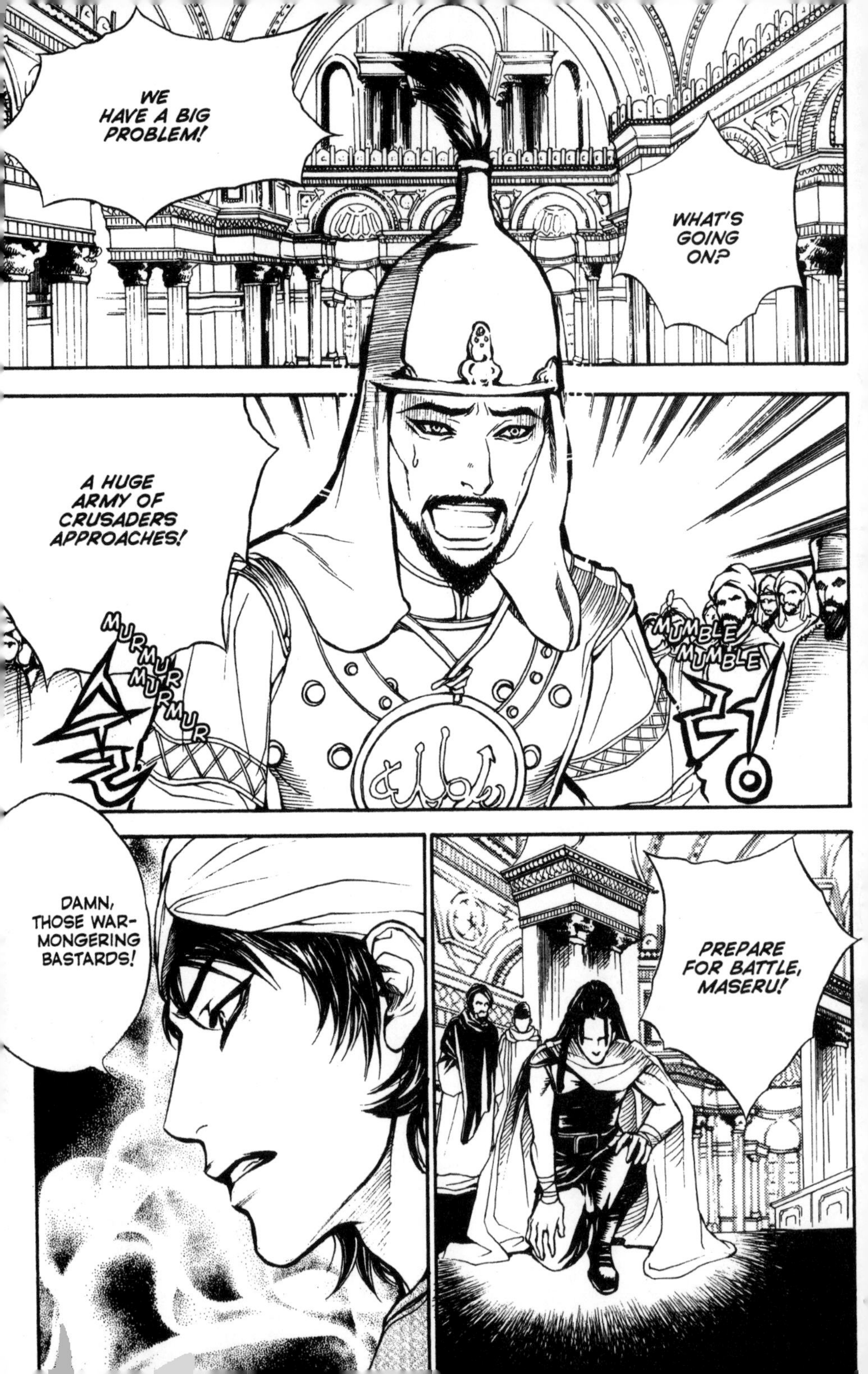
WE HAVE A BIG PROBLEM!
WHAT'S GOING ON?
A HUGE ARMY OF CRUSADERS APPROACHES!
MURMUR MURMUR MURMUR
MUMBLE MUMBLE
DAMN, THOSE WAR-MONGERING BASTARDS!
PREPARE FOR BATTLE, MASERU!

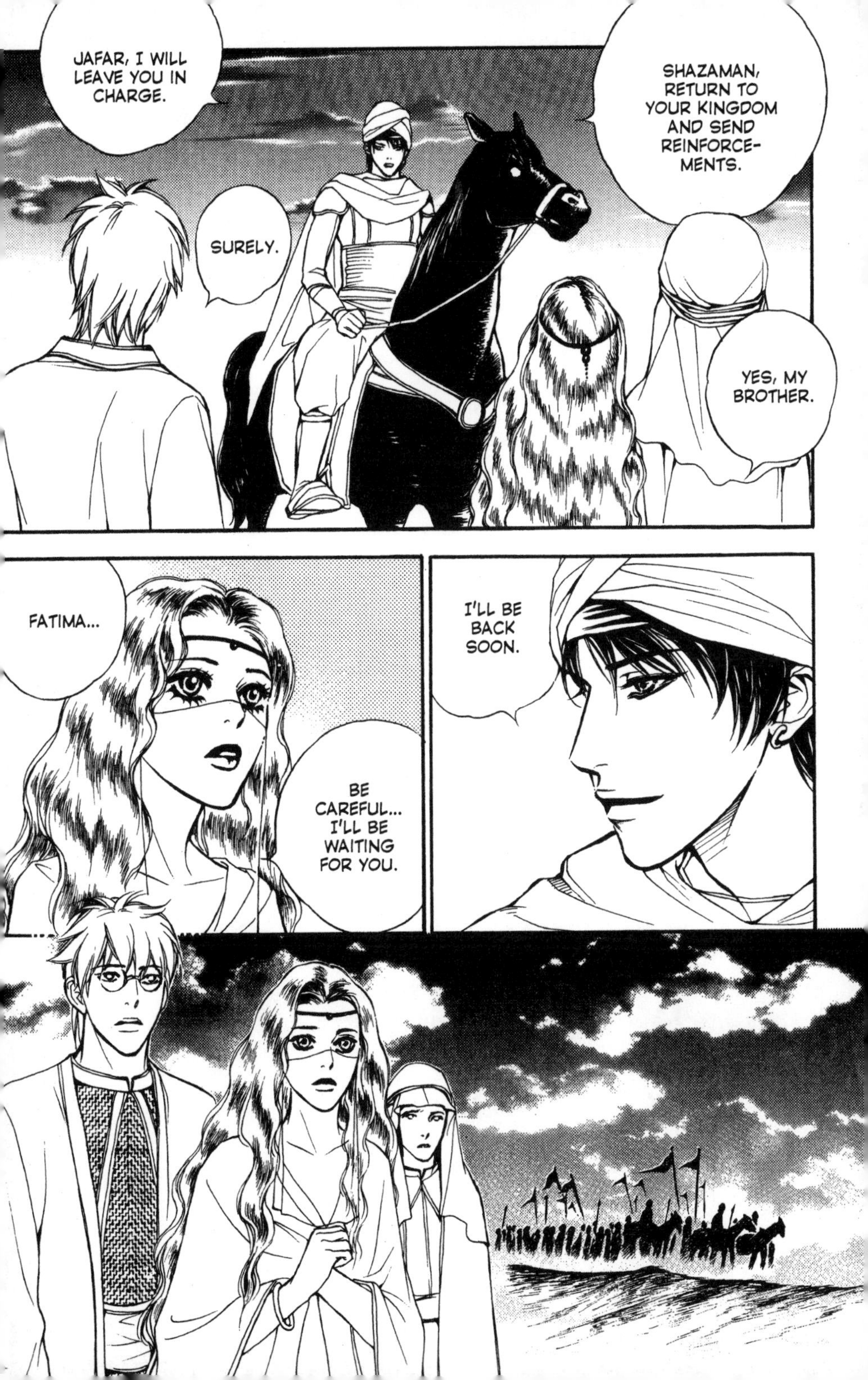
JAFAR, I WILL LEAVE YOU IN CHARGE.
SURELY.
SHAZAMAN, RETURN TO YOUR KINGDOM AND SEND REINFORCE-MENTS.
YES, MY BROTHER.
FATIMA...
BE CAREFUL... I'LL BE WAITING FOR YOU.
I'LL BE BACK SOON.

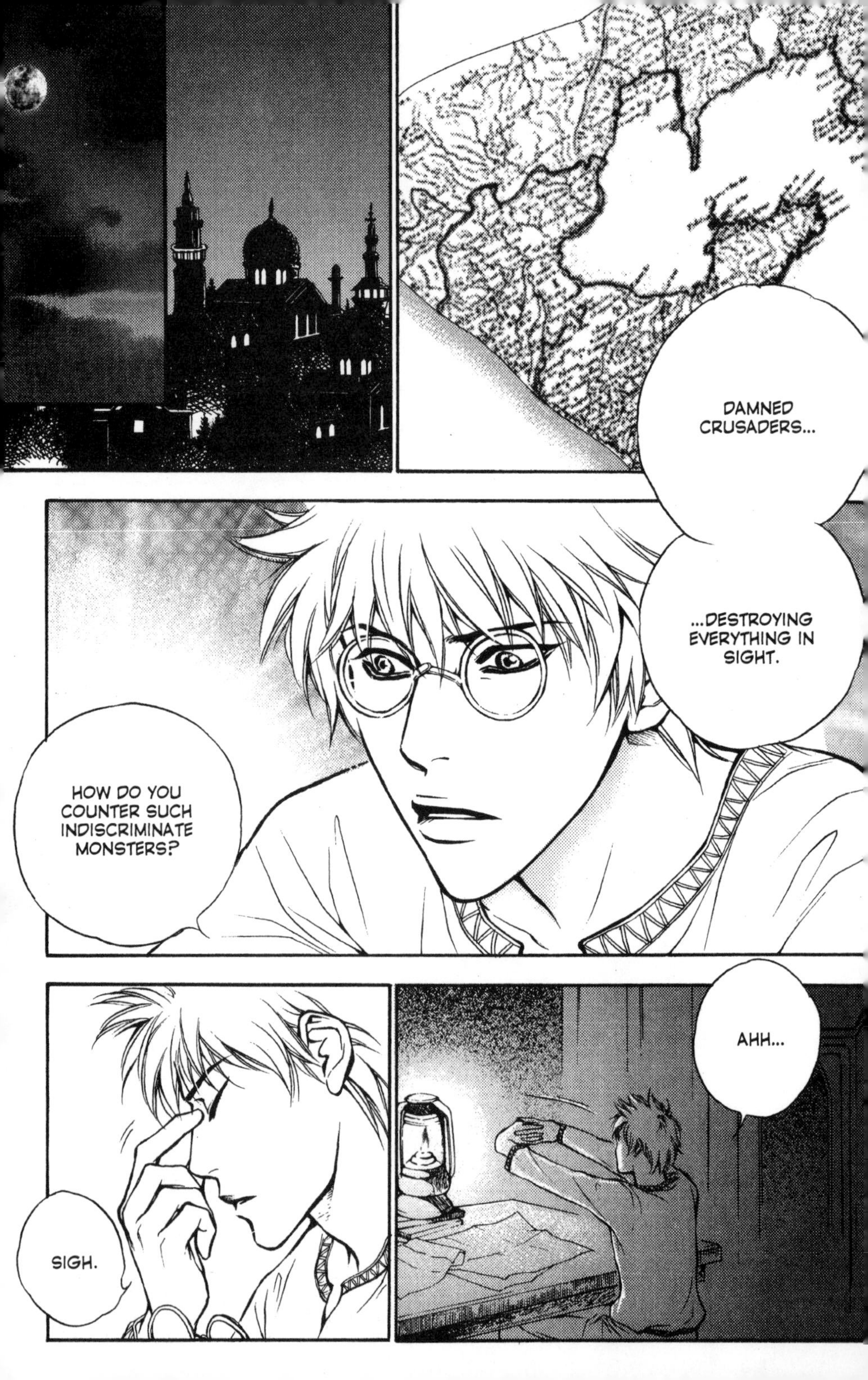
DAMNED CRUSADERS...
...DESTROYING EVERYTHING IN SIGHT.
HOW DO YOU COUNTER SUCH INDISCRIMINATE MONSTERS?
SIGH.
AHH...

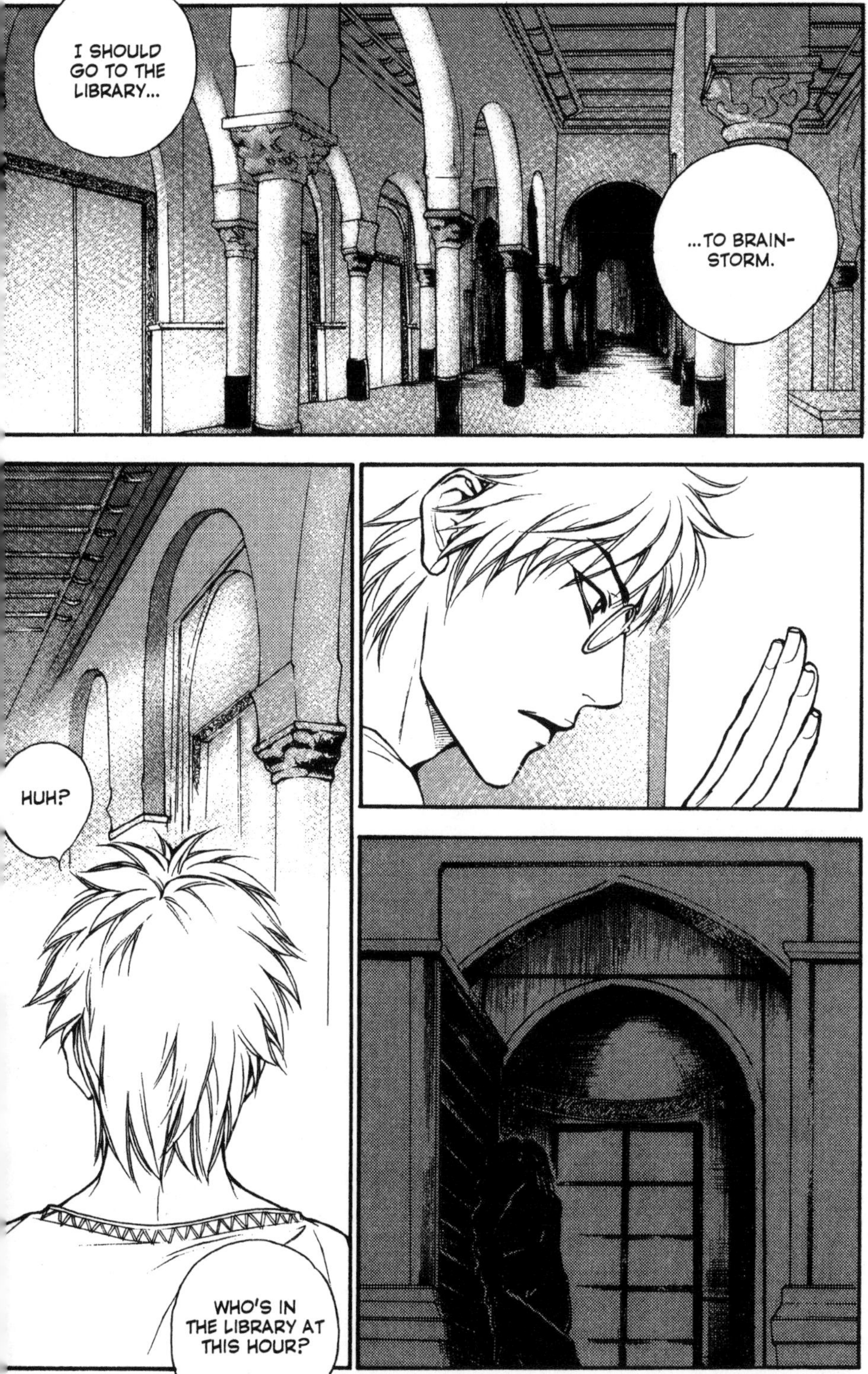
I SHOULD GO TO THE LIBRARY...
...TO BRAIN-STORM.
HUH?
WHO'S IN THE LIBRARY AT THIS HOUR?

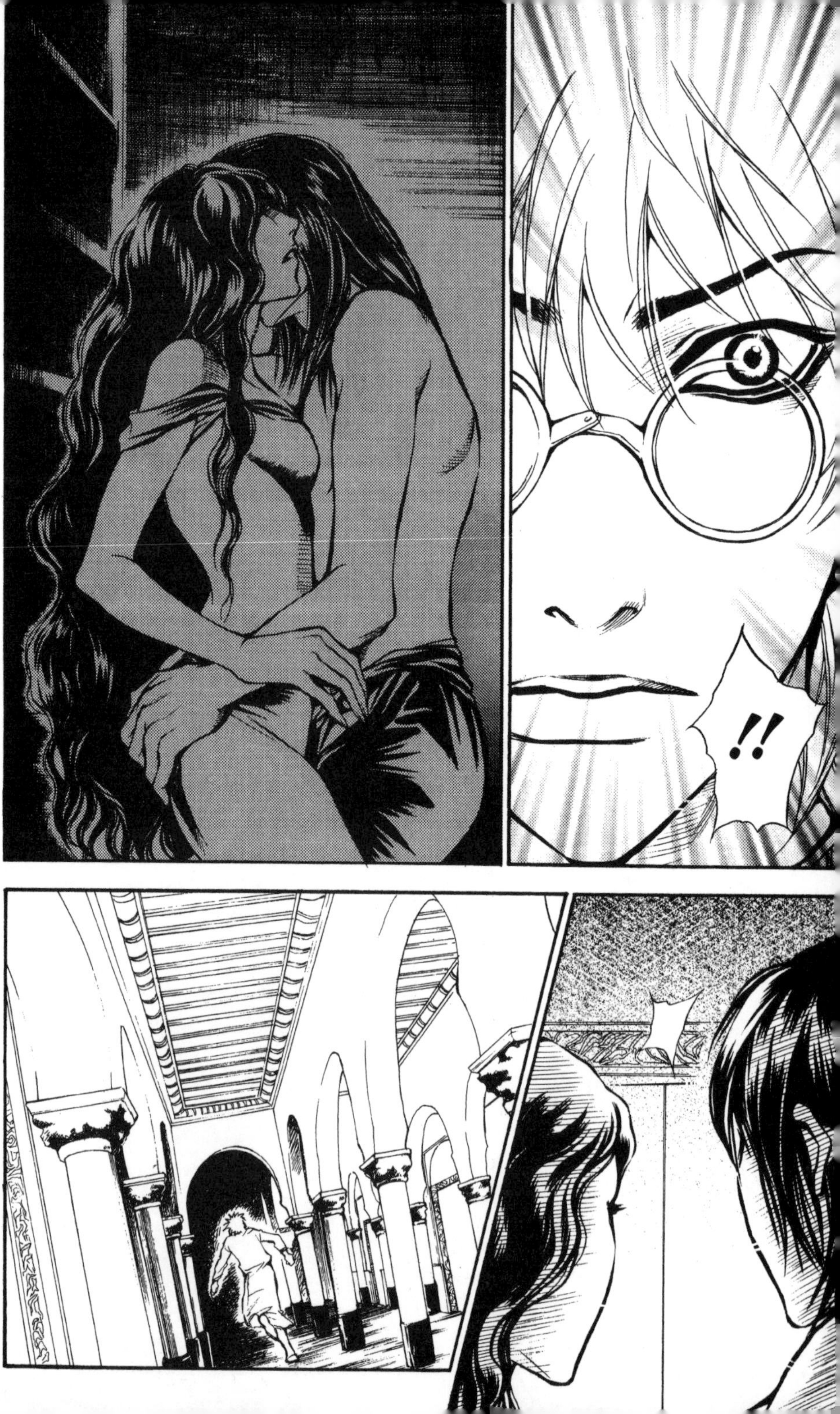
!!

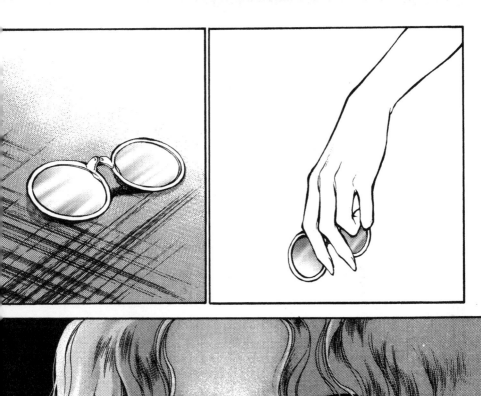

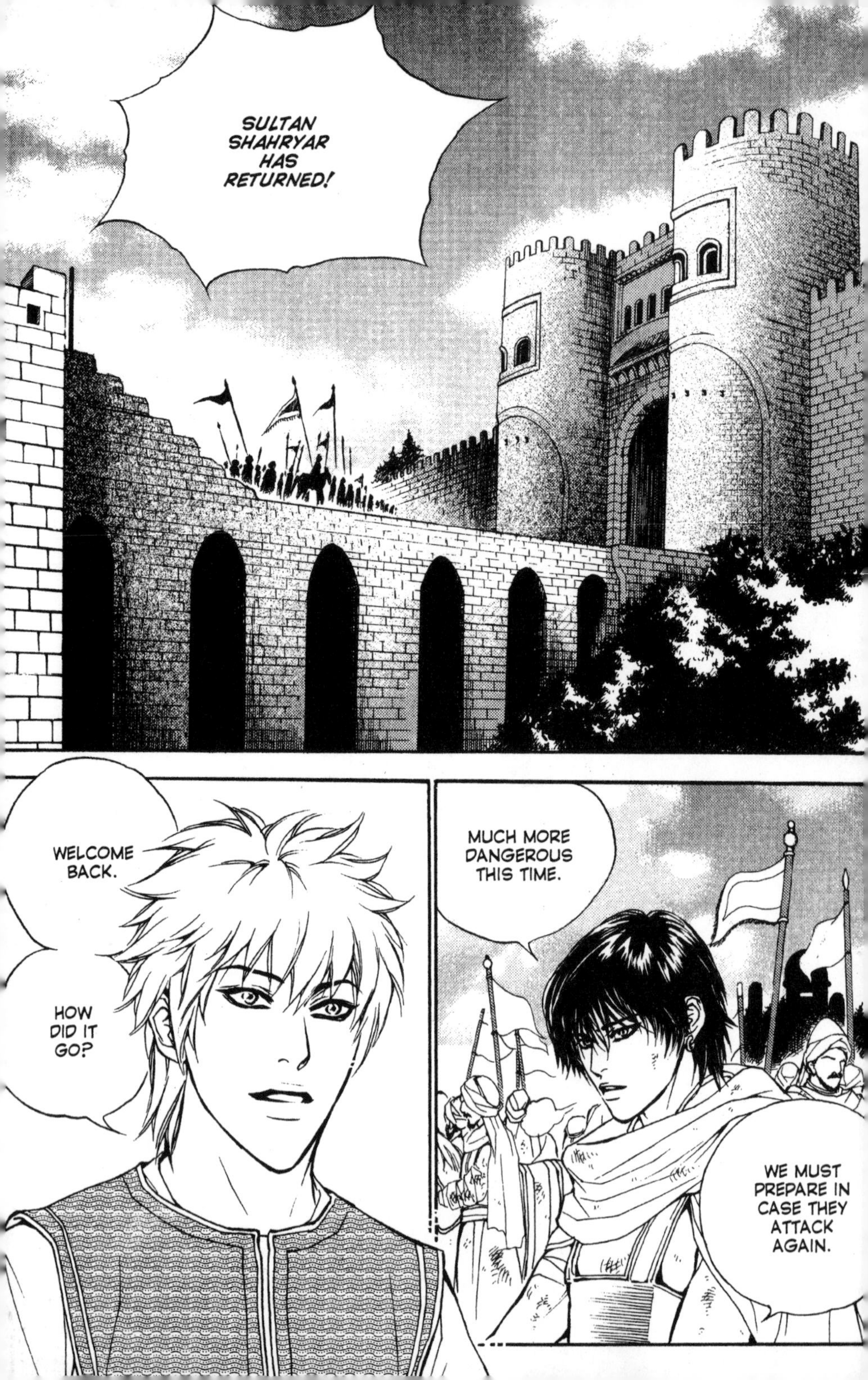
SULTAN SHAHRYAR HAS RETURNED!
WELCOME BACK.
HOW DID IT GO?
MUCH MORE DANGEROUS THIS TIME.
WE MUST PREPARE IN CASE THEY ATTACK AGAIN.

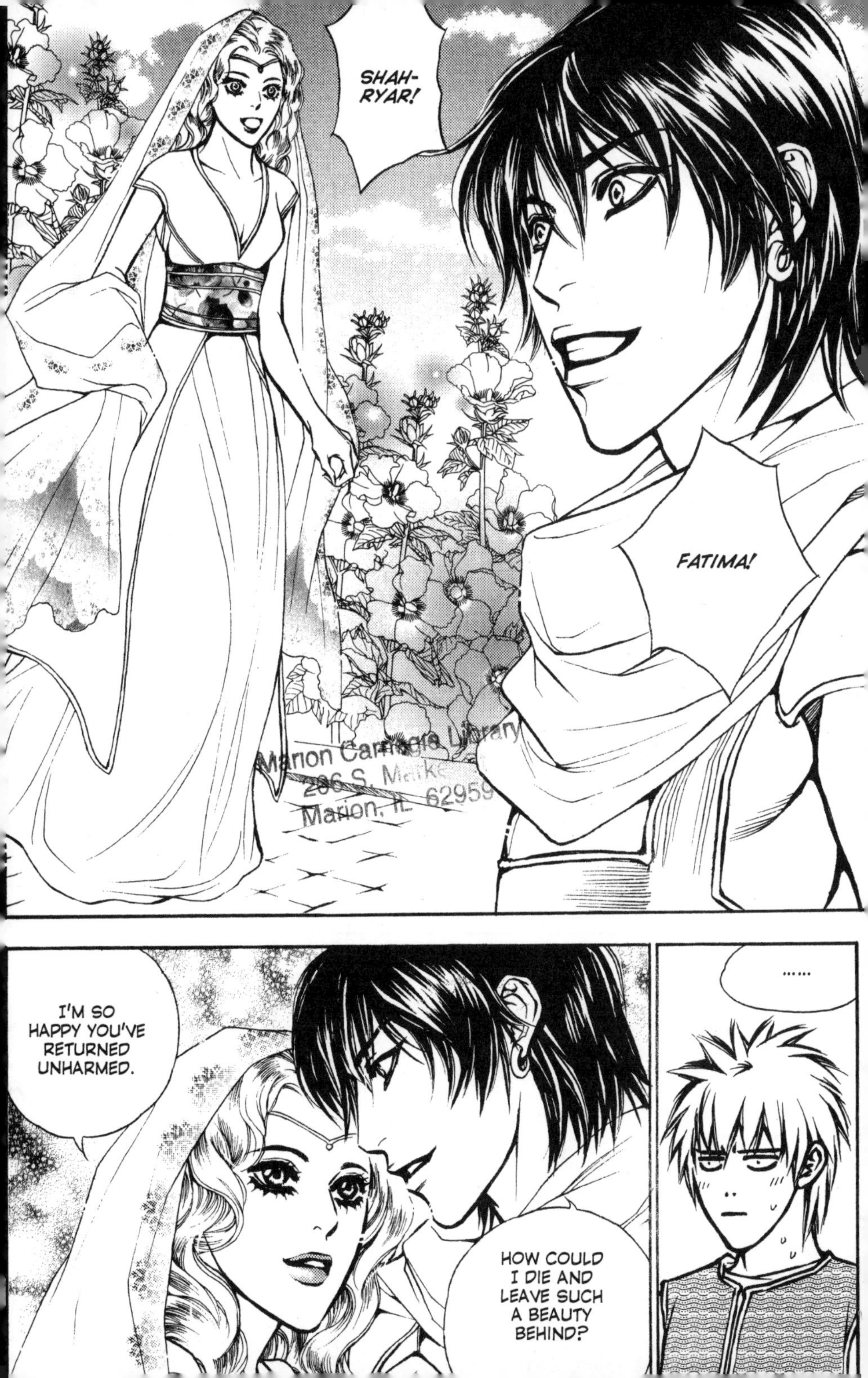
SHAH-RYAR!
FATIMA!
I'M SO HAPPY YOU'VE RETURNED UNHARMED.
HOW COULD I DIE AND LEAVE SUCH A BEAUTY BEHIND?
......

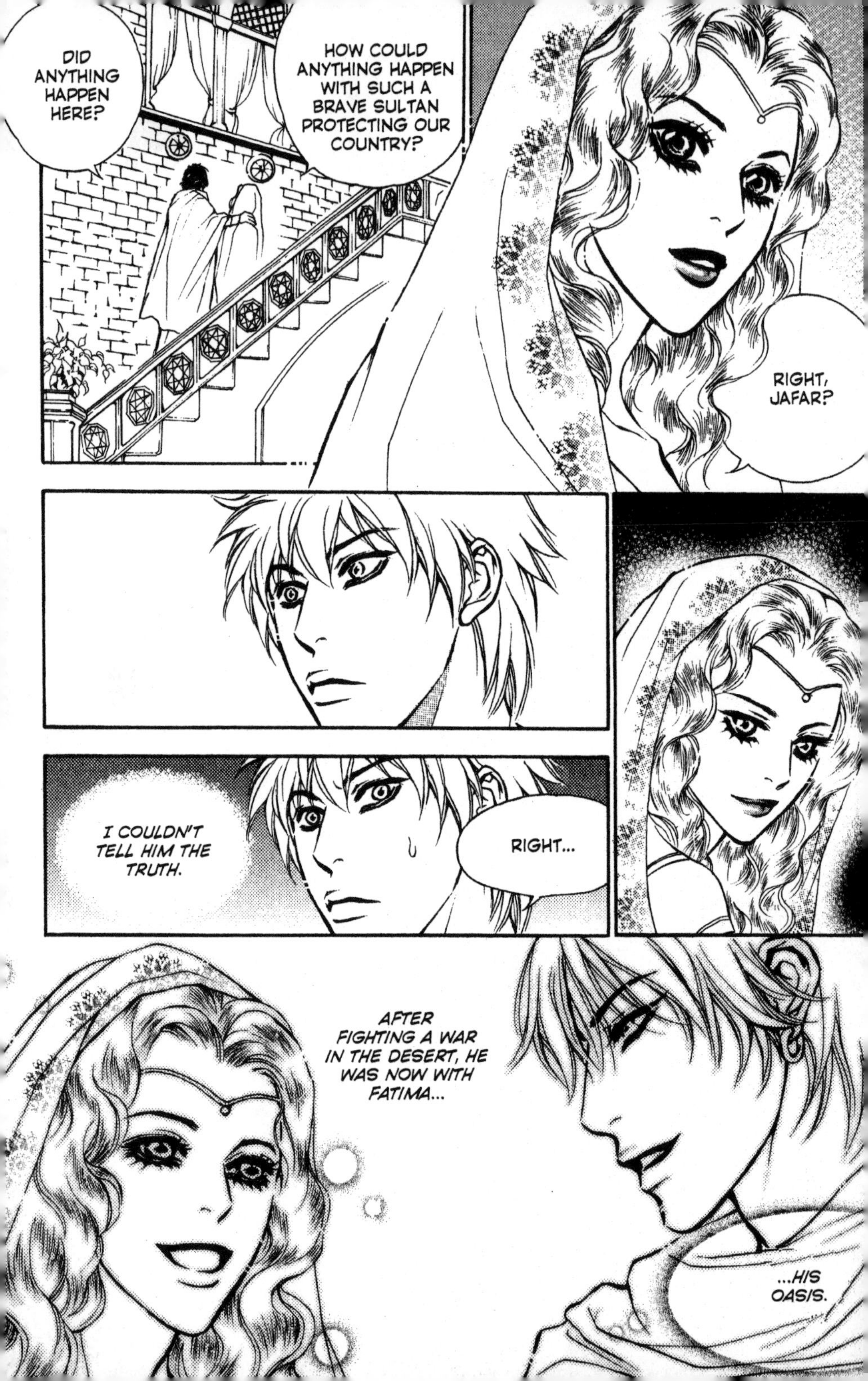
DID ANYTHING HAPPEN HERE?
HOW COULD ANYTHING HAPPEN WITH SUCH A BRAVE SULTAN PROTECTING OUR COUNTRY?
RIGHT, JAFAR?
I COULDN'T TELL HIM THE TRUTH.
RIGHT...
AFTER FIGHTING A WAR IN THE DESERT, HE WAS NOW WITH FATIMA...
...HIS OASIS.

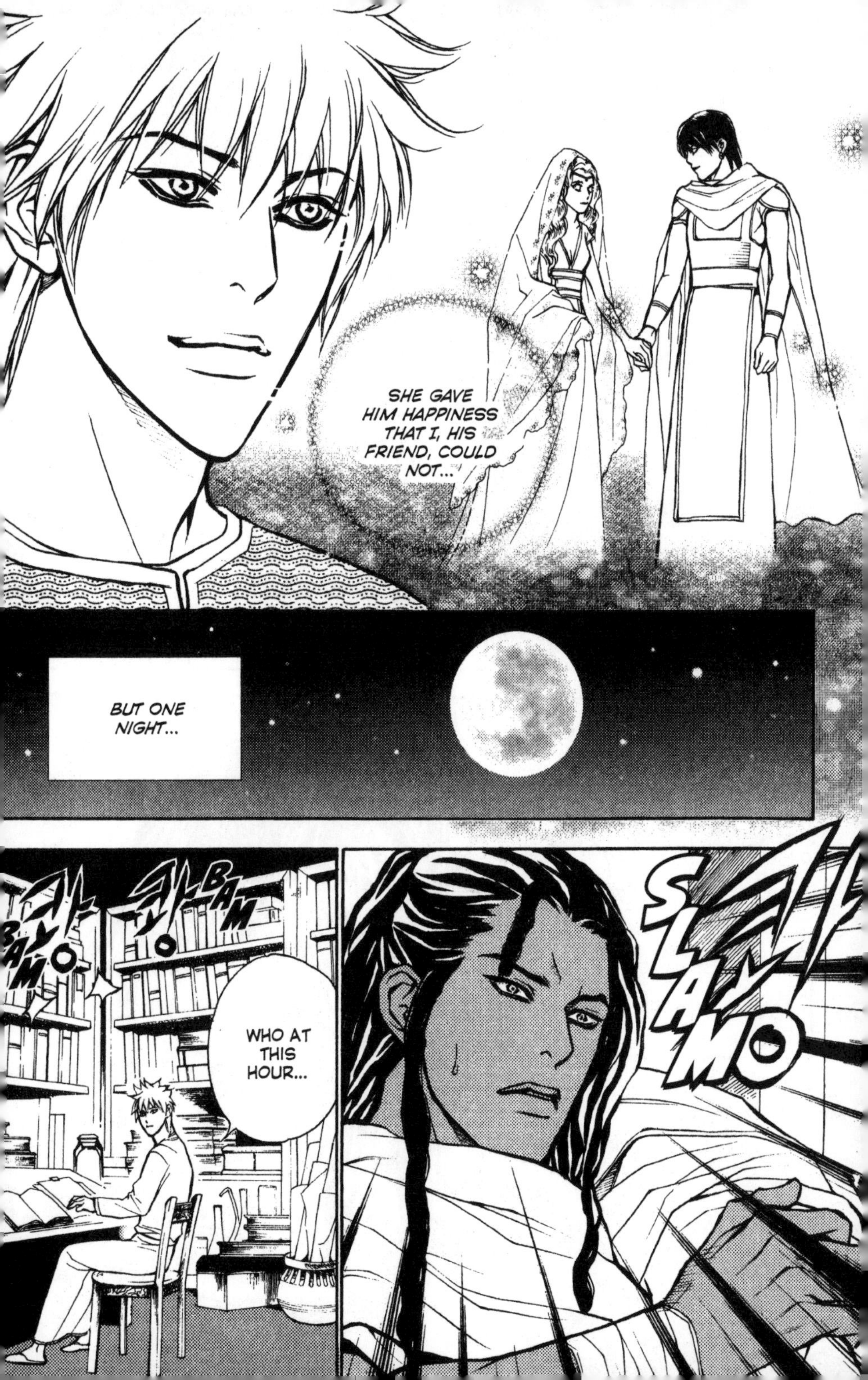
SHE GAVE HIM HAPPINESS THAT I, HIS FRIEND, COULD NOT...
BUT ONE NIGHT...
BAM
BAM
WHO AT THIS HOUR...
SLAM

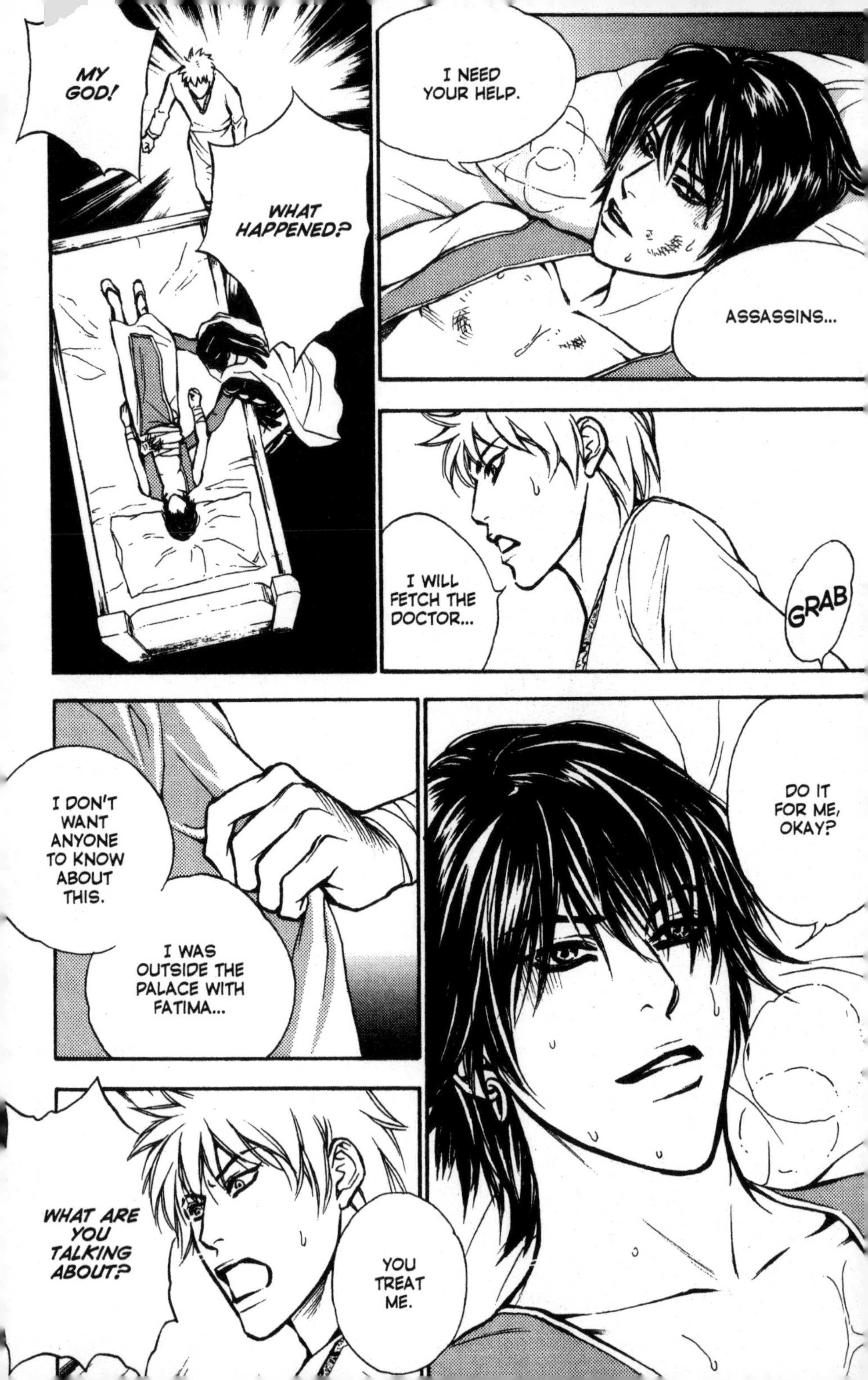
MY GOD!
WHAT HAPPENED?
I NEED YOUR HELP.
ASSASSINS...
I WILL FETCH THE DOCTOR...
GRAB
I DON'T WANT ANYONE TO KNOW ABOUT THIS.
I WAS OUTSIDE THE PALACE WITH FATIMA...
WHAT ARE YOU TALKING ABOUT?
YOU TREAT ME.
DO IT FOR ME, OKAY?

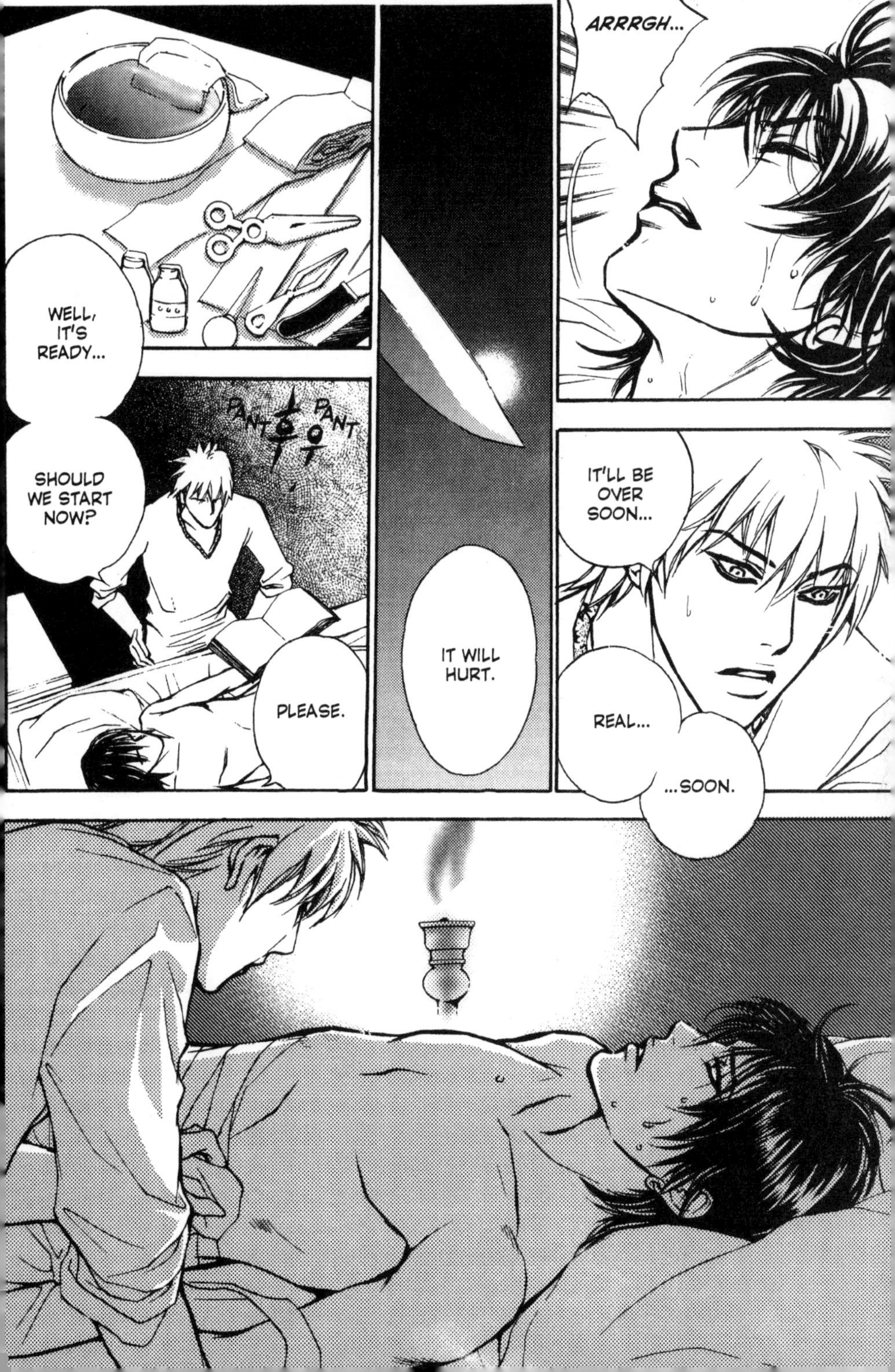
WELL, IT'S READY...
SHOULD WE START NOW?
PANT PANT
PLEASE.
IT WILL HURT.
ARRRGH...
IT'LL BE OVER SOON...
REAL...
...SOON.

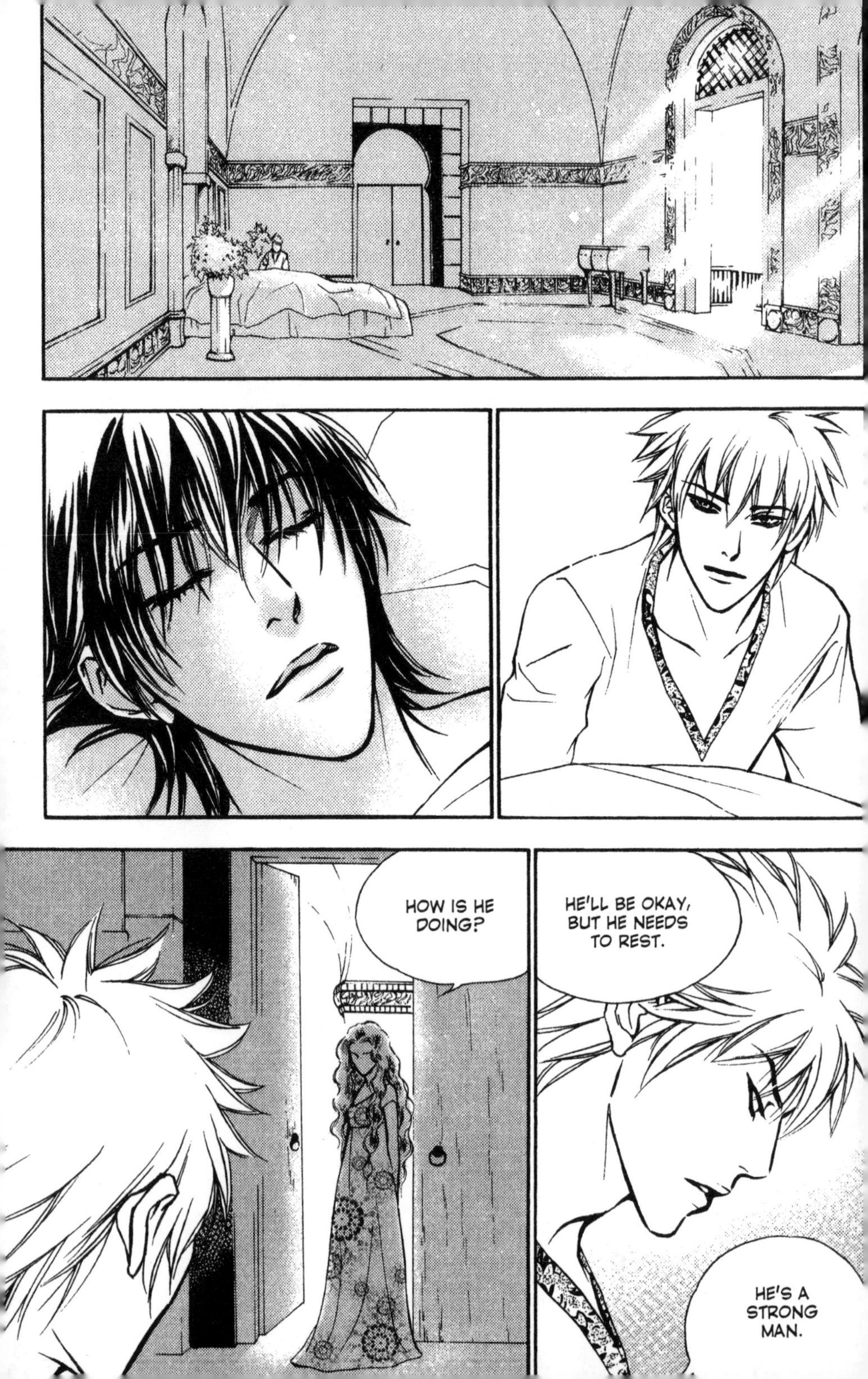
HOW IS HE DOING?
HE'LL BE OKAY, BUT HE NEEDS TO REST.
HE'S A STRONG MAN.

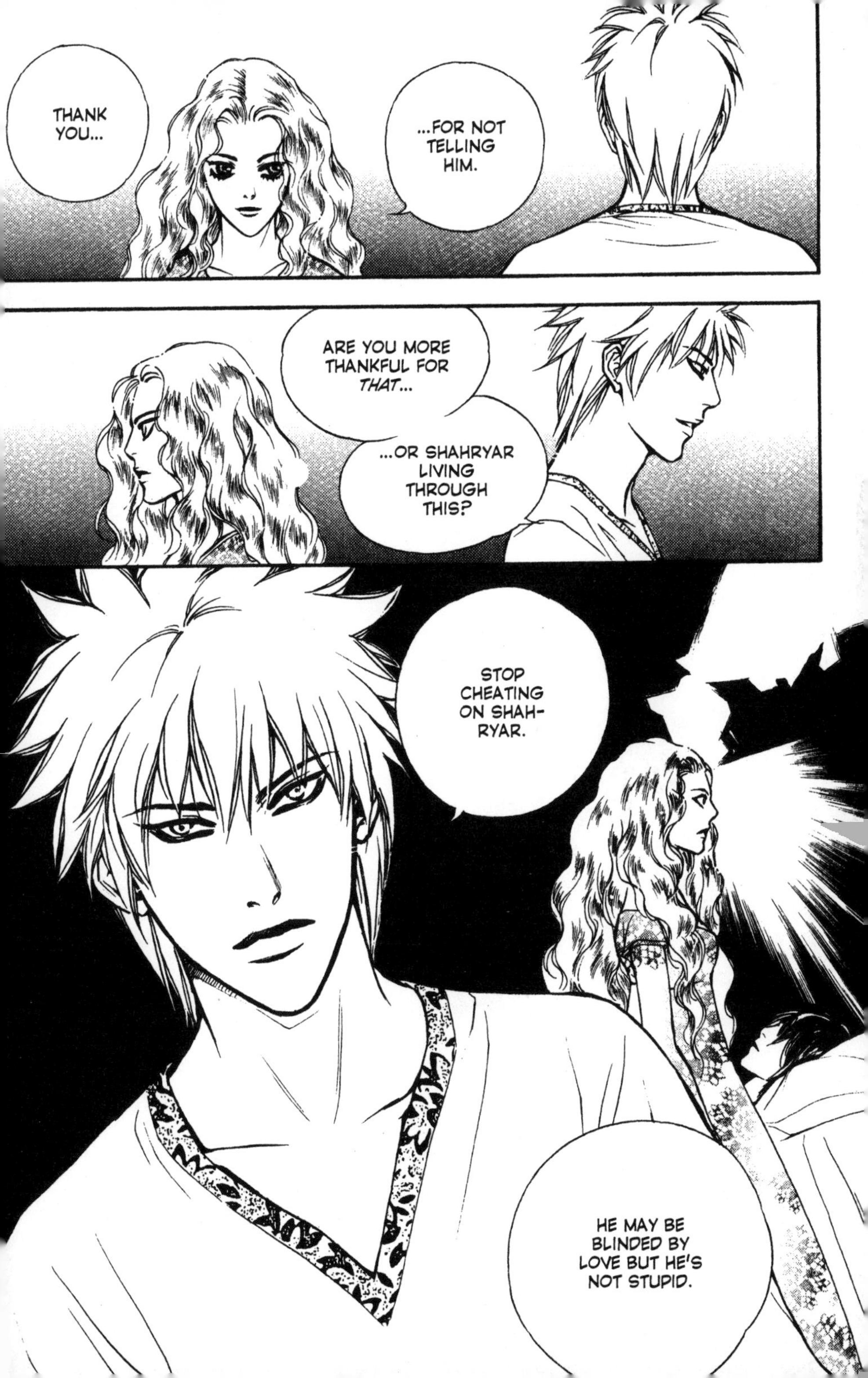
THANK YOU...
...FOR NOT TELLING HIM.
ARE YOU MORE THANKFUL FOR *THAT*...
...OR SHAHRYAR LIVING THROUGH THIS?
STOP CHEATING ON SHAH-RYAR.
HE MAY BE BLINDED BY LOVE BUT HE'S NOT STUPID.

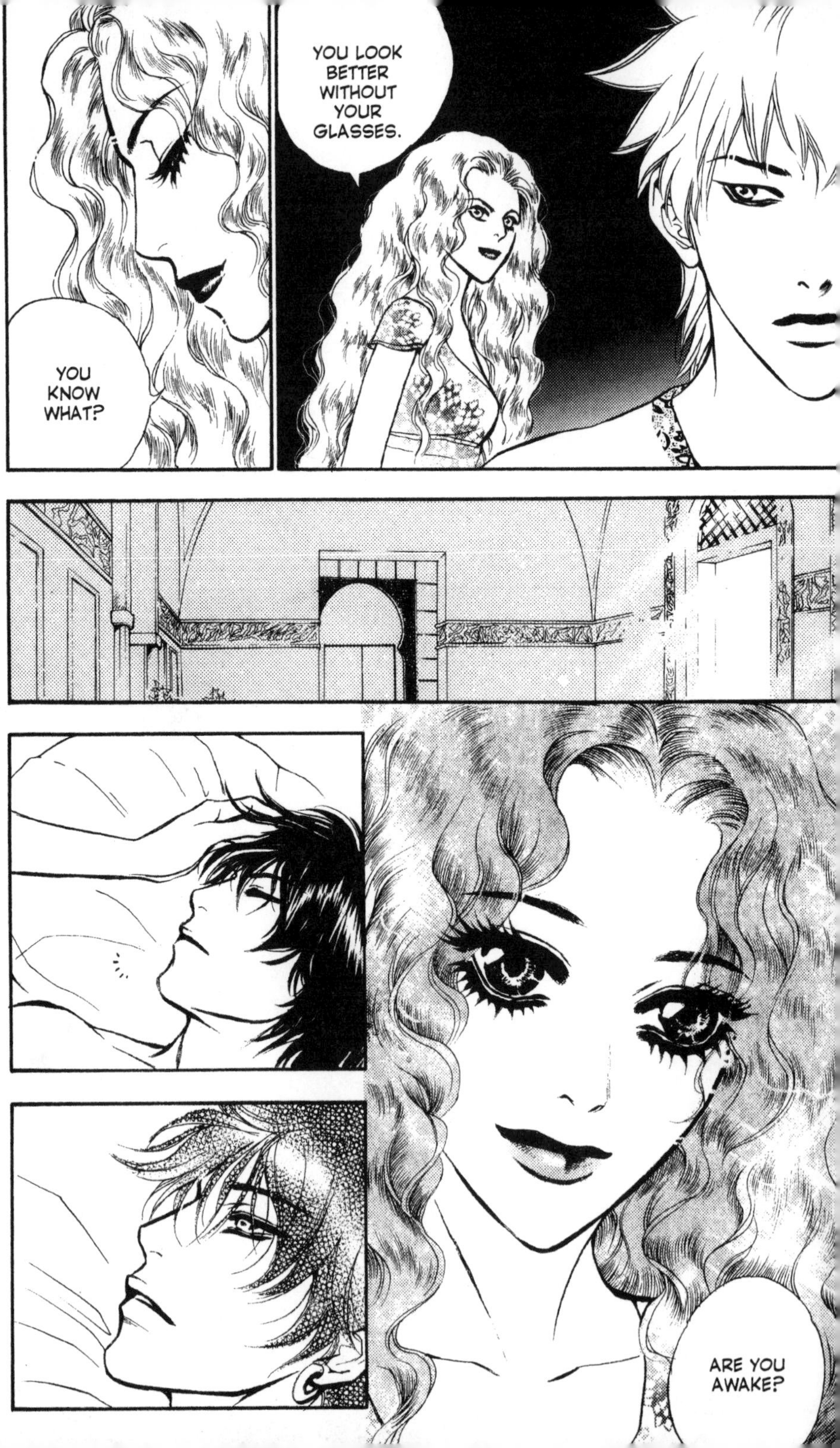
YOU KNOW WHAT?
YOU LOOK BETTER WITHOUT YOUR GLASSES.
ARE YOU AWAKE?

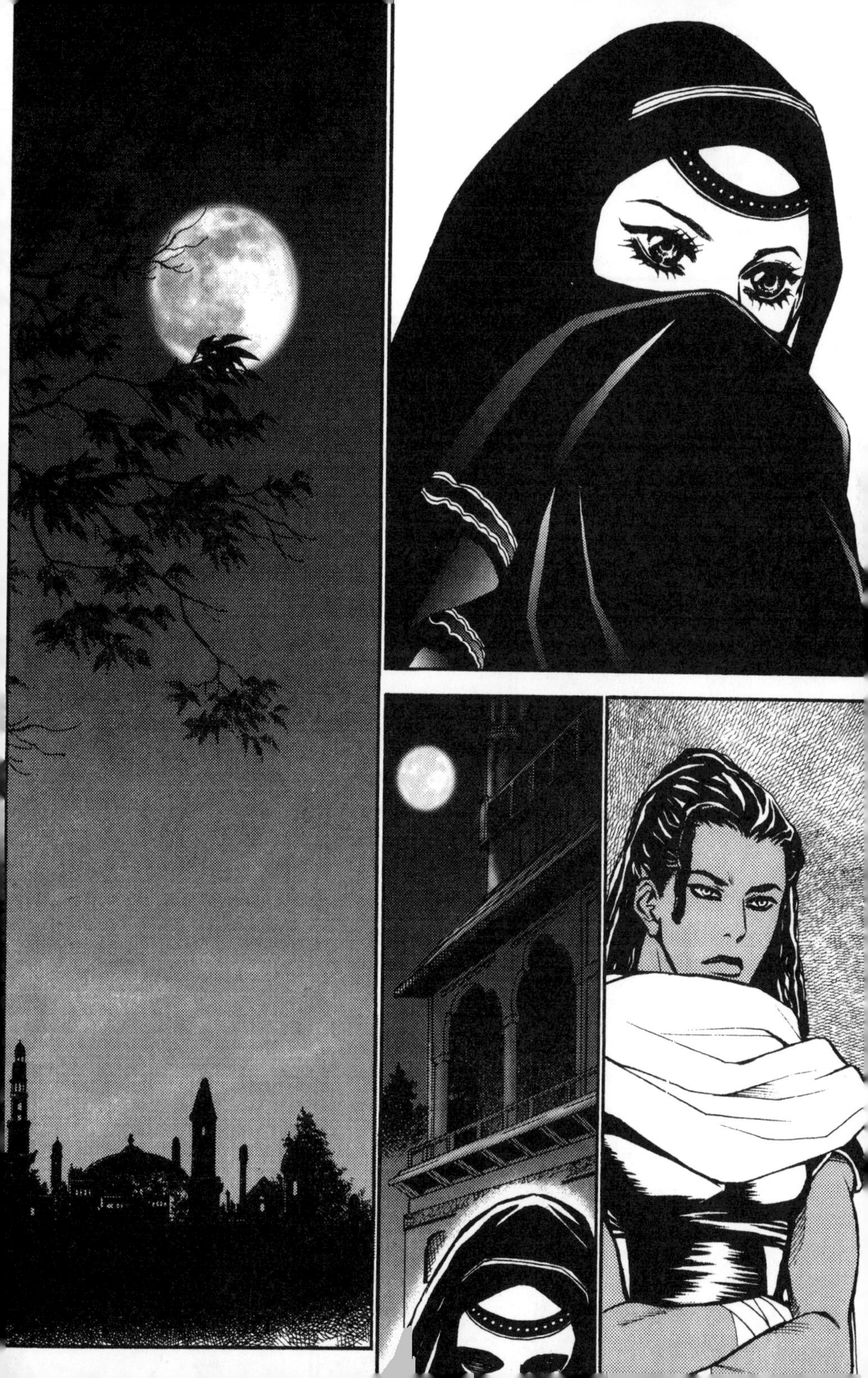

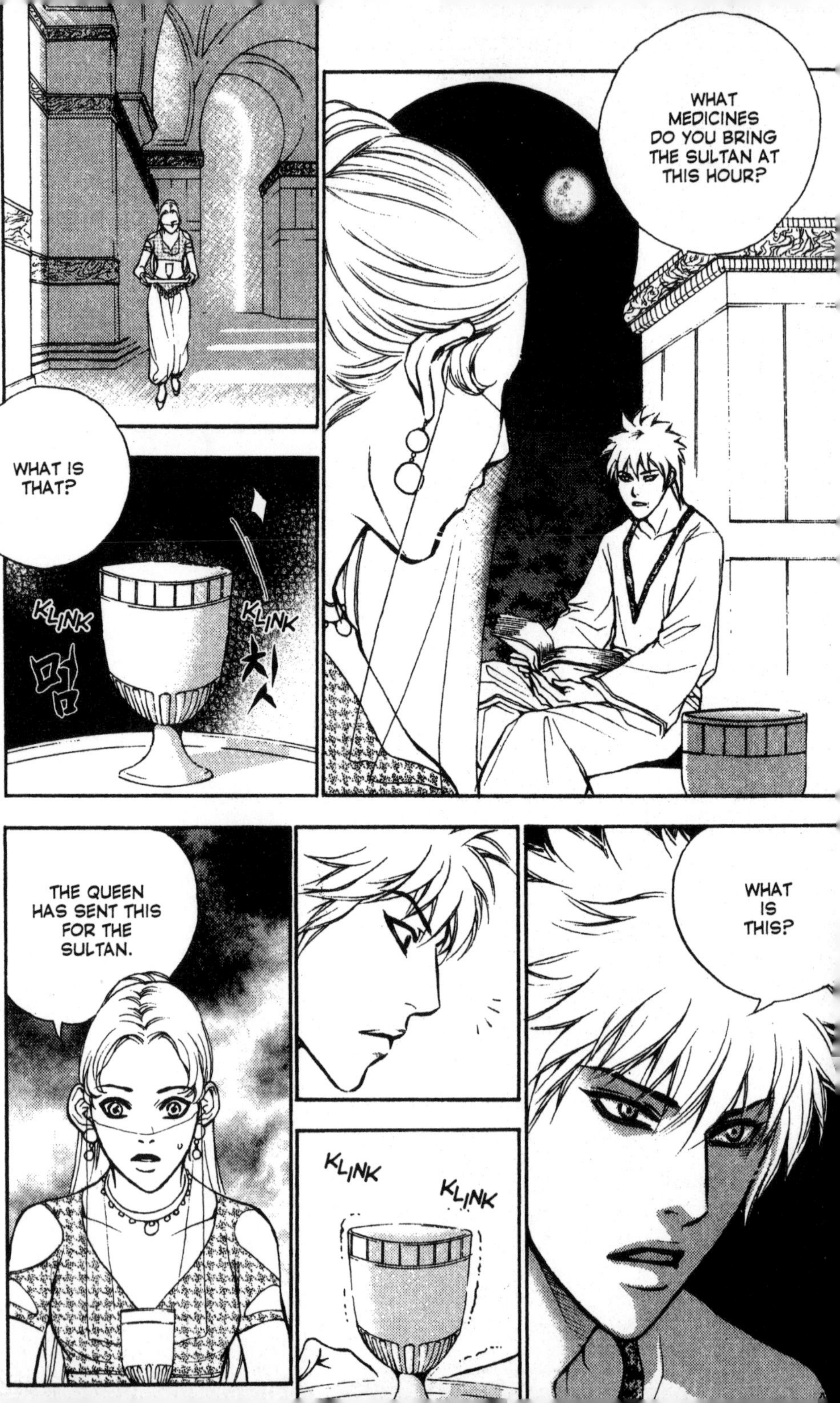
WHAT IS THAT?
KLINK
KLINK
WHAT MEDICINES DO YOU BRING THE SULTAN AT THIS HOUR?
THE QUEEN HAS SENT THIS FOR THE SULTAN.
KLINK
KLINK
WHAT IS THIS?

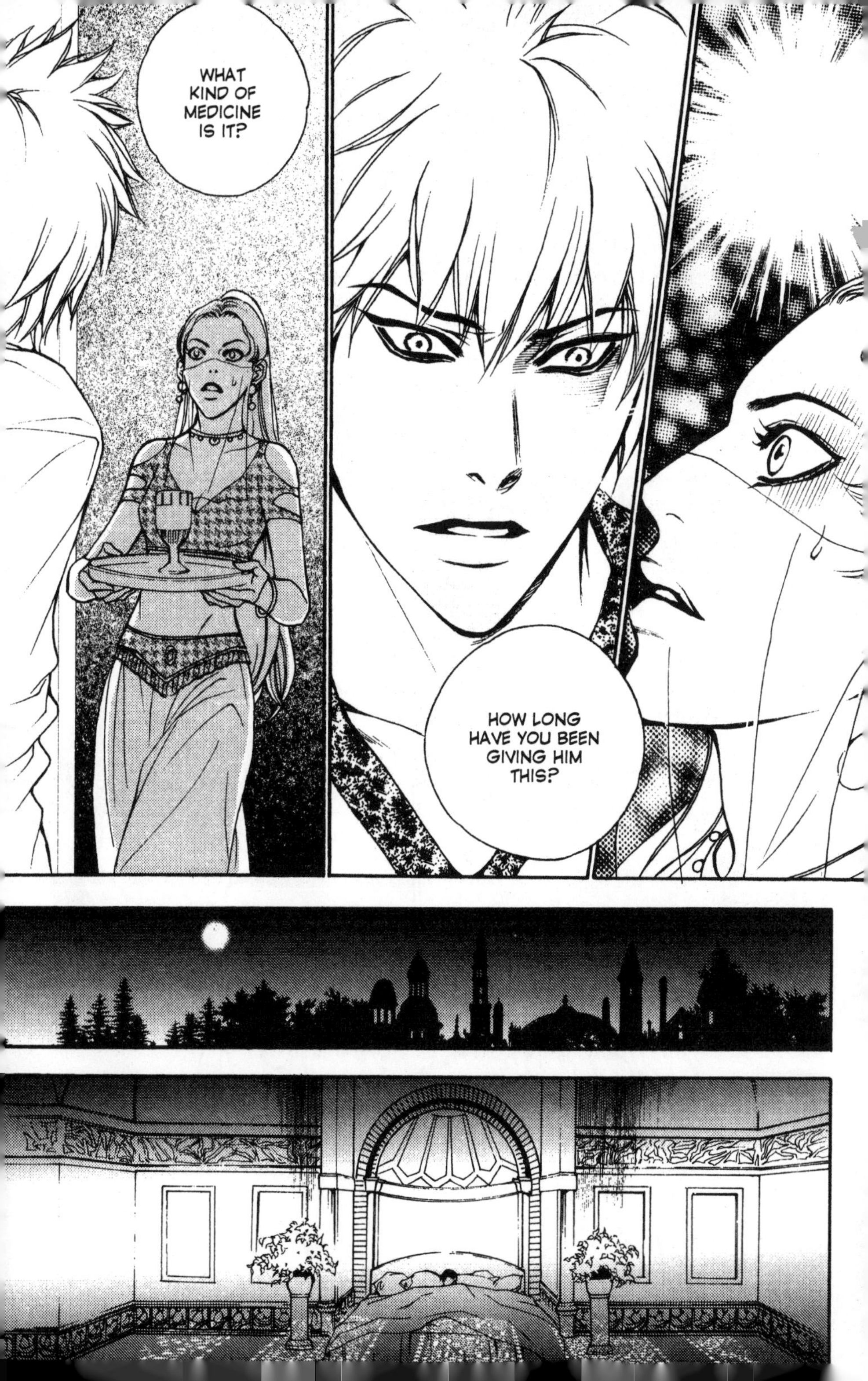
WHAT KIND OF MEDICINE IS IT?
HOW LONG HAVE YOU BEEN GIVING HIM THIS?

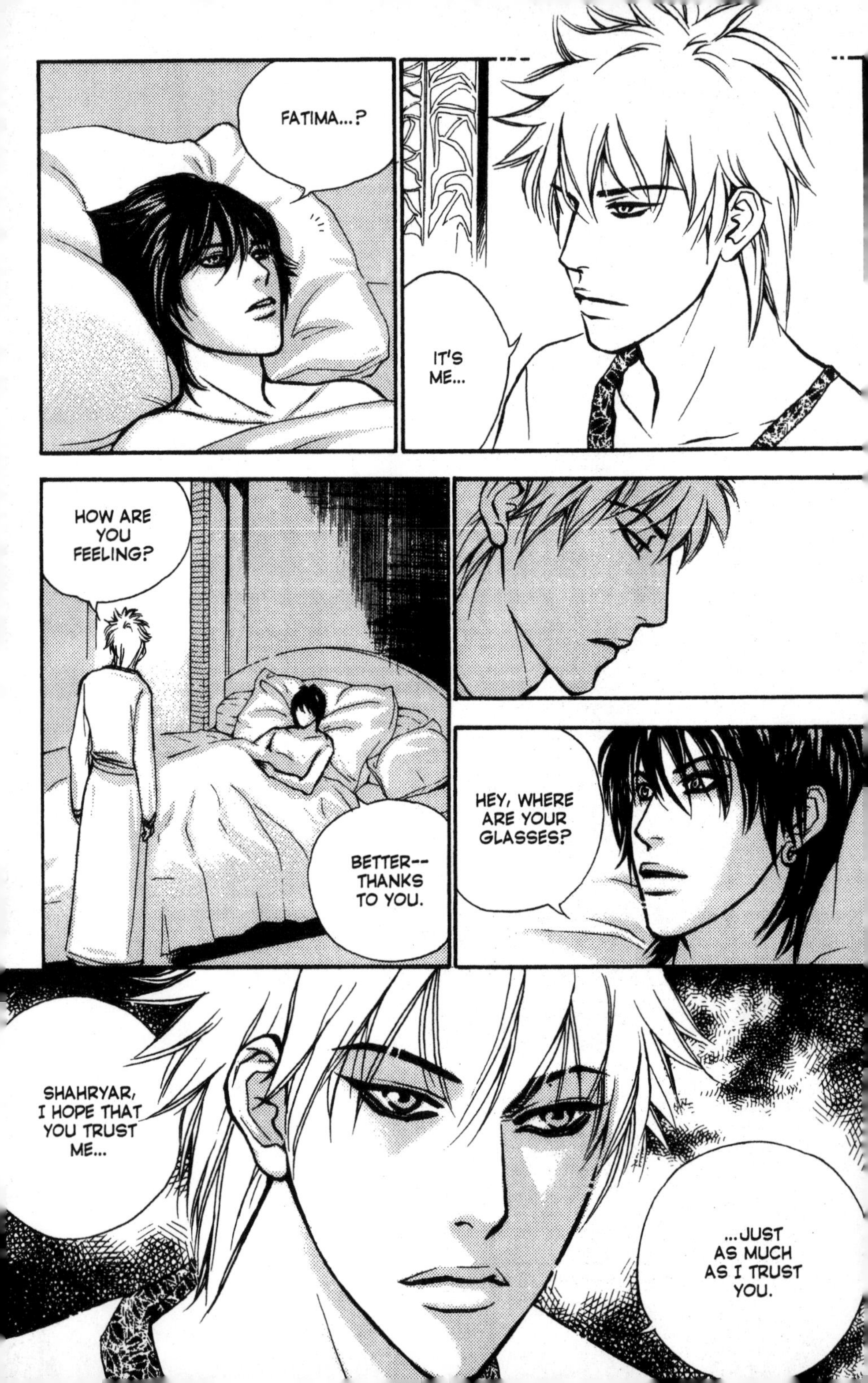
FATIMA...?
IT'S ME...
HOW ARE YOU FEELING?
BETTER-- THANKS TO YOU.
HEY, WHERE ARE YOUR GLASSES?
SHAHRYAR, I HOPE THAT YOU TRUST ME...
...JUST AS MUCH AS I TRUST YOU.

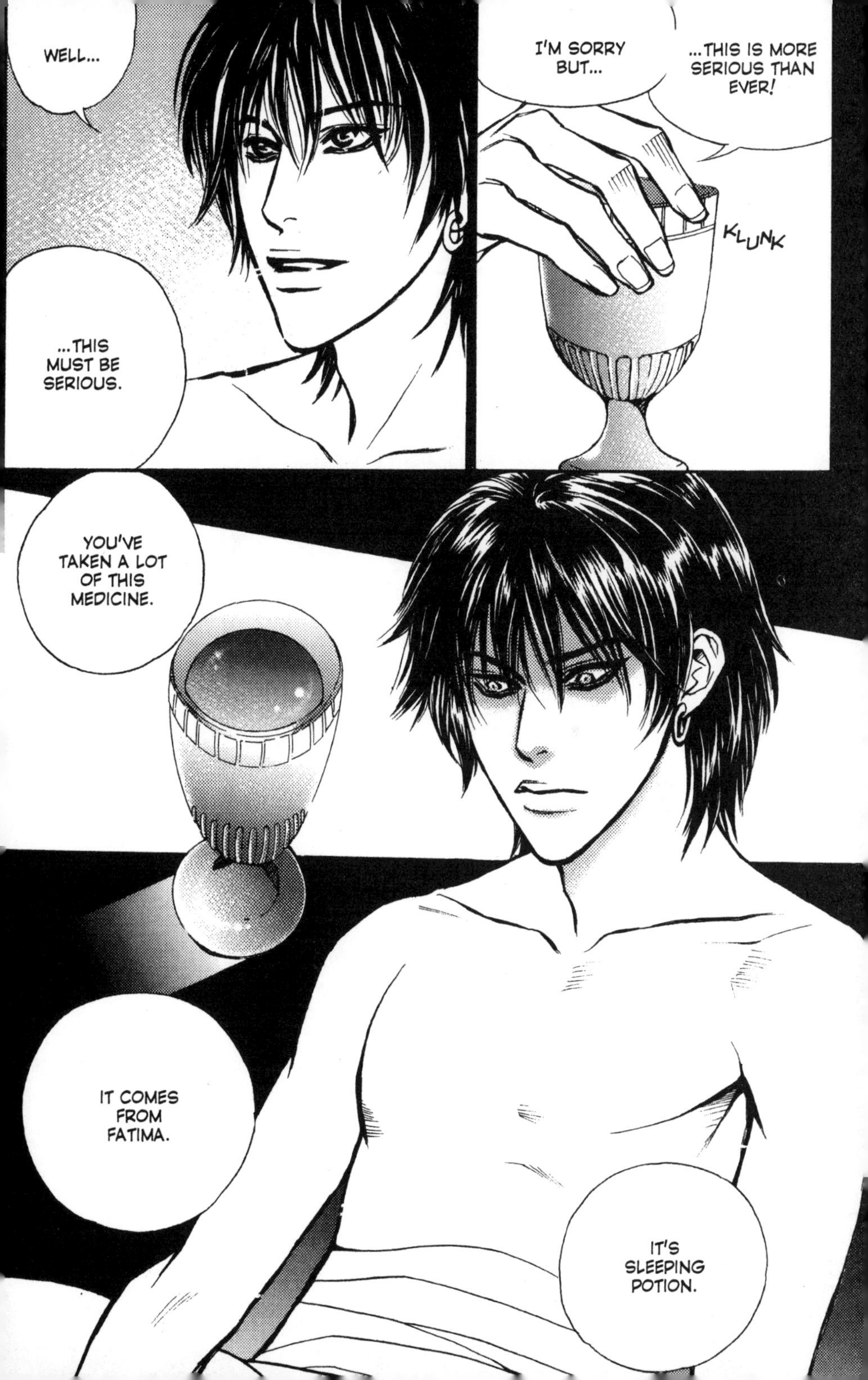
WELL...
...THIS MUST BE SERIOUS.
I'M SORRY BUT...
...THIS IS MORE SERIOUS THAN EVER!
KLUNK
YOU'VE TAKEN A LOT OF THIS MEDICINE.
IT COMES FROM FATIMA.
IT'S SLEEPING POTION.

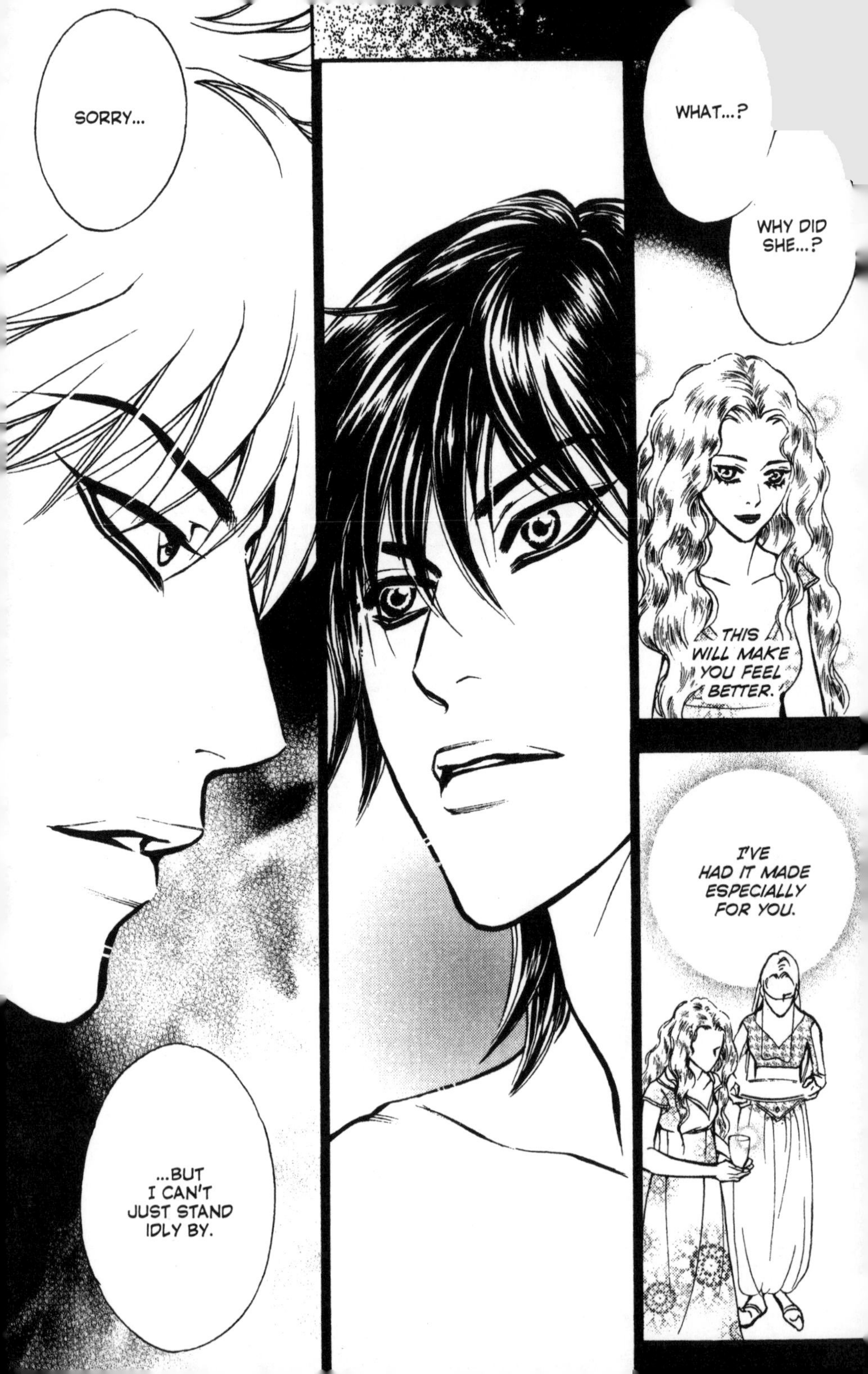
SORRY...
...BUT I CAN'T JUST STAND IDLY BY.
WHAT...?
WHY DID SHE...?
THIS WILL MAKE YOU FEEL BETTER.
I'VE HAD IT MADE ESPECIALLY FOR YOU.

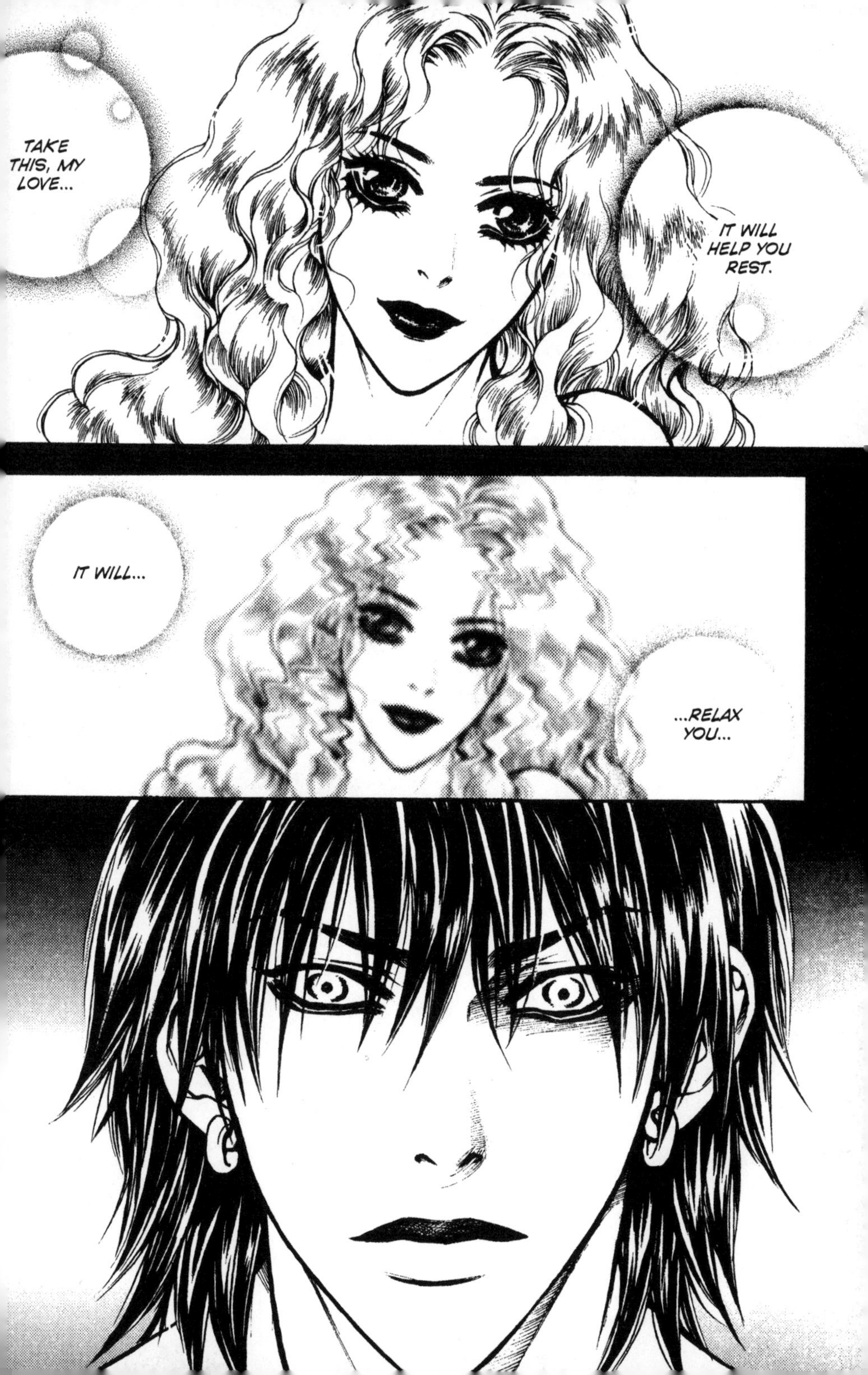
TAKE THIS, MY LOVE...
IT WILL HELP YOU REST.
IT WILL...
...RELAX YOU...

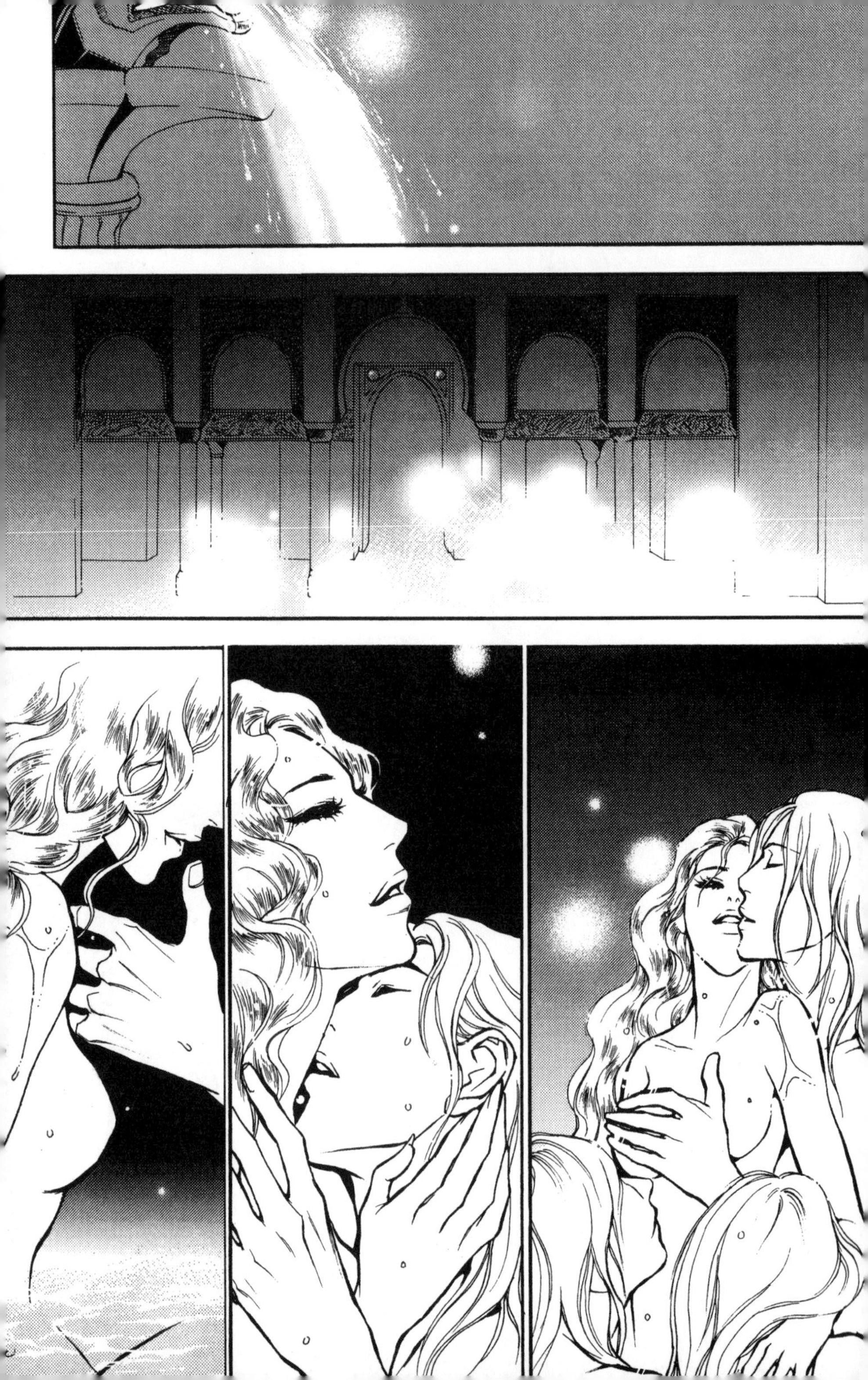

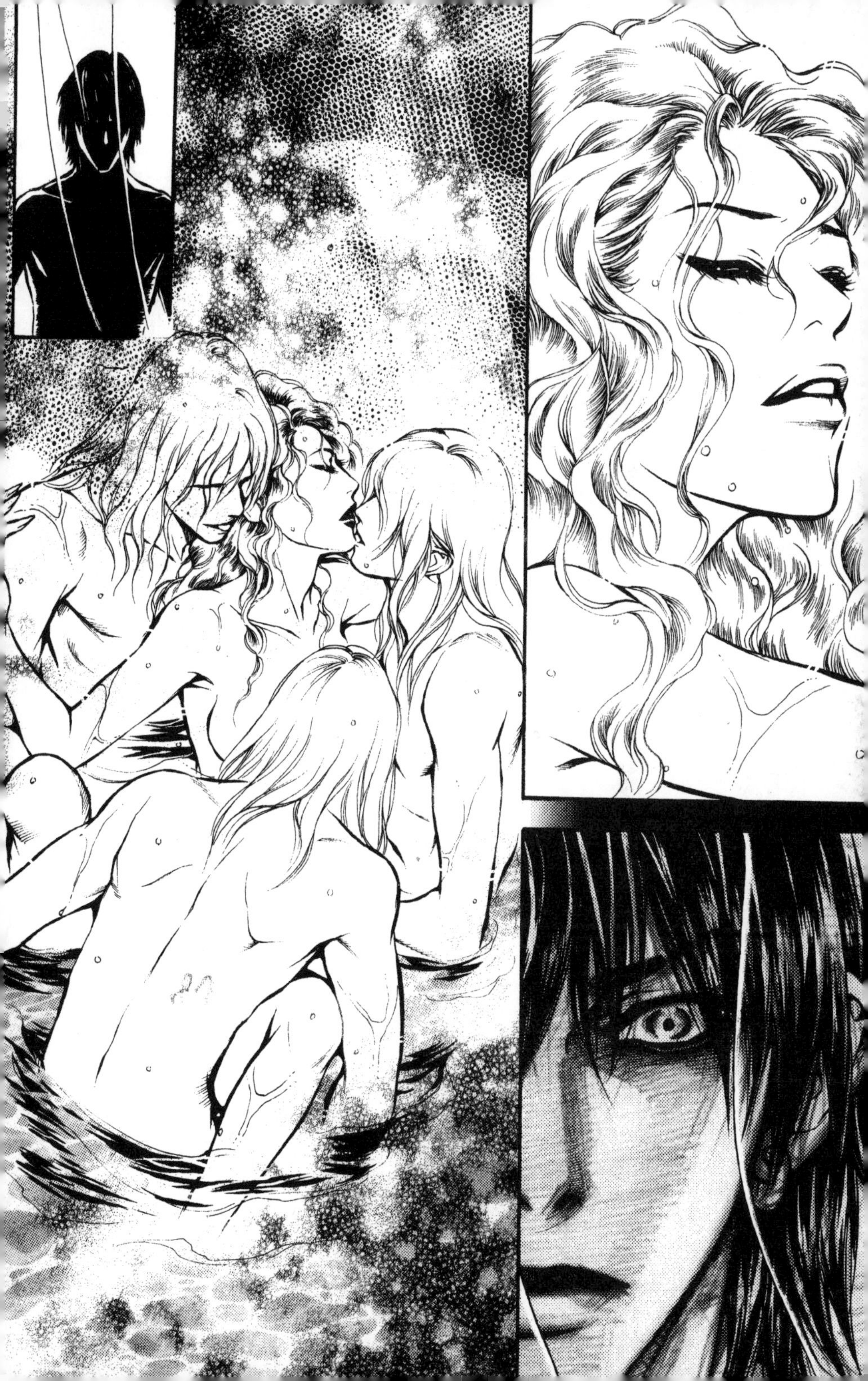

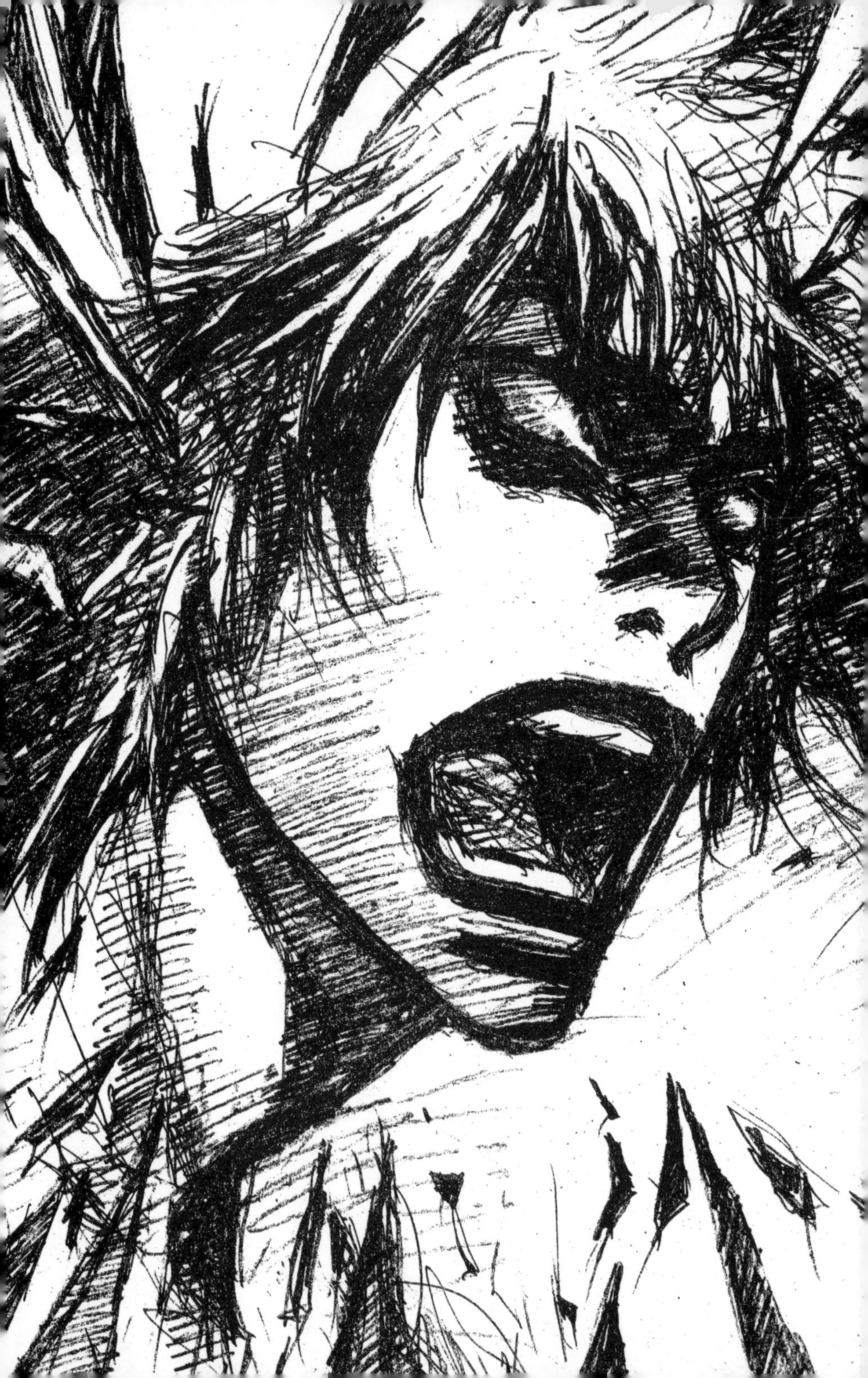

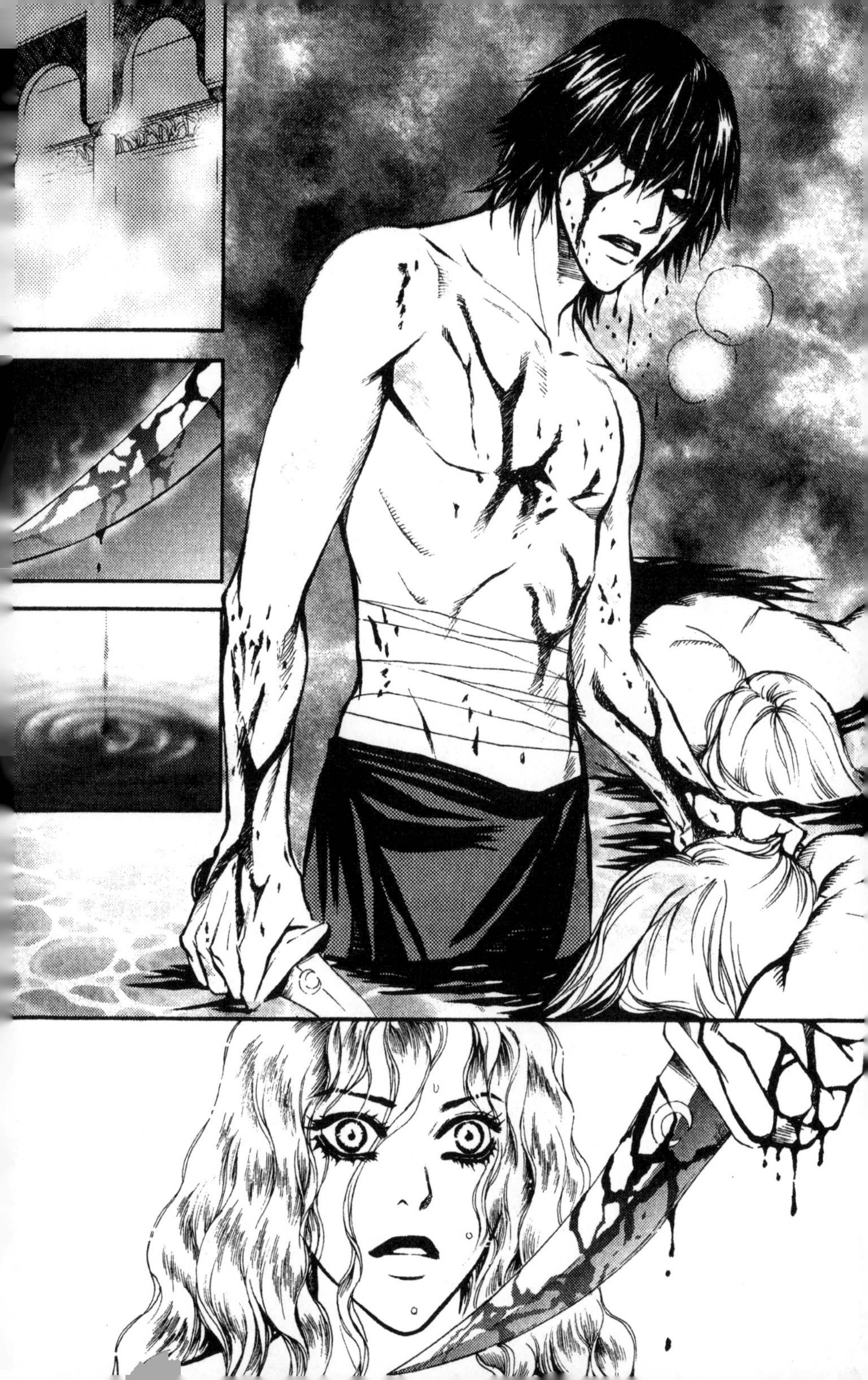

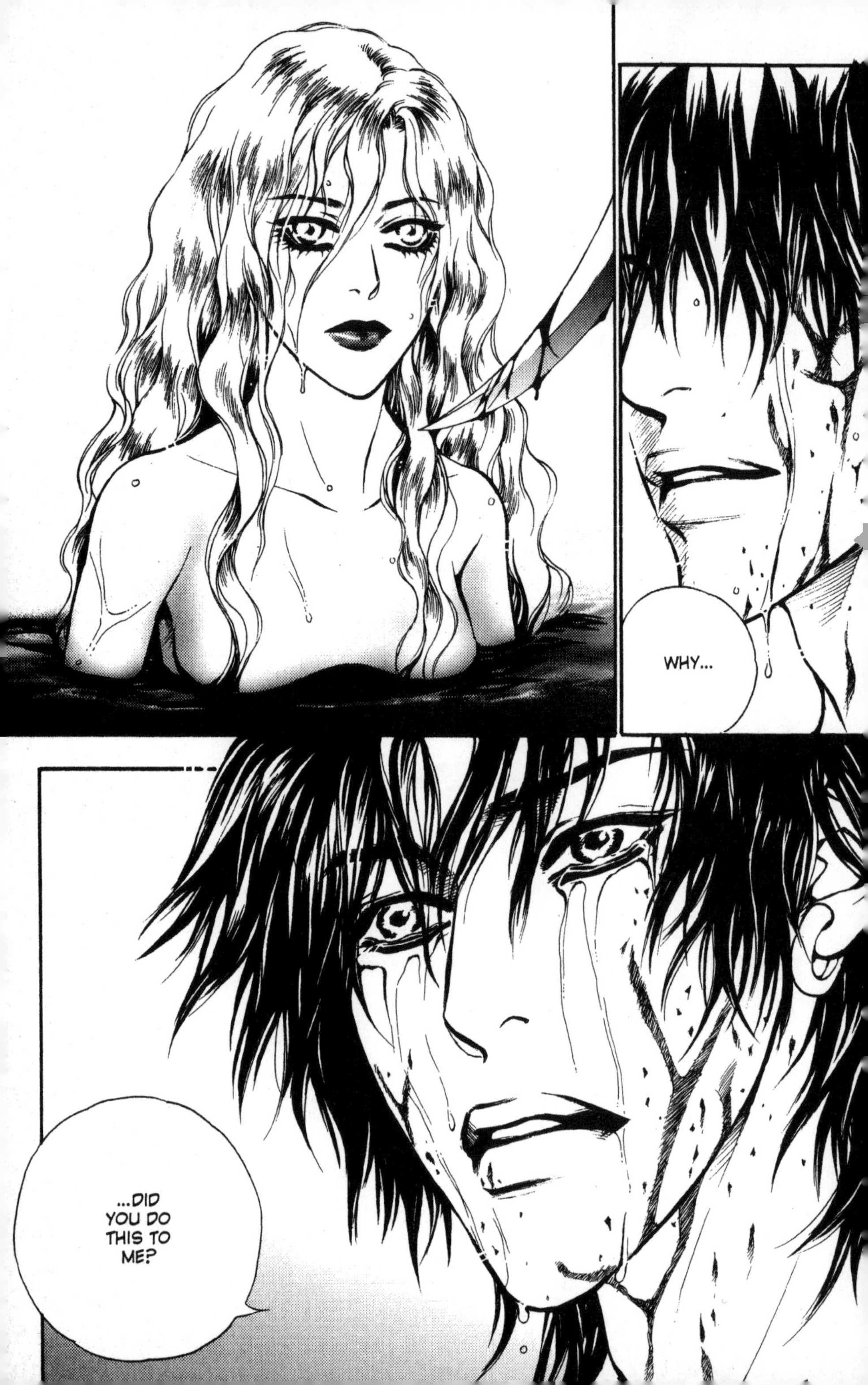
WHY...
...DID YOU DO THIS TO ME?

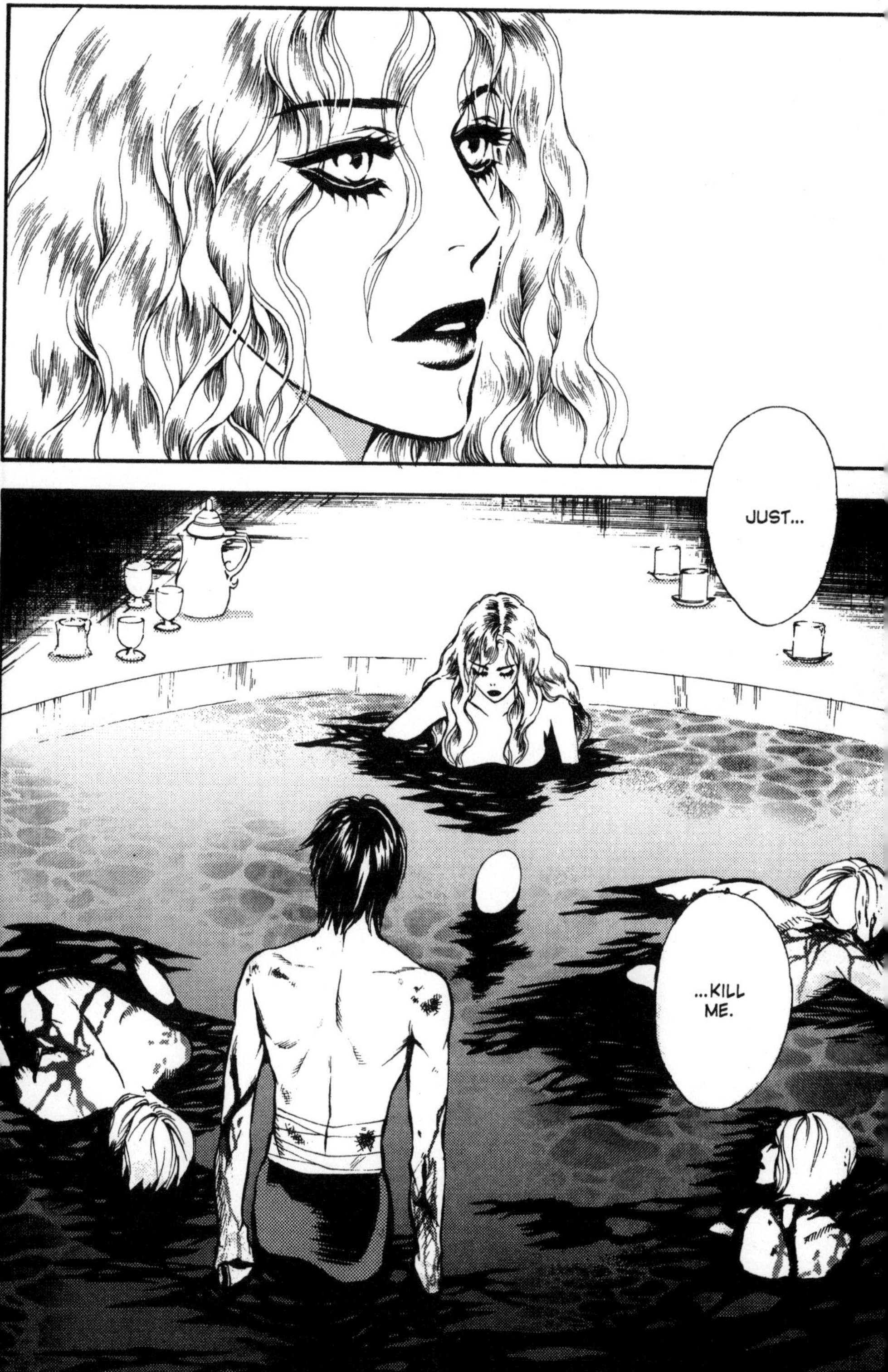
JUST...
...KILL ME.

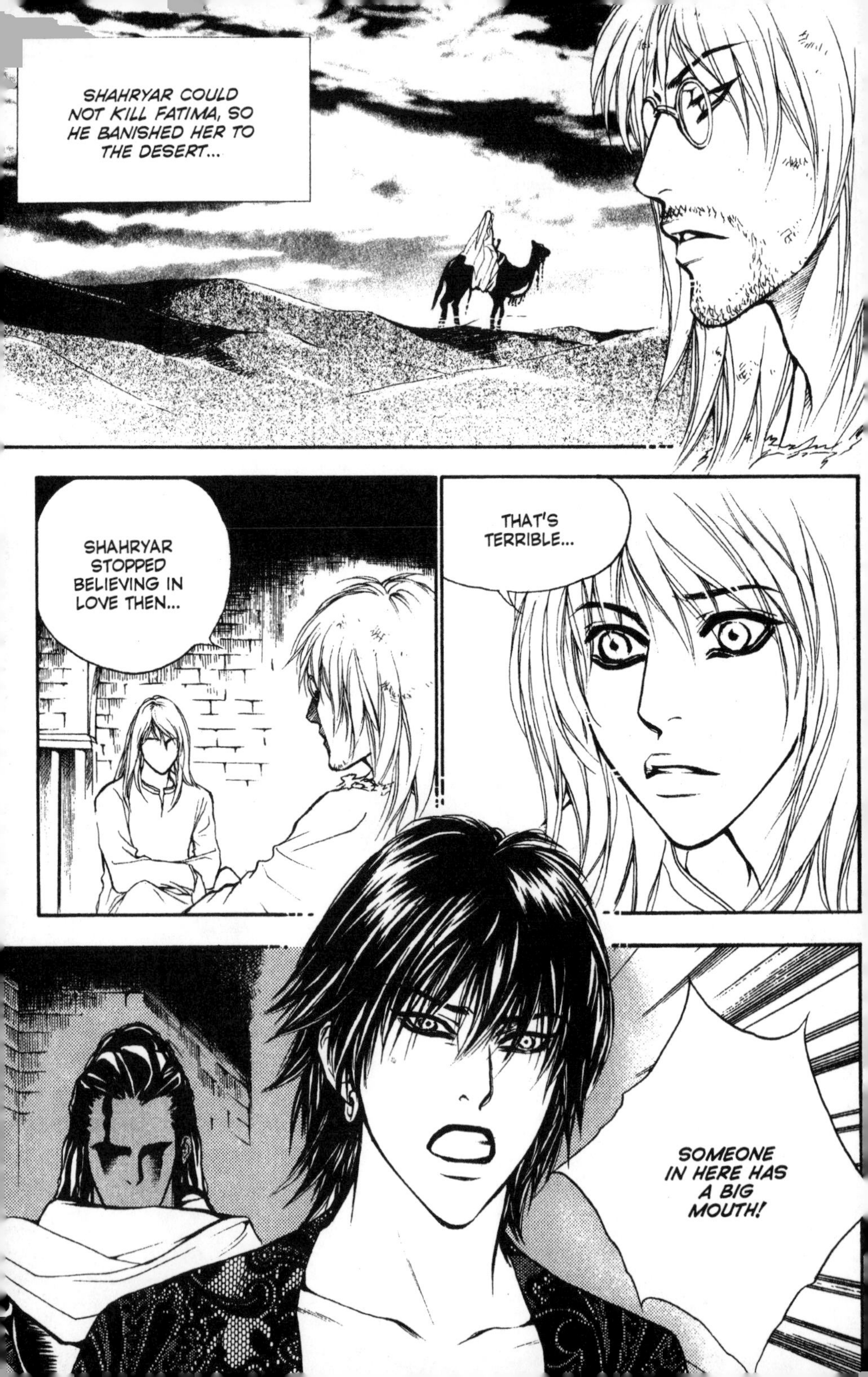
SHAHRYAR COULD NOT KILL FATIMA, SO HE BANISHED HER TO THE DESERT...
SHAHRYAR STOPPED BELIEVING IN LOVE THEN...
THAT'S TERRIBLE...
SOMEONE IN HERE HAS A BIG MOUTH!

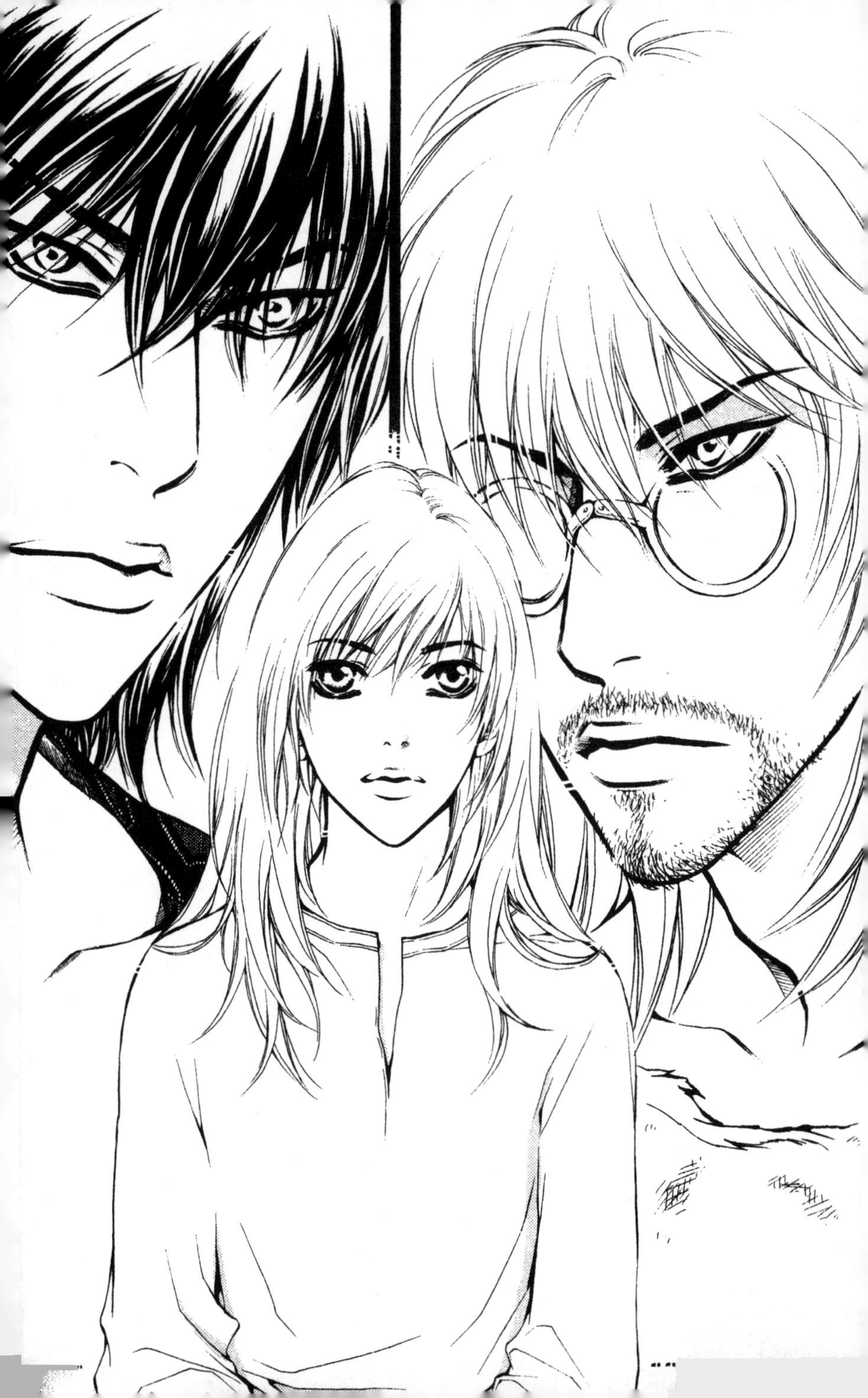

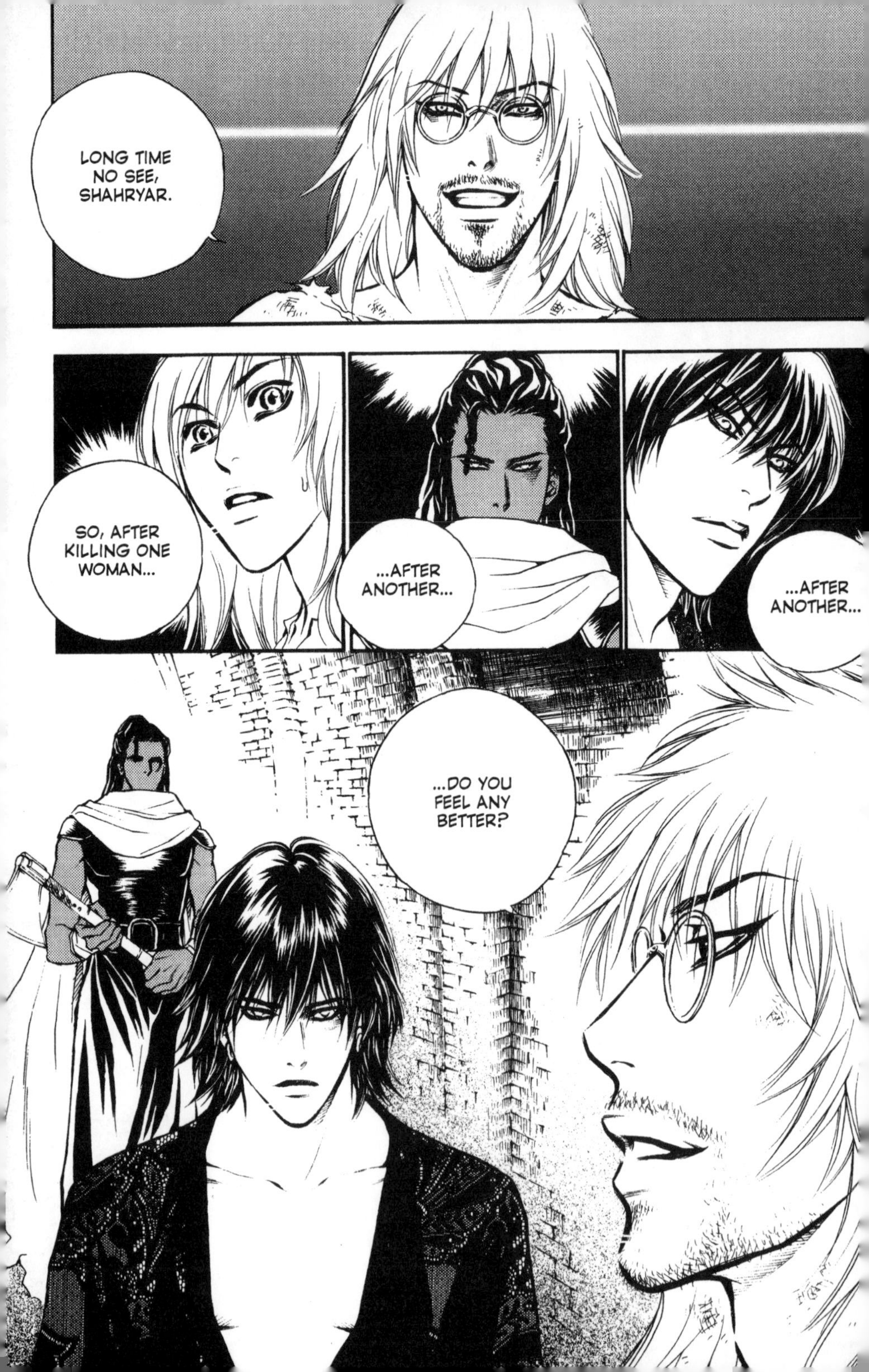
LONG TIME NO SEE, SHAHRYAR.
SO, AFTER KILLING ONE WOMAN...
...AFTER ANOTHER...
...AFTER ANOTHER...
...DO YOU FEEL ANY BETTER?

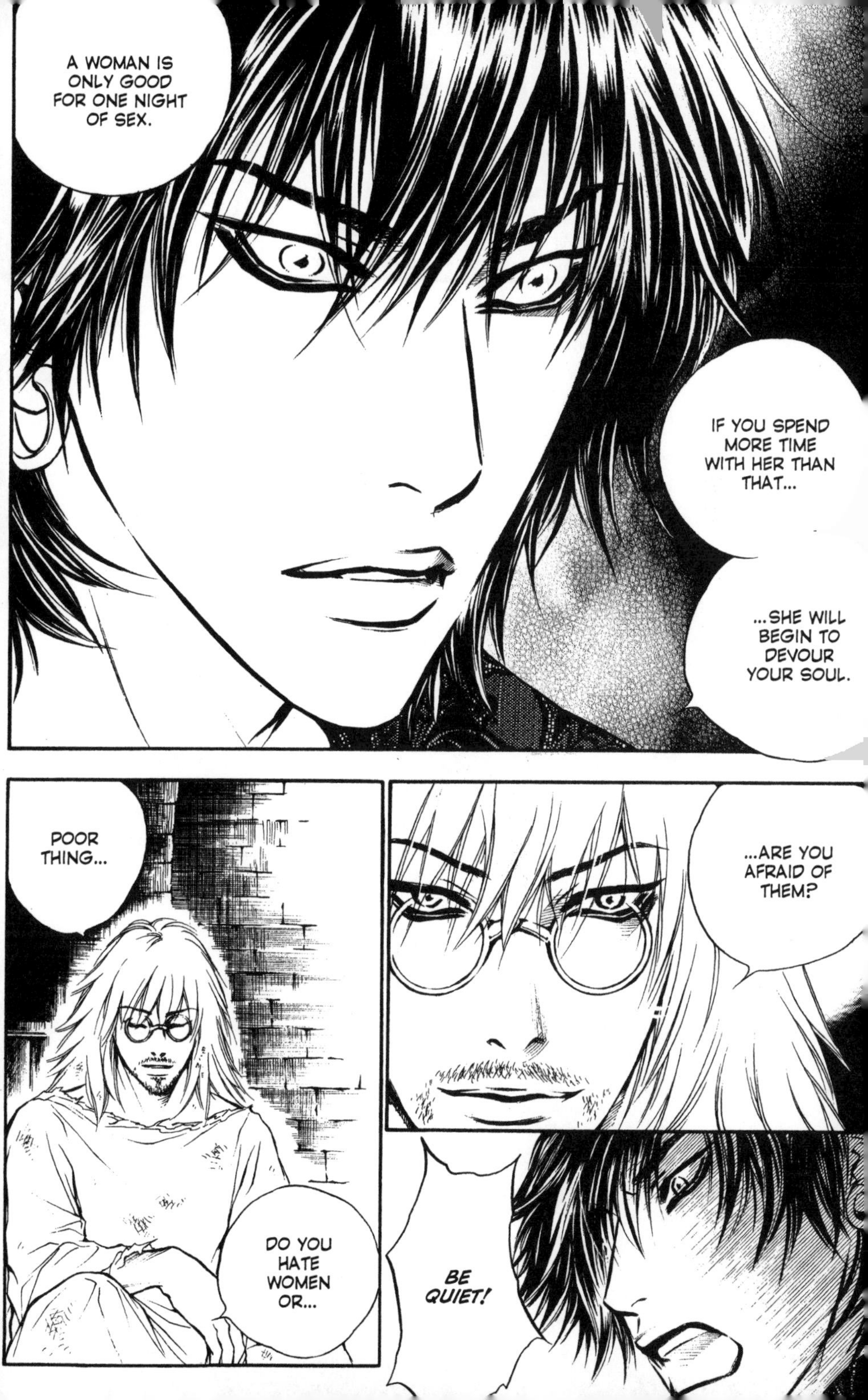
A WOMAN IS ONLY GOOD FOR ONE NIGHT OF SEX.
IF YOU SPEND MORE TIME WITH HER THAN THAT...
...SHE WILL BEGIN TO DEVOUR YOUR SOUL.
...ARE YOU AFRAID OF THEM?
POOR THING...
BE QUIET!
DO YOU HATE WOMEN OR...

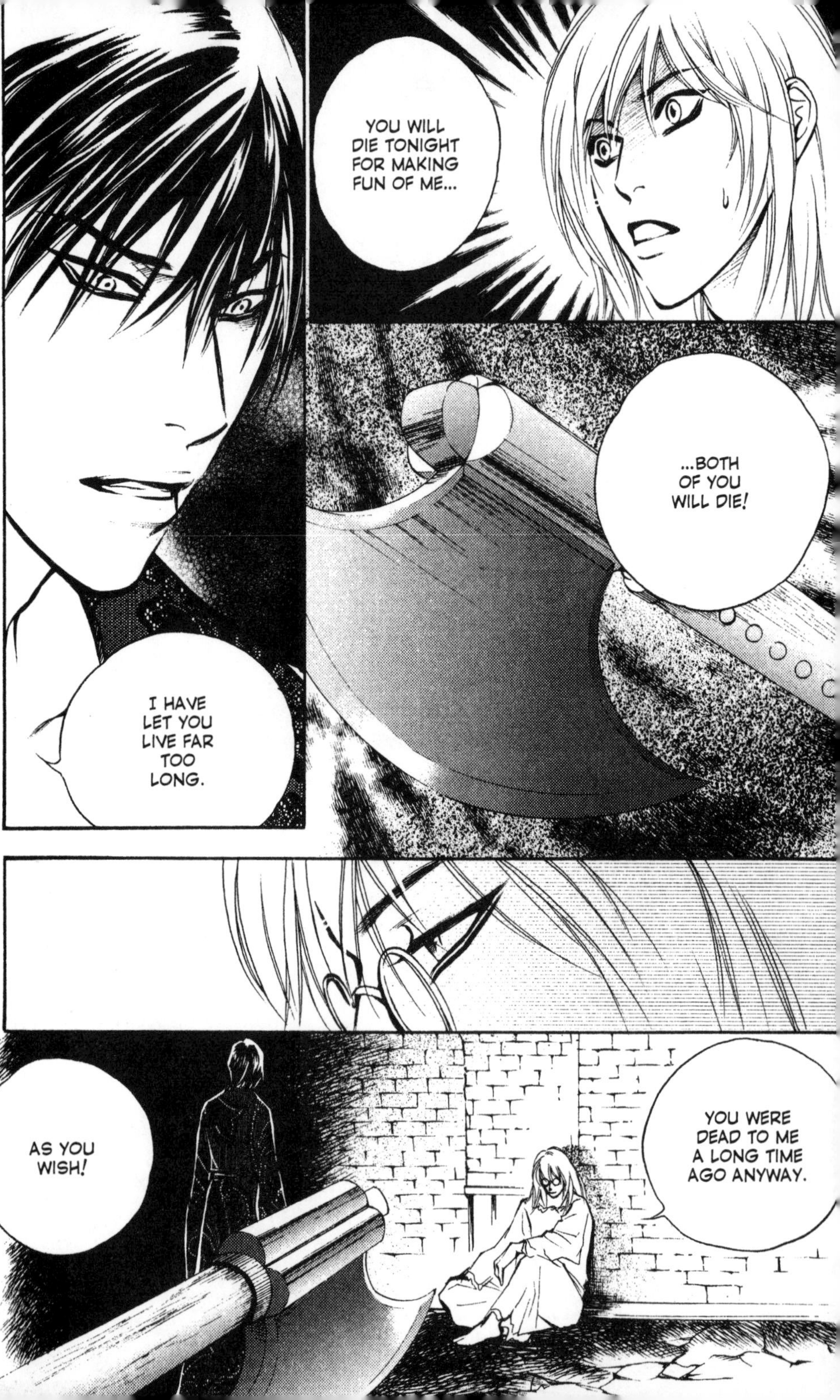
I HAVE LET YOU LIVE FAR TOO LONG.
YOU WILL DIE TONIGHT FOR MAKING FUN OF ME...
...BOTH OF YOU WILL DIE!
AS YOU WISH!
YOU WERE DEAD TO ME A LONG TIME AGO ANYWAY.

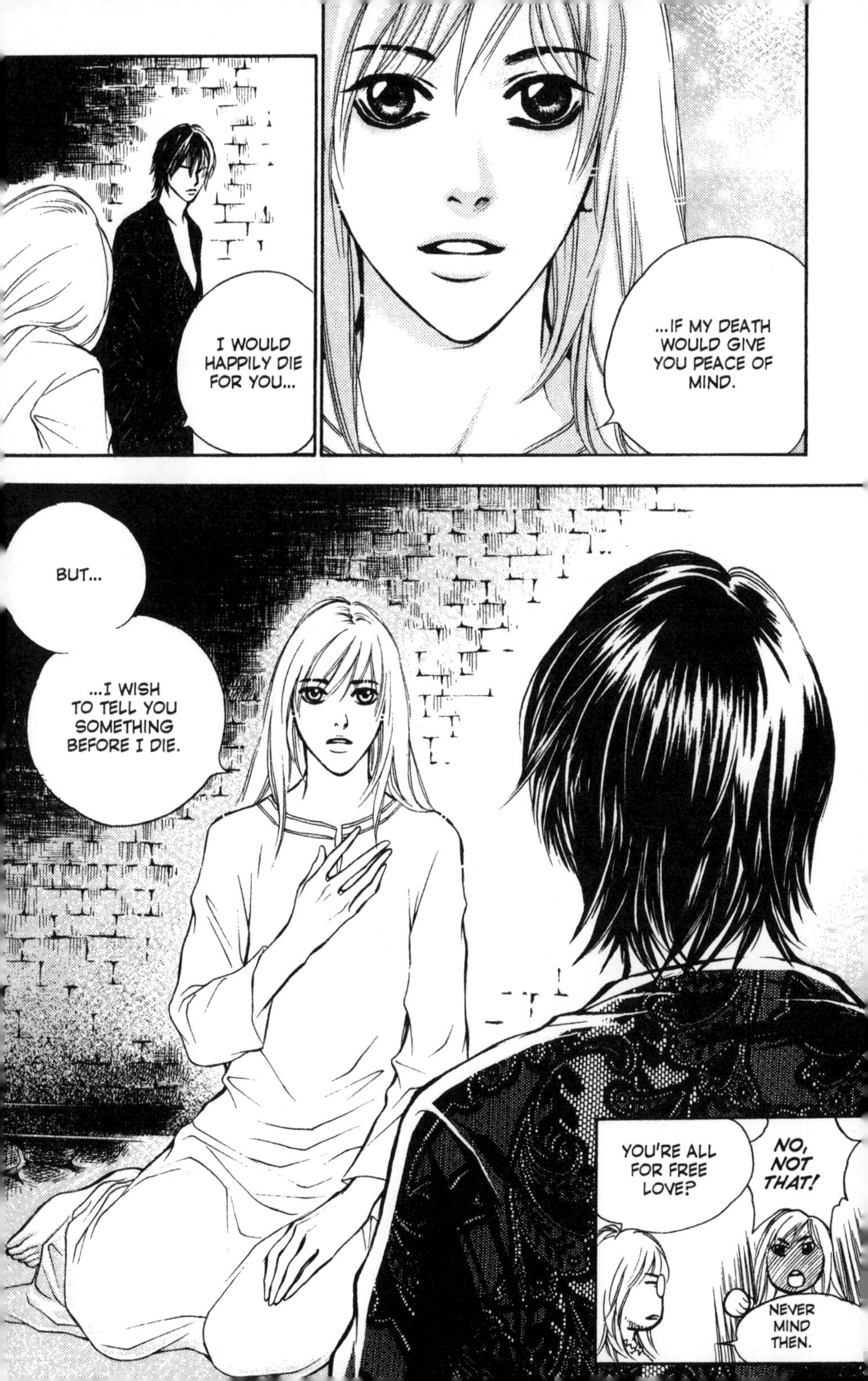
I WOULD HAPPILY DIE FOR YOU...
...IF MY DEATH WOULD GIVE YOU PEACE OF MIND.
BUT...
...I WISH TO TELL YOU SOMETHING BEFORE I DIE.
YOU'RE ALL FOR FREE LOVE?
NO, NOT THAT!
NEVER MIND THEN.

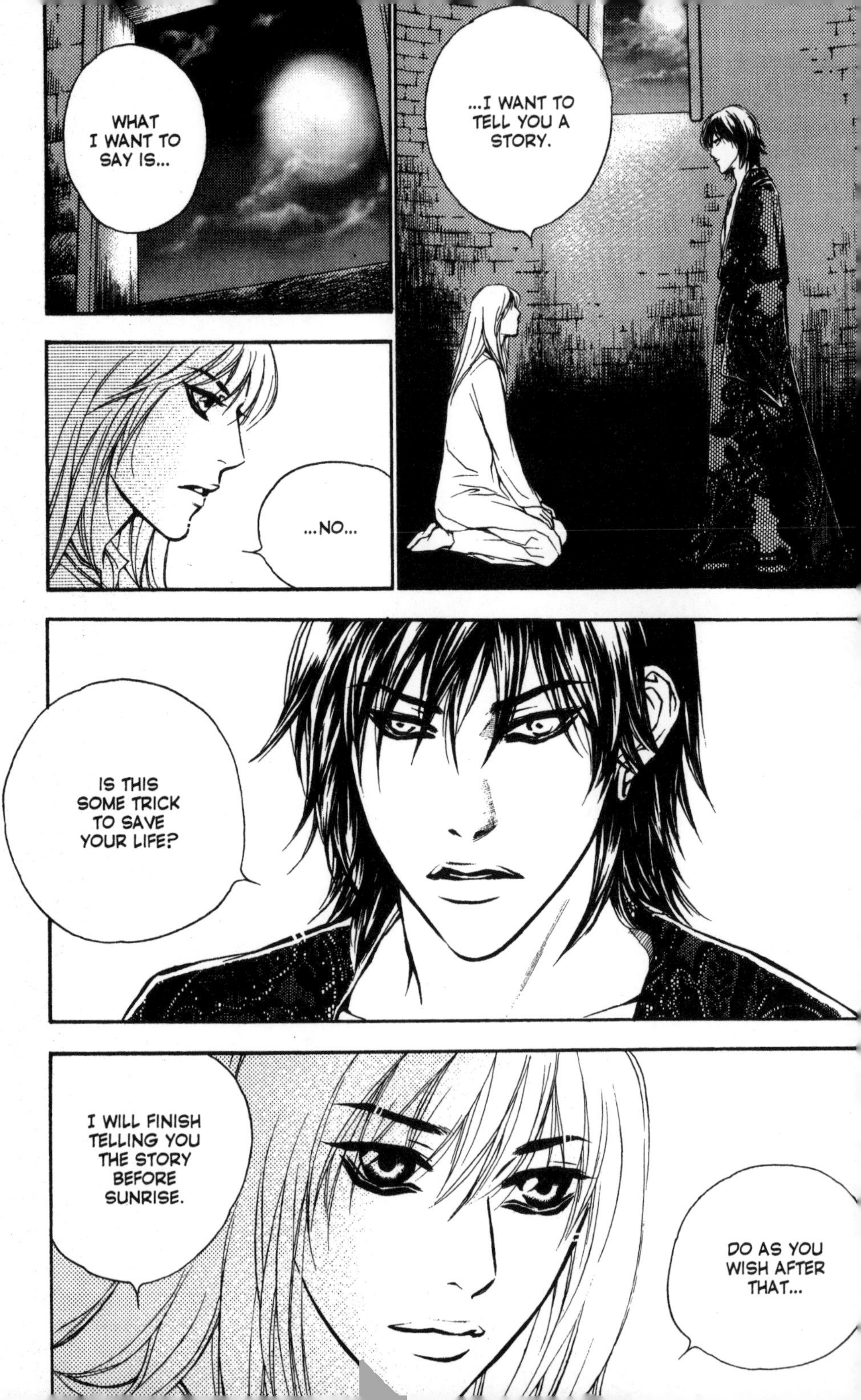
WHAT I WANT TO SAY IS...
...I WANT TO TELL YOU A STORY.
...NO...
IS THIS SOME TRICK TO SAVE YOUR LIFE?
I WILL FINISH TELLING YOU THE STORY BEFORE SUNRISE.
DO AS YOU WISH AFTER THAT...

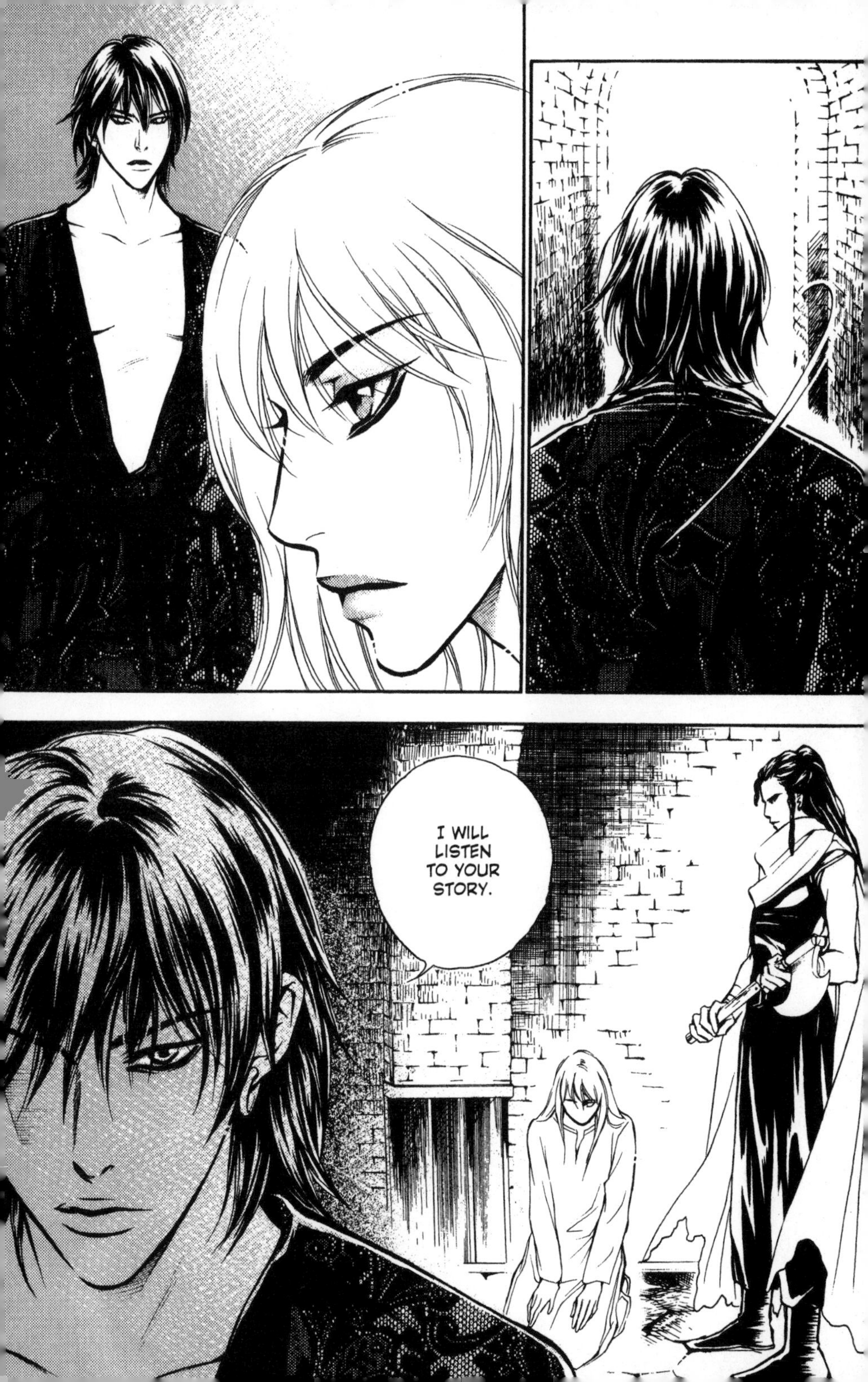
I WILL LISTEN TO YOUR STORY.

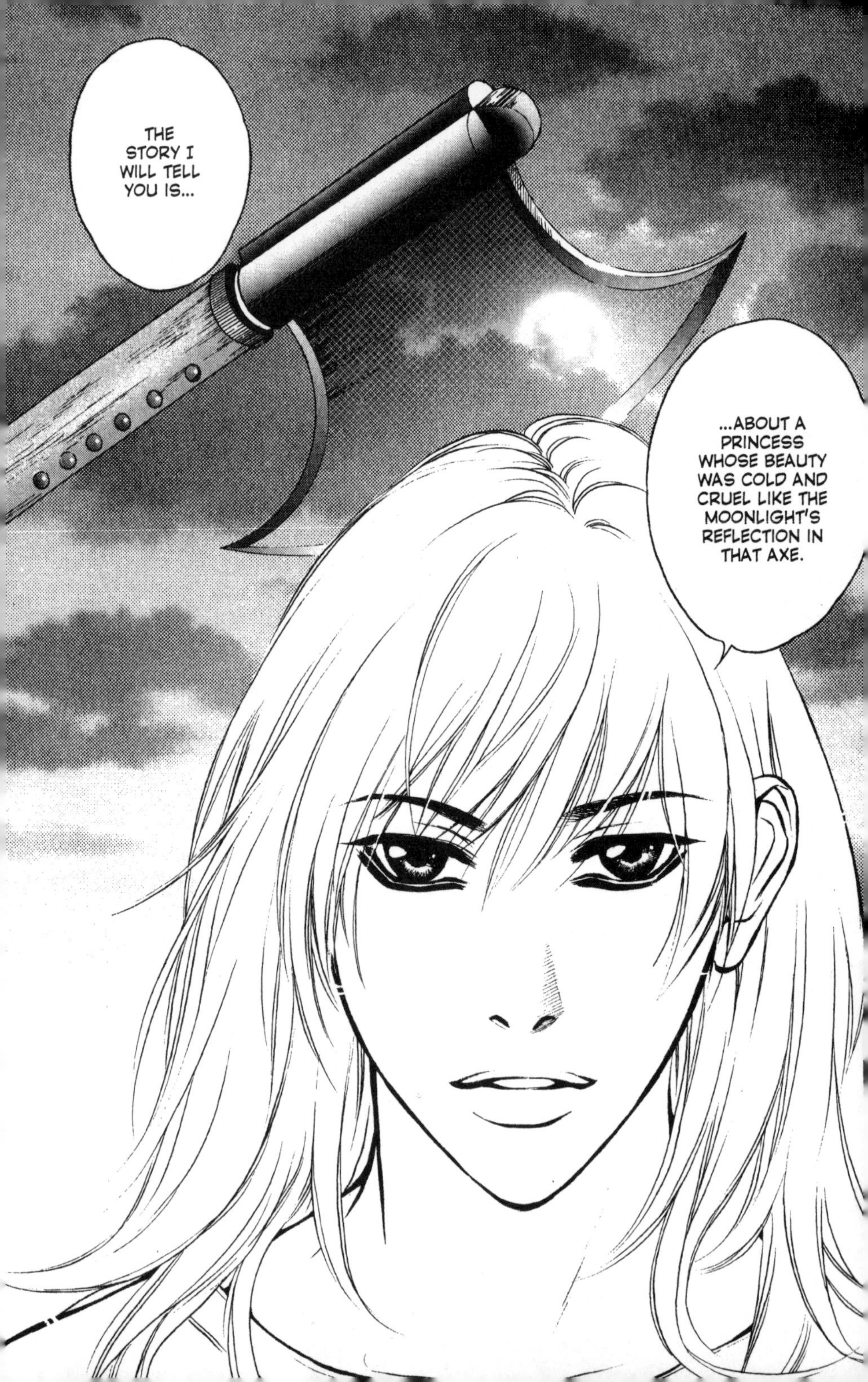
THE STORY I WILL TELL YOU IS...
...ABOUT A PRINCESS WHOSE BEAUTY WAS COLD AND CRUEL LIKE THE MOONLIGHT'S REFLECTION IN THAT AXE.

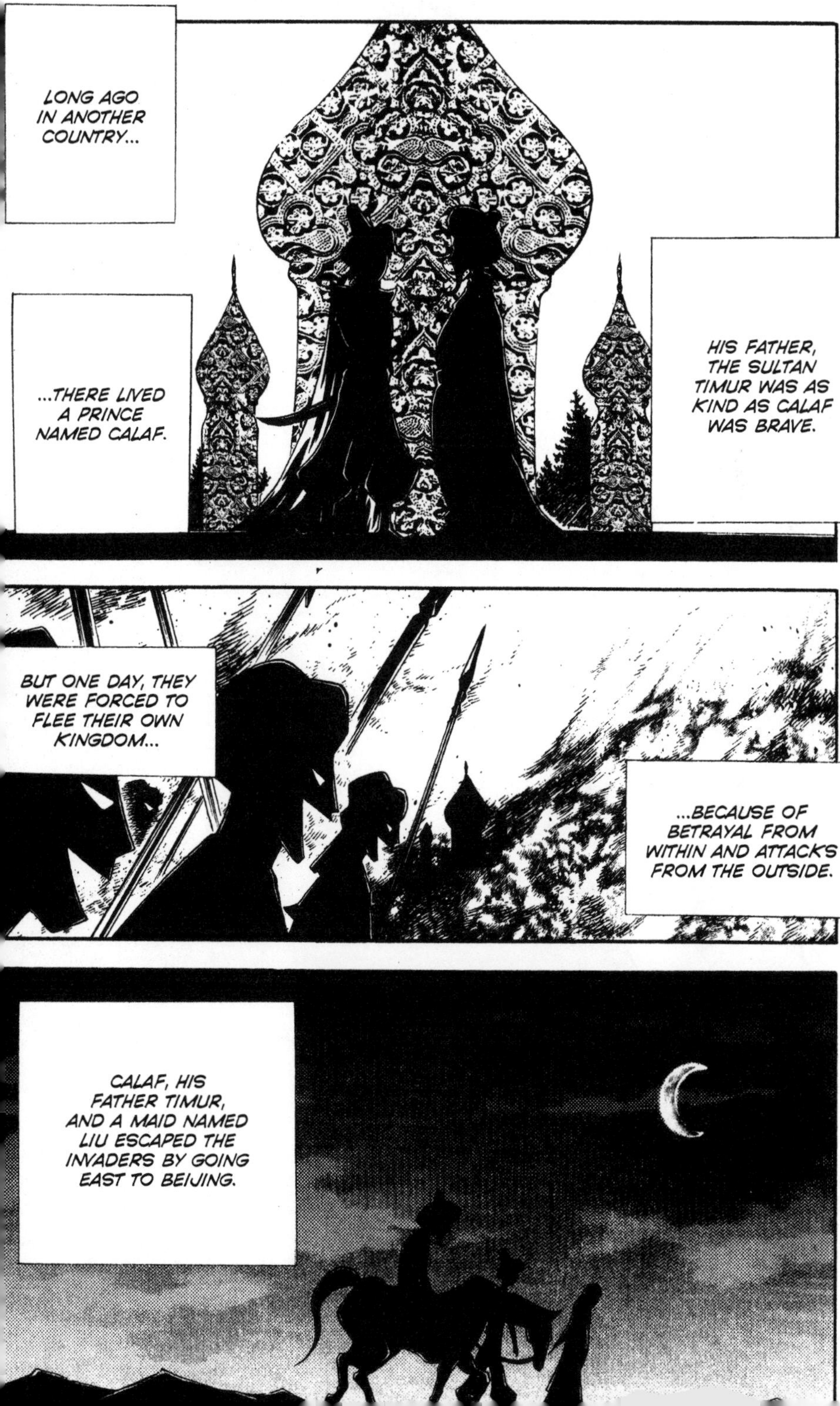
LONG AGO IN ANOTHER COUNTRY...
...THERE LIVED A PRINCE NAMED CALAF.
HIS FATHER, THE SULTAN TIMUR WAS AS KIND AS CALAF WAS BRAVE.
BUT ONE DAY, THEY WERE FORCED TO FLEE THEIR OWN KINGDOM...
...BECAUSE OF BETRAYAL FROM WITHIN AND ATTACKS FROM THE OUTSIDE.
CALAF, HIS FATHER TIMUR, AND A MAID NAMED LIU ESCAPED THE INVADERS BY GOING EAST TO BEIJING.

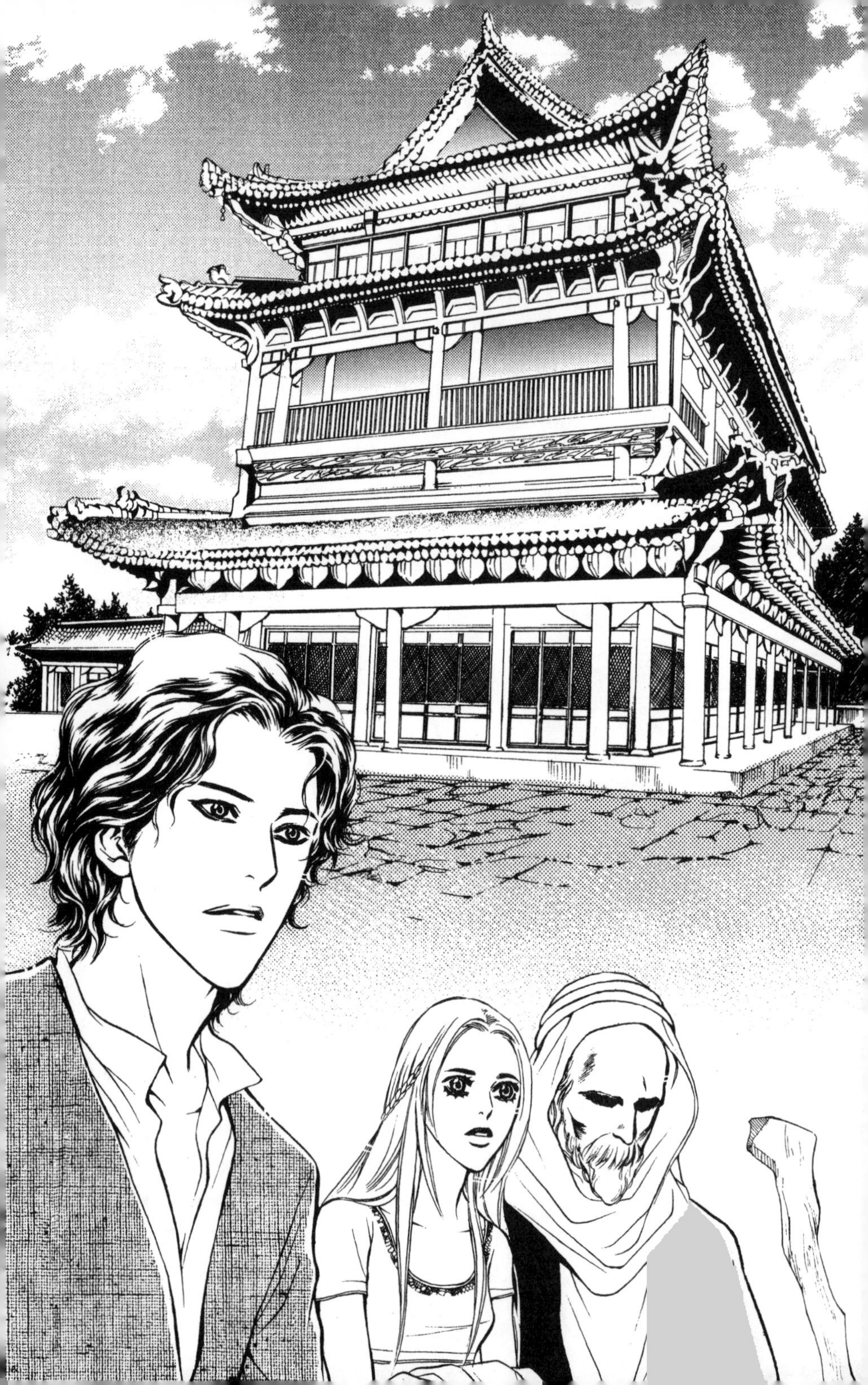

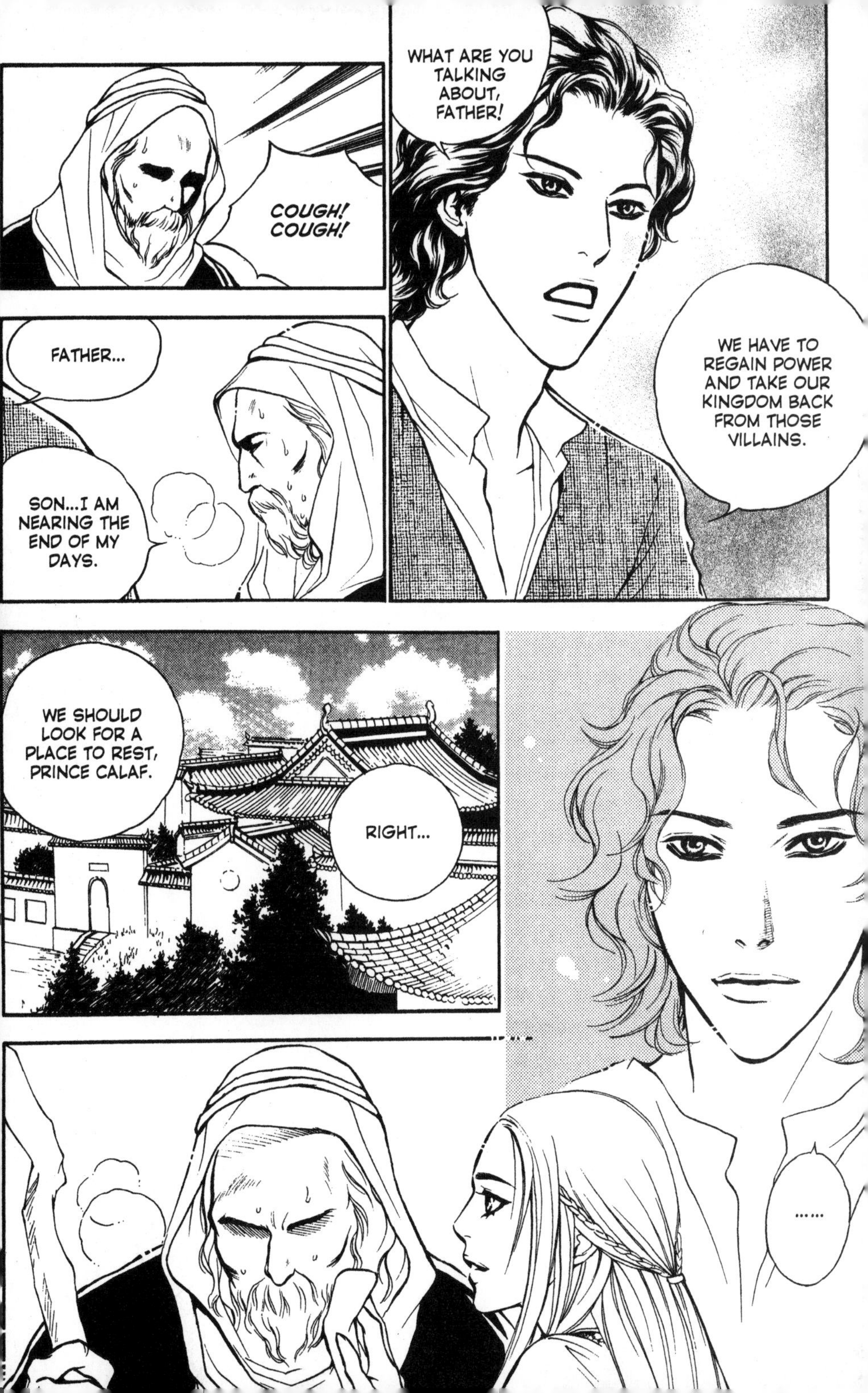
COUGH! COUGH!
FATHER...
SON...I AM NEARING THE END OF MY DAYS.
WHAT ARE YOU TALKING ABOUT, FATHER!
WE HAVE TO REGAIN POWER AND TAKE OUR KINGDOM BACK FROM THOSE VILLAINS.
WE SHOULD LOOK FOR A PLACE TO REST, PRINCE CALAF.
RIGHT...
......

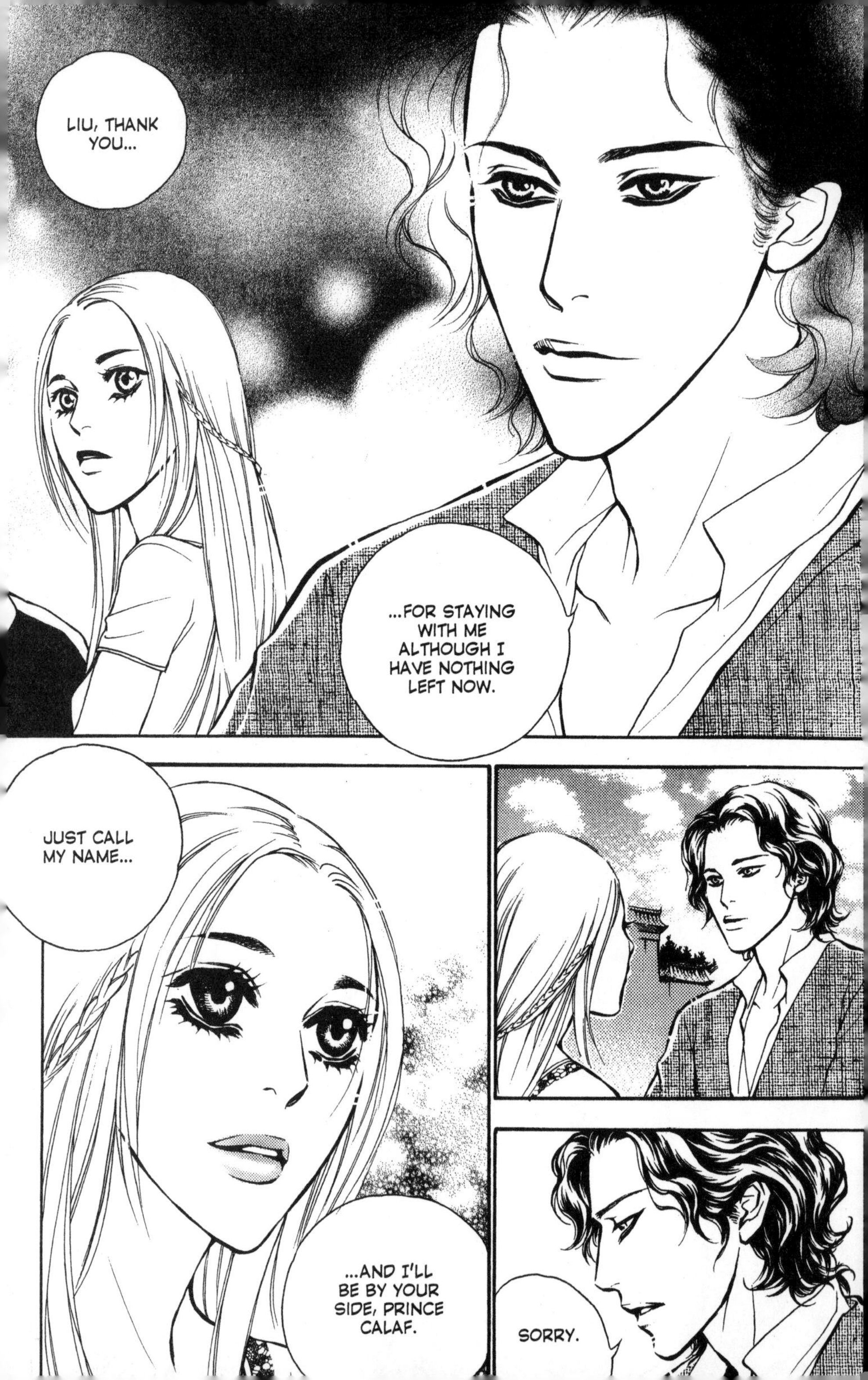
LIU, THANK YOU...
...FOR STAYING WITH ME ALTHOUGH I HAVE NOTHING LEFT NOW.
JUST CALL MY NAME...
...AND I'LL BE BY YOUR SIDE, PRINCE CALAF.
SORRY.

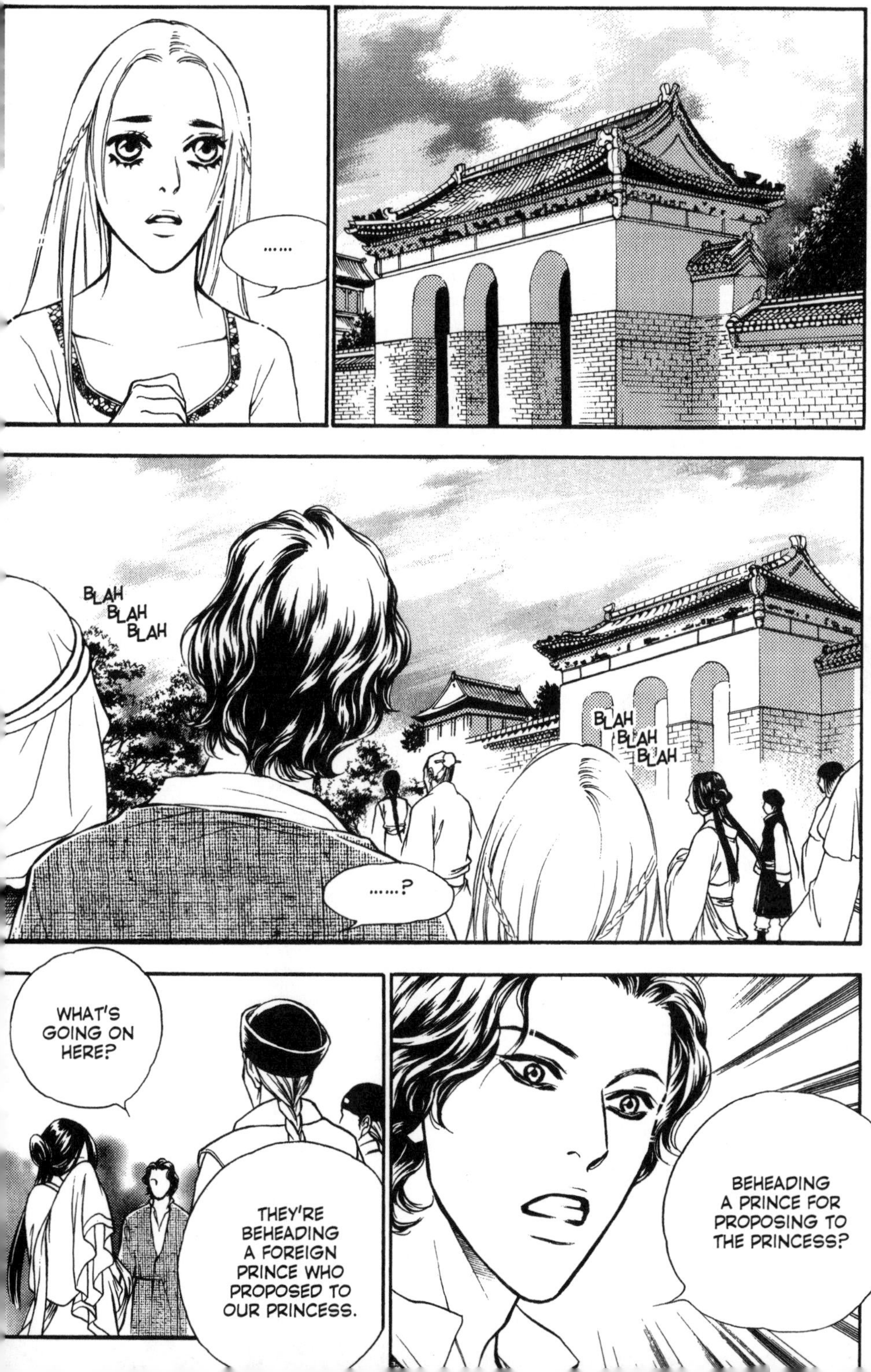
……
BLAH BLAH BLAH
BLAH BLAH BLAH
……?
WHAT'S GOING ON HERE?
THEY'RE BEHEADING A FOREIGN PRINCE WHO PROPOSED TO OUR PRINCESS.
BEHEADING A PRINCE FOR PROPOSING TO THE PRINCESS?

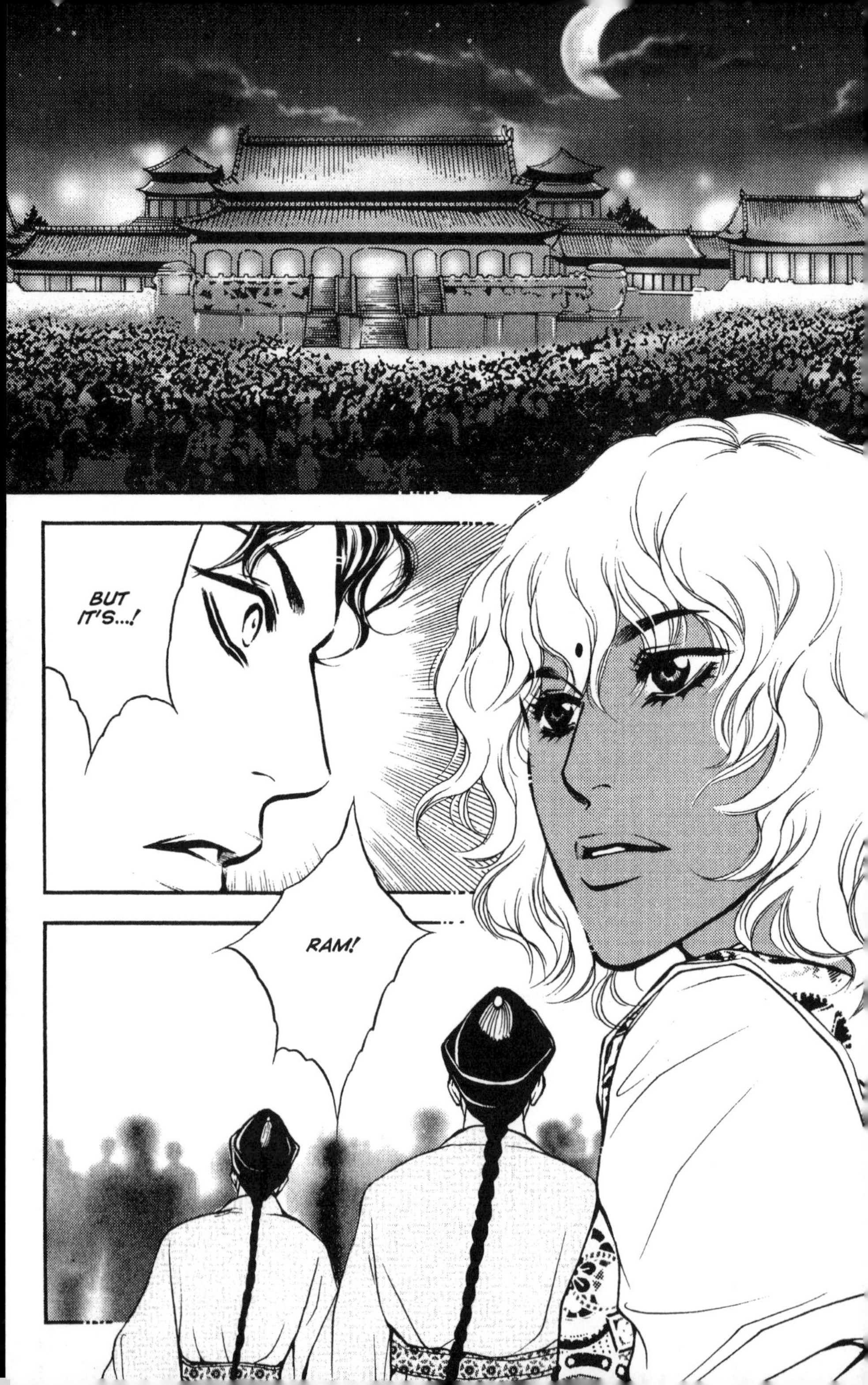
BUT IT'S...!
RAM!

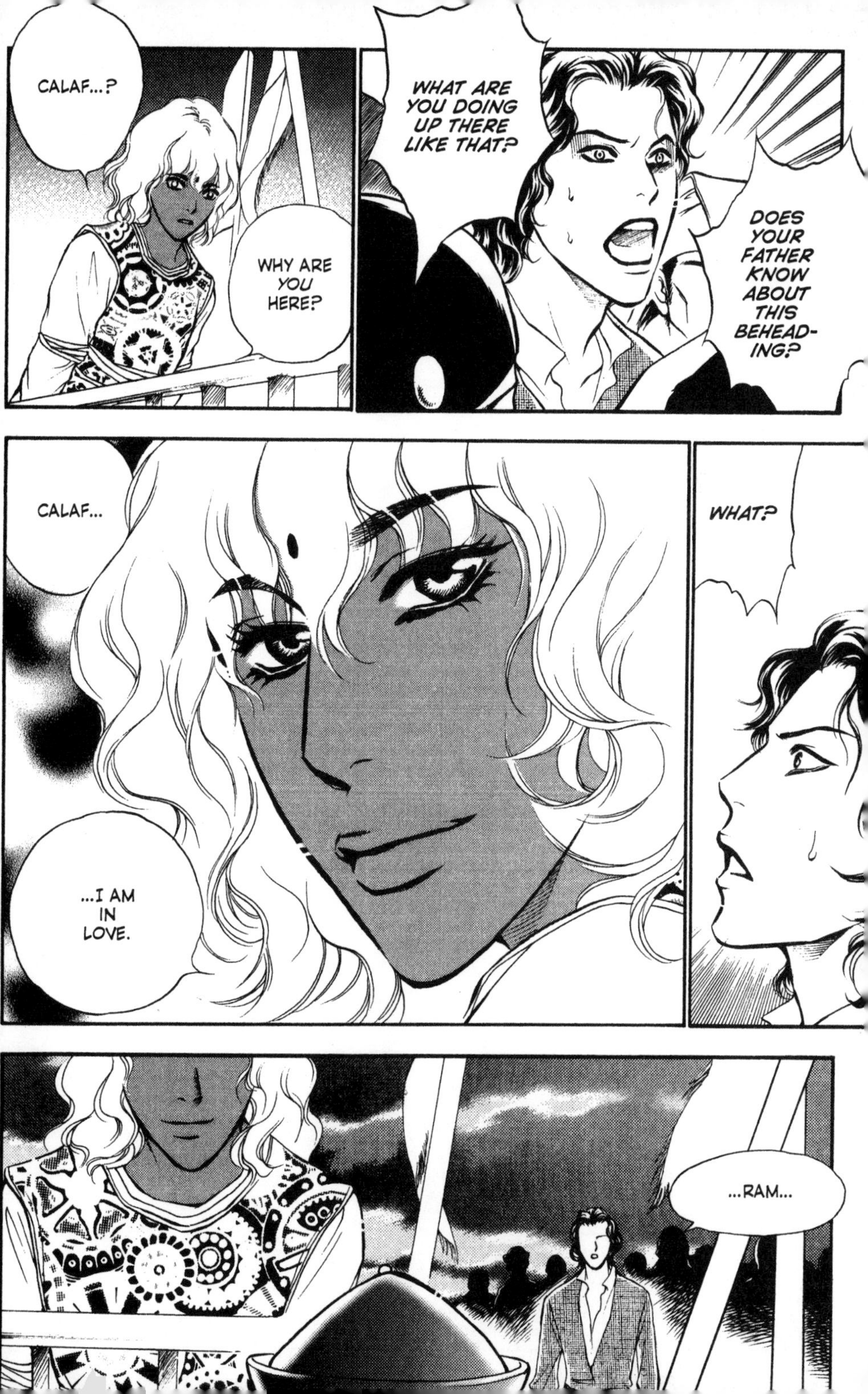
CALAF...?
WHY ARE YOU HERE?
WHAT ARE YOU DOING UP THERE LIKE THAT?
DOES YOUR FATHER KNOW ABOUT THIS BEHEAD-ING?
CALAF...
...I AM IN LOVE.
WHAT?
...RAM...

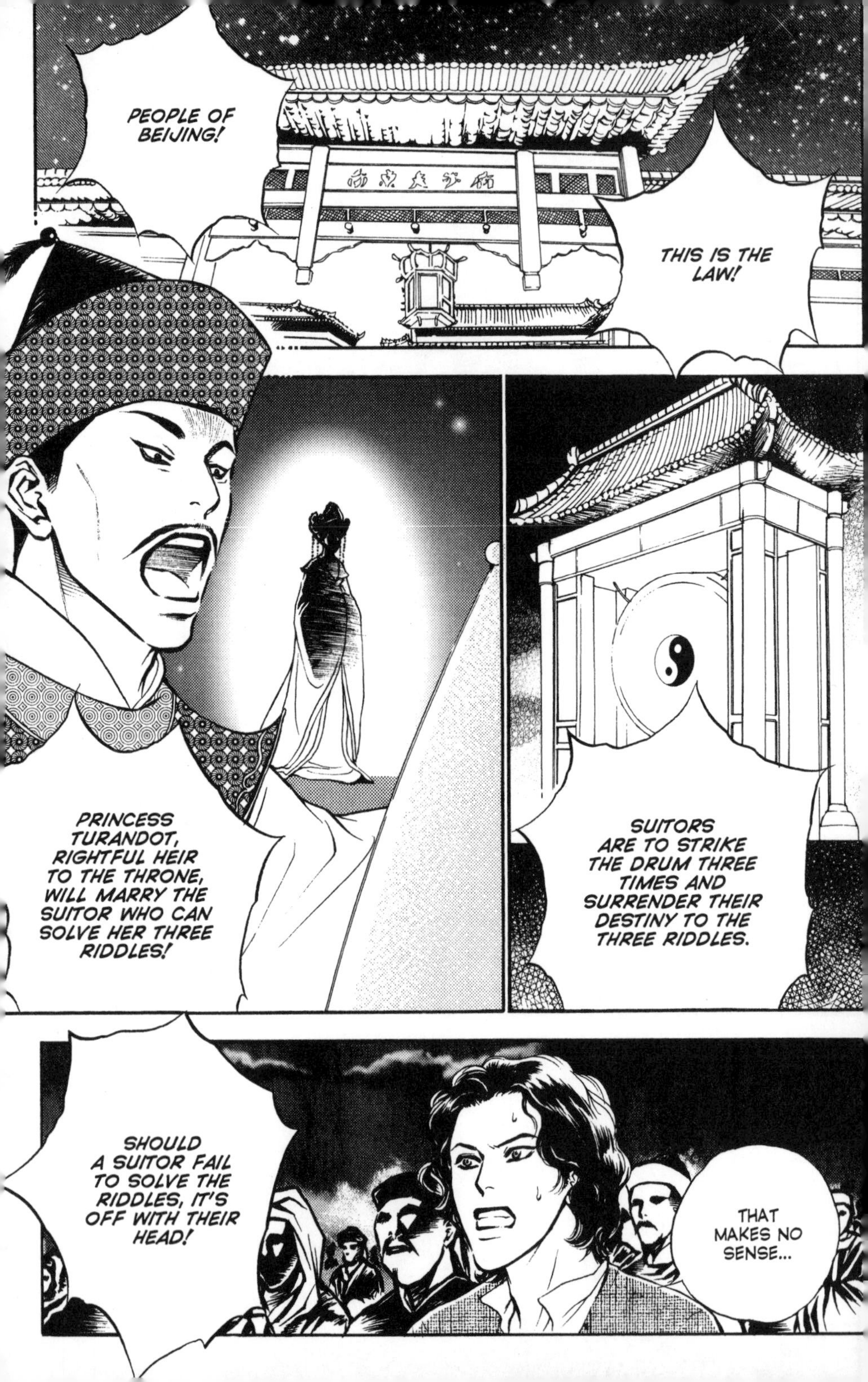
PEOPLE OF BEIJING!
THIS IS THE LAW!
PRINCESS TURANDOT, RIGHTFUL HEIR TO THE THRONE, WILL MARRY THE SUITOR WHO CAN SOLVE HER THREE RIDDLES!
SUITORS ARE TO STRIKE THE DRUM THREE TIMES AND SURRENDER THEIR DESTINY TO THE THREE RIDDLES.
SHOULD A SUITOR FAIL TO SOLVE THE RIDDLES, IT'S OFF WITH THEIR HEAD!
THAT MAKES NO SENSE...

THIS PRINCE FROM INDIA PROPOSED TO THE PRINCESS YESTERDAY BUT FAILED TO SOLVE THE RIDDLES!

NOW, HE WILL PAY WITH HIS LIFE!

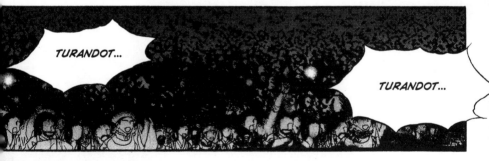

TURANDOT...

TURANDOT...

TURANDOT!

TURANDOT!

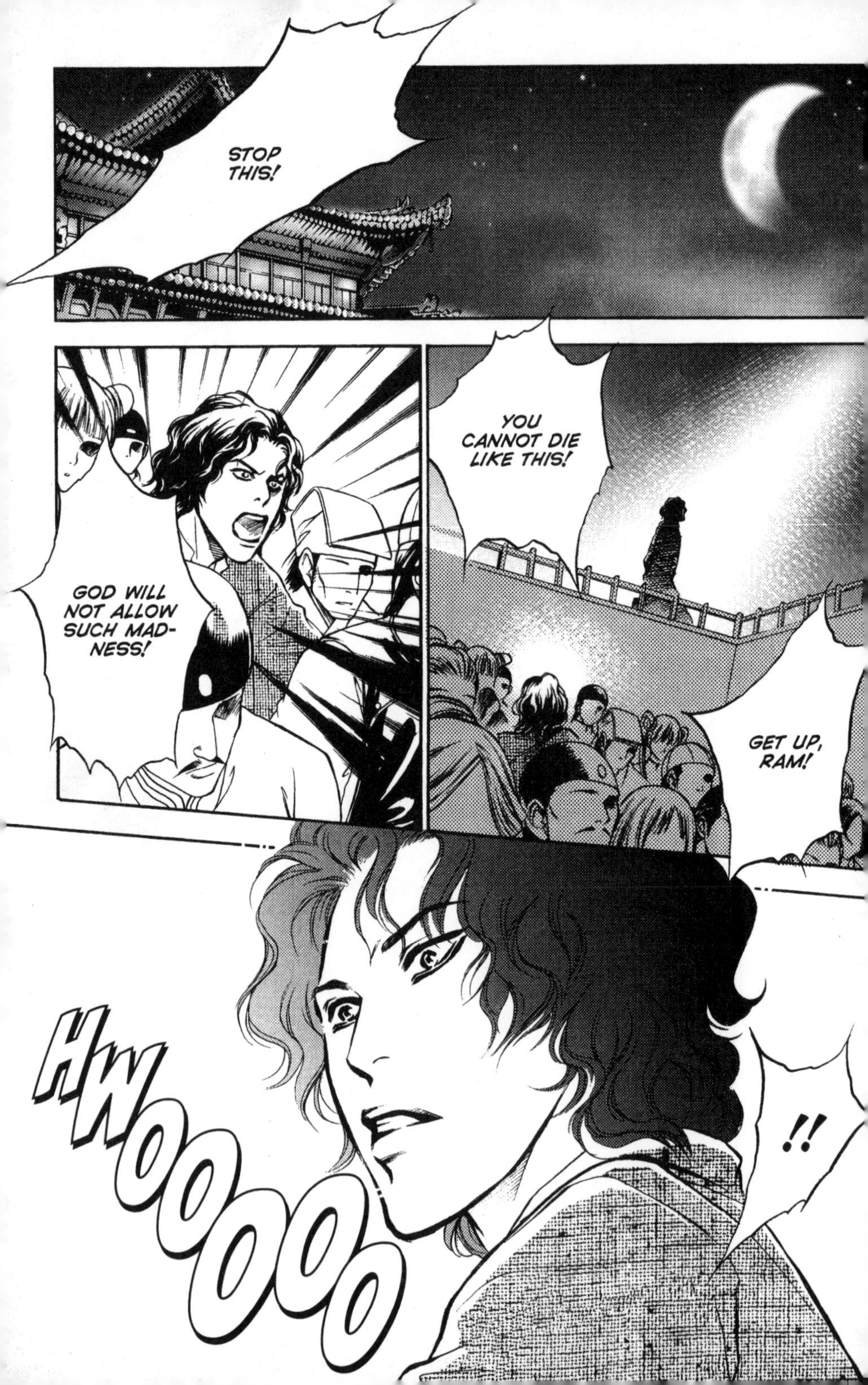
STOP THIS!
GOD WILL NOT ALLOW SUCH MAD-NESS!
YOU CANNOT DIE LIKE THIS!
GET UP, RAM!
HWOOOOO
!!

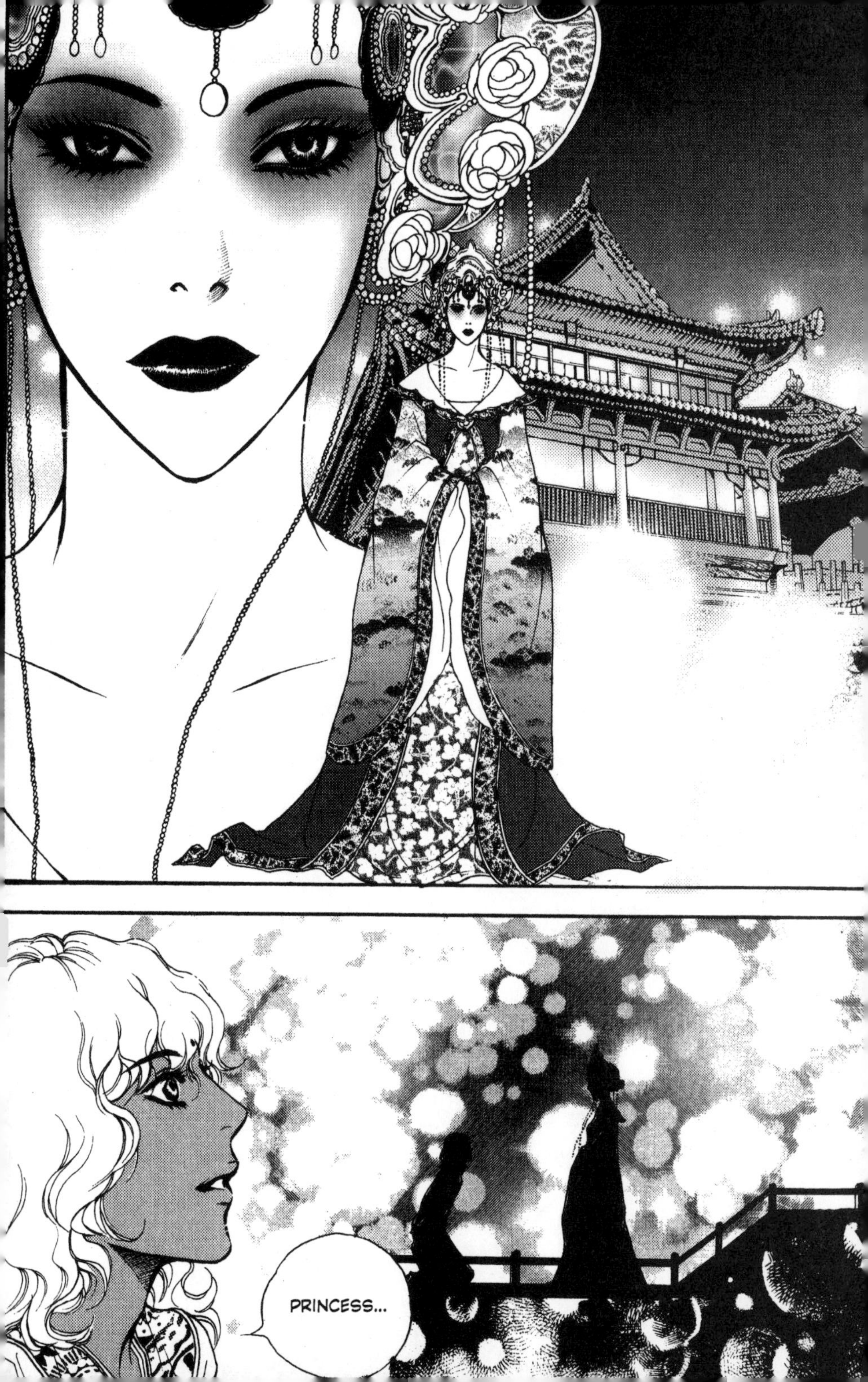
PRINCESS...

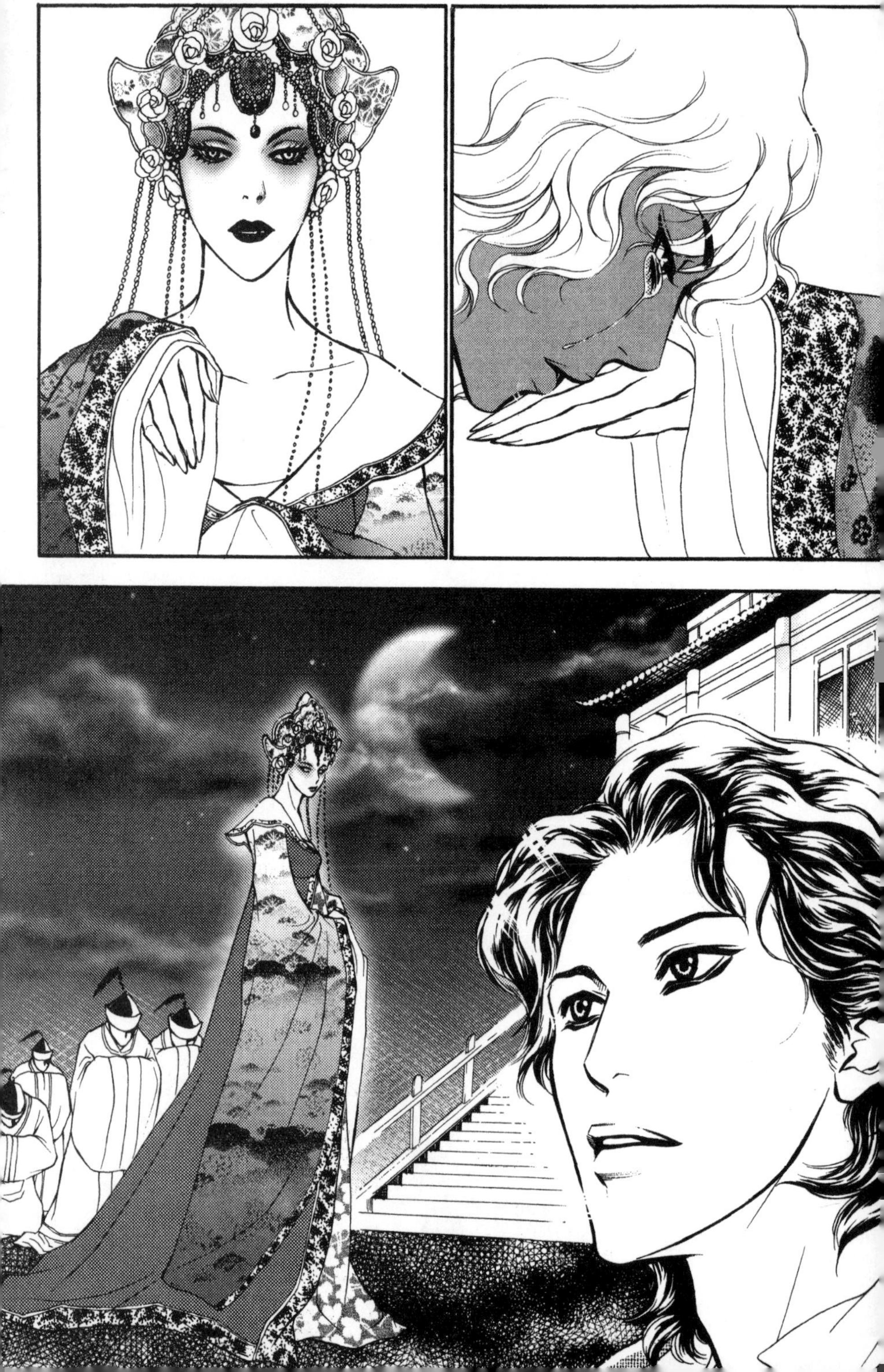

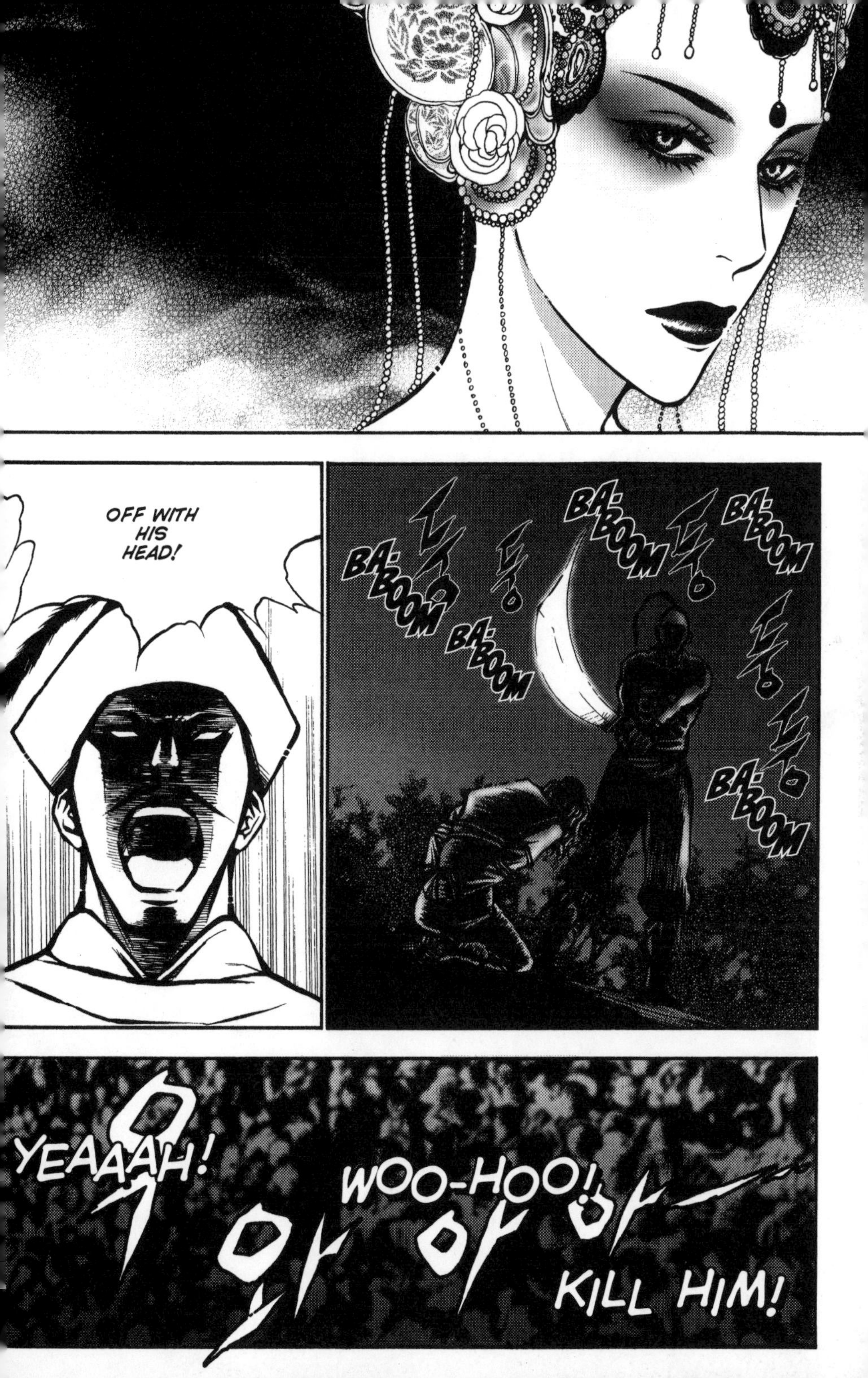
OFF WITH HIS HEAD!
BA-BOOM
BA-BOOM
BA-BOOM
BA-BOOM
BA-BOOM
YEAAAH!
WOO-HOO!
KILL HIM!

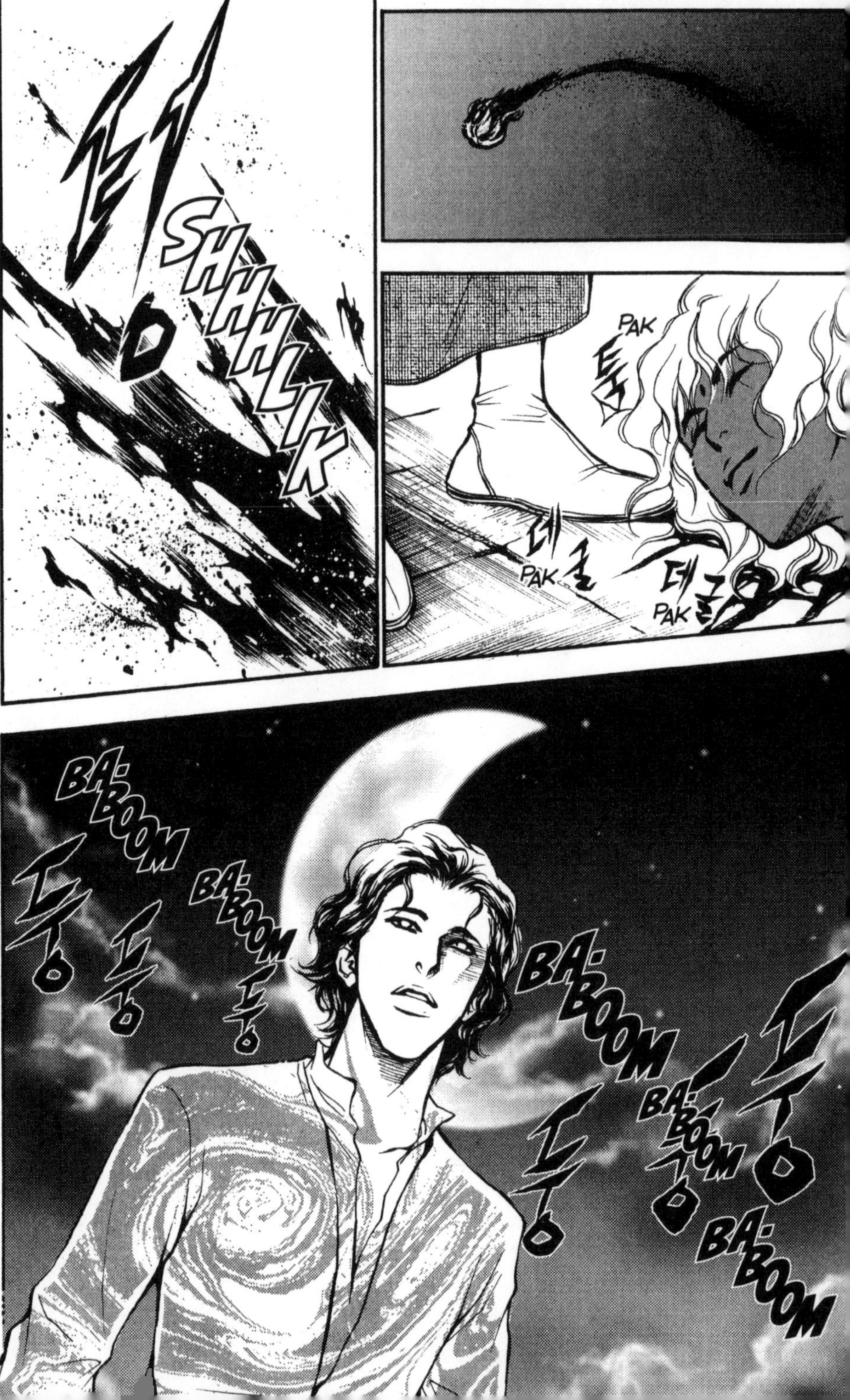
SHHHLIK
PAK
탁
데굴
PAK
데굴
PAK
BA-BOOM
BA-BOOM
BA-BOOM
BA-BOOM
BA-BOOM

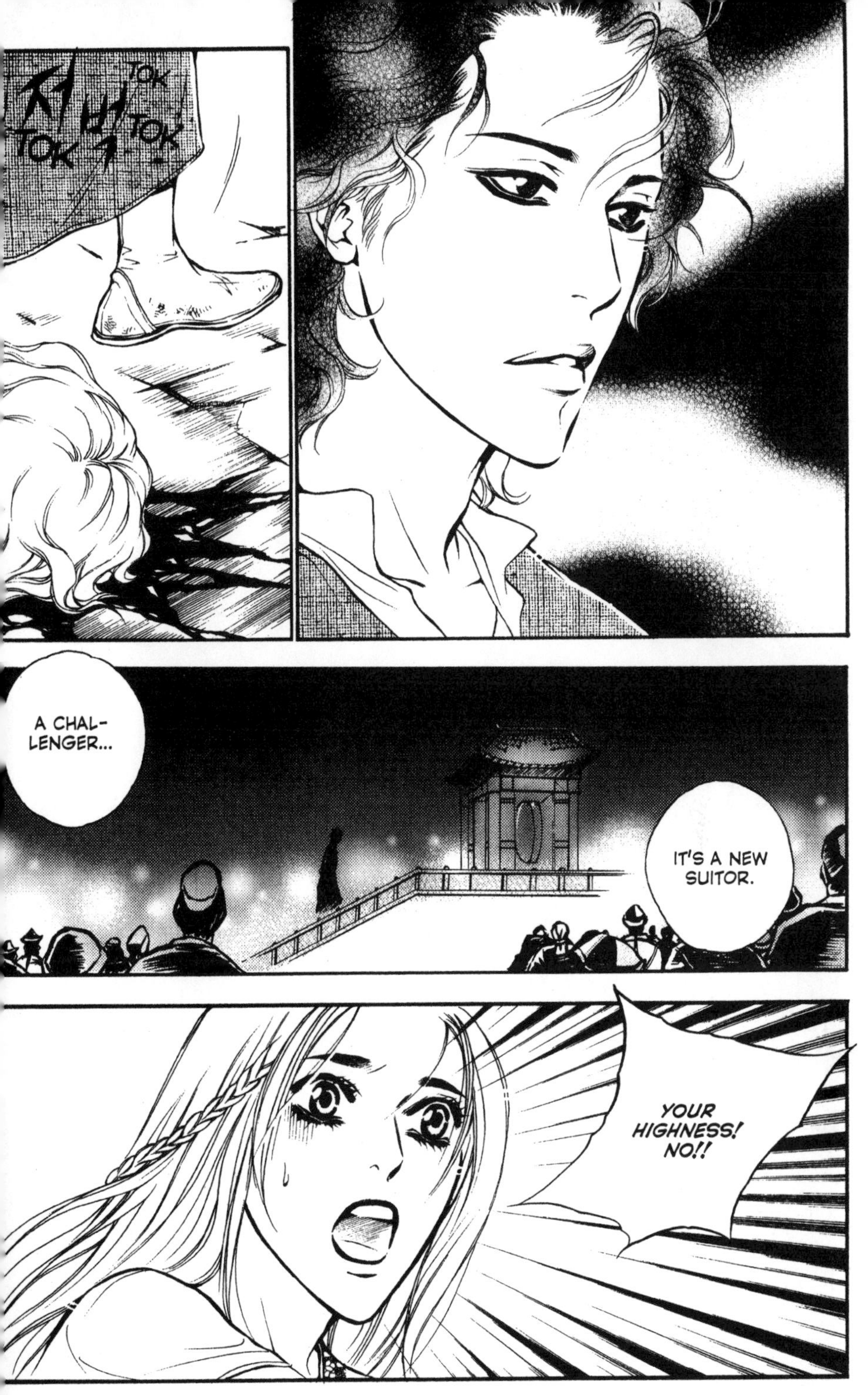
저벅
TOK TOK TOK
A CHAL-LENGER...
IT'S A NEW SUITOR.
YOUR HIGHNESS! NO!!

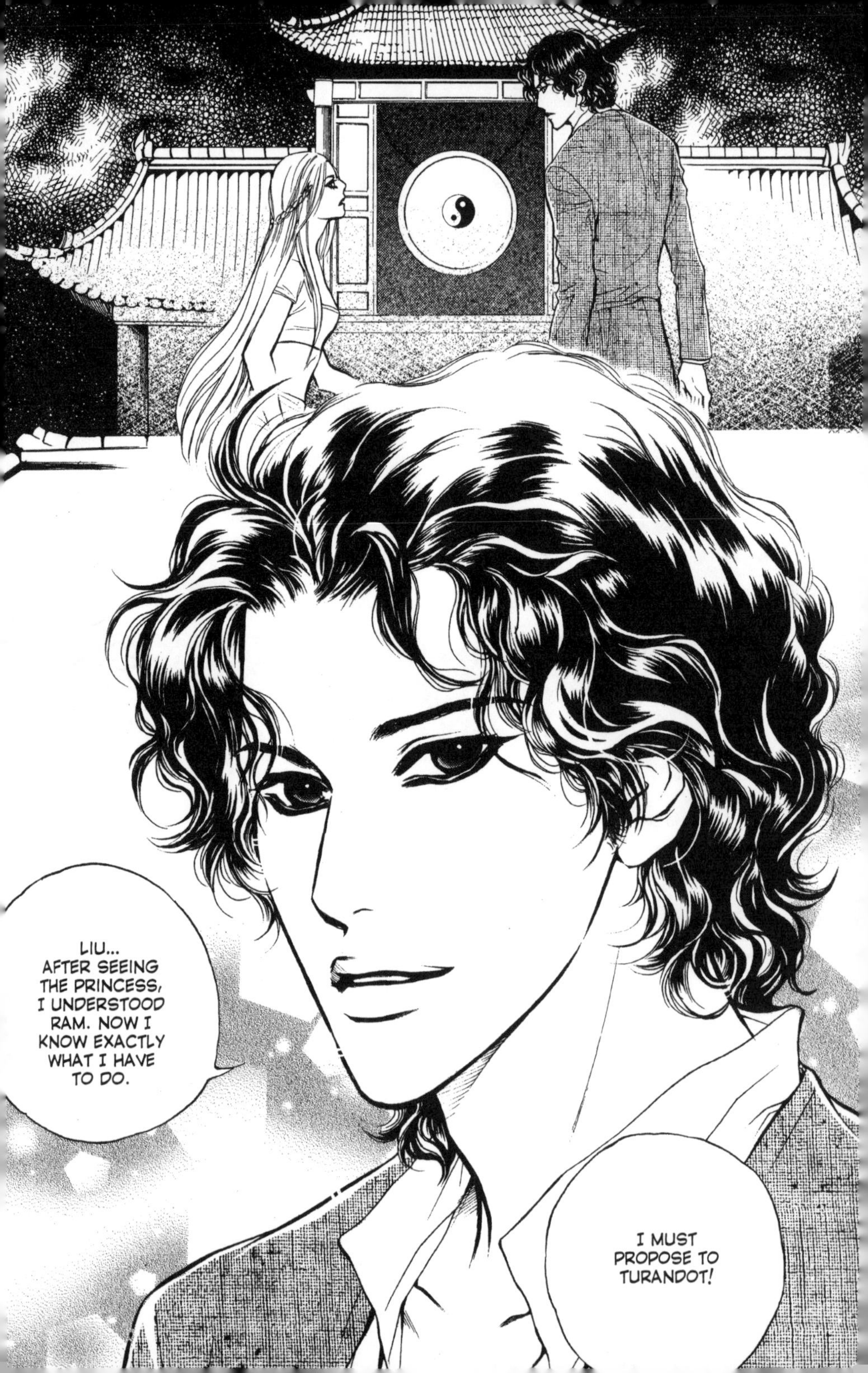
LIU... AFTER SEEING THE PRINCESS, I UNDERSTOOD RAM. NOW I KNOW EXACTLY WHAT I HAVE TO DO.
I MUST PROPOSE TO TURANDOT!

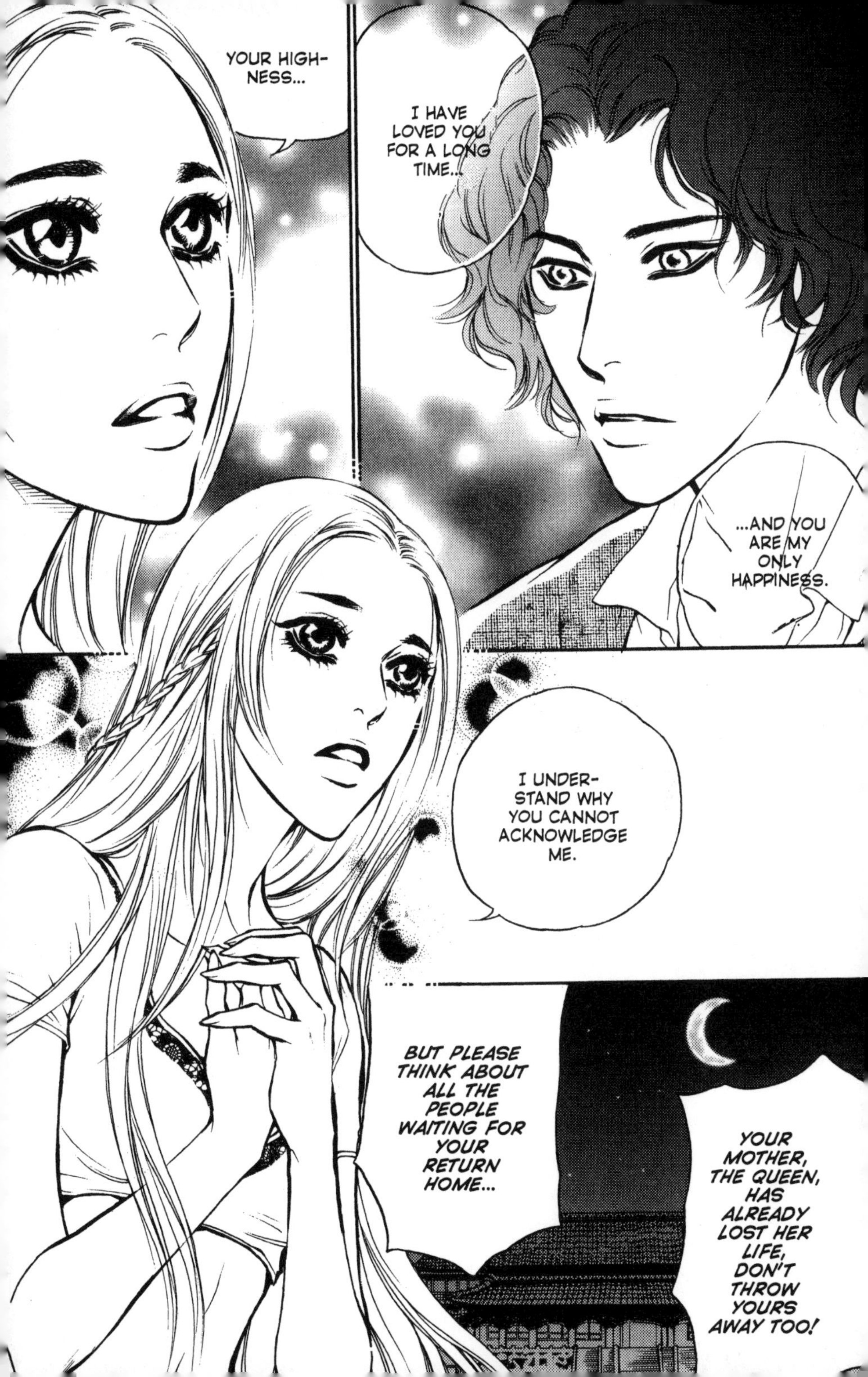
YOUR HIGH-NESS...
I HAVE LOVED YOU FOR A LONG TIME...
...AND YOU ARE MY ONLY HAPPINESS.
I UNDER-STAND WHY YOU CANNOT ACKNOWLEDGE ME.
BUT PLEASE THINK ABOUT ALL THE PEOPLE WAITING FOR YOUR RETURN HOME...
YOUR MOTHER, THE QUEEN, HAS ALREADY LOST HER LIFE, DON'T THROW YOURS AWAY TOO!

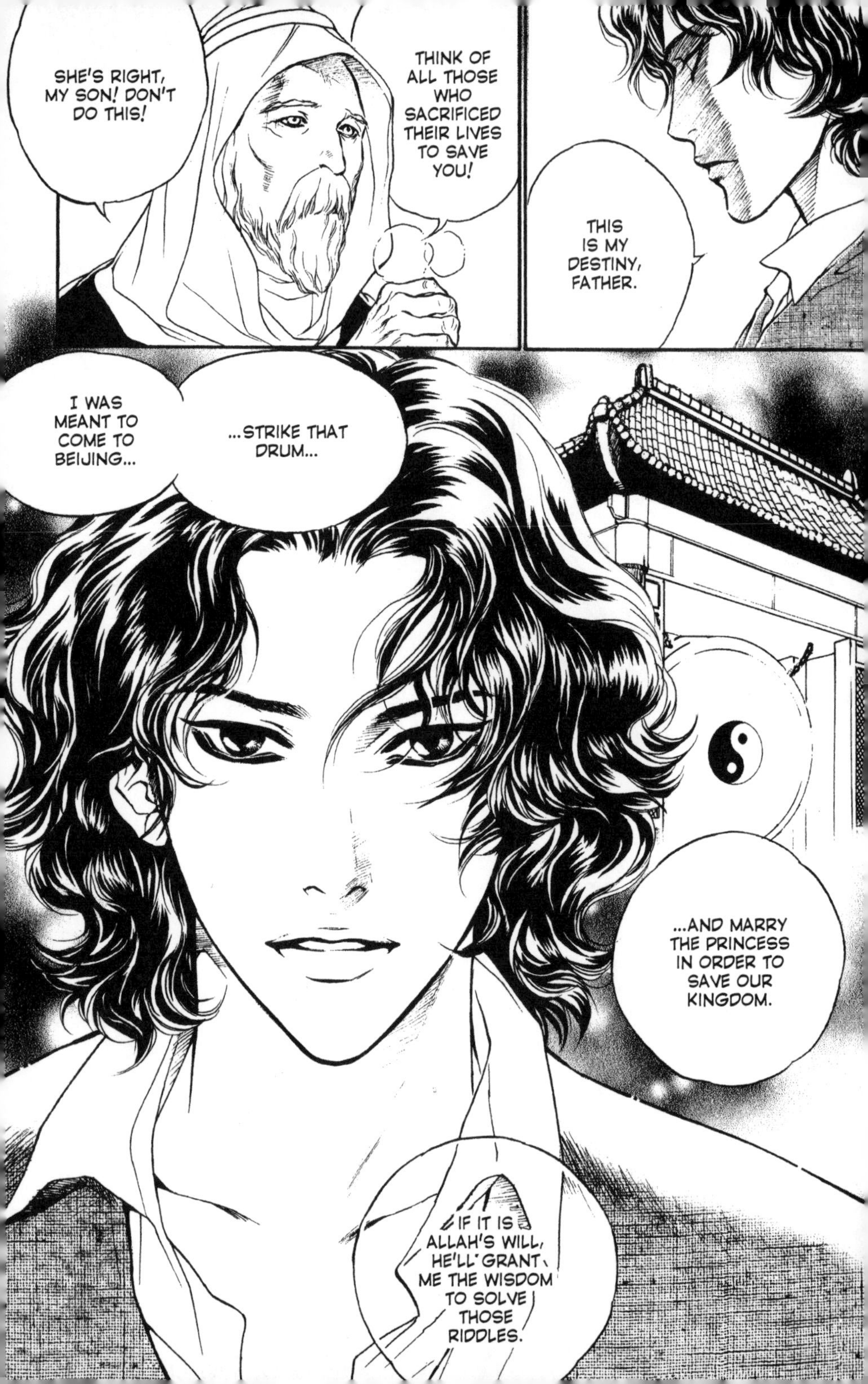
SHE'S RIGHT, MY SON! DON'T DO THIS!
THINK OF ALL THOSE WHO SACRIFICED THEIR LIVES TO SAVE YOU!
THIS IS MY DESTINY, FATHER.
I WAS MEANT TO COME TO BEIJING...
...STRIKE THAT DRUM...
...AND MARRY THE PRINCESS IN ORDER TO SAVE OUR KINGDOM.
IF IT IS ALLAH'S WILL, HE'LL GRANT ME THE WISDOM TO SOLVE THOSE RIDDLES.

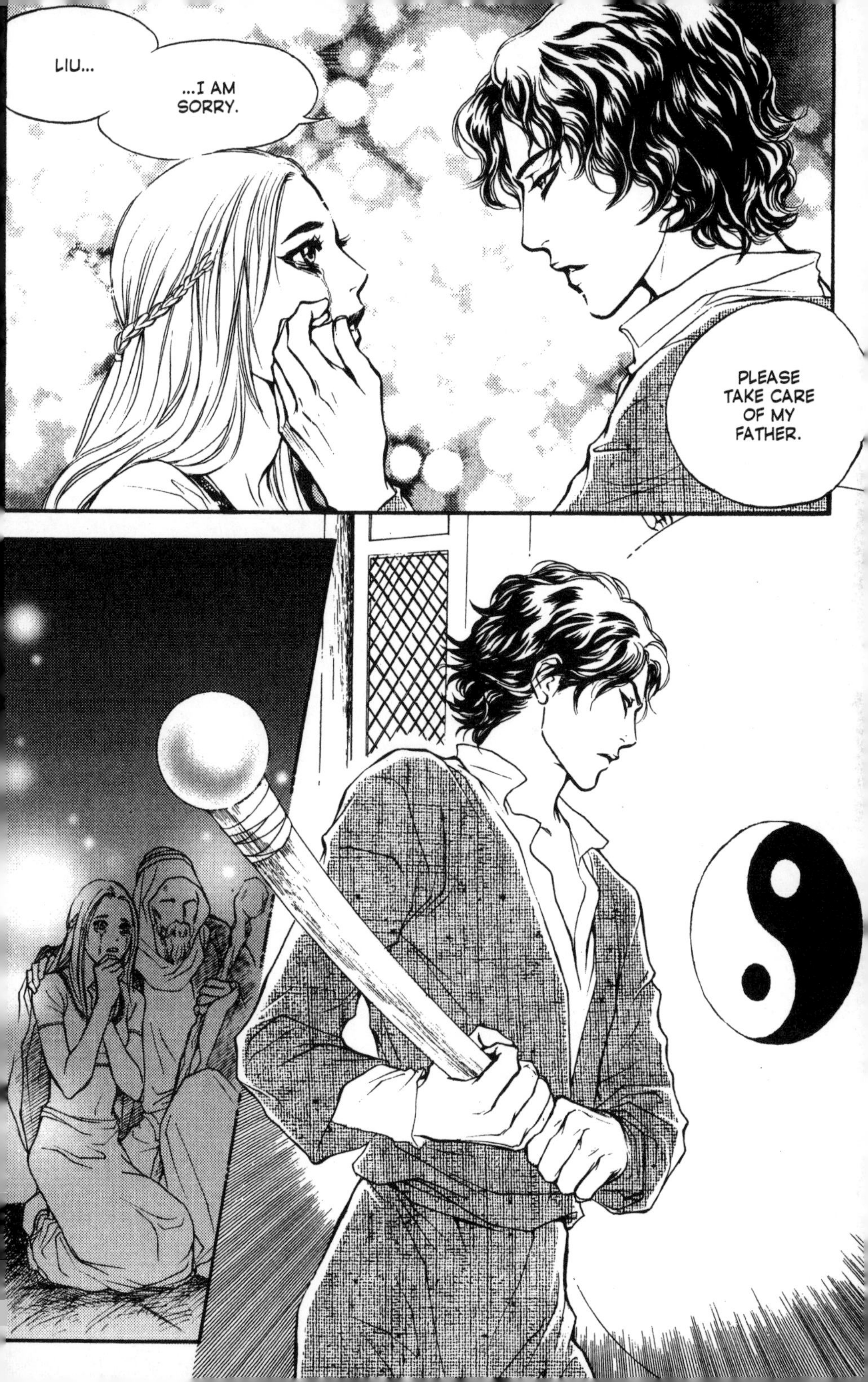
LIU...
...I AM SORRY.
PLEASE TAKE CARE OF MY FATHER.

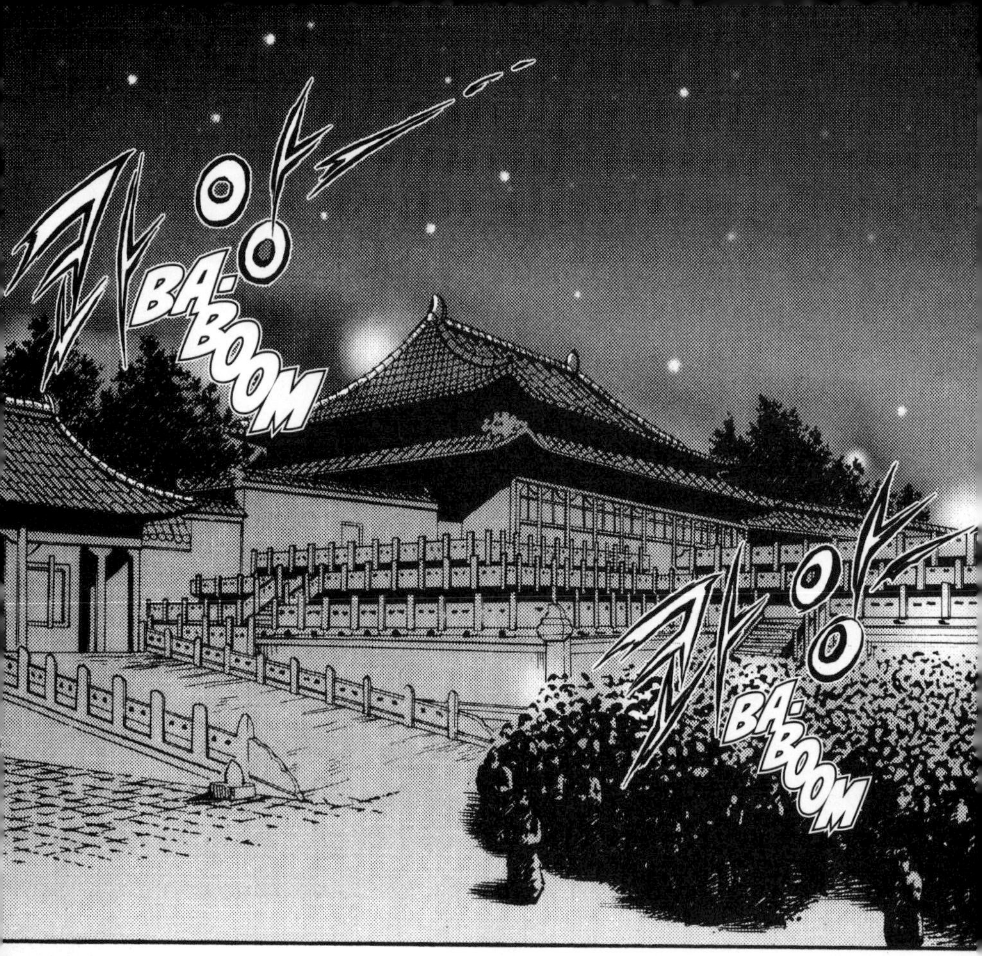
콰앙—
BA-BOOM
콰앙
BA-BOOM
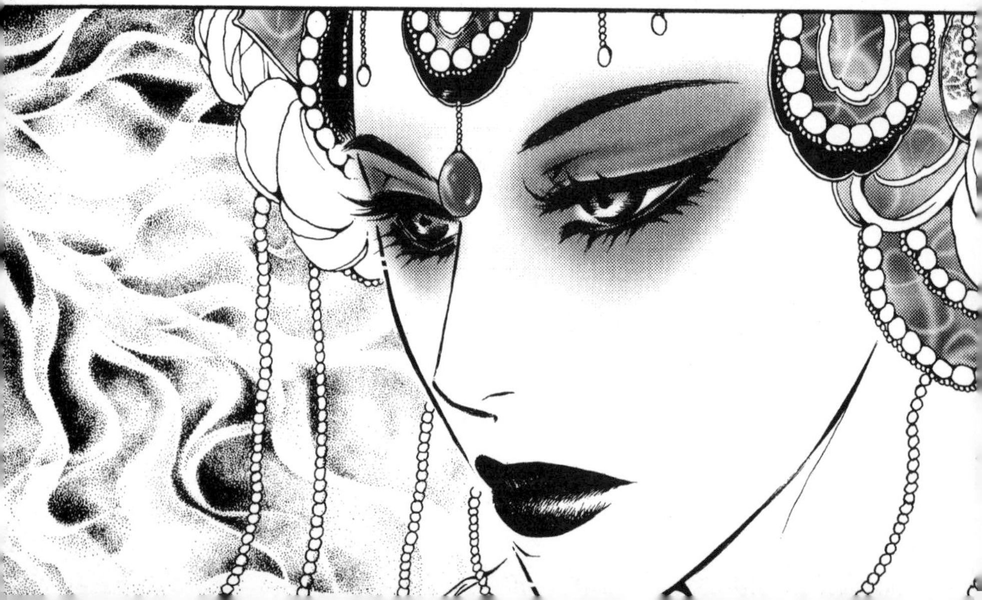

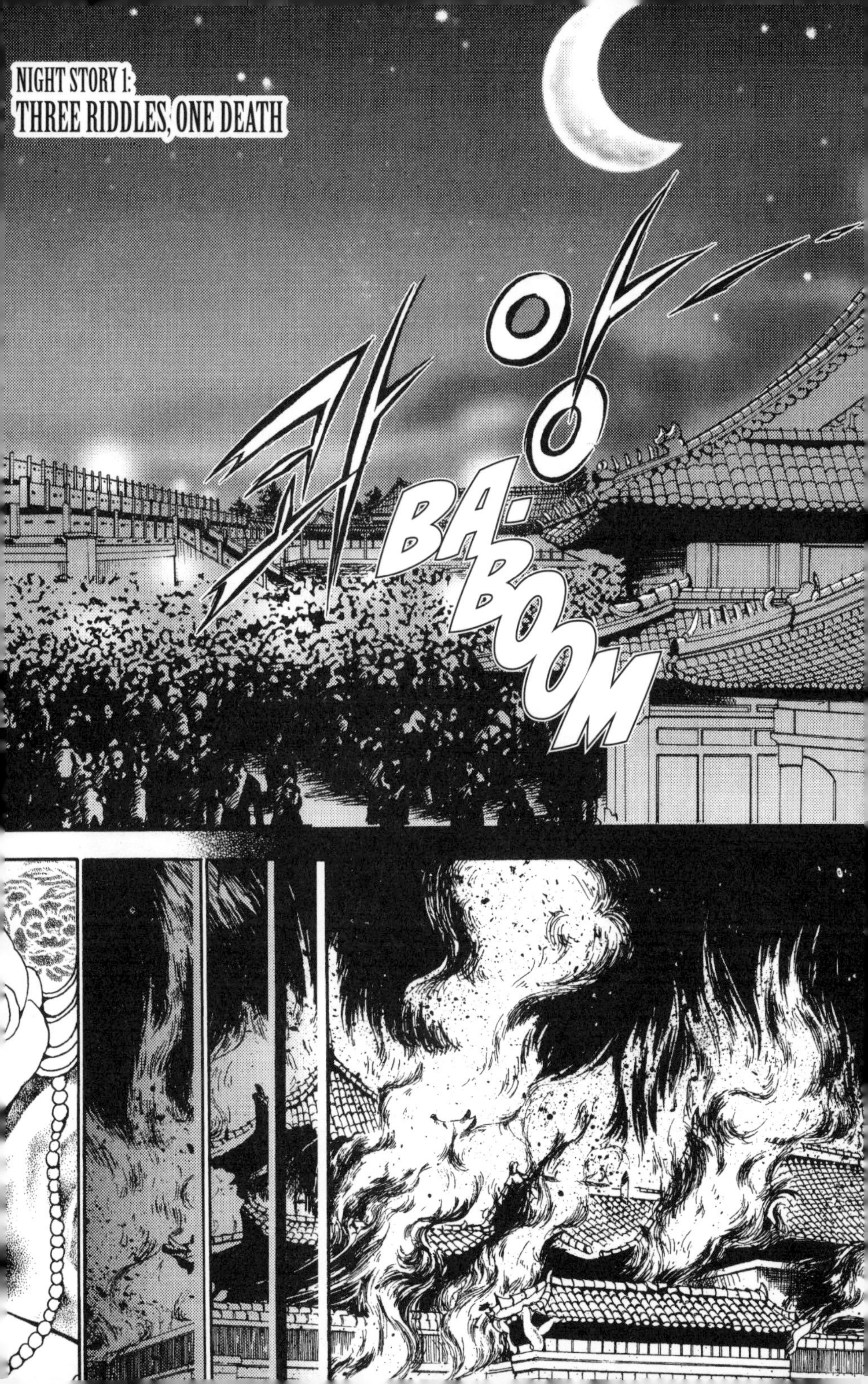
NIGHT STORY 1:
THREE RIDDLES, ONE DEATH
BA-BOOOM

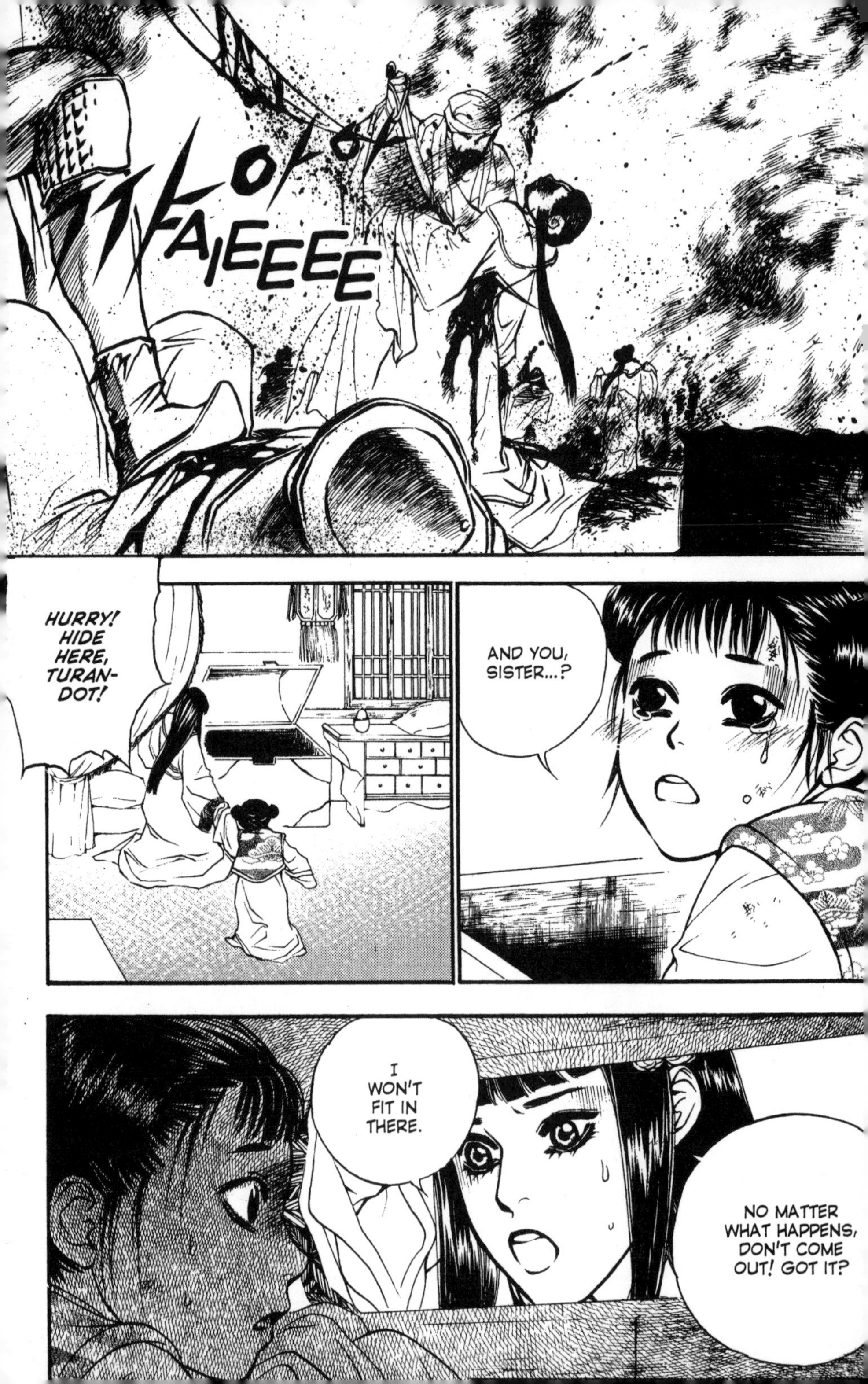

AIEEEEE
HURRY! HIDE HERE, TURAN-DOT!
AND YOU, SISTER...?
I WON'T FIT IN THERE.
NO MATTER WHAT HAPPENS, DON'T COME OUT! GOT IT?

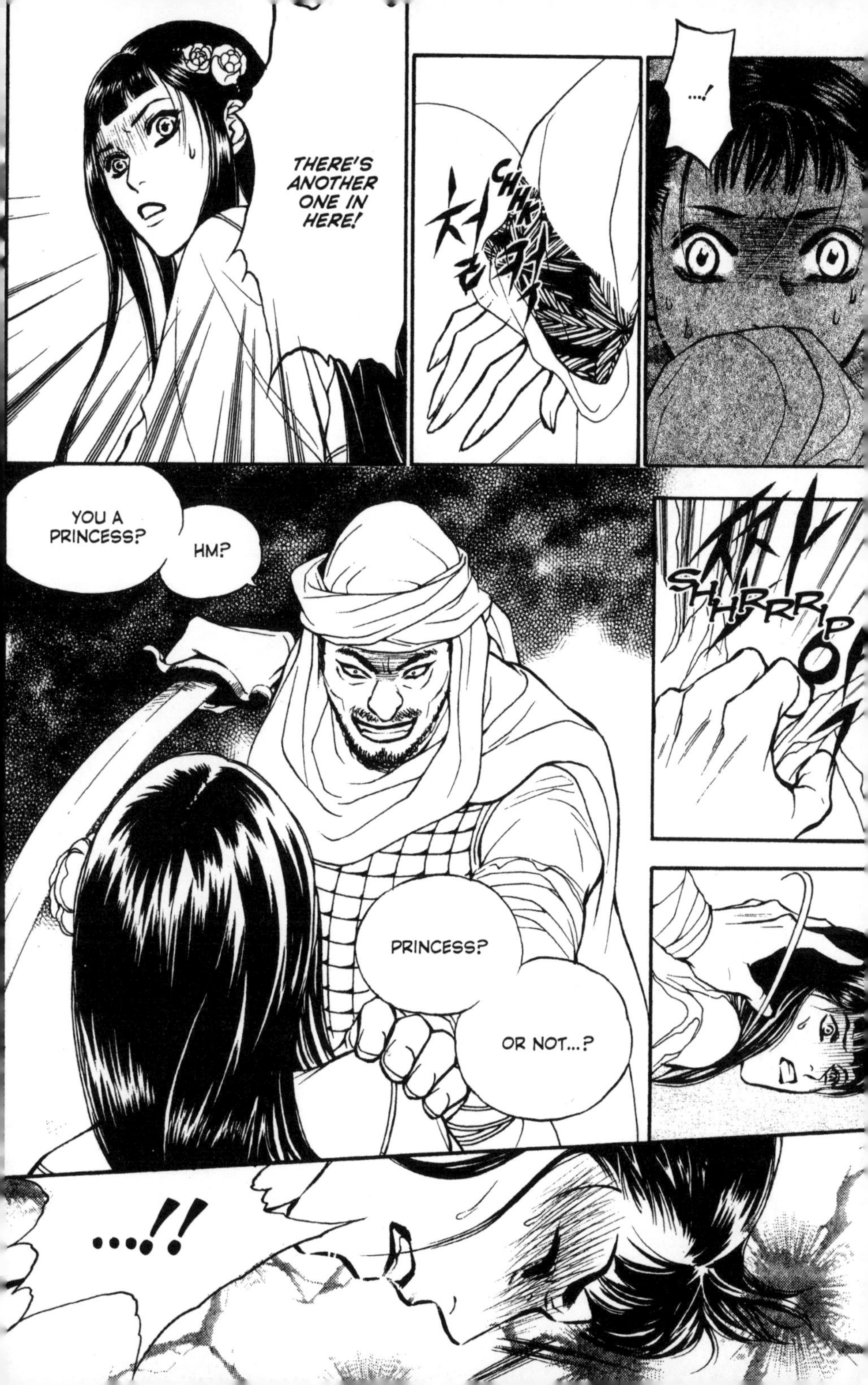
...!
THERE'S ANOTHER ONE IN HERE!
CHHK
YOU A PRINCESS?
HM?
SHHRRRIP
PRINCESS?
OR NOT...?
...!!

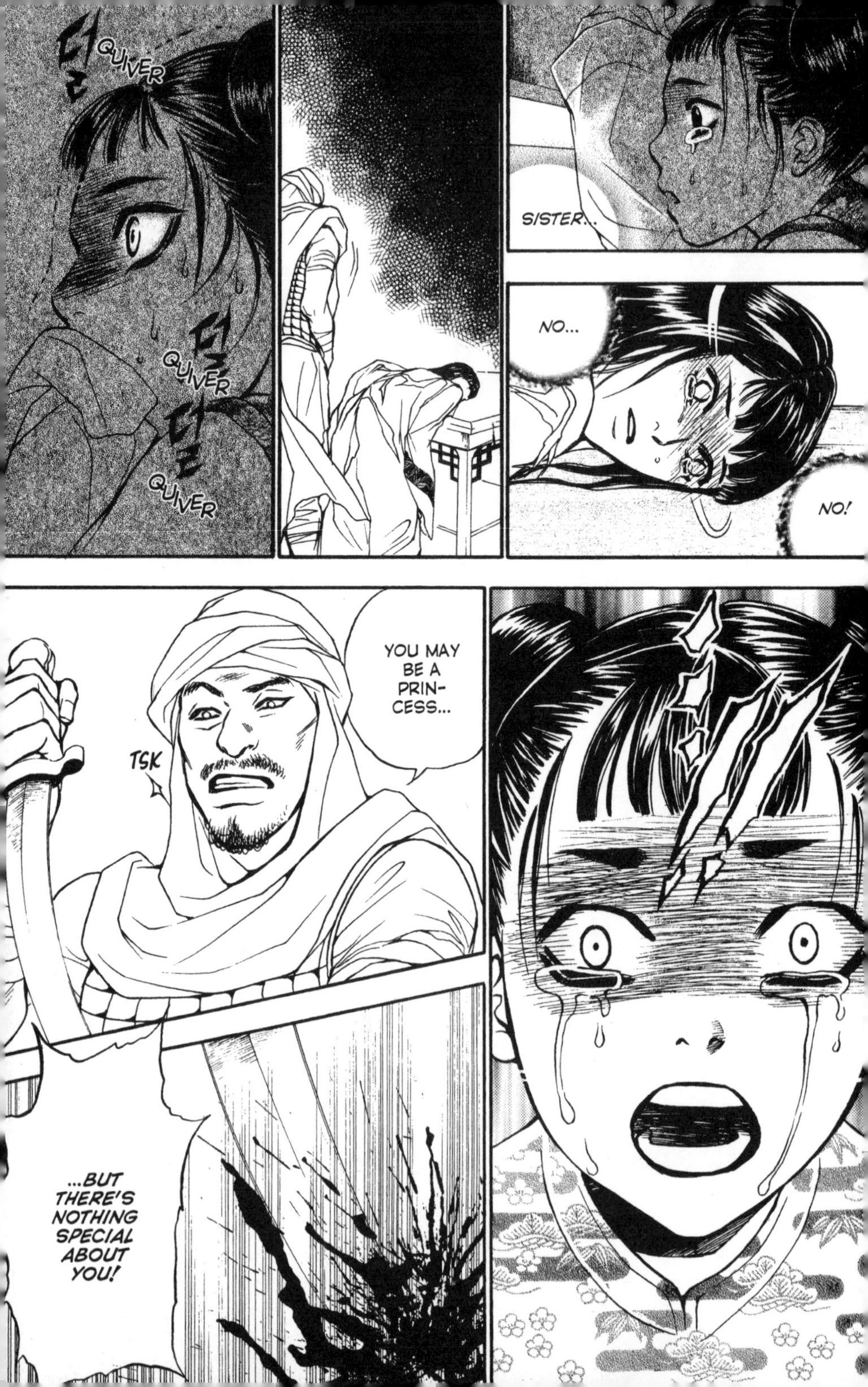
떨
QUIVER
떨
QUIVER
떨
QUIVER
SISTER...
NO...
NO!
YOU MAY BE A PRINCESS...
TSK
...BUT THERE'S NOTHING SPECIAL ABOUT YOU!

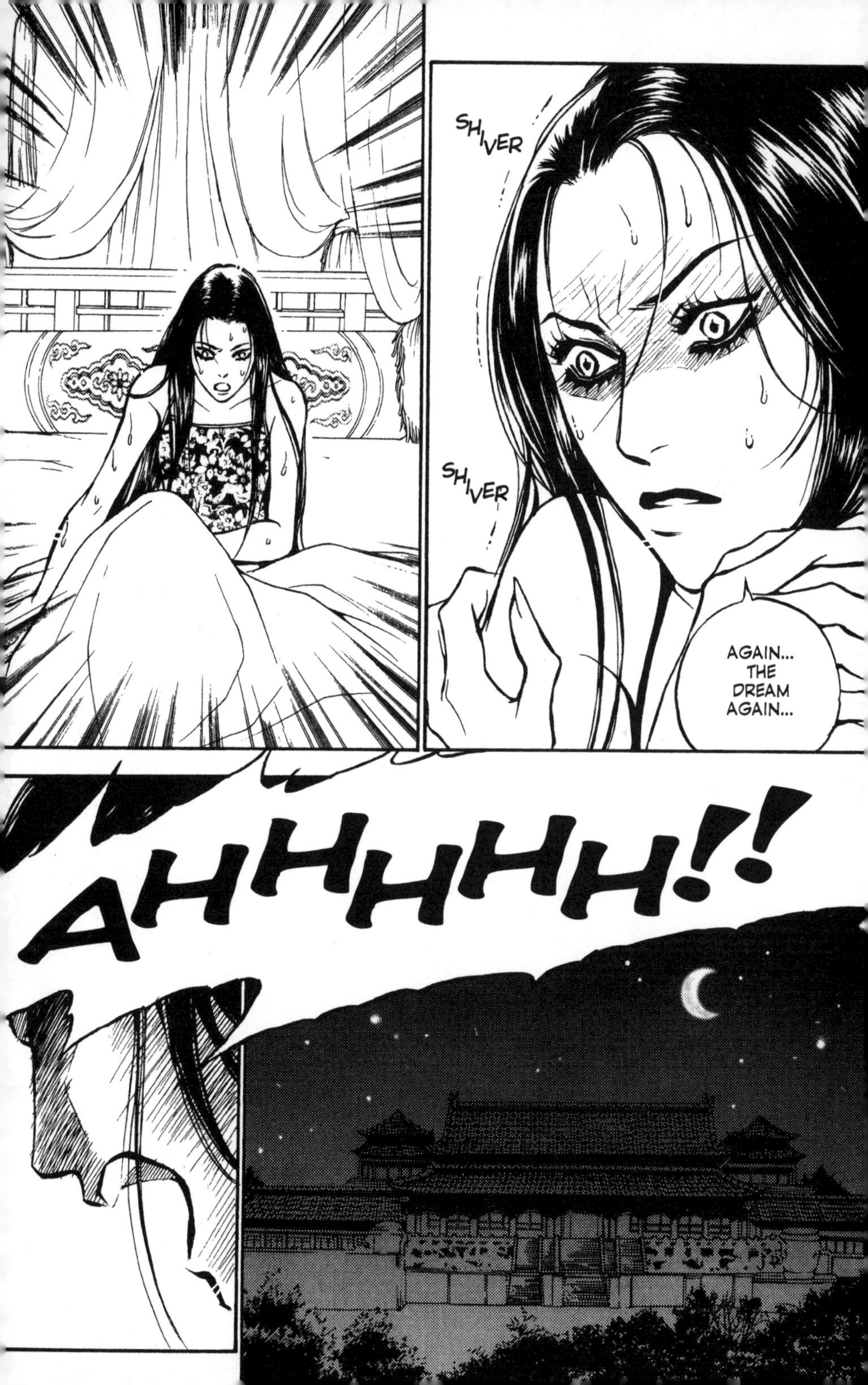
SHIVER
SHIVER
AGAIN... THE DREAM AGAIN...
AHHHHH!!

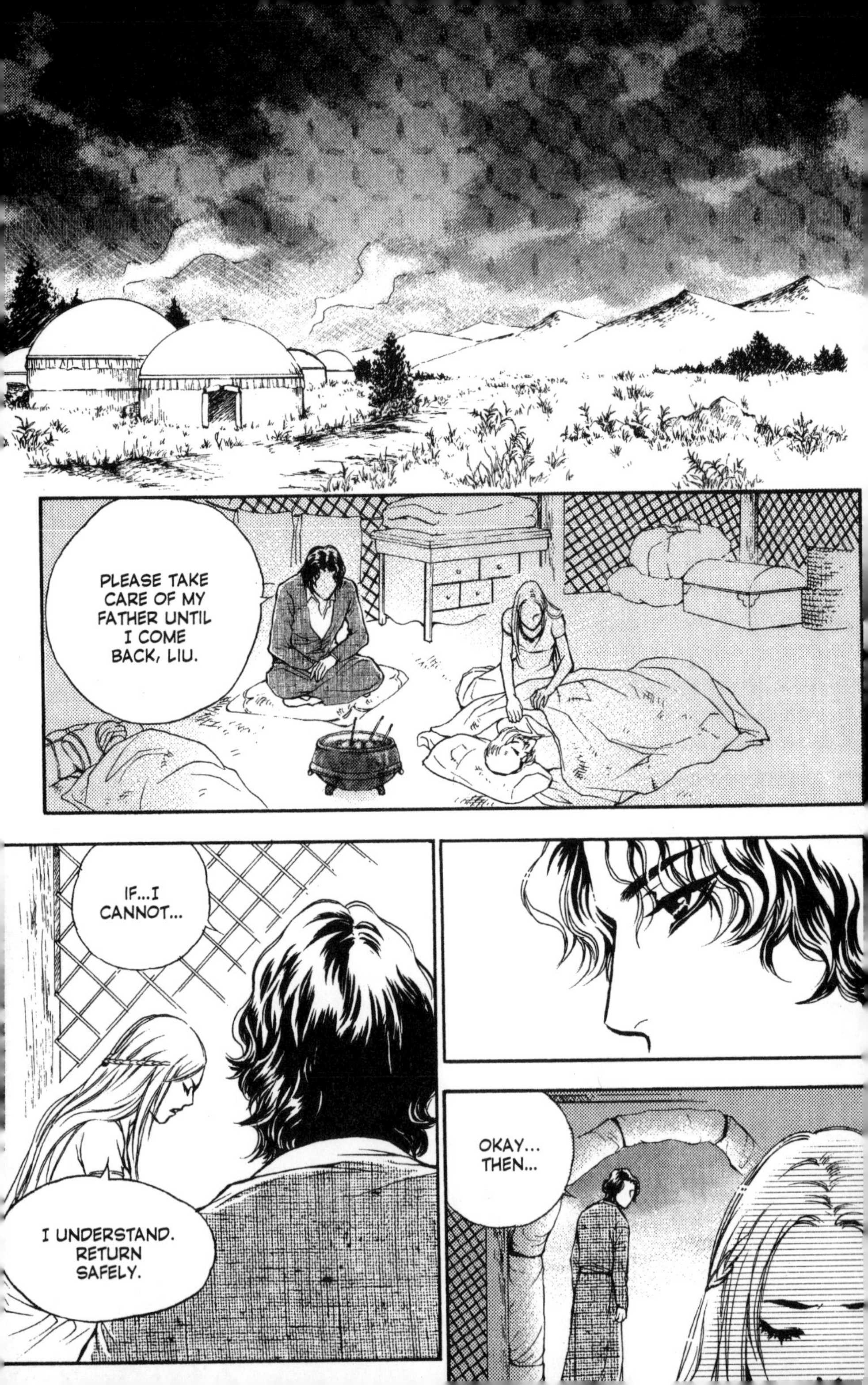
PLEASE TAKE CARE OF MY FATHER UNTIL I COME BACK, LIU.
IF...I CANNOT...
I UNDERSTAND. RETURN SAFELY.
OKAY... THEN...

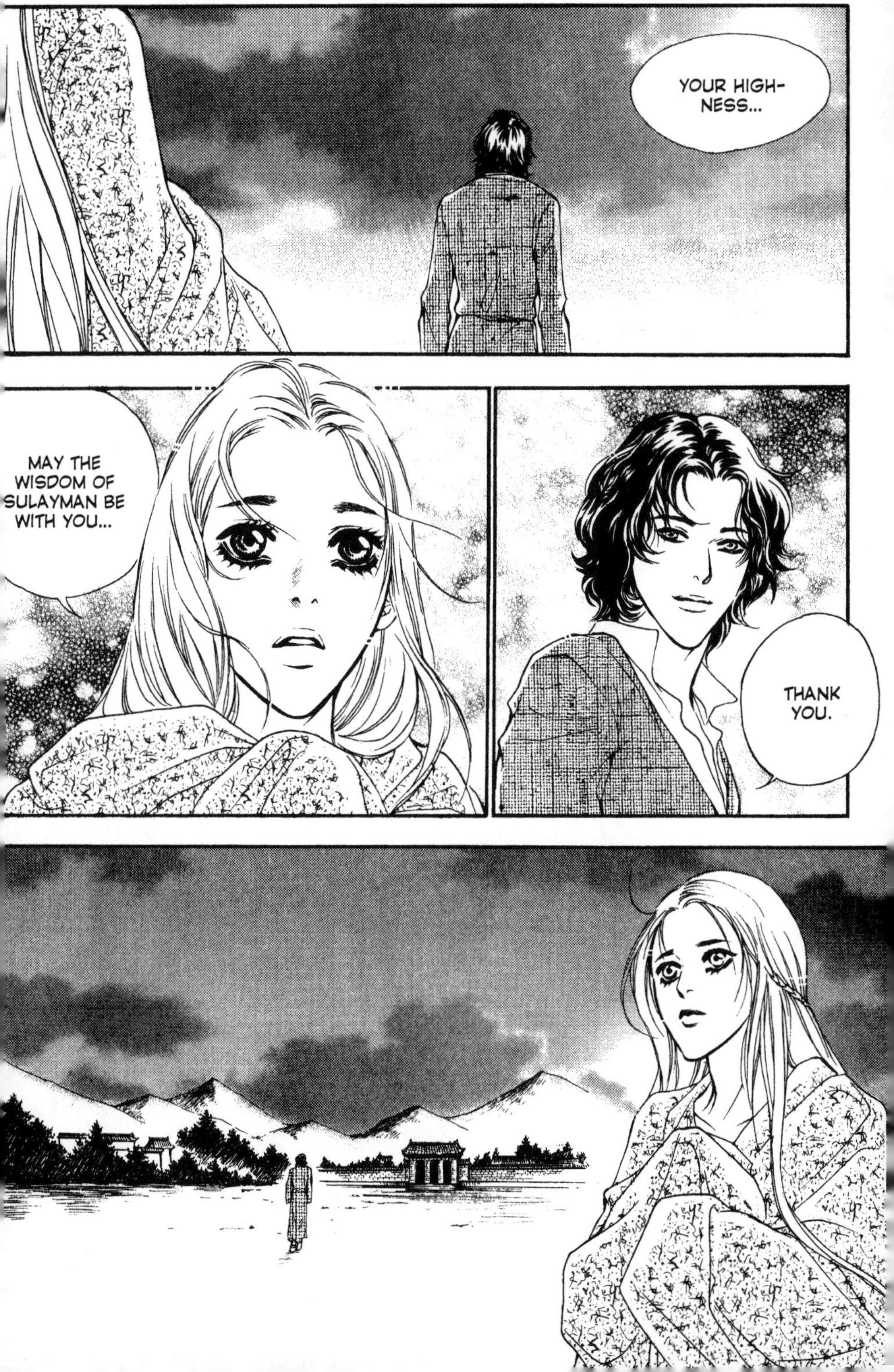
YOUR HIGH-NESS...
MAY THE WISDOM OF SULAYMAN BE WITH YOU...
THANK YOU.

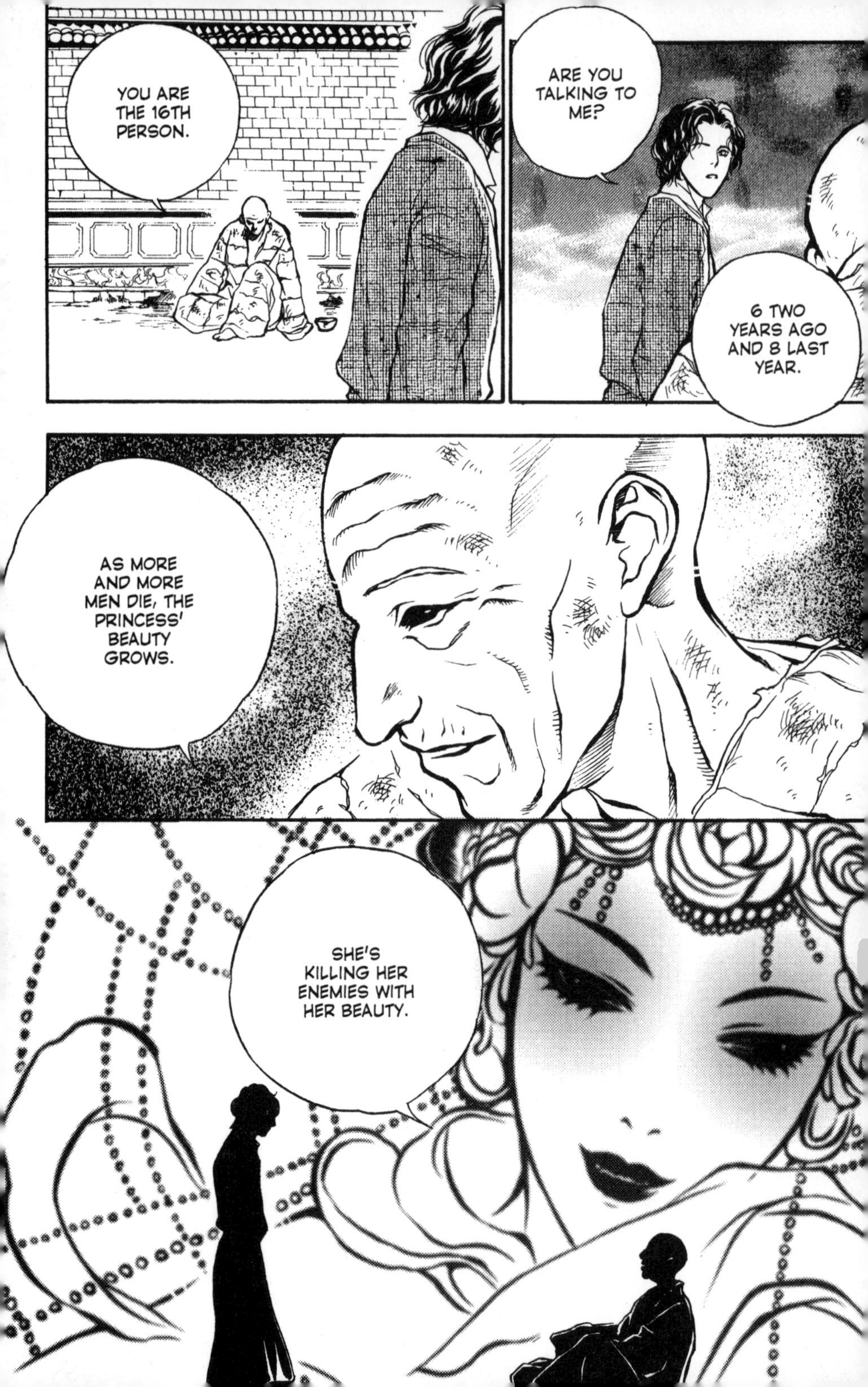
YOU ARE THE 16TH PERSON.
ARE YOU TALKING TO ME?
6 TWO YEARS AGO AND 8 LAST YEAR.
AS MORE AND MORE MEN DIE, THE PRINCESS' BEAUTY GROWS.
SHE'S KILLING HER ENEMIES WITH HER BEAUTY.

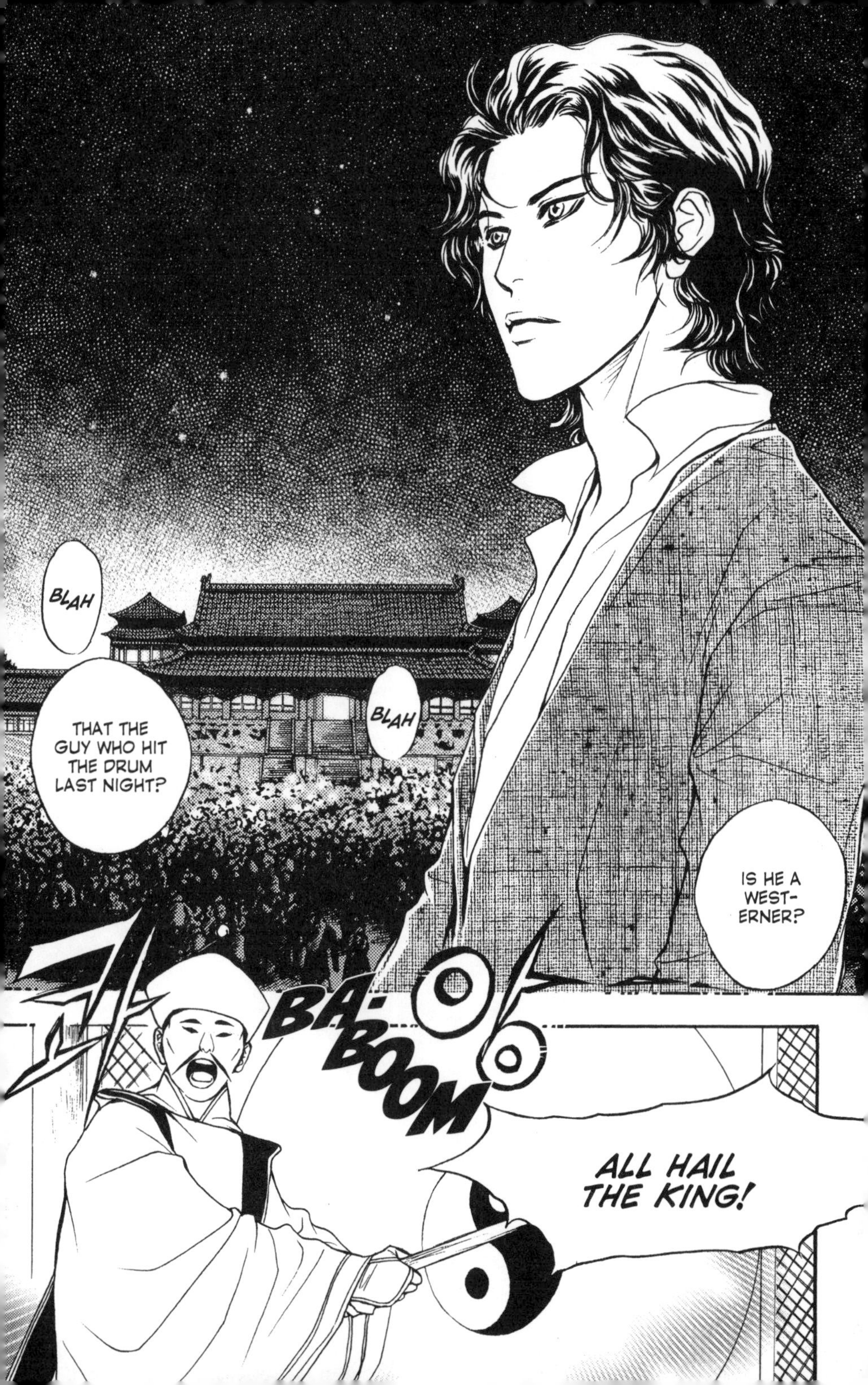
BLAH
THAT THE GUY WHO HIT THE DRUM LAST NIGHT?
BLAH
IS HE A WEST-ERNER?
BA-BOOM
ALL HAIL THE KING!

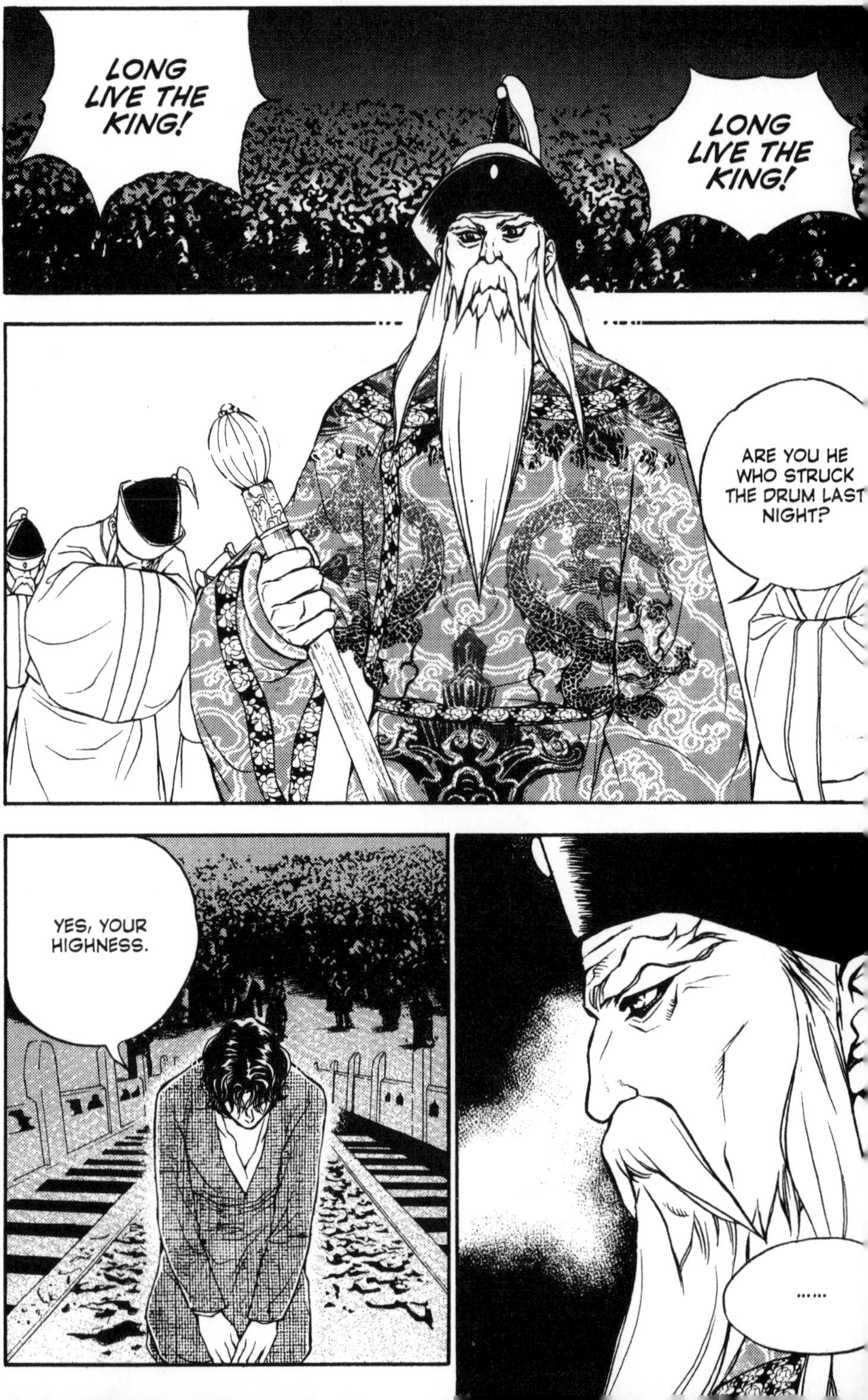
LONG LIVE THE KING!
LONG LIVE THE KING!
ARE YOU HE WHO STRUCK THE DRUM LAST NIGHT?
YES, YOUR HIGHNESS.
......

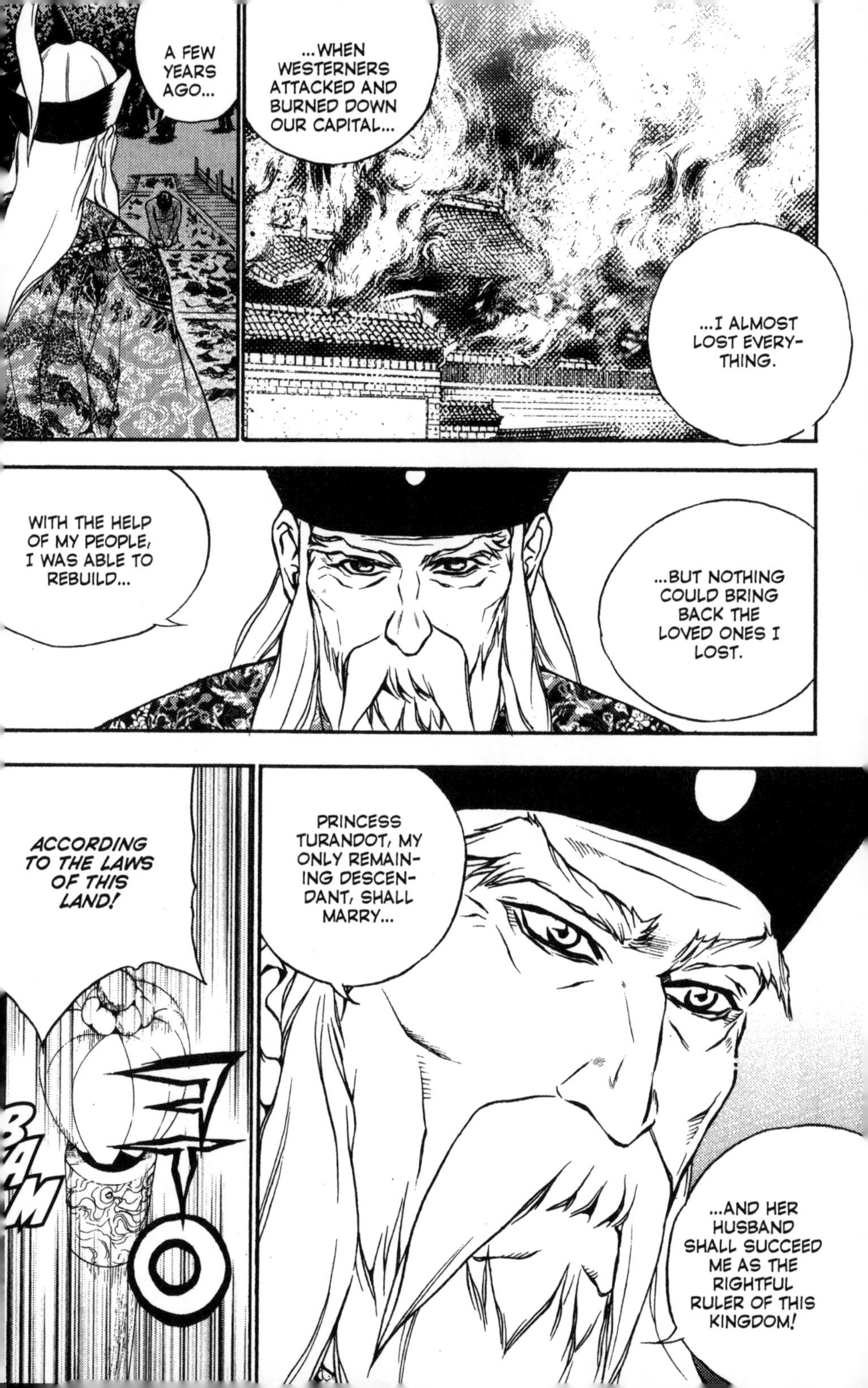
A FEW YEARS AGO...
...WHEN WESTERNERS ATTACKED AND BURNED DOWN OUR CAPITAL...
...I ALMOST LOST EVERY-THING.
WITH THE HELP OF MY PEOPLE, I WAS ABLE TO REBUILD...
...BUT NOTHING COULD BRING BACK THE LOVED ONES I LOST.
ACCORDING TO THE LAWS OF THIS LAND!
BAM
PRINCESS TURANDOT, MY ONLY REMAIN-ING DESCEN-DANT, SHALL MARRY...
...AND HER HUSBAND SHALL SUCCEED ME AS THE RIGHTFUL RULER OF THIS KINGDOM!

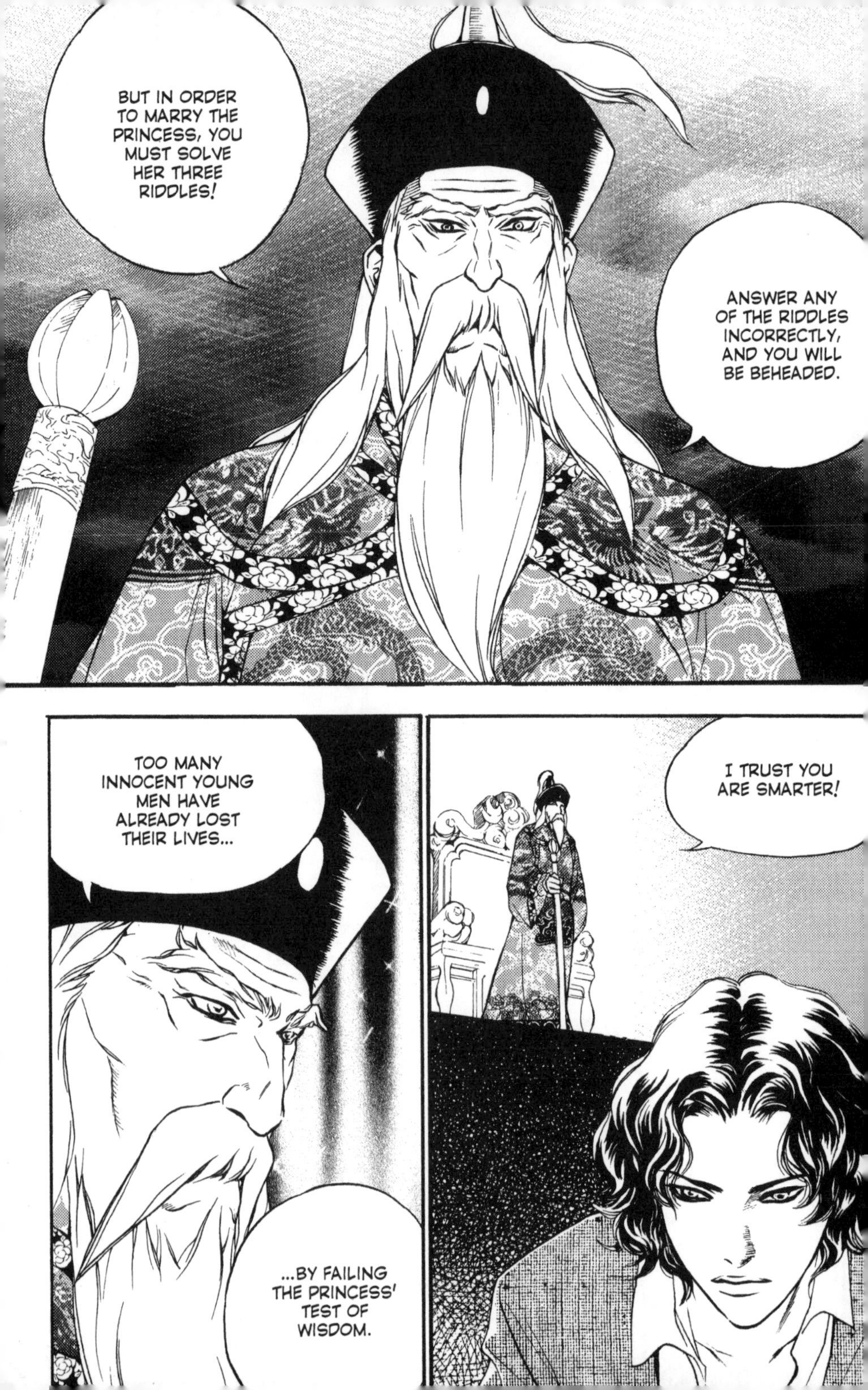
BUT IN ORDER TO MARRY THE PRINCESS, YOU MUST SOLVE HER THREE RIDDLES!
ANSWER ANY OF THE RIDDLES INCORRECTLY, AND YOU WILL BE BEHEADED.
TOO MANY INNOCENT YOUNG MEN HAVE ALREADY LOST THEIR LIVES...
...BY FAILING THE PRINCESS' TEST OF WISDOM.
I TRUST YOU ARE SMARTER!

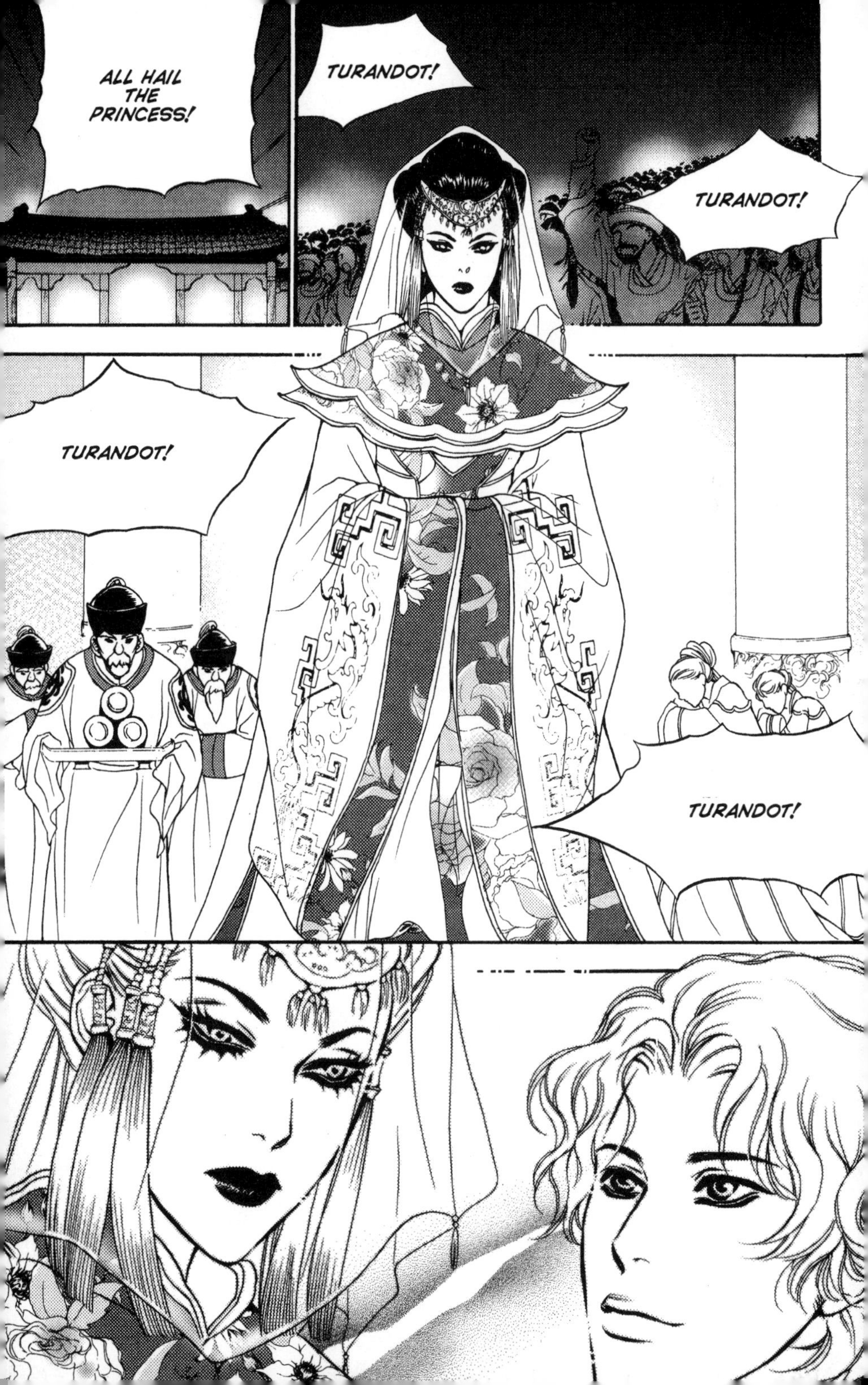
ALL HAIL THE PRINCESS!
TURANDOT!
TURANDOT!
TURANDOT!
TURANDOT!

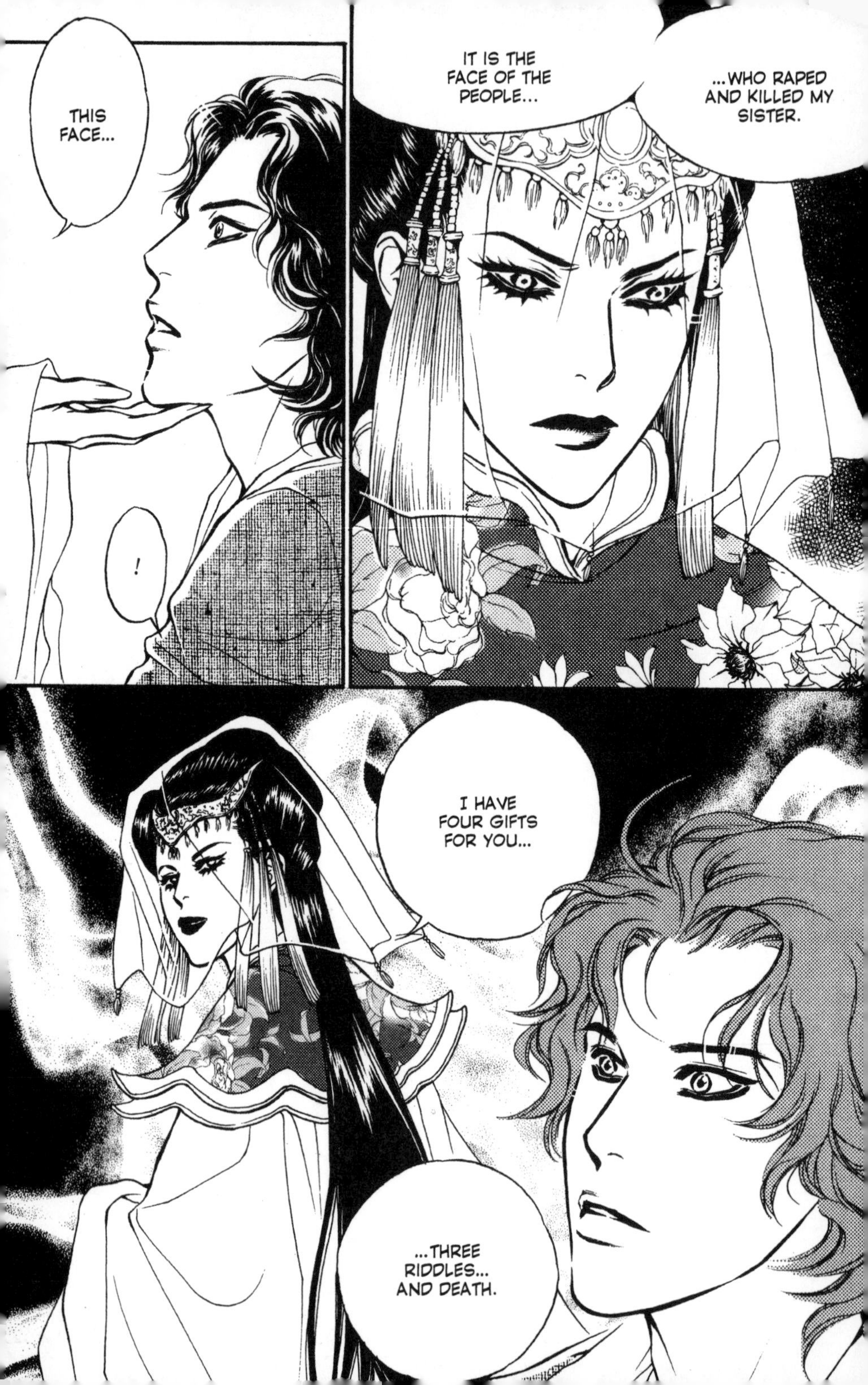
THIS FACE...
!
IT IS THE FACE OF THE PEOPLE...
...WHO RAPED AND KILLED MY SISTER.
I HAVE FOUR GIFTS FOR YOU...
...THREE RIDDLES... AND DEATH.

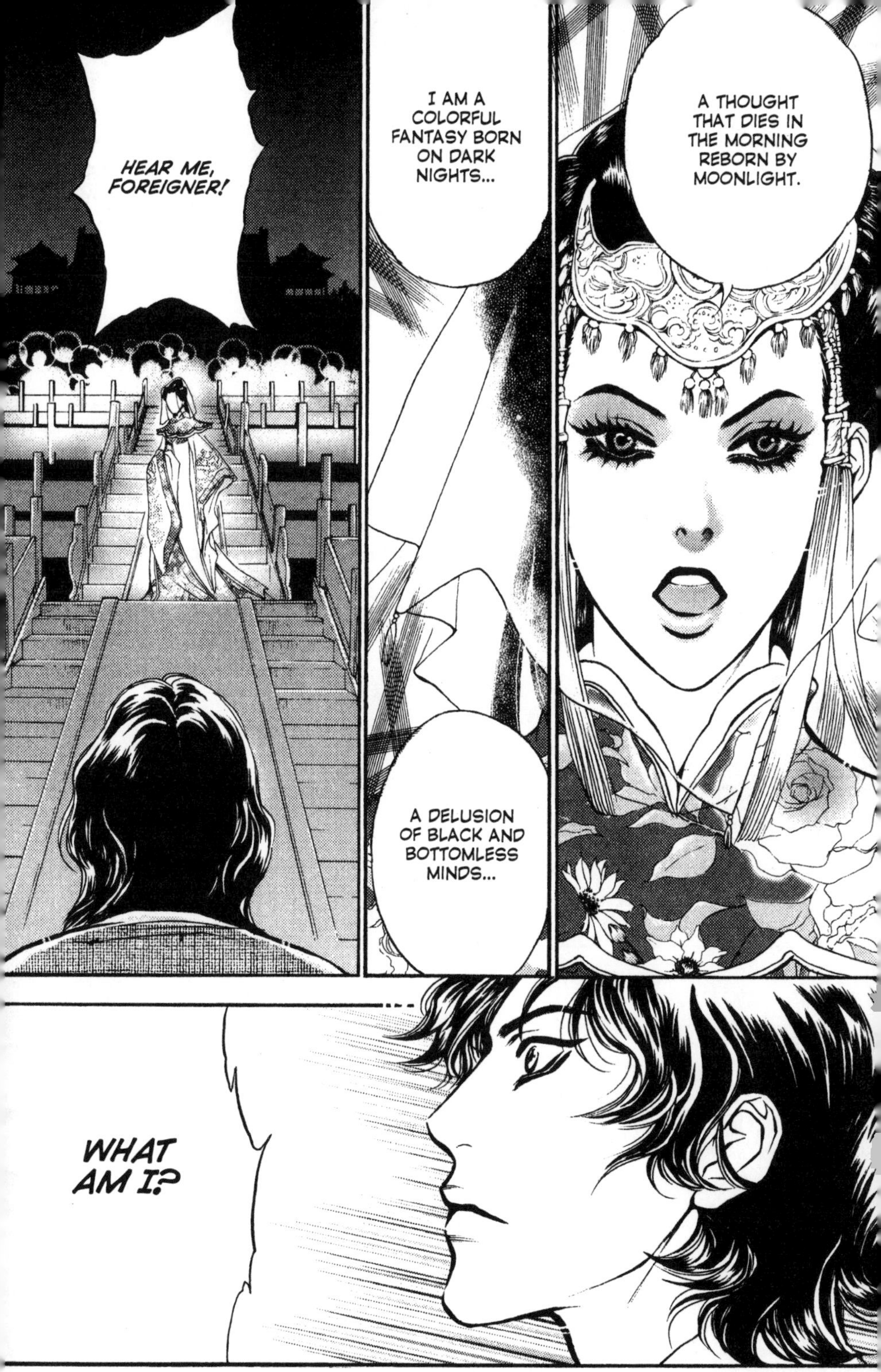
HEAR ME, FOREIGNER!
I AM A COLORFUL FANTASY BORN ON DARK NIGHTS...
A DELUSION OF BLACK AND BOTTOMLESS MINDS...
A THOUGHT THAT DIES IN THE MORNING REBORN BY MOONLIGHT.
WHAT AM I?

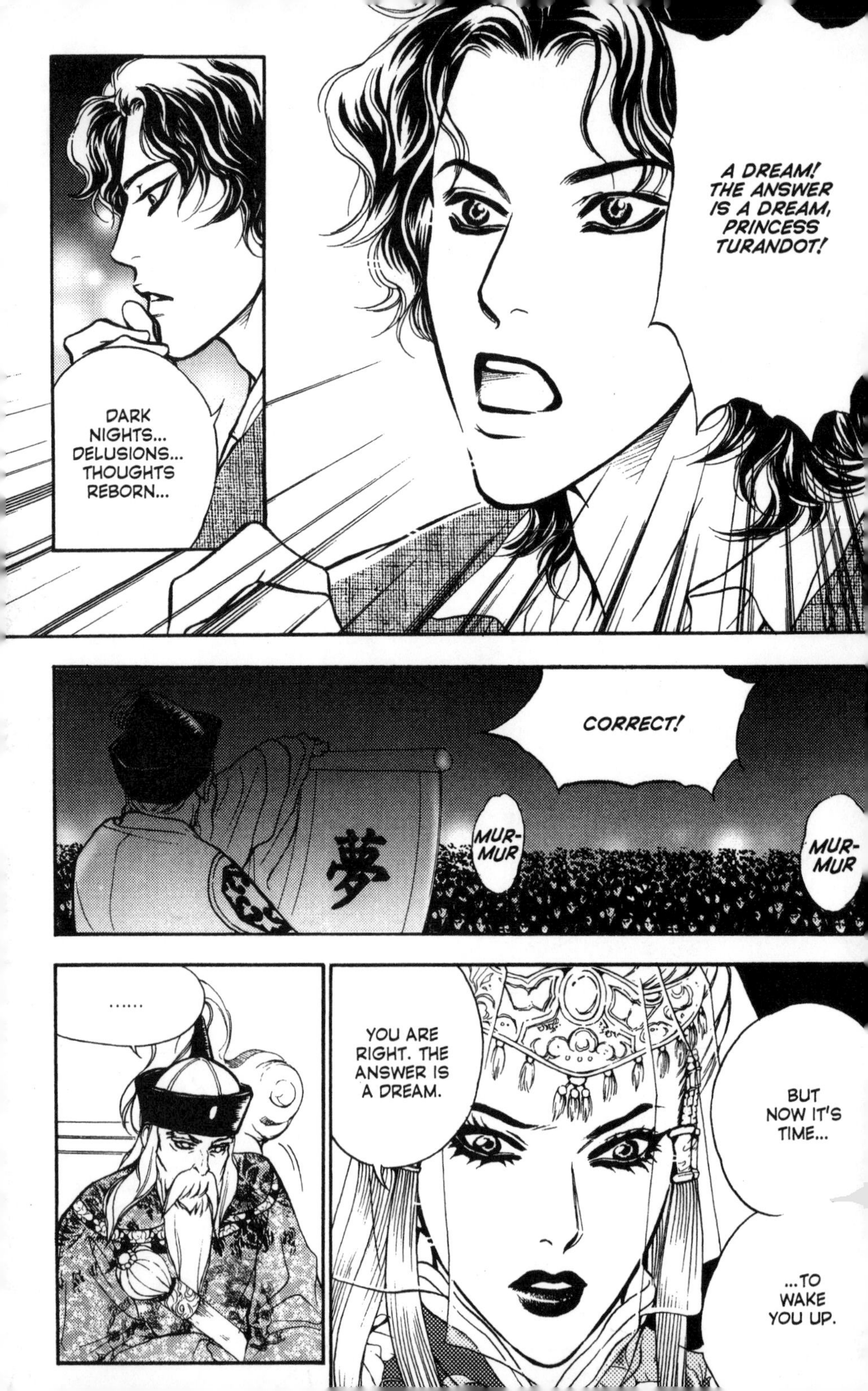
DARK NIGHTS... DELUSIONS... THOUGHTS REBORN...
A DREAM! THE ANSWER IS A DREAM, PRINCESS TURANDOT!
CORRECT!
夢
MUR-MUR
MUR-MUR
......
YOU ARE RIGHT. THE ANSWER IS A DREAM.
BUT NOW IT'S TIME...
...TO WAKE YOU UP.

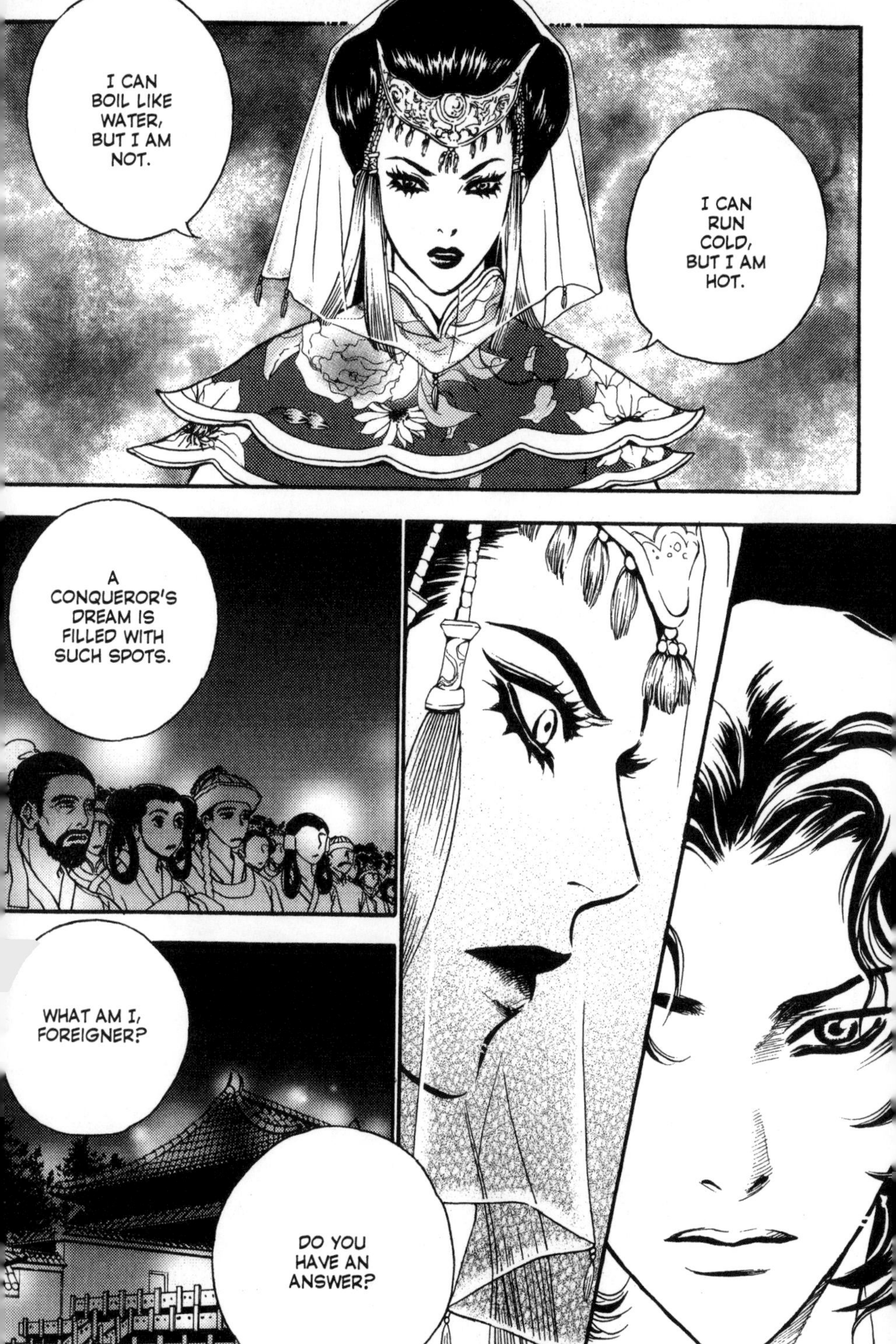
I CAN BOIL LIKE WATER, BUT I AM NOT.
I CAN RUN COLD, BUT I AM HOT.
A CONQUEROR'S DREAM IS FILLED WITH SUCH SPOTS.
WHAT AM I, FOREIGNER?
DO YOU HAVE AN ANSWER?

SHH!
QUIET!
COLD... CONQUER... SPOTS...
THE ANSWER IS BLOOD!
AND MAY NONE OF MINE BE SPILLED HERE TODAY!
CORRECT!
OHHHHHH

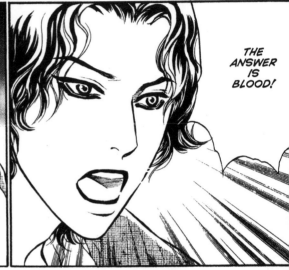

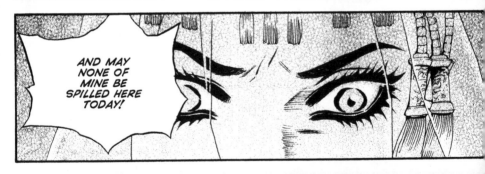

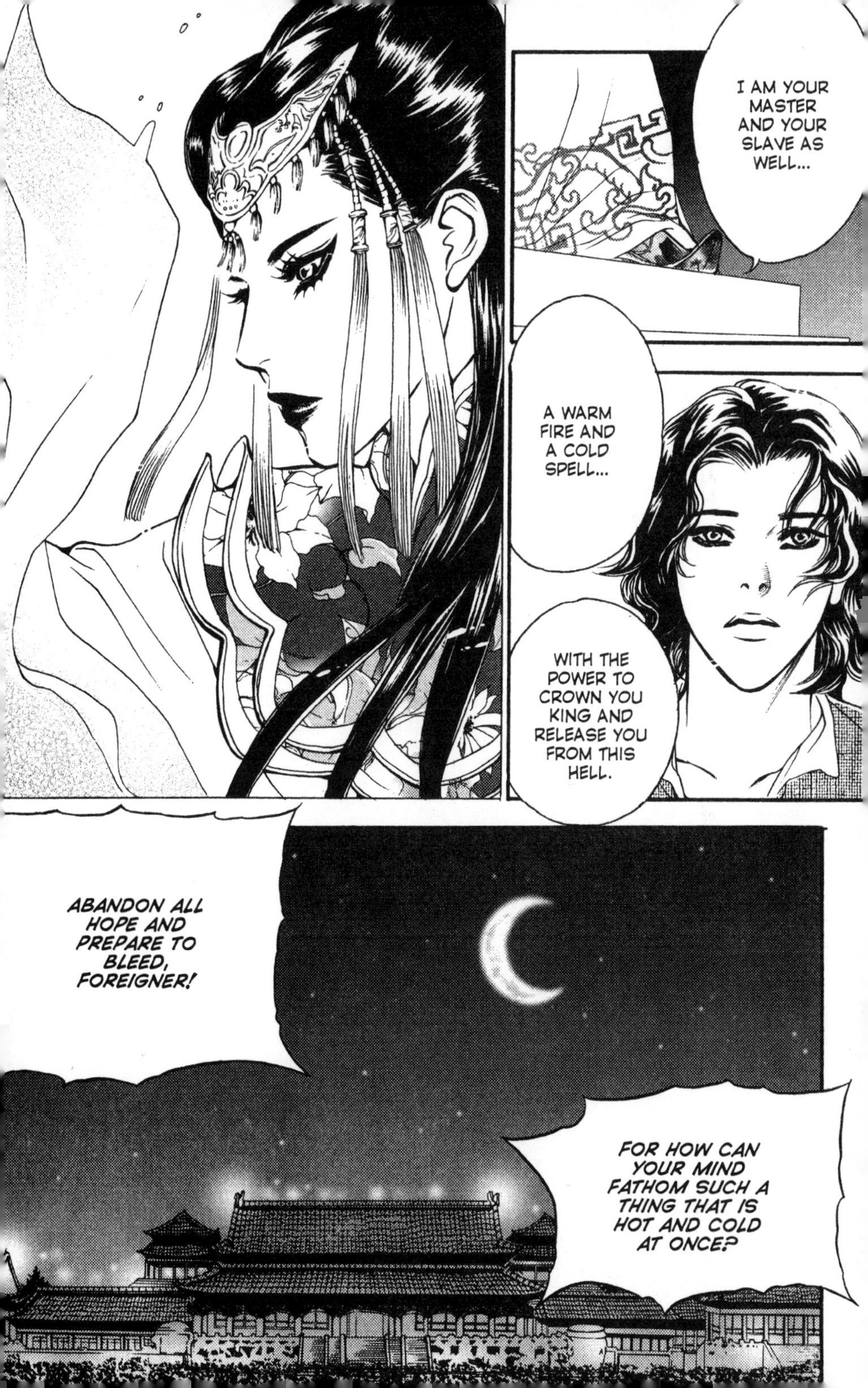
I AM YOUR MASTER AND YOUR SLAVE AS WELL...
A WARM FIRE AND A COLD SPELL...
WITH THE POWER TO CROWN YOU KING AND RELEASE YOU FROM THIS HELL.
ABANDON ALL HOPE AND PREPARE TO BLEED, FOREIGNER!
FOR HOW CAN YOUR MIND FATHOM SUCH A THING THAT IS HOT AND COLD AT ONCE?

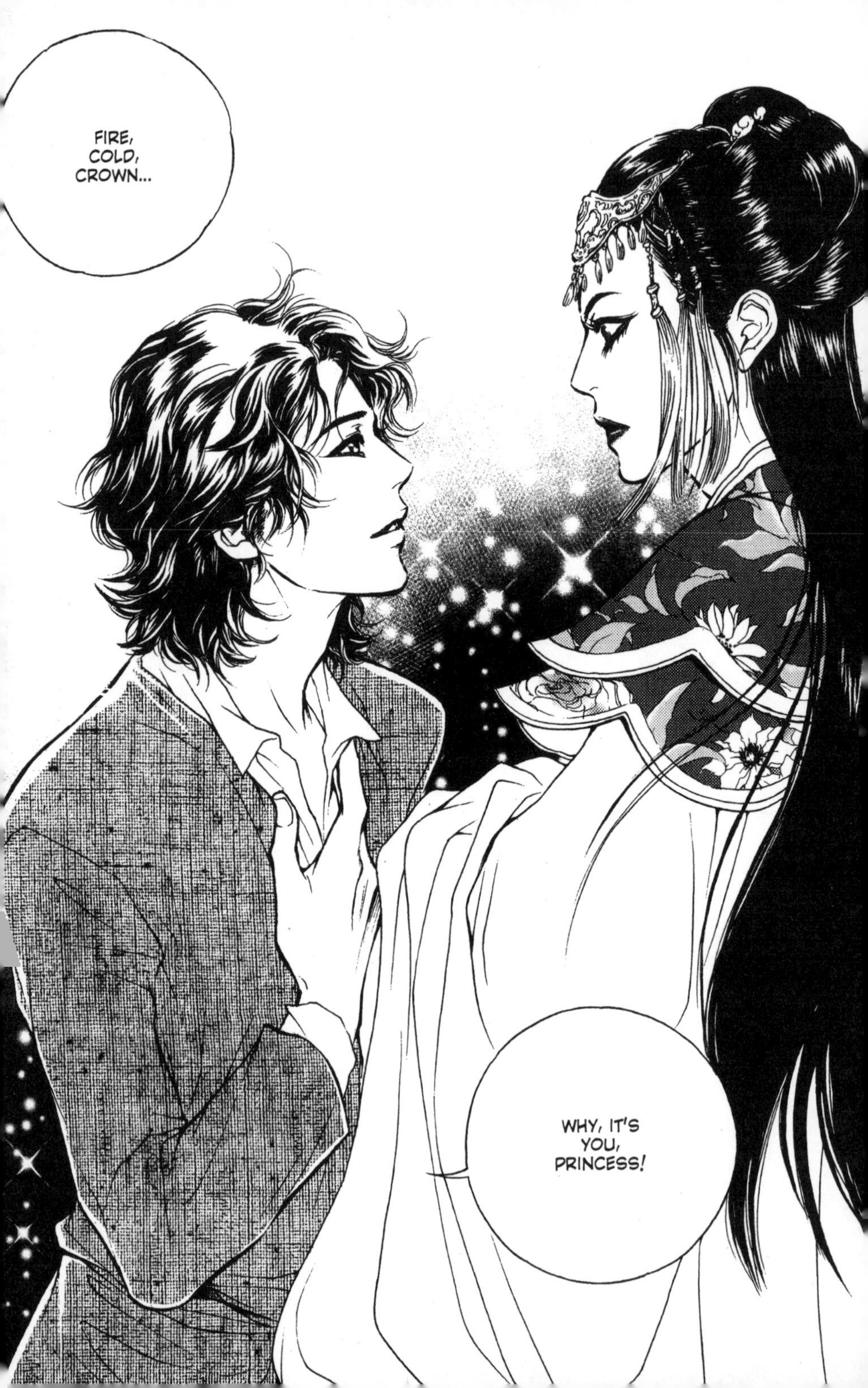
FIRE, COLD, CROWN...
WHY, IT'S YOU, PRINCESS!

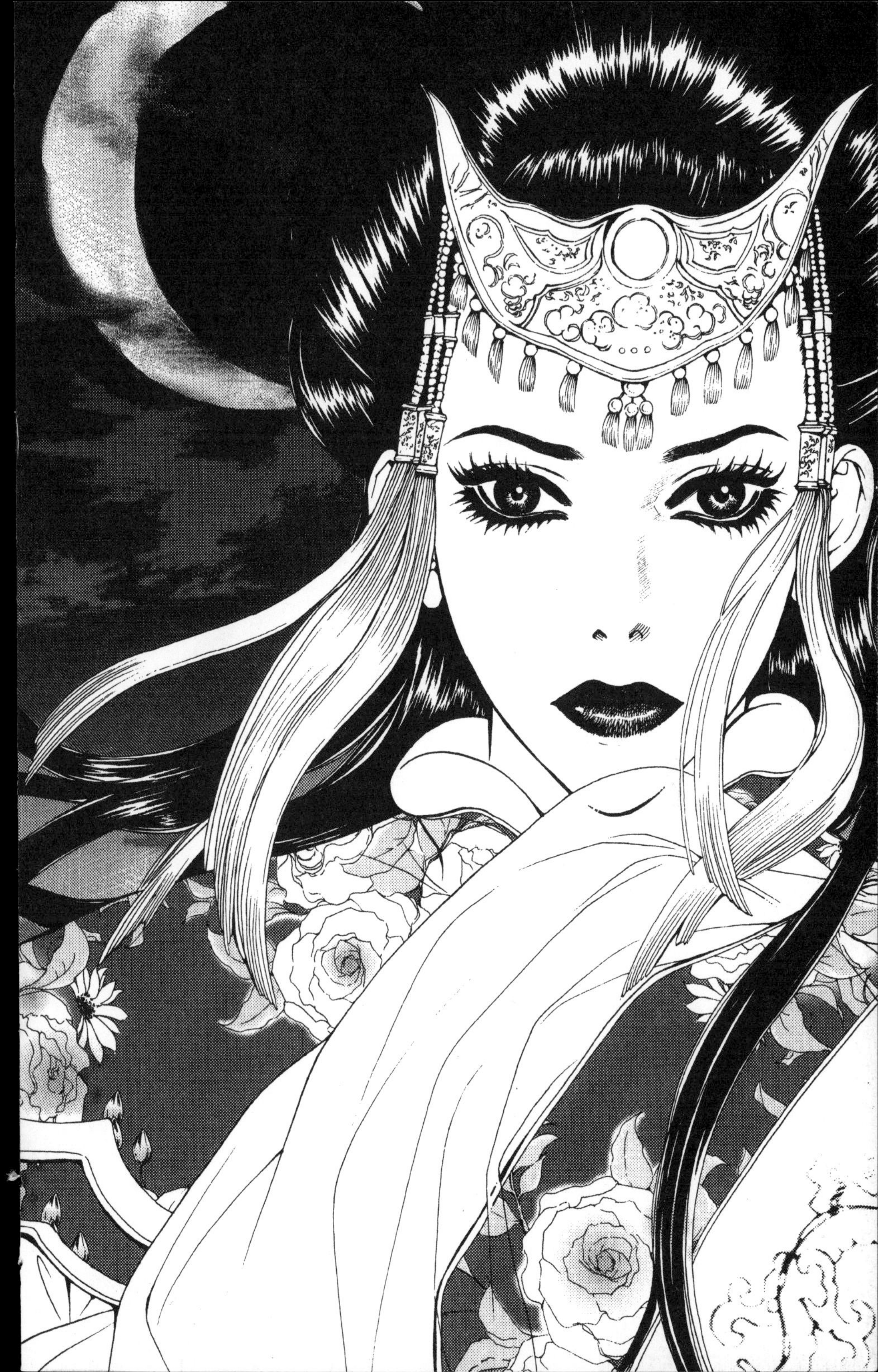

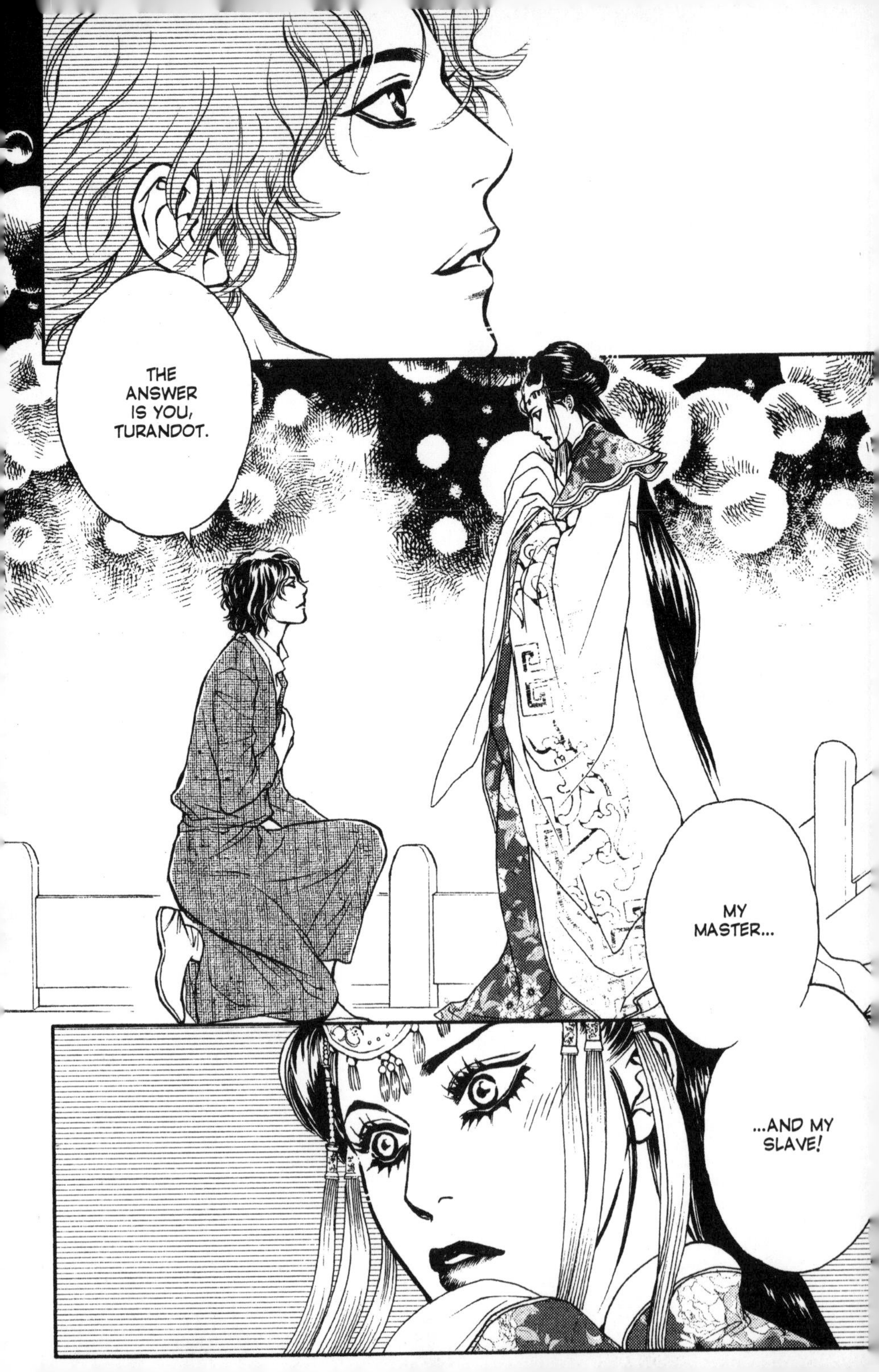
THE ANSWER IS YOU, TURANDOT.
MY MASTER...
...AND MY SLAVE!

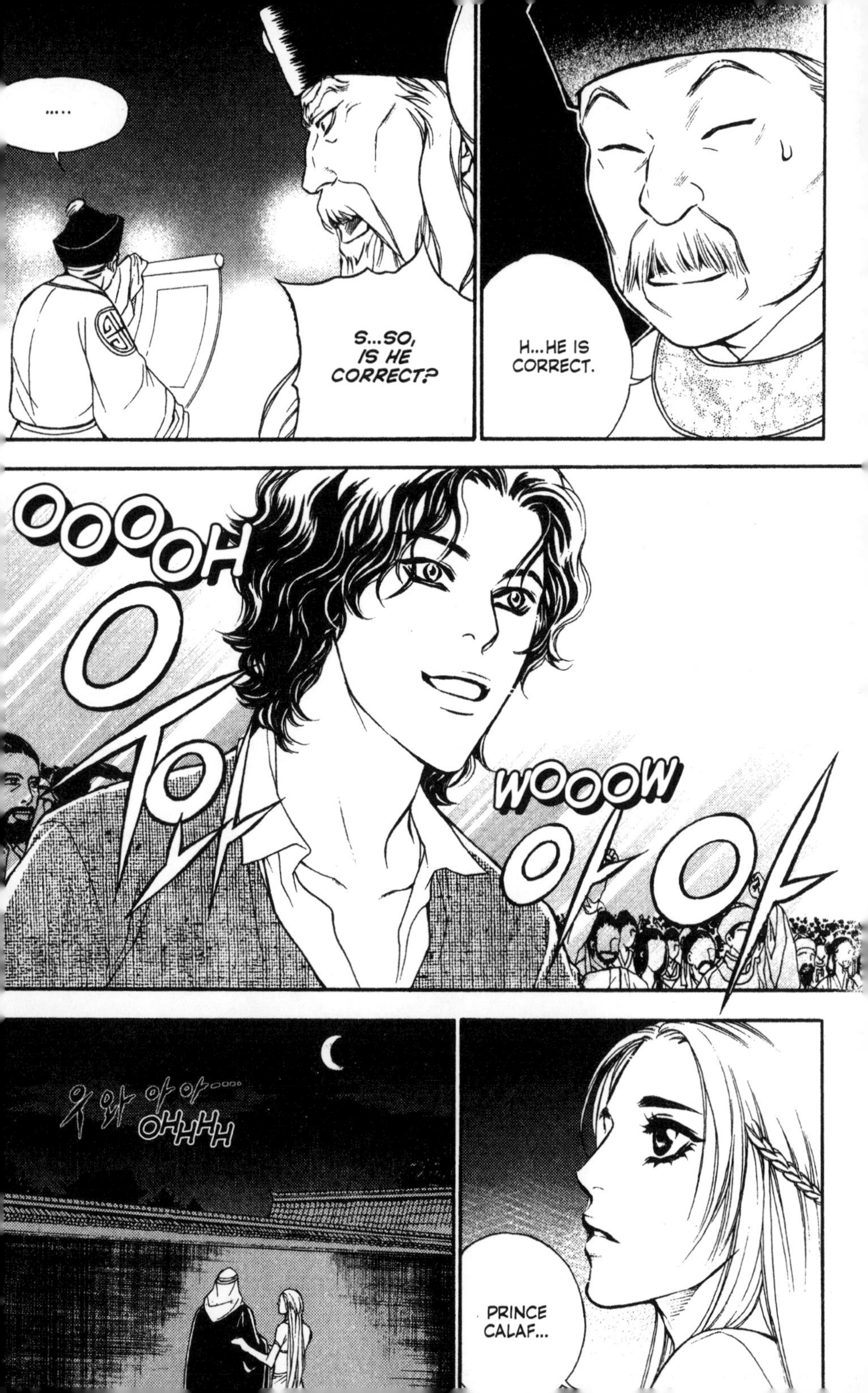
.....
S...SO, IS HE CORRECT?
H...HE IS CORRECT.
OOOOH
WOOOW
우와 아아.....
OHHHH
PRINCE CALAF...

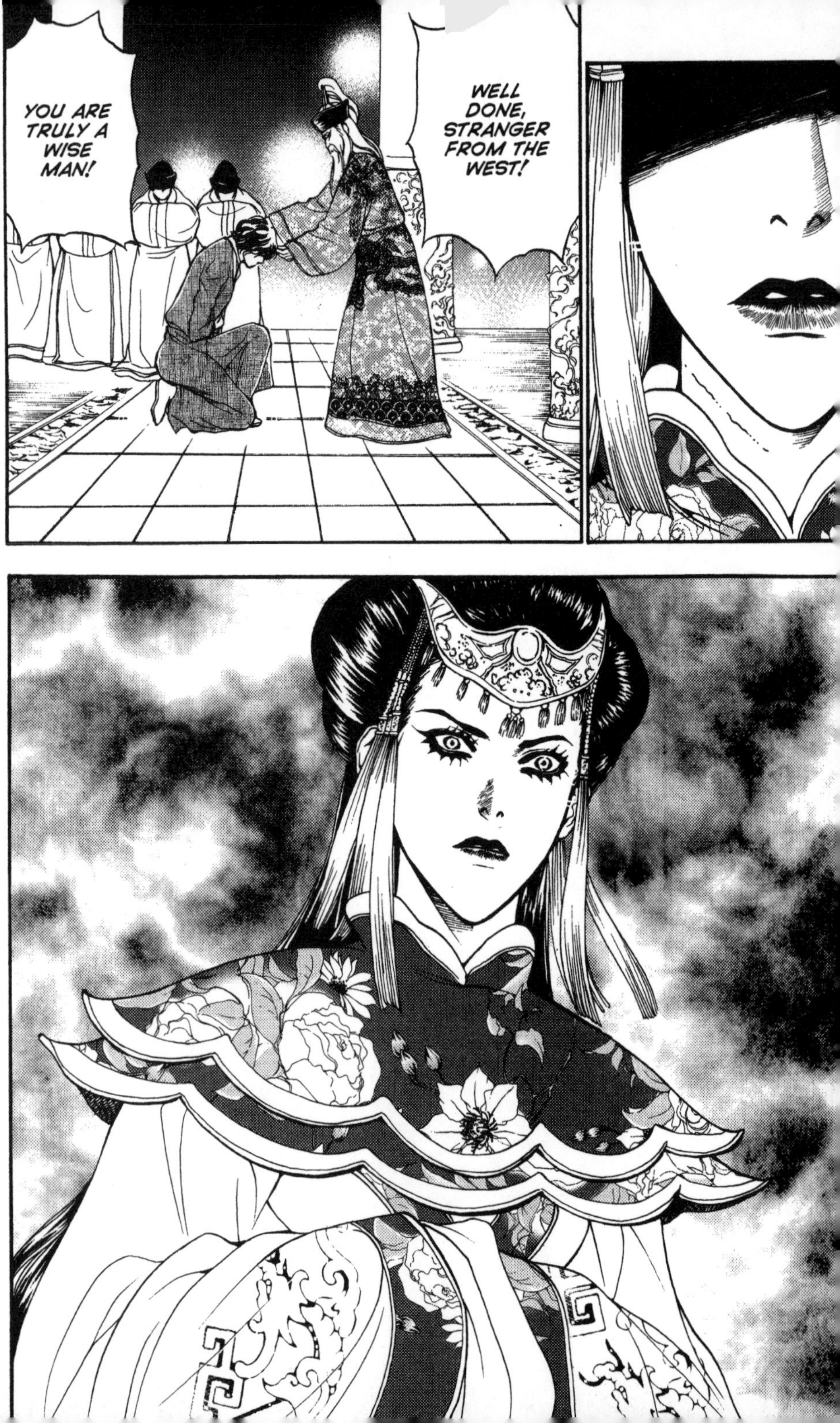
YOU ARE TRULY A WISE MAN!
WELL DONE, STRANGER FROM THE WEST!

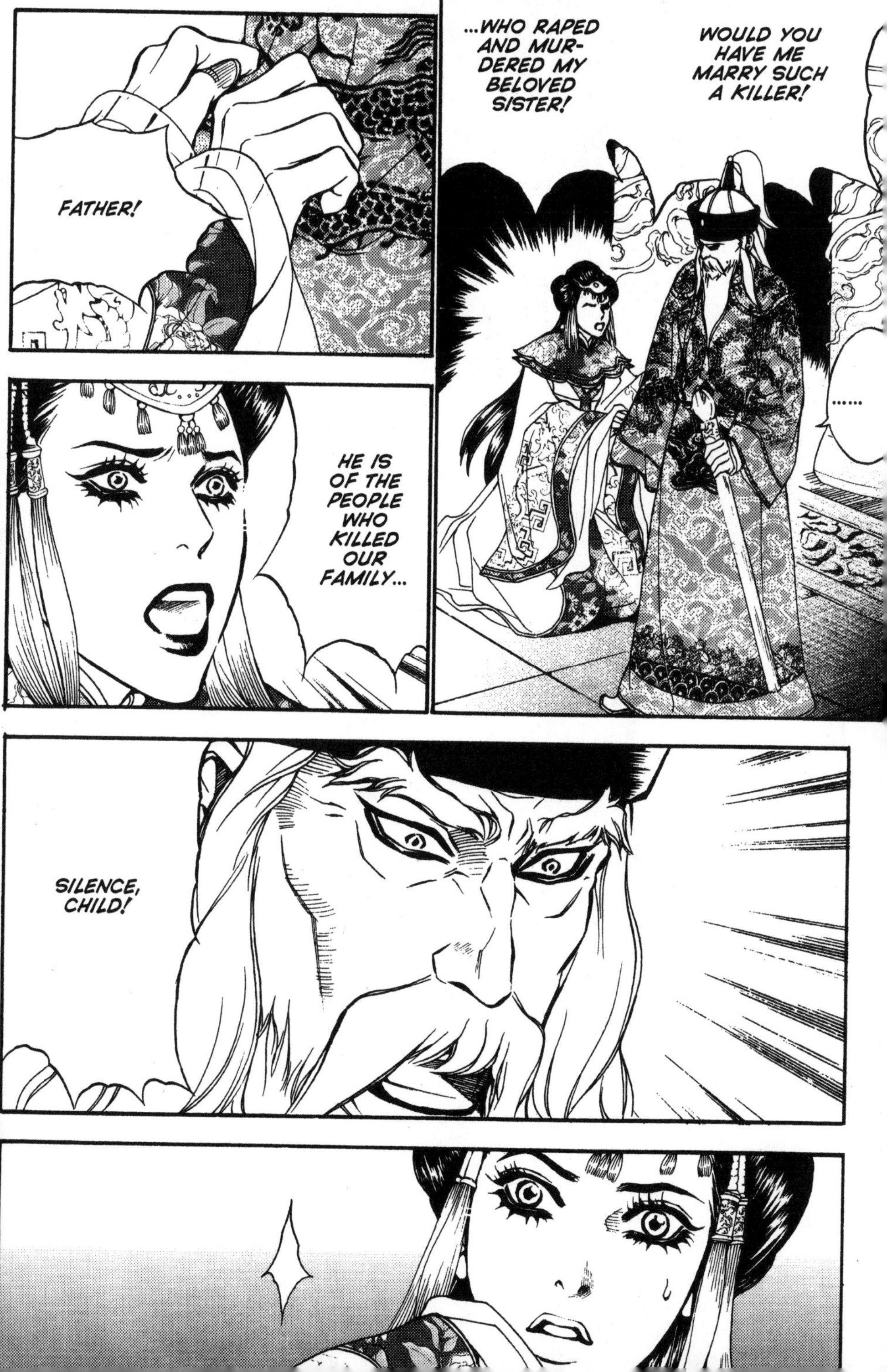
FATHER!
HE IS OF THE PEOPLE WHO KILLED OUR FAMILY...
...WHO RAPED AND MURDERED MY BELOVED SISTER!
WOULD YOU HAVE ME MARRY SUCH A KILLER!
......
SILENCE, CHILD!

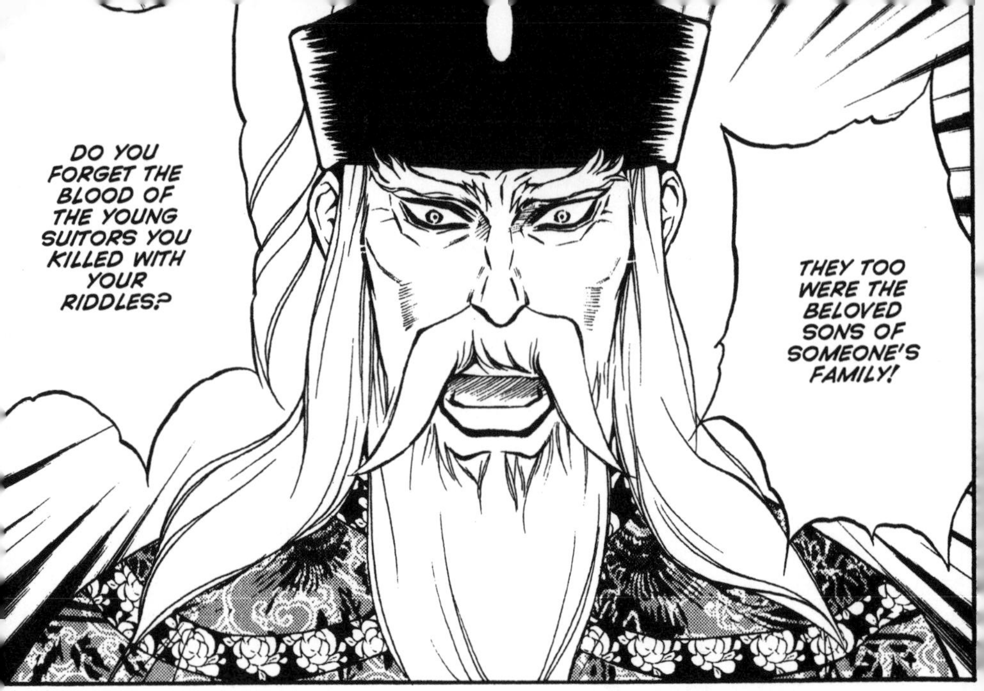
DO YOU FORGET THE BLOOD OF THE YOUNG SUITORS YOU KILLED WITH YOUR RIDDLES?
THEY TOO WERE THE BELOVED SONS OF SOMEONE'S FAMILY!
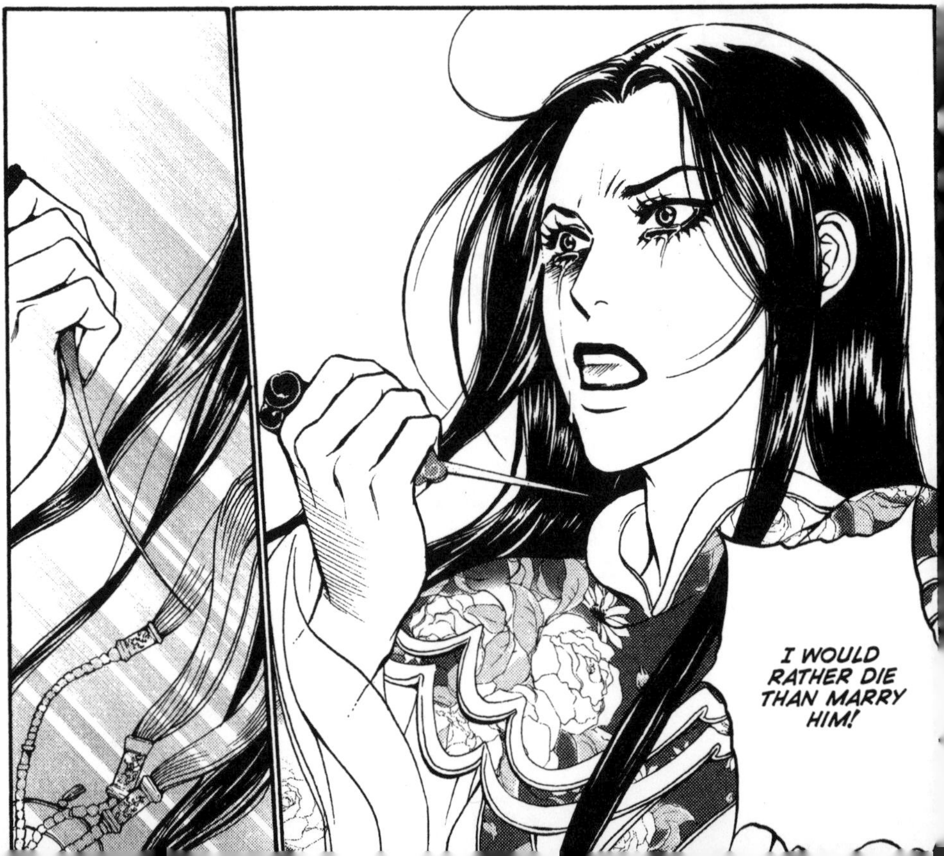
I WOULD RATHER DIE THAN MARRY HIM!

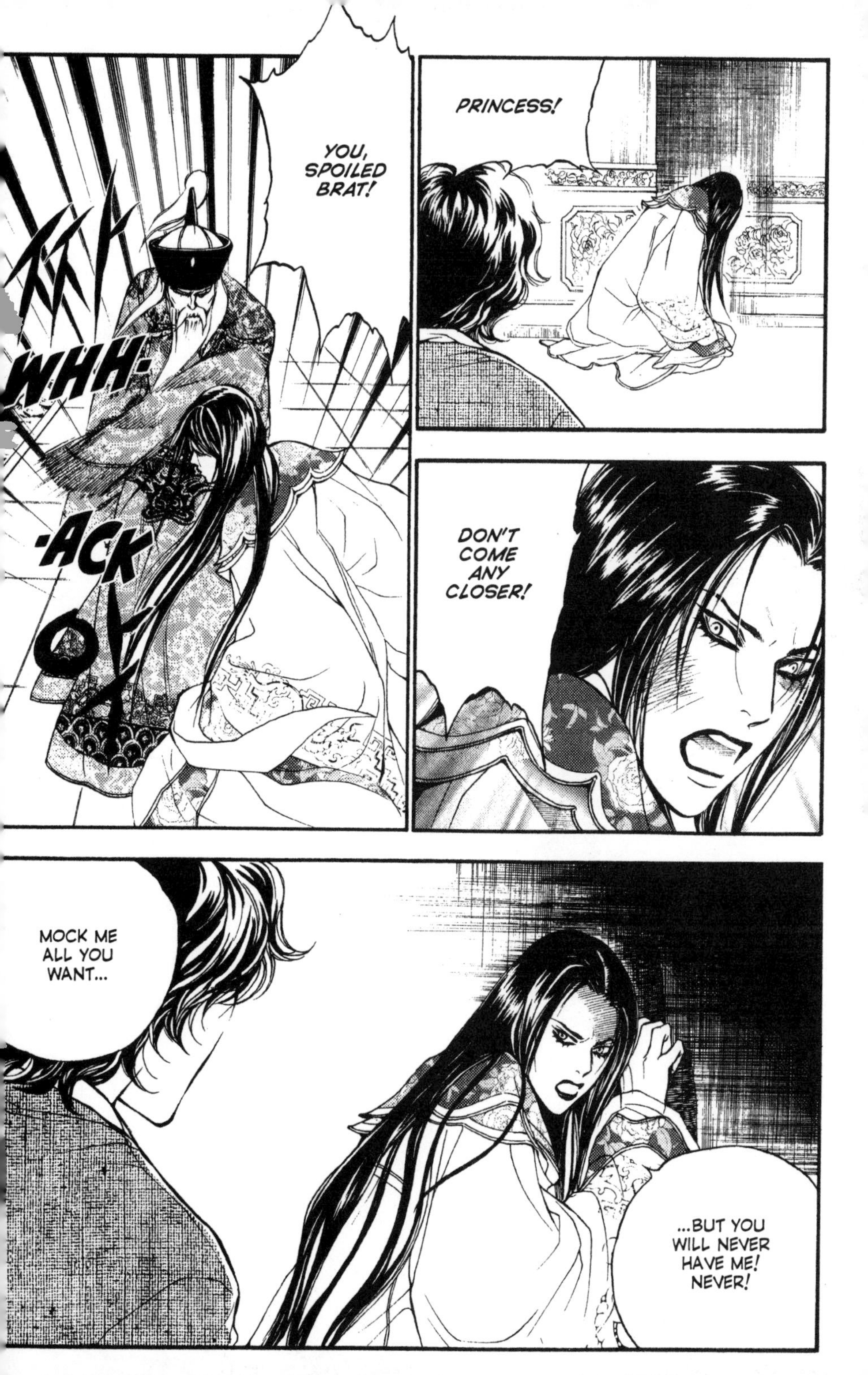
YOU, SPOILED BRAT!
WHH-
-ACK
PRINCESS!
DON'T COME ANY CLOSER!
MOCK ME ALL YOU WANT...
...BUT YOU WILL NEVER HAVE ME! NEVER!

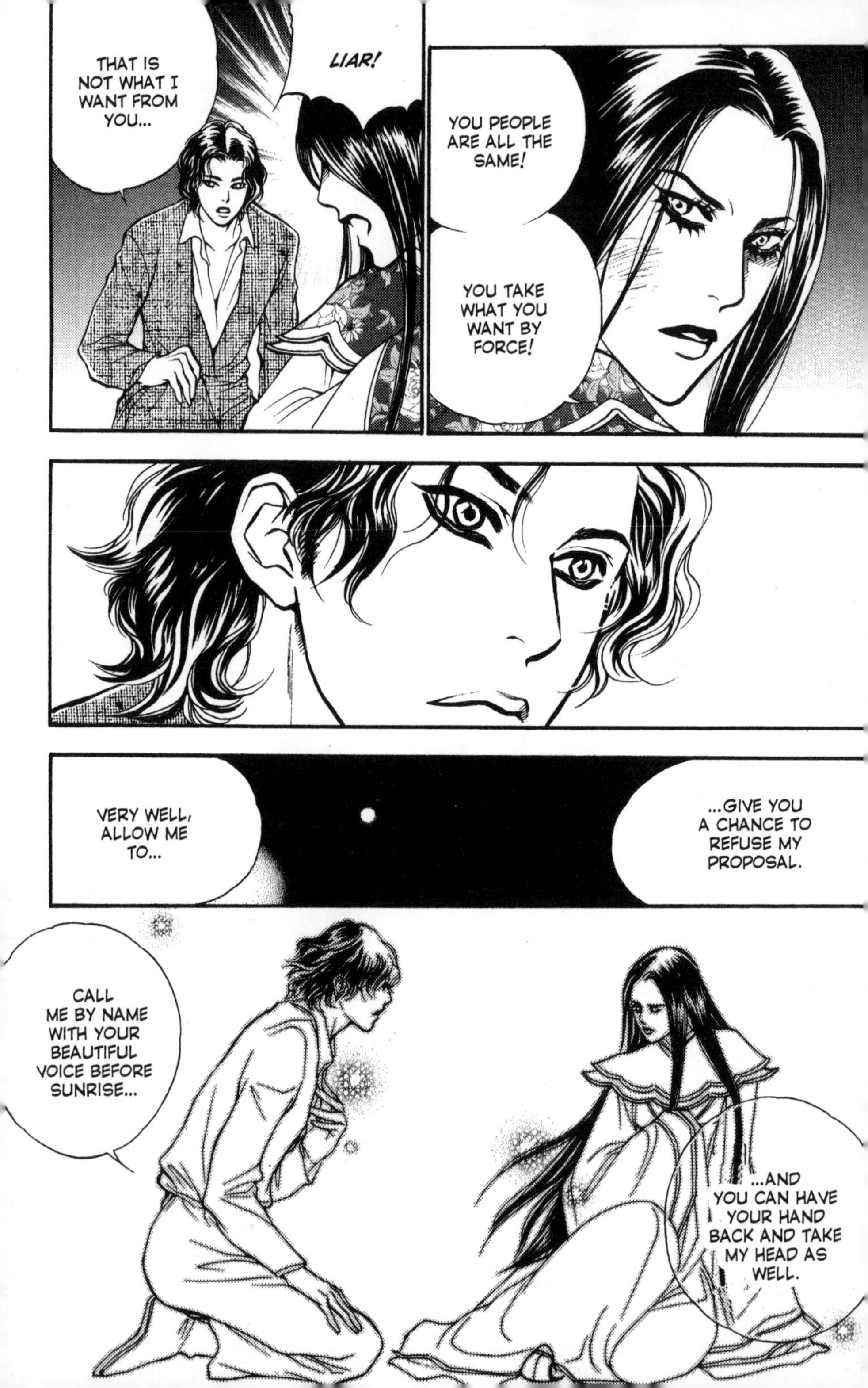
THAT IS NOT WHAT I WANT FROM YOU...
LIAR!
YOU PEOPLE ARE ALL THE SAME!
YOU TAKE WHAT YOU WANT BY FORCE!
VERY WELL, ALLOW ME TO...
...GIVE YOU A CHANCE TO REFUSE MY PROPOSAL.
CALL ME BY NAME WITH YOUR BEAUTIFUL VOICE BEFORE SUNRISE...
...AND YOU CAN HAVE YOUR HAND BACK AND TAKE MY HEAD AS WELL.

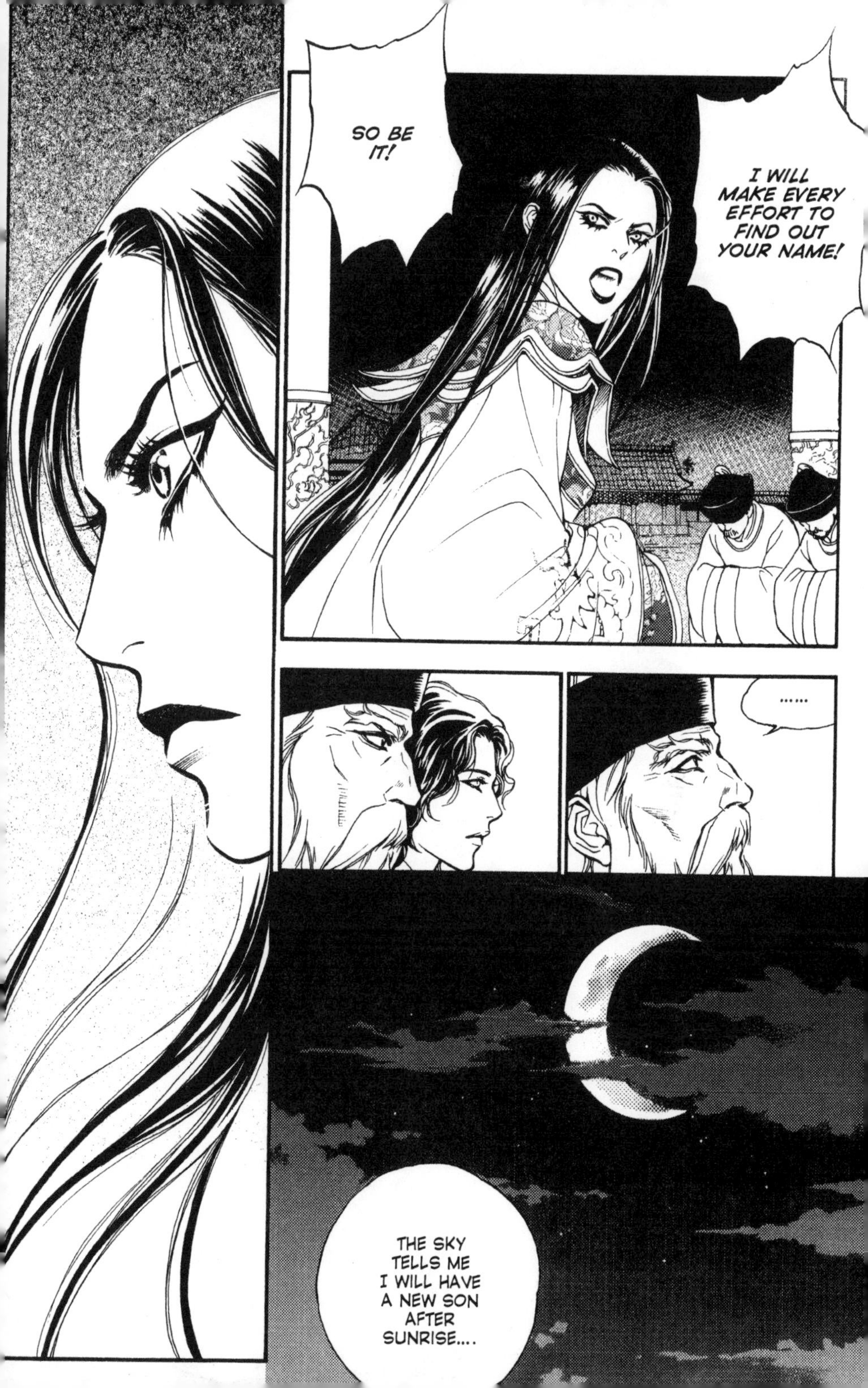
SO BE IT!
I WILL MAKE EVERY EFFORT TO FIND OUT YOUR NAME!
……
THE SKY TELLS ME I WILL HAVE A NEW SON AFTER SUNRISE....

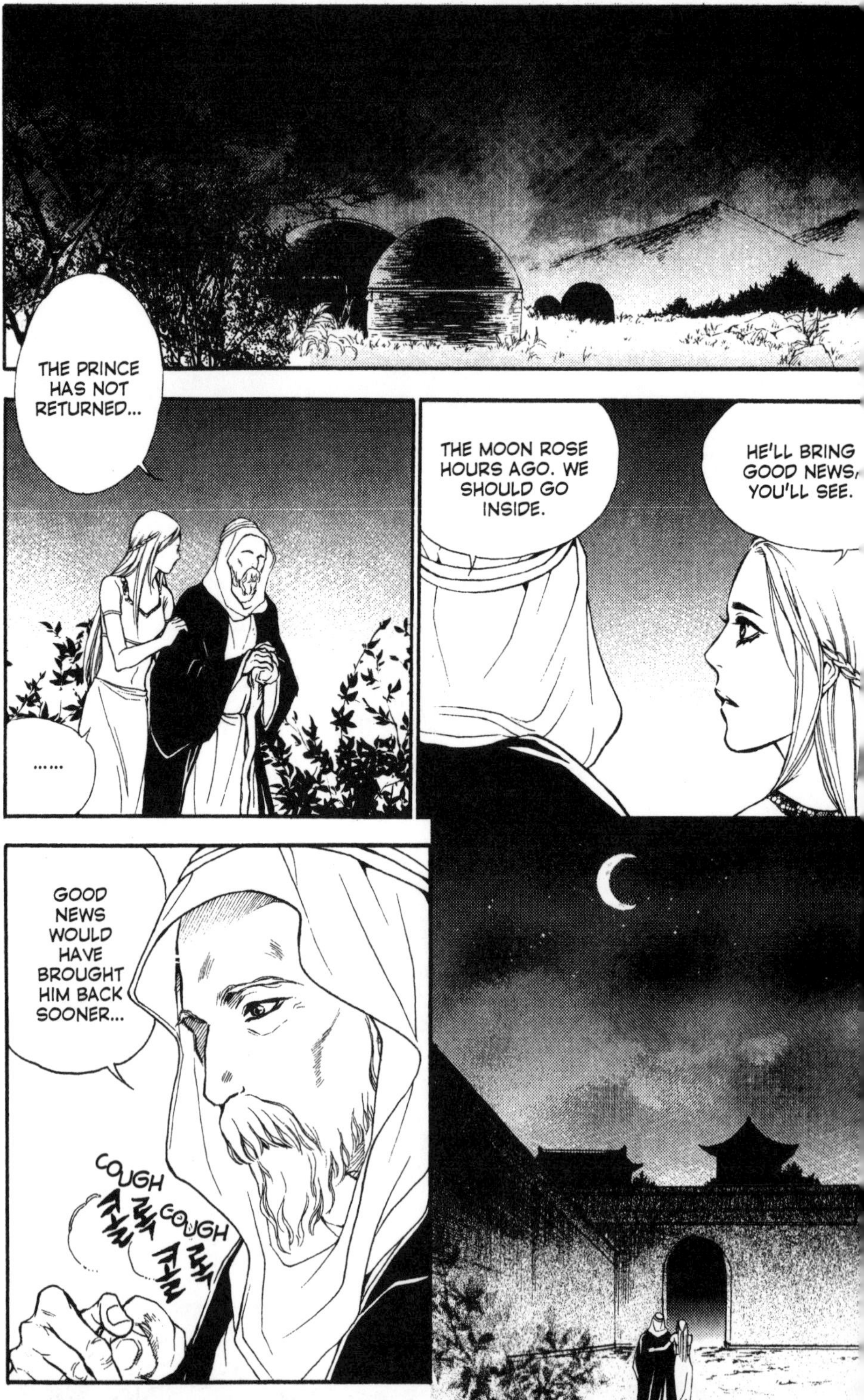
THE PRINCE HAS NOT RETURNED...
......
THE MOON ROSE HOURS AGO. WE SHOULD GO INSIDE.
HE'LL BRING GOOD NEWS, YOU'LL SEE.
GOOD NEWS WOULD HAVE BROUGHT HIM BACK SOONER...
COUGH
콜록
COUGH
콜록

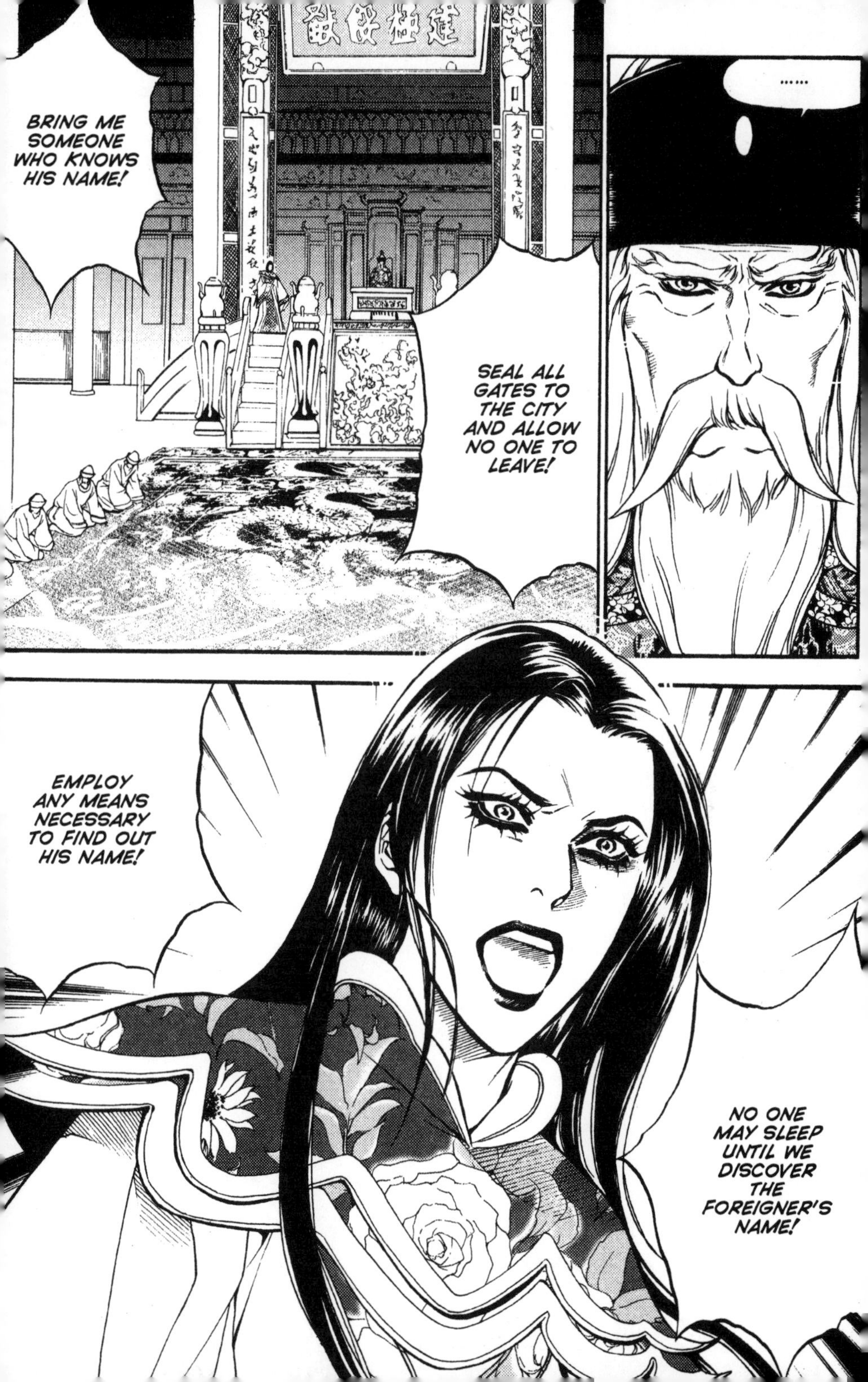
BRING ME SOMEONE WHO KNOWS HIS NAME!
SEAL ALL GATES TO THE CITY AND ALLOW NO ONE TO LEAVE!
......
EMPLOY ANY MEANS NECESSARY TO FIND OUT HIS NAME!
NO ONE MAY SLEEP UNTIL WE DISCOVER THE FOREIGNER'S NAME!

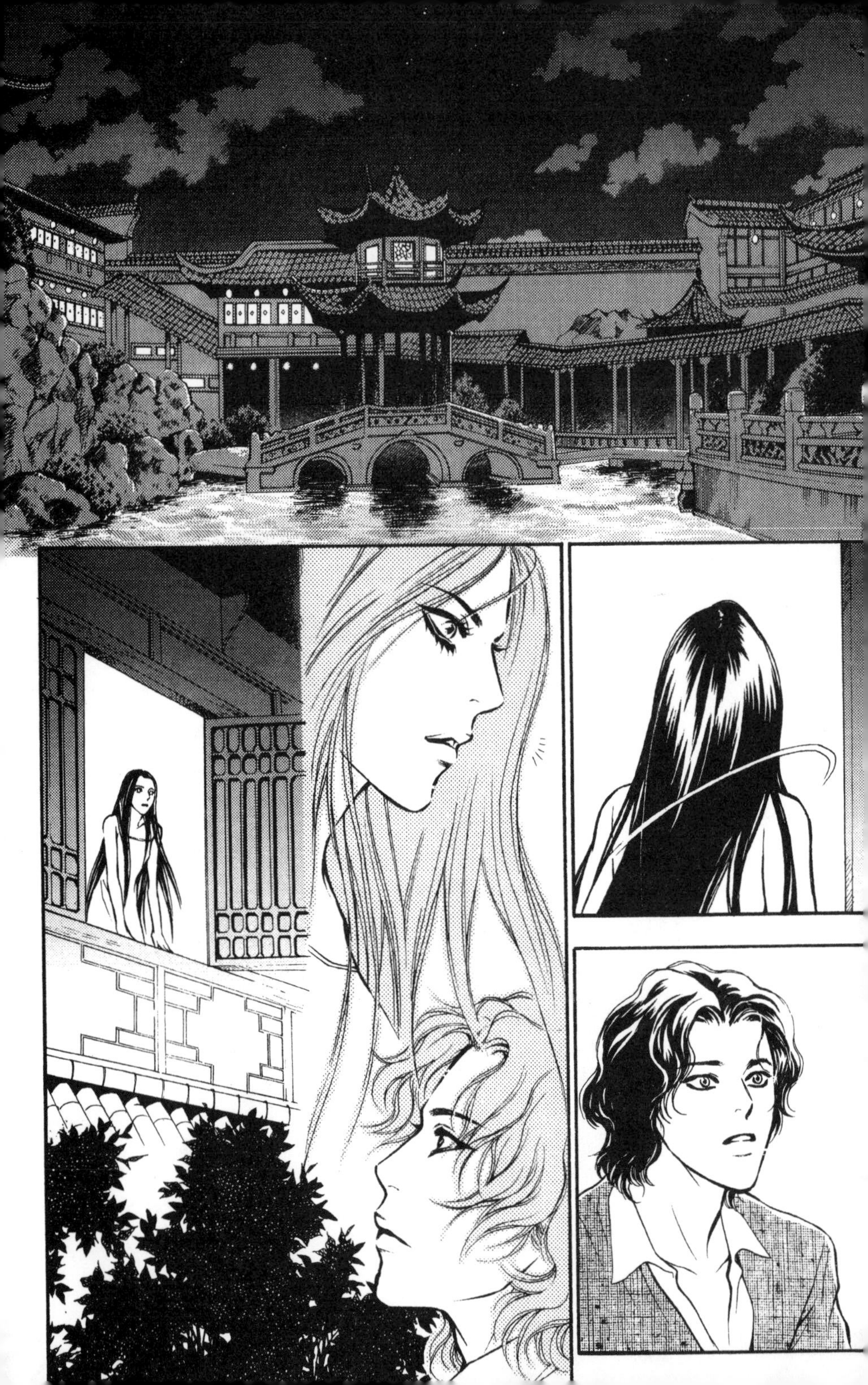

YOU WERE QUITE IMPRESSIVE.

NOT ONE PERSON HAS SOLVED ANY ONE OF HER RIDDLES, AND YOU SOLVED THEM ALL.

WHAT DO YOU WANT?

YOU'RE NOT THE AVERAGE TRAVELER...

I SMELL NOBLE BLOOD.

WHAT ARE YOU TALKING ABOUT?

......

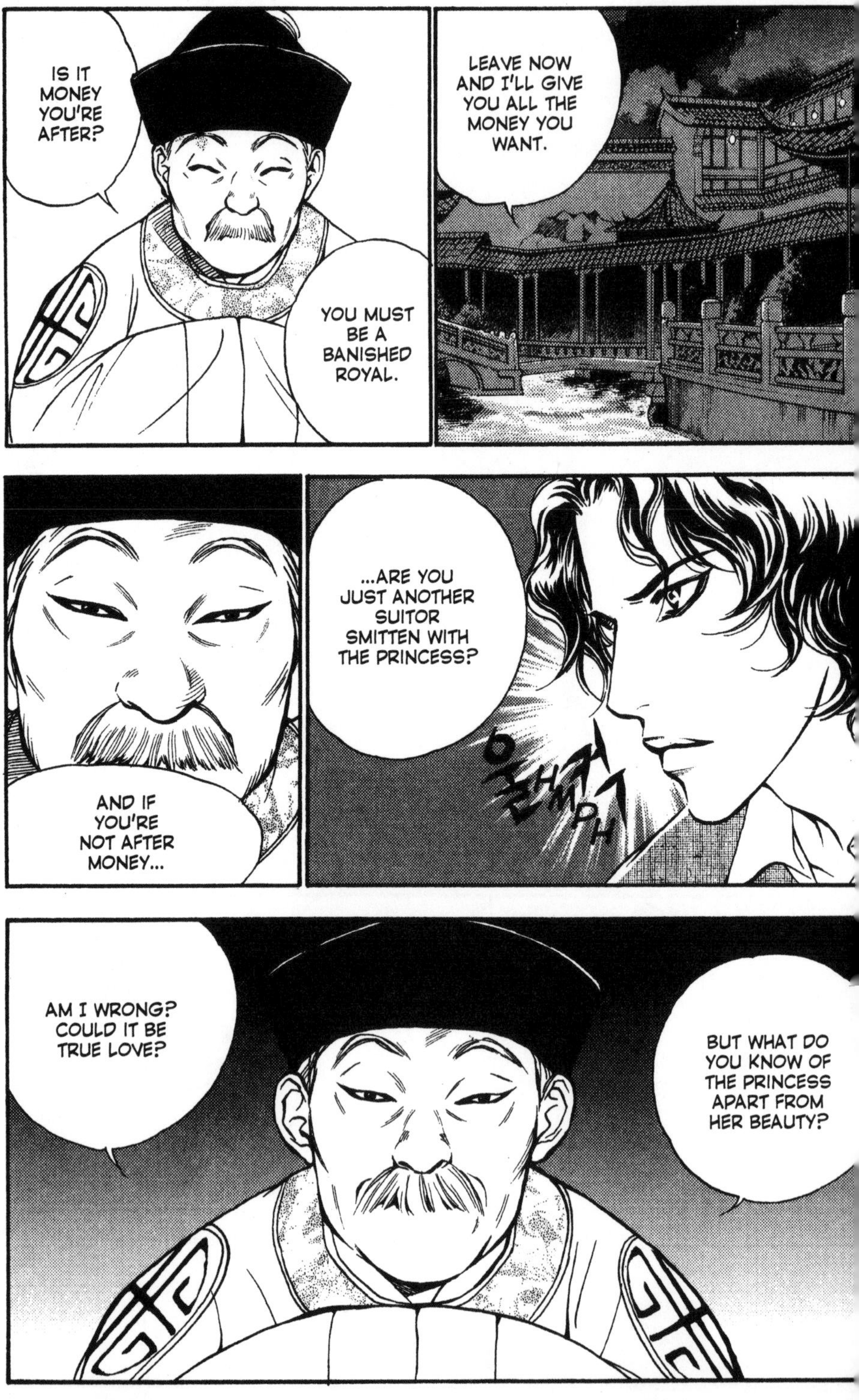
IS IT MONEY YOU'RE AFTER?
YOU MUST BE A BANISHED ROYAL.
LEAVE NOW AND I'LL GIVE YOU ALL THE MONEY YOU WANT.
AND IF YOU'RE NOT AFTER MONEY...
...ARE YOU JUST ANOTHER SUITOR SMITTEN WITH THE PRINCESS?
HMPH
AM I WRONG? COULD IT BE TRUE LOVE?
BUT WHAT DO YOU KNOW OF THE PRINCESS APART FROM HER BEAUTY?

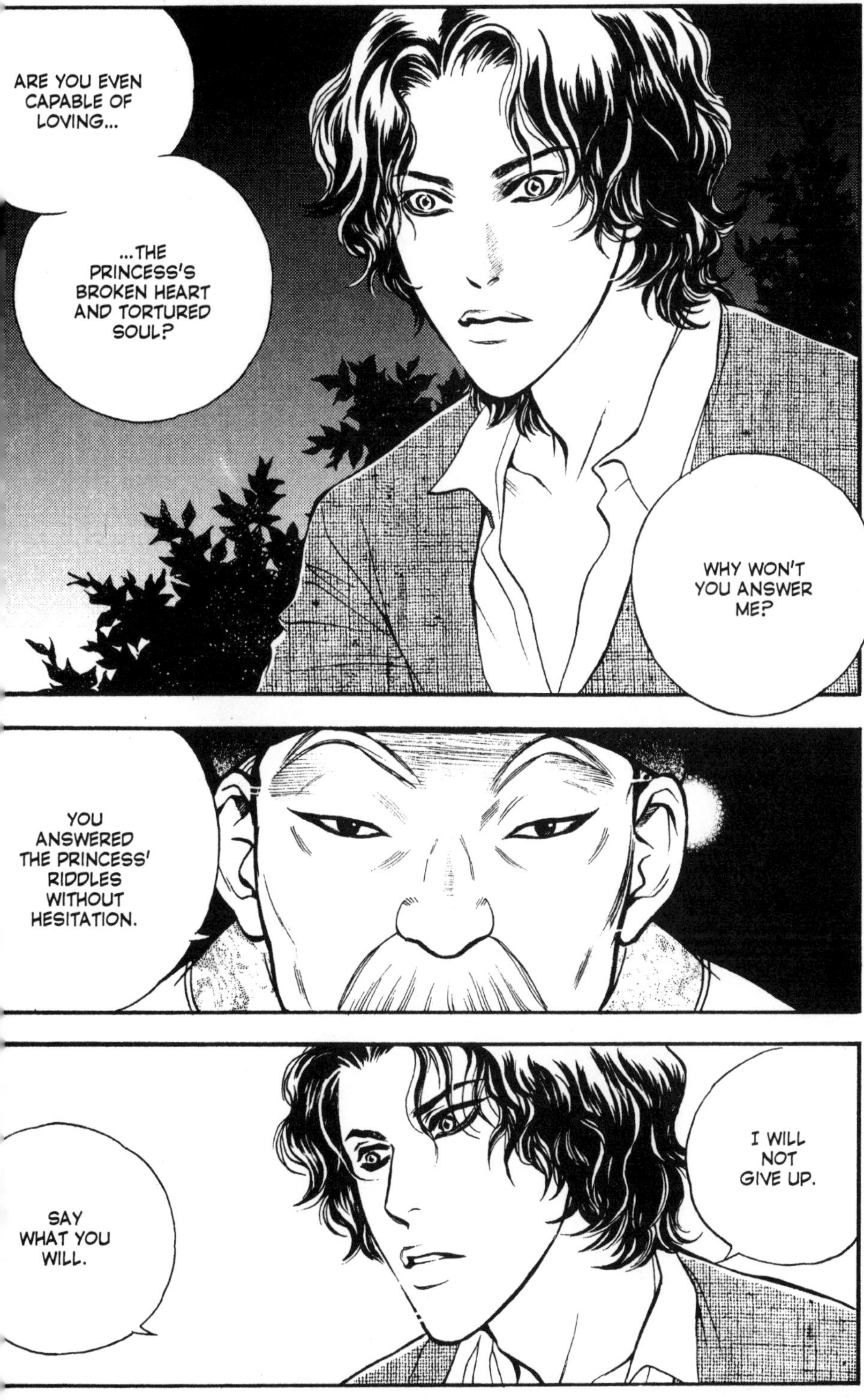

ARE YOU EVEN CAPABLE OF LOVING...
...THE PRINCESS'S BROKEN HEART AND TORTURED SOUL?
WHY WON'T YOU ANSWER ME?
YOU ANSWERED THE PRINCESS' RIDDLES WITHOUT HESITATION.
SAY WHAT YOU WILL.
I WILL NOT GIVE UP.

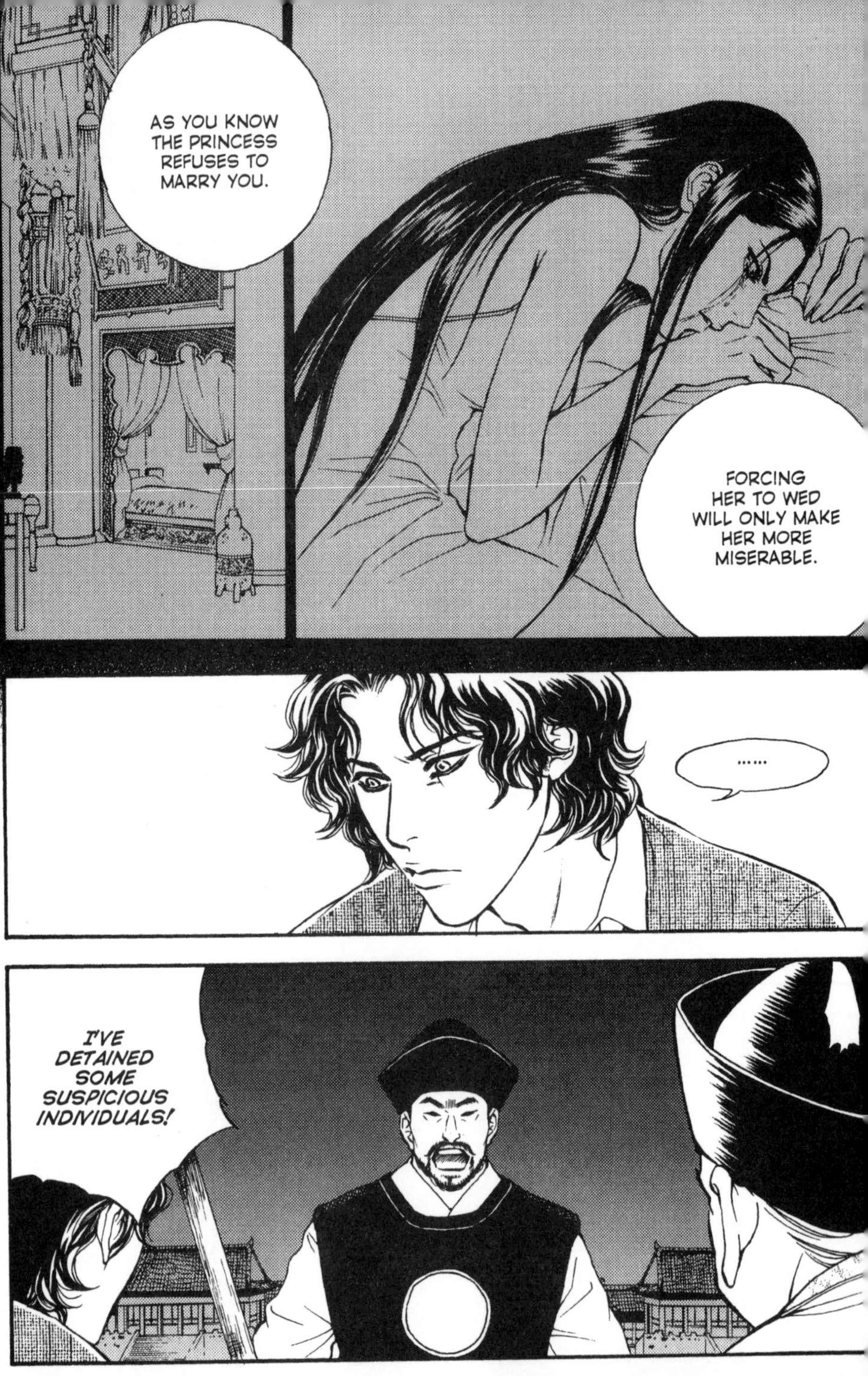
AS YOU KNOW THE PRINCESS REFUSES TO MARRY YOU.
FORCING HER TO WED WILL ONLY MAKE HER MORE MISERABLE.
......
I'VE DETAINED SOME SUSPICIOUS INDIVIDUALS!

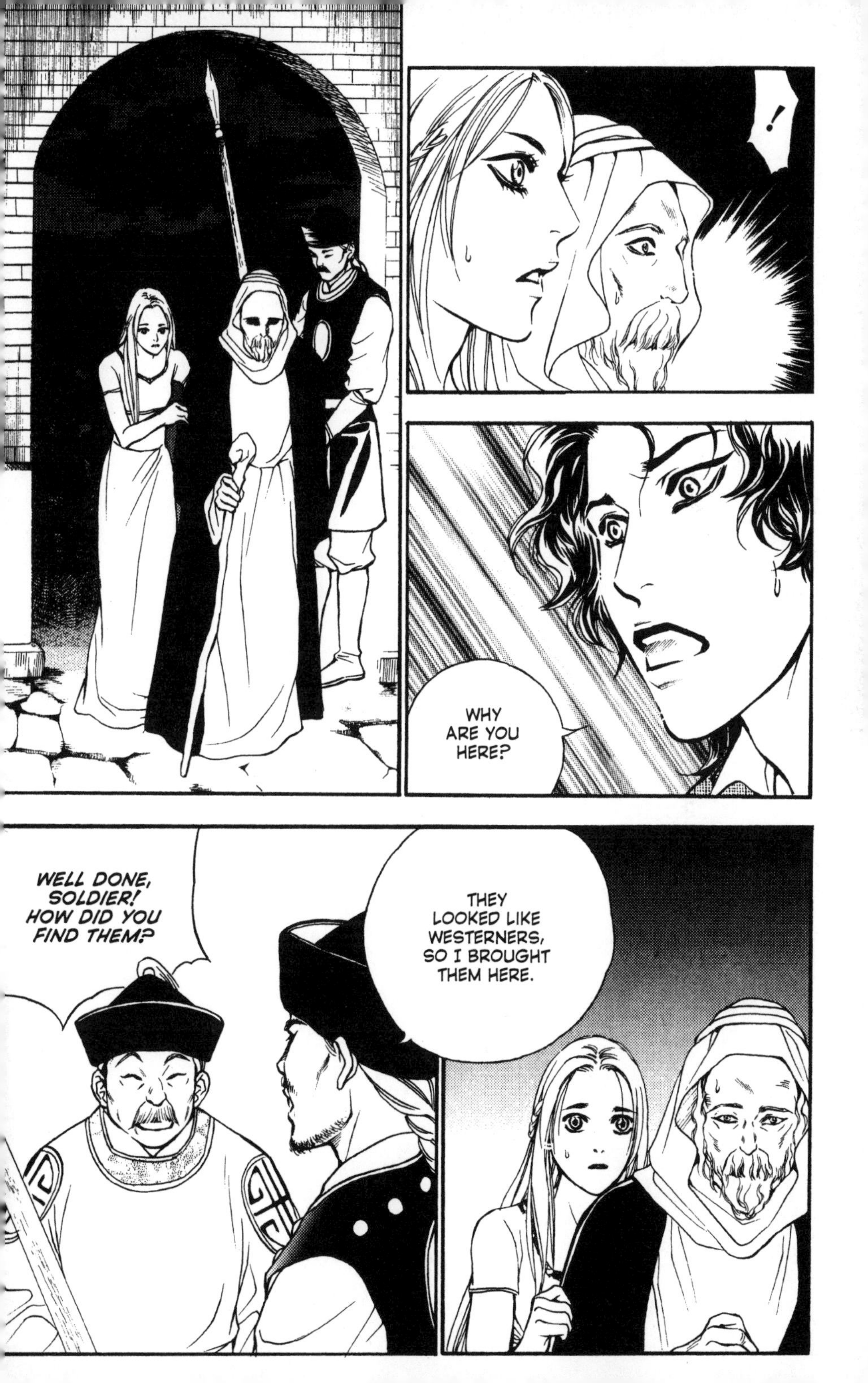
!
WHY ARE YOU HERE?
WELL DONE, SOLDIER! HOW DID YOU FIND THEM?
THEY LOOKED LIKE WESTERNERS, SO I BROUGHT THEM HERE.

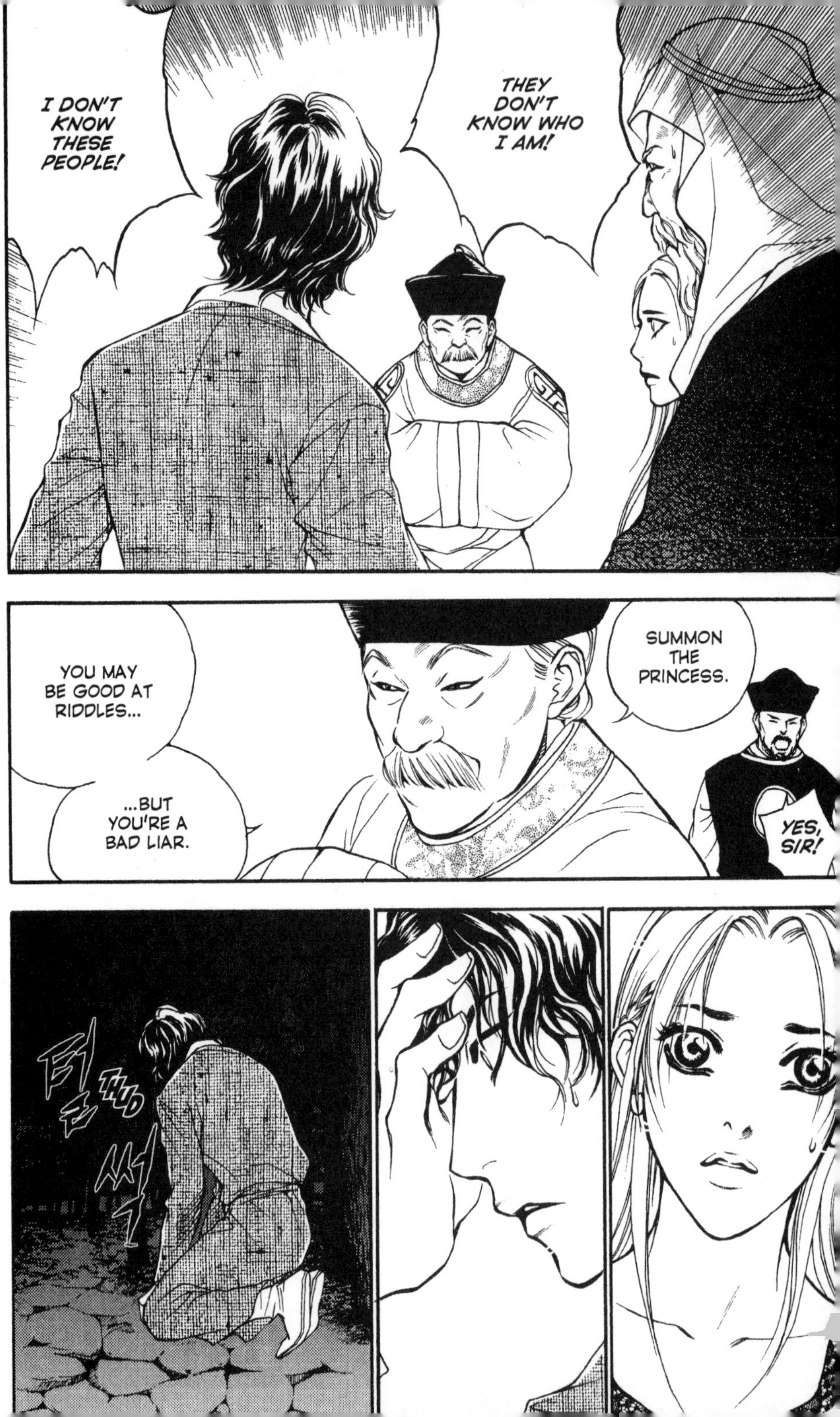
I DON'T KNOW THESE PEOPLE!
THEY DON'T KNOW WHO I AM!
YOU MAY BE GOOD AT RIDDLES...
...BUT YOU'RE A BAD LIAR.
SUMMON THE PRINCESS.
YES, SIR!
THUD

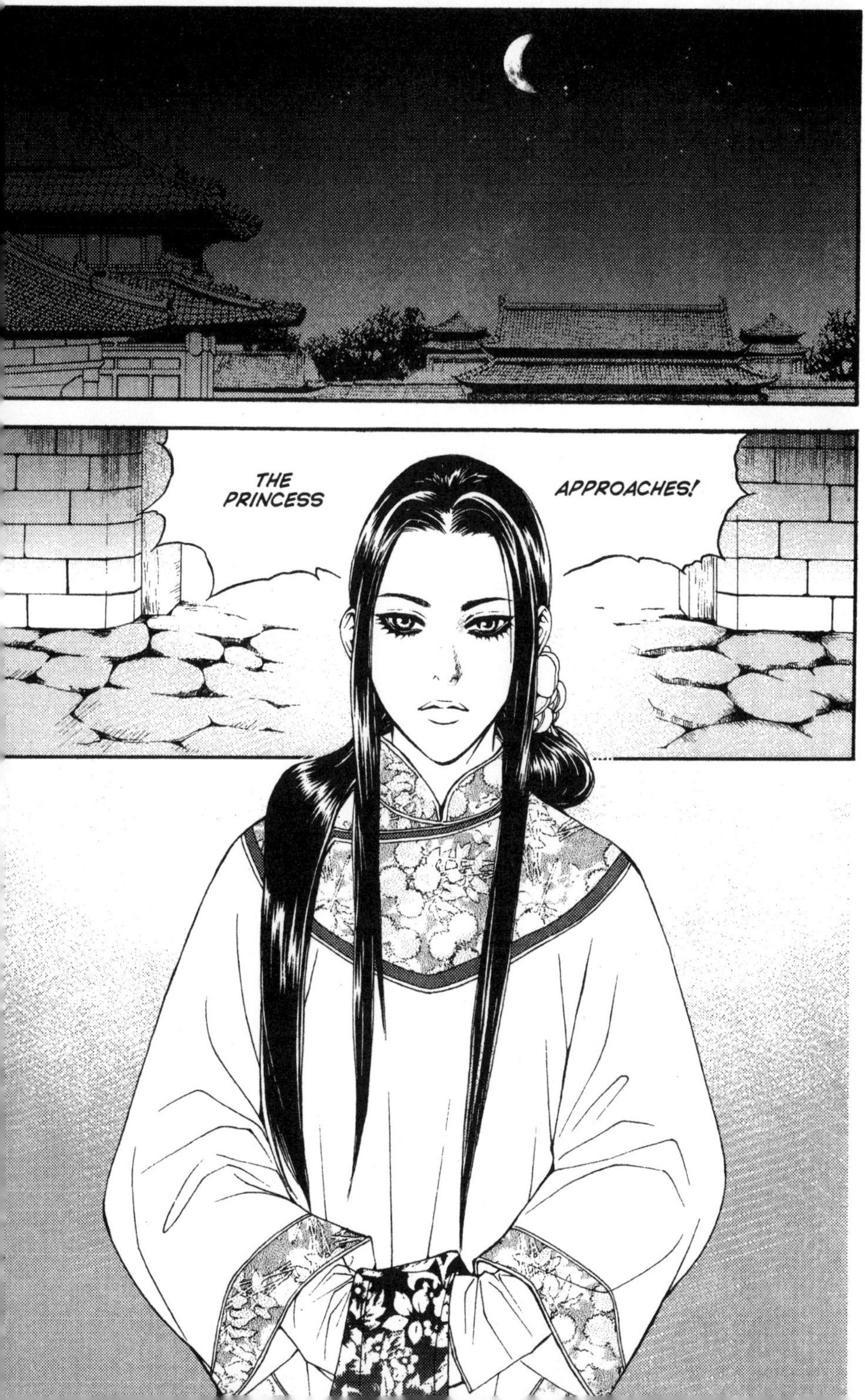
THE PRINCESS
APPROACHES!

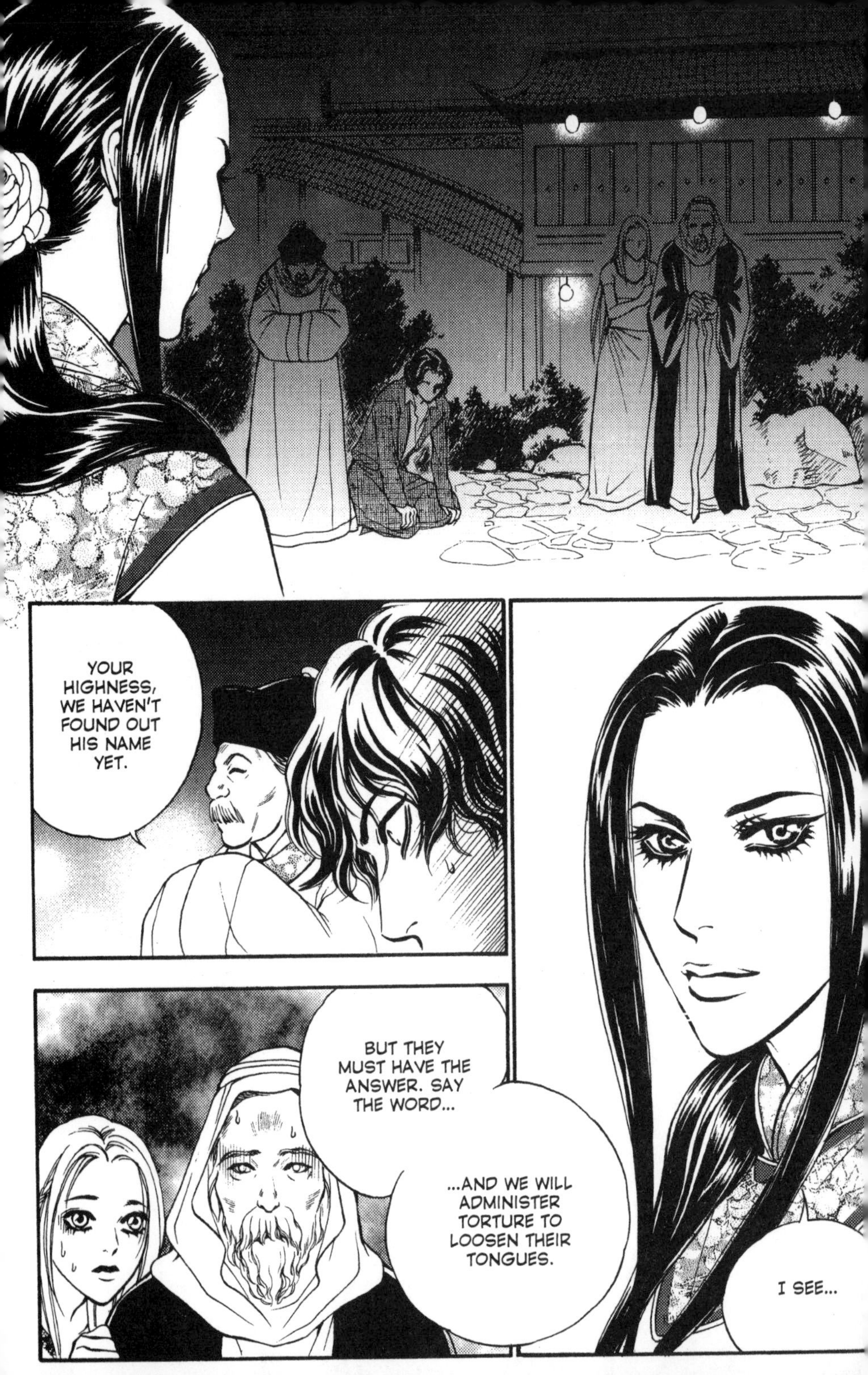
YOUR HIGHNESS, WE HAVEN'T FOUND OUT HIS NAME YET.
BUT THEY MUST HAVE THE ANSWER. SAY THE WORD...
...AND WE WILL ADMINISTER TORTURE TO LOOSEN THEIR TONGUES.
I SEE...

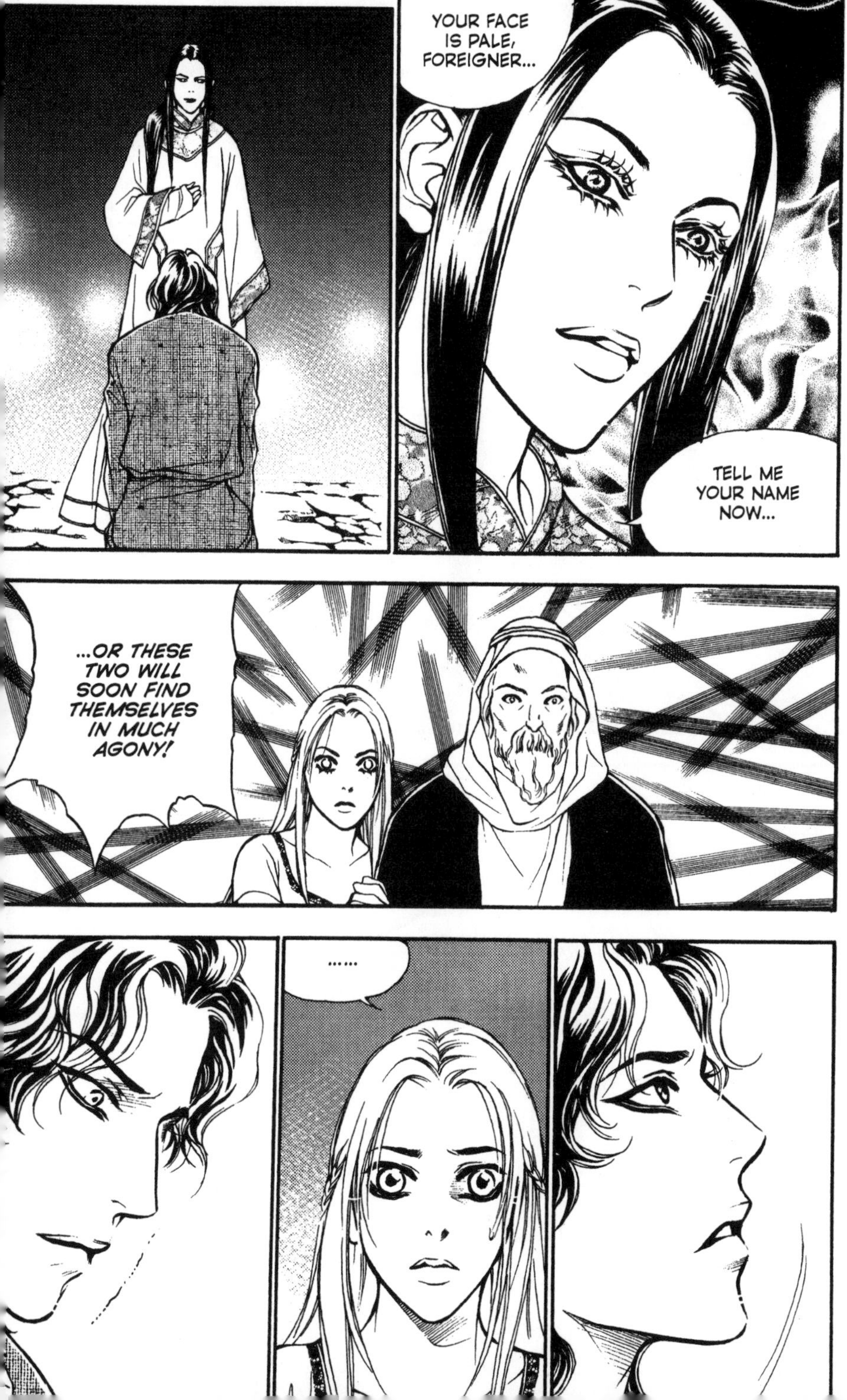
YOUR FACE IS PALE, FOREIGNER...
TELL ME YOUR NAME NOW...
...OR THESE TWO WILL SOON FIND THEMSELVES IN MUCH AGONY!
......

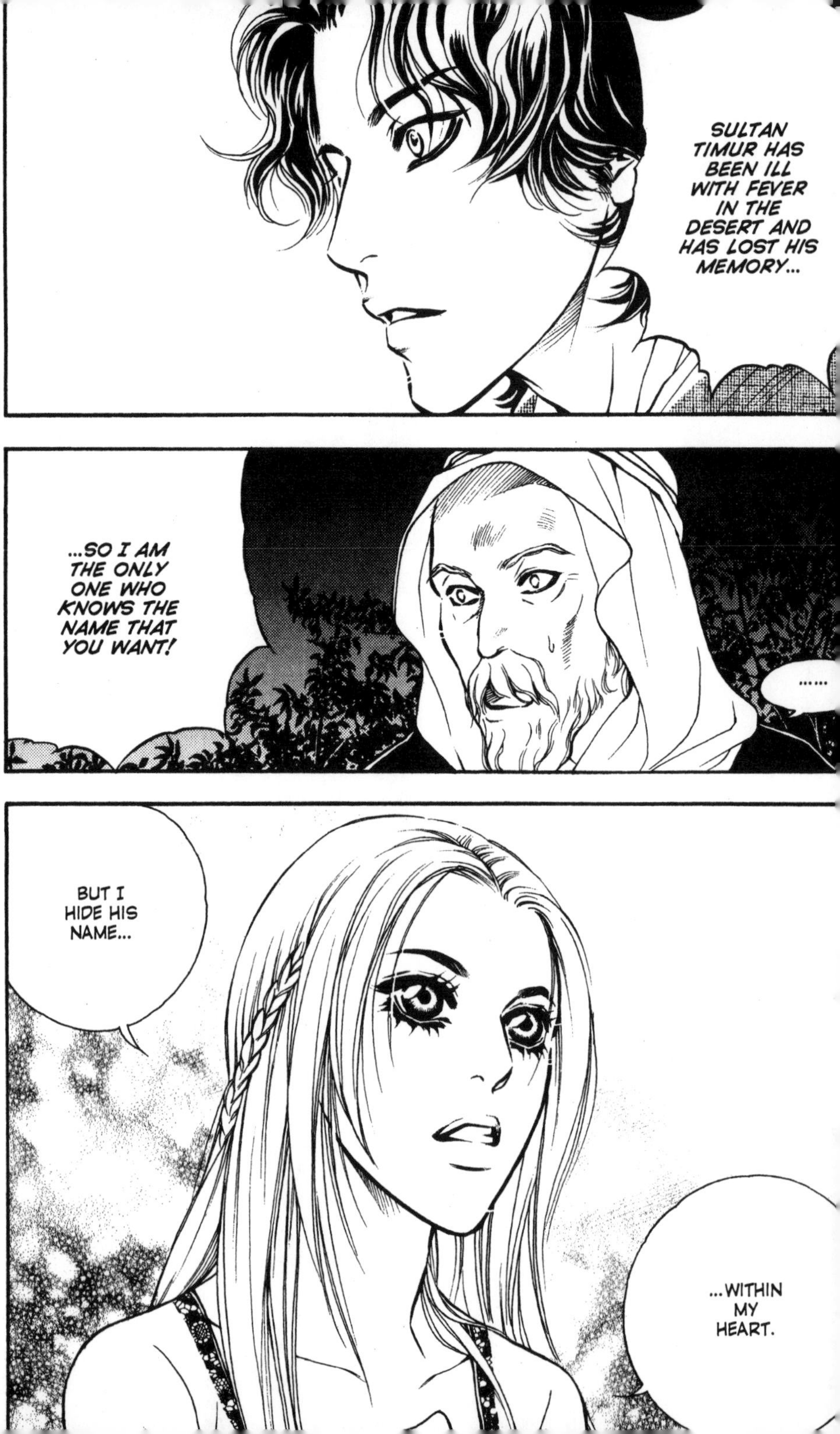
SULTAN TIMUR HAS BEEN ILL WITH FEVER IN THE DESERT AND HAS LOST HIS MEMORY...
...SO I AM THE ONLY ONE WHO KNOWS THE NAME THAT YOU WANT!
......
BUT I HIDE HIS NAME...
...WITHIN MY HEART.

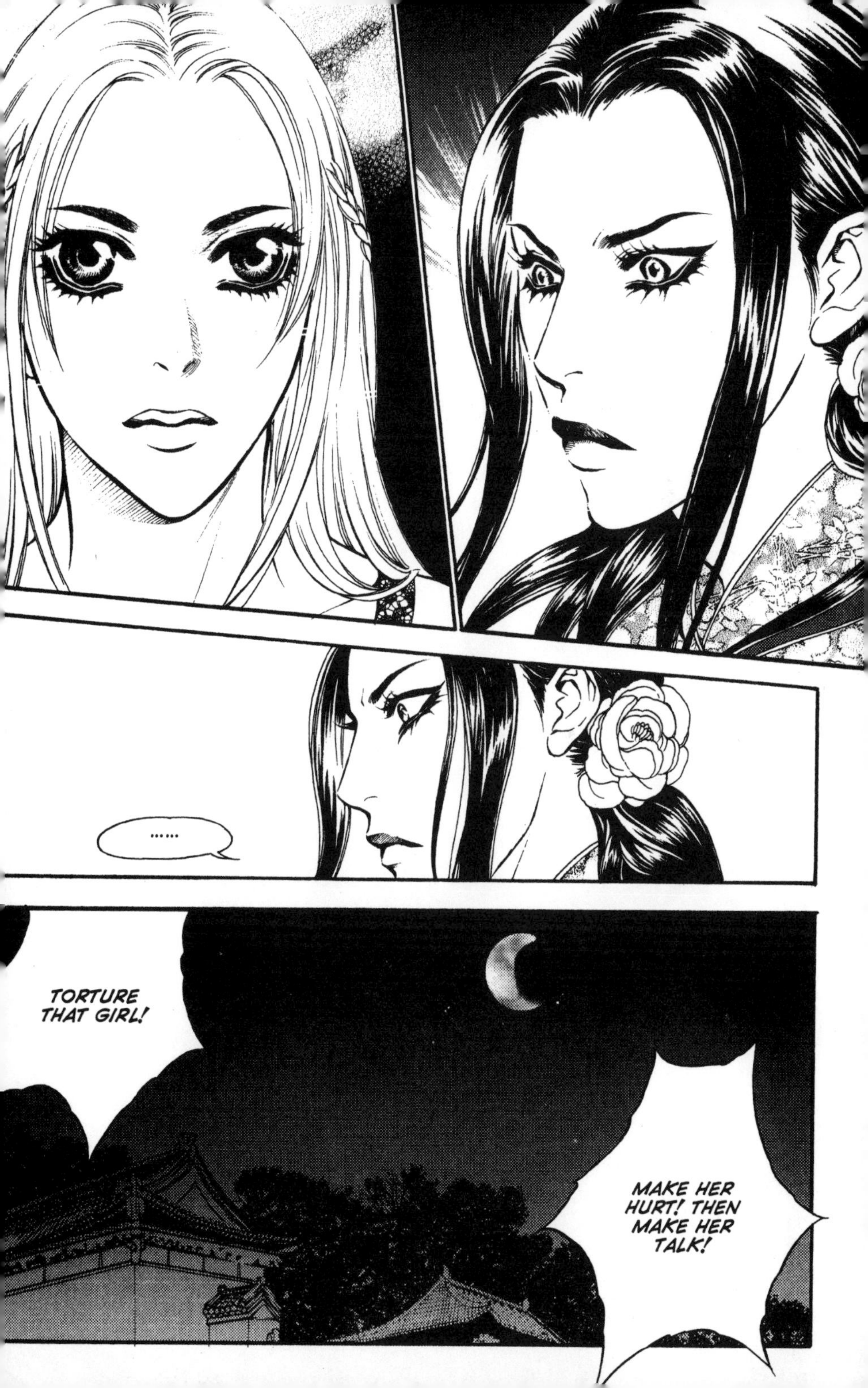
......
TORTURE THAT GIRL!
MAKE HER HURT! THEN MAKE HER TALK!

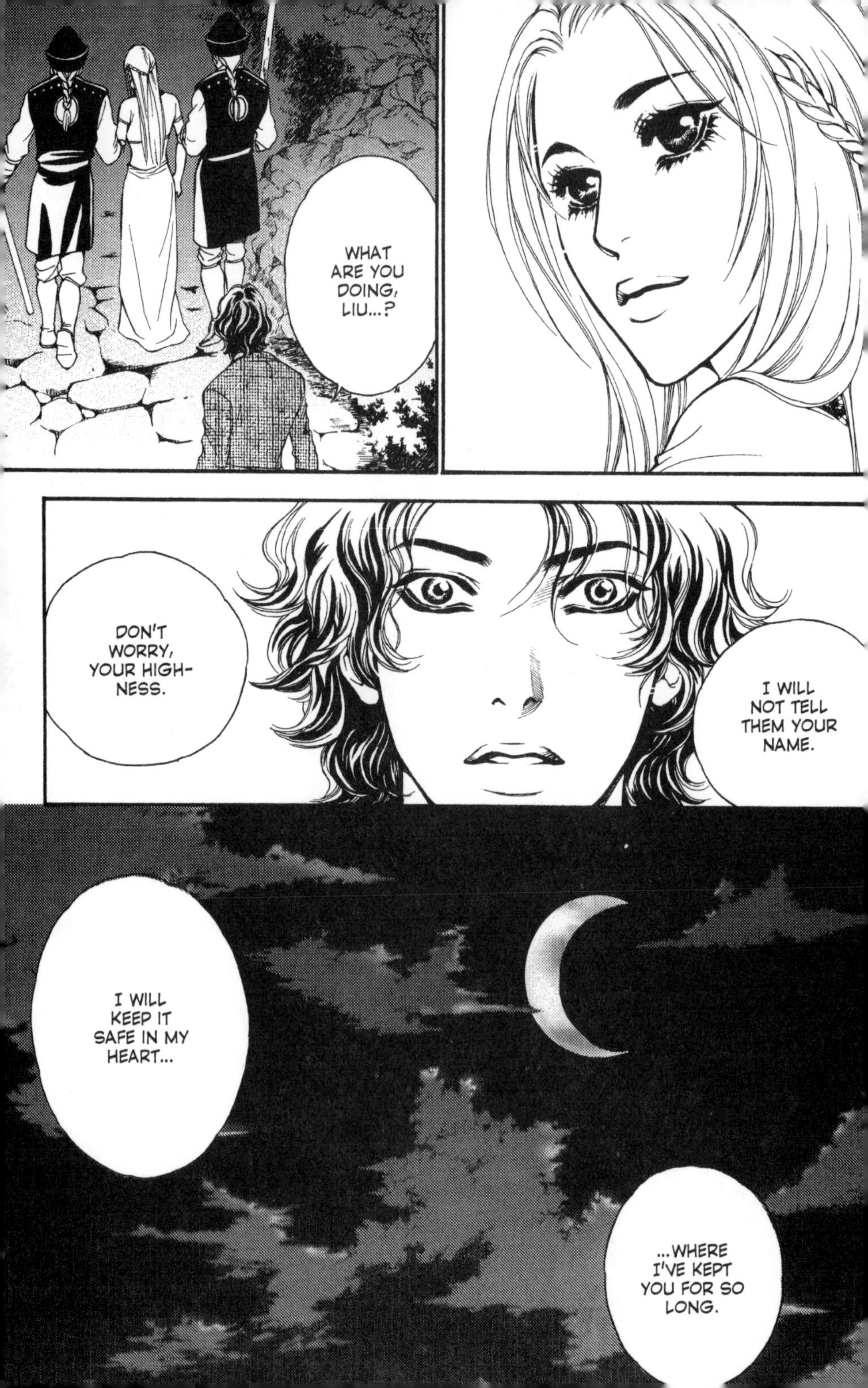
WHAT ARE YOU DOING, LIU...?
DON'T WORRY, YOUR HIGH-NESS.
I WILL NOT TELL THEM YOUR NAME.
I WILL KEEP IT SAFE IN MY HEART...
...WHERE I'VE KEPT YOU FOR SO LONG.

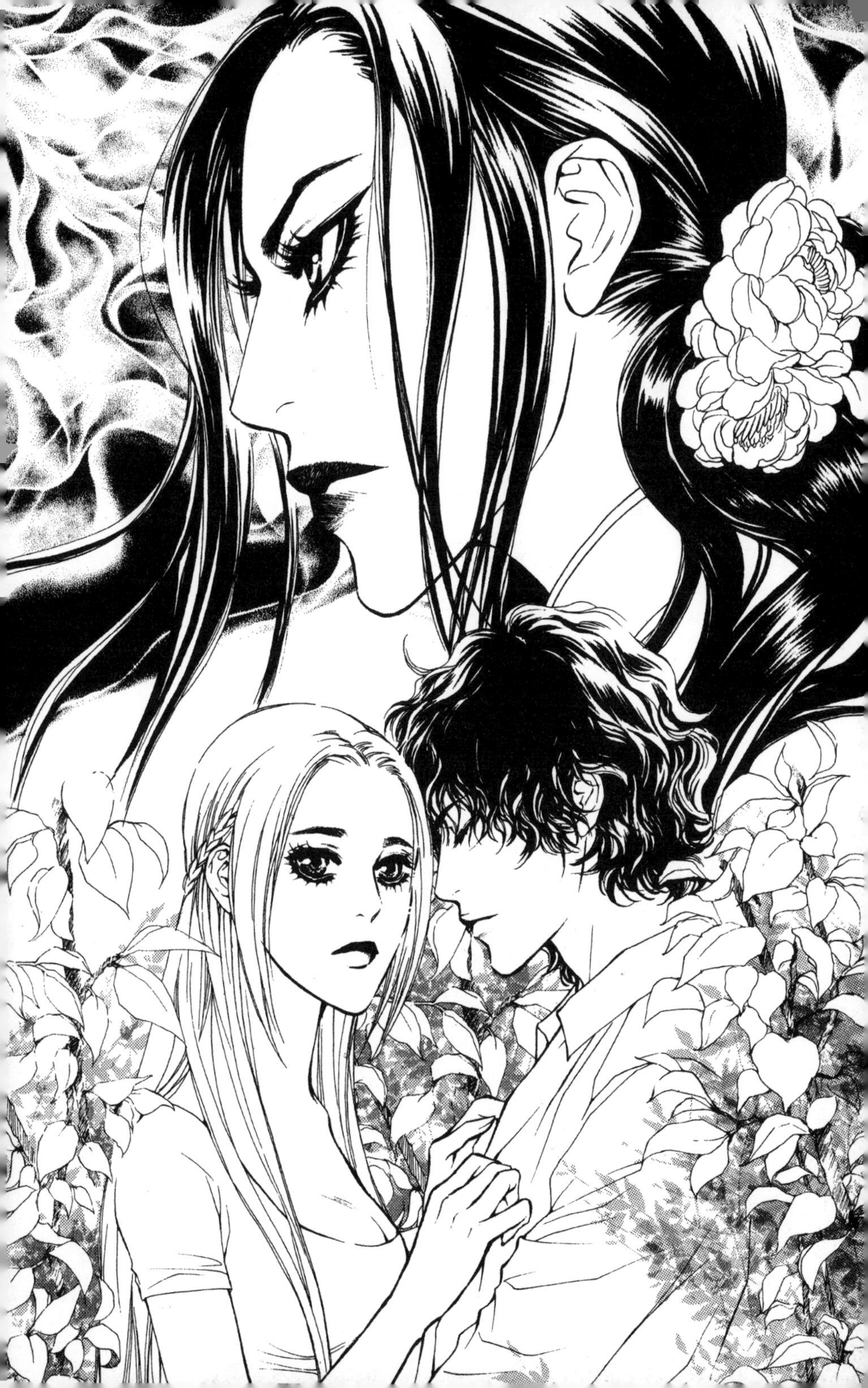

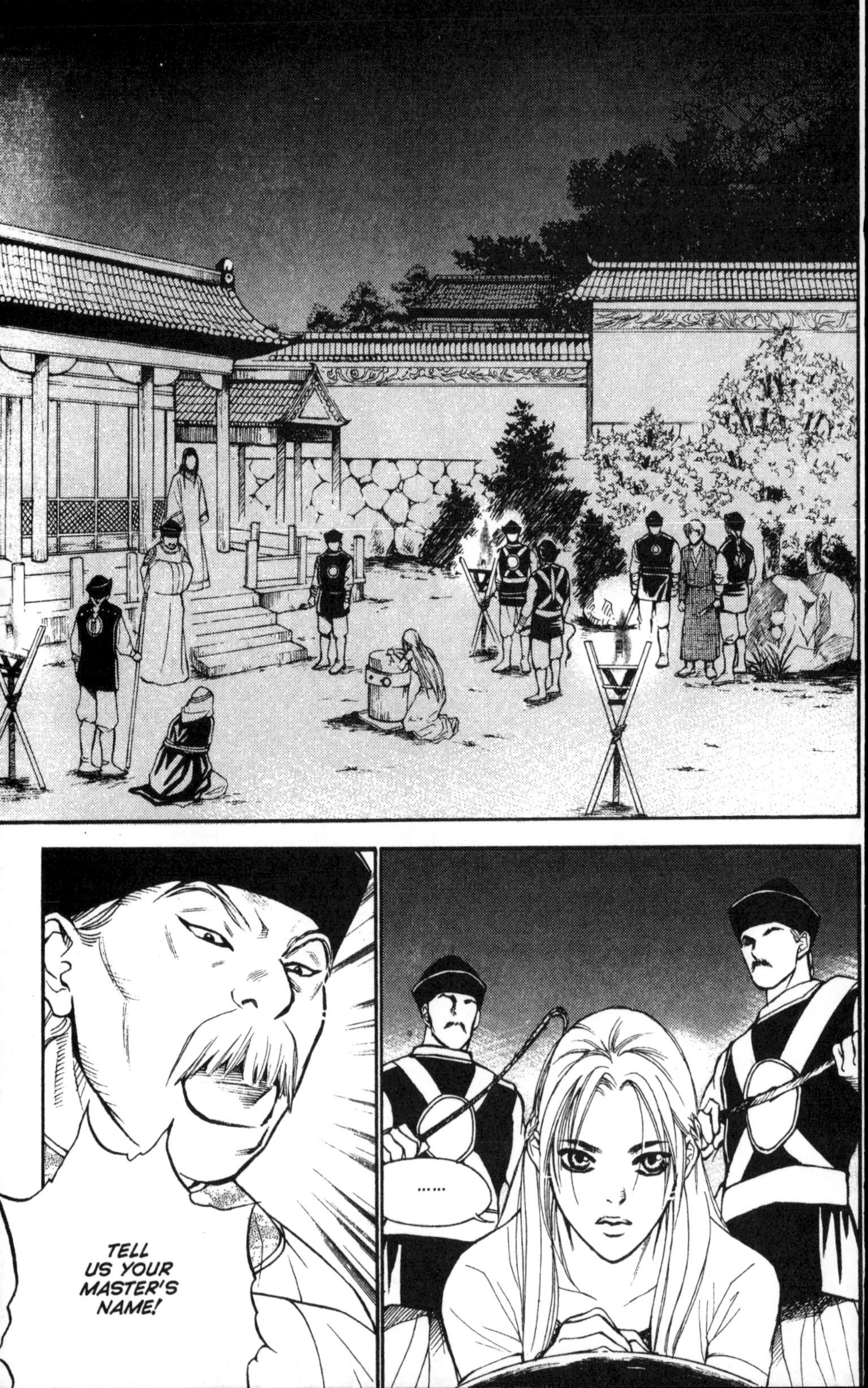
TELL US YOUR MASTER'S NAME!
……

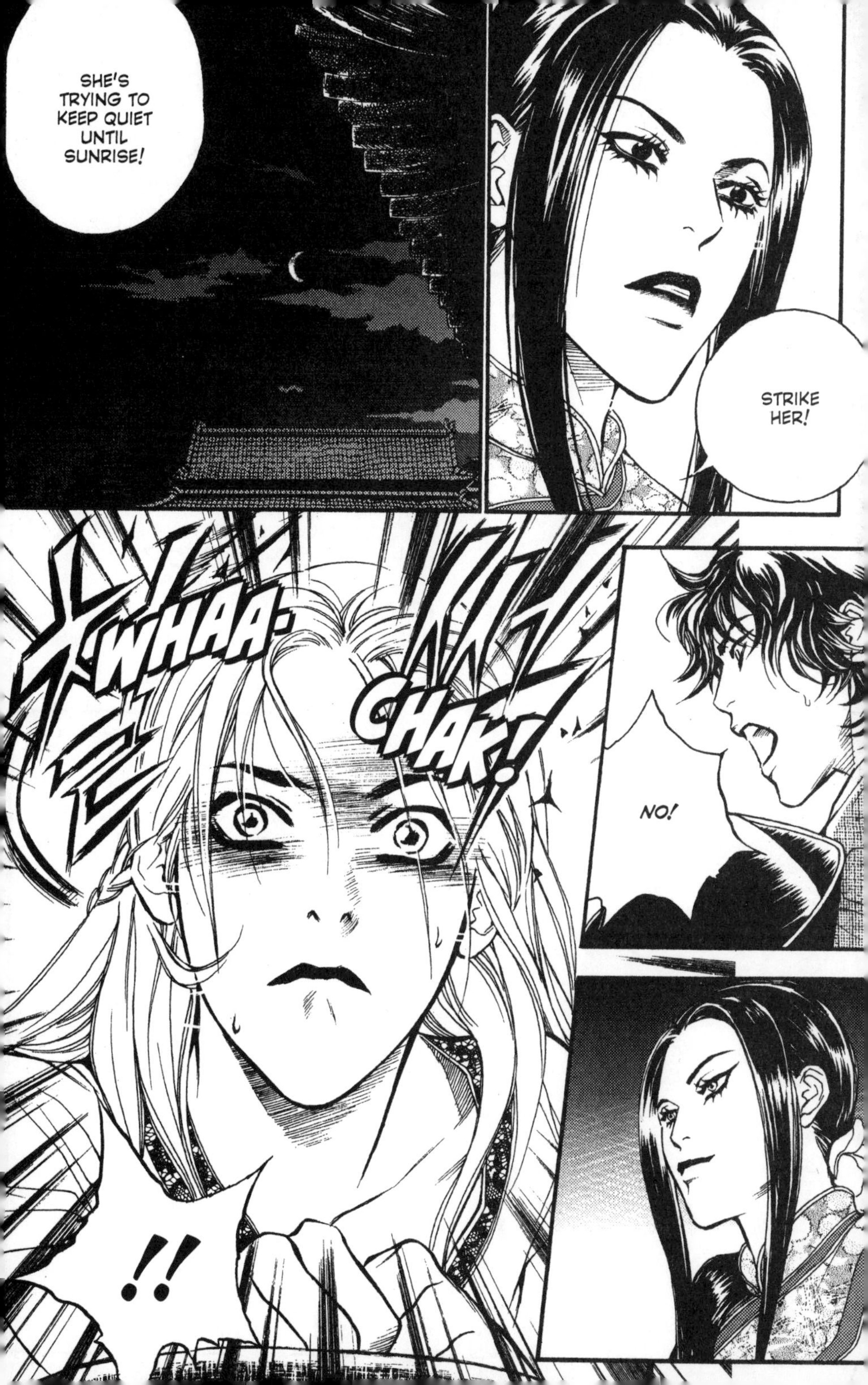
SHE'S TRYING TO KEEP QUIET UNTIL SUNRISE!
STRIKE HER!
WHAA-
CHAK!
!!
NO!

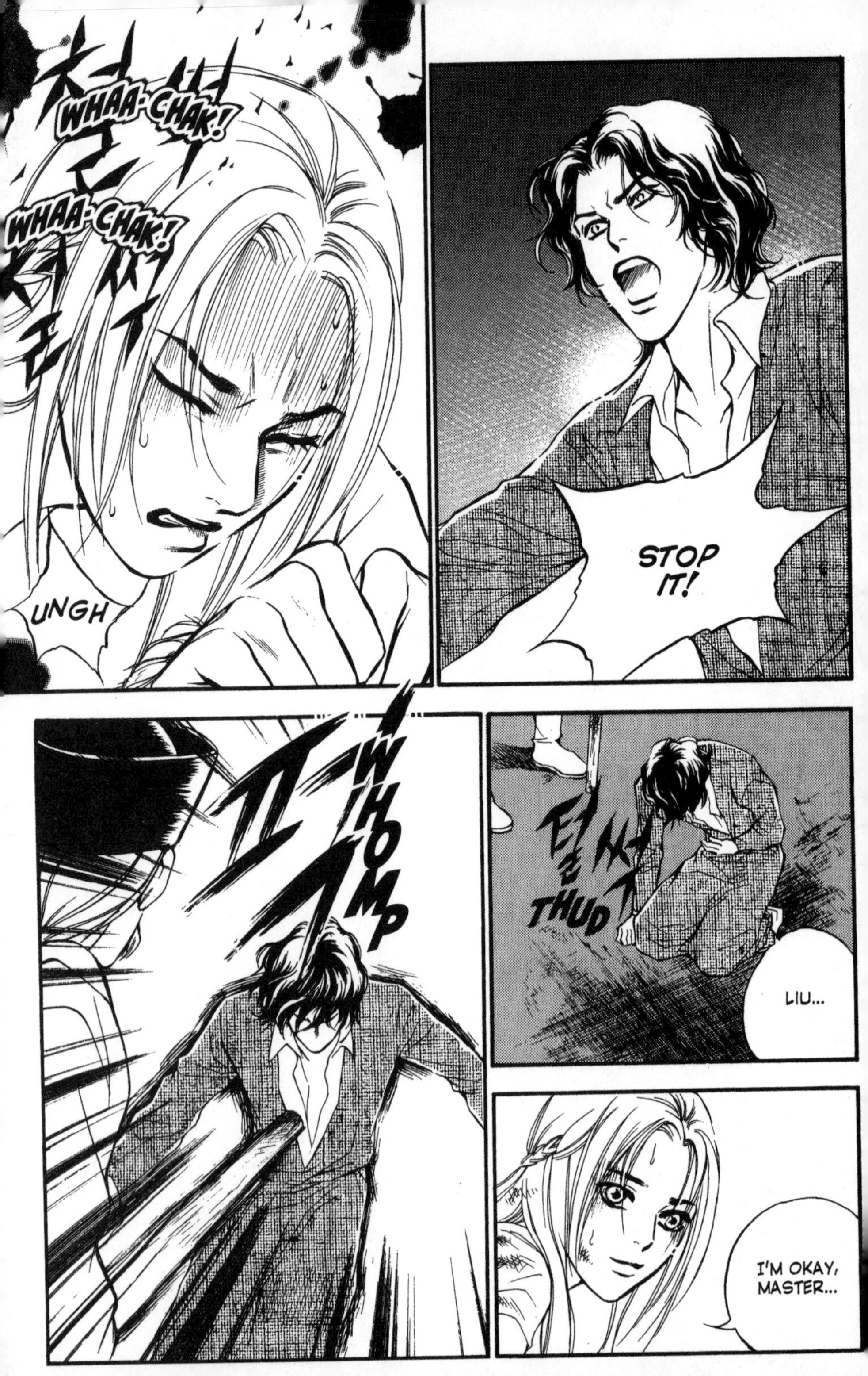

WHAA-CHAK!
WHAA-CHAK!
UNGH
STOP IT!
WHOMP
THUD
LIU...
I'M OKAY, MASTER...

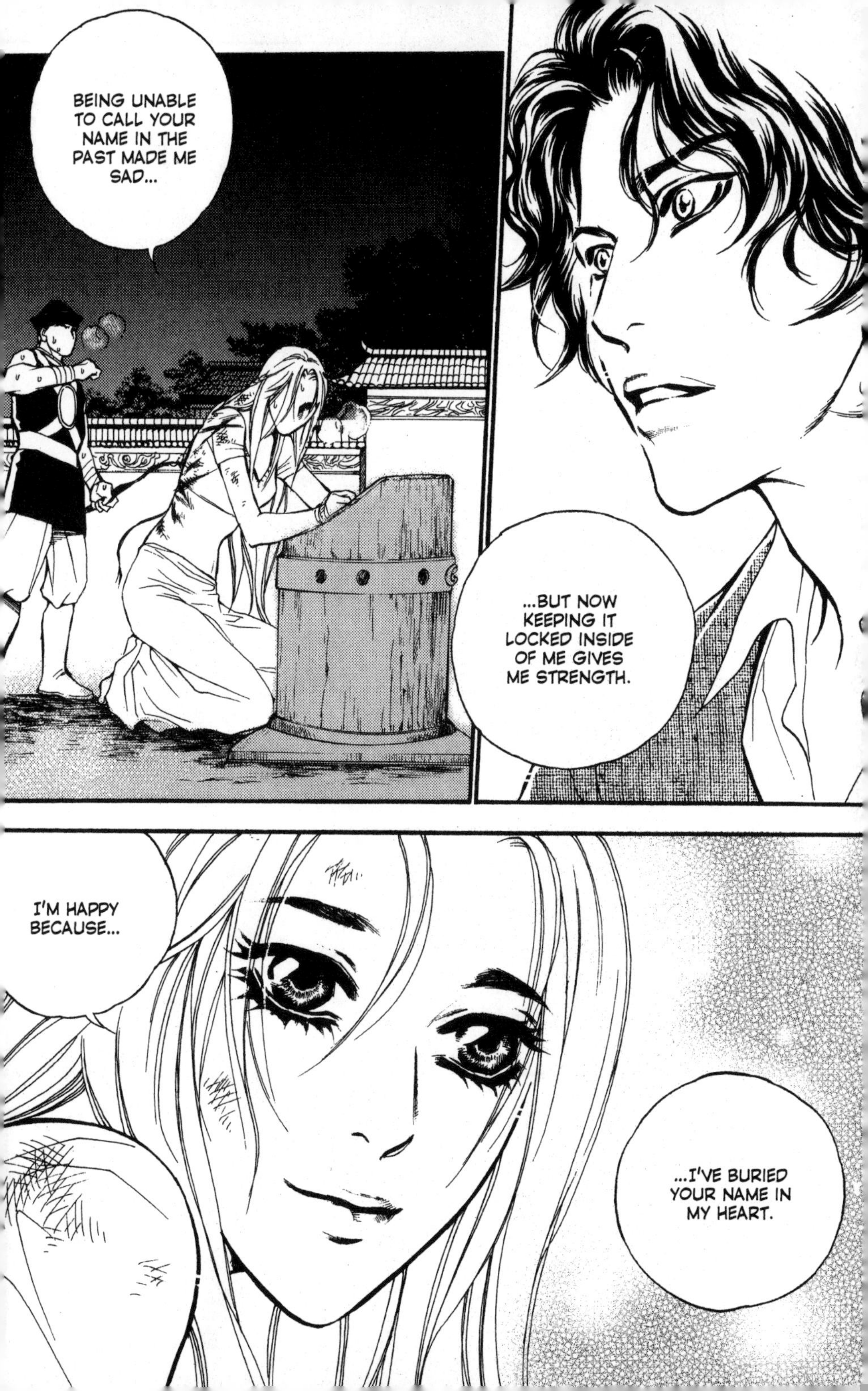
BEING UNABLE TO CALL YOUR NAME IN THE PAST MADE ME SAD...
...BUT NOW KEEPING IT LOCKED INSIDE OF ME GIVES ME STRENGTH.
I'M HAPPY BECAUSE...
...I'VE BURIED YOUR NAME IN MY HEART.

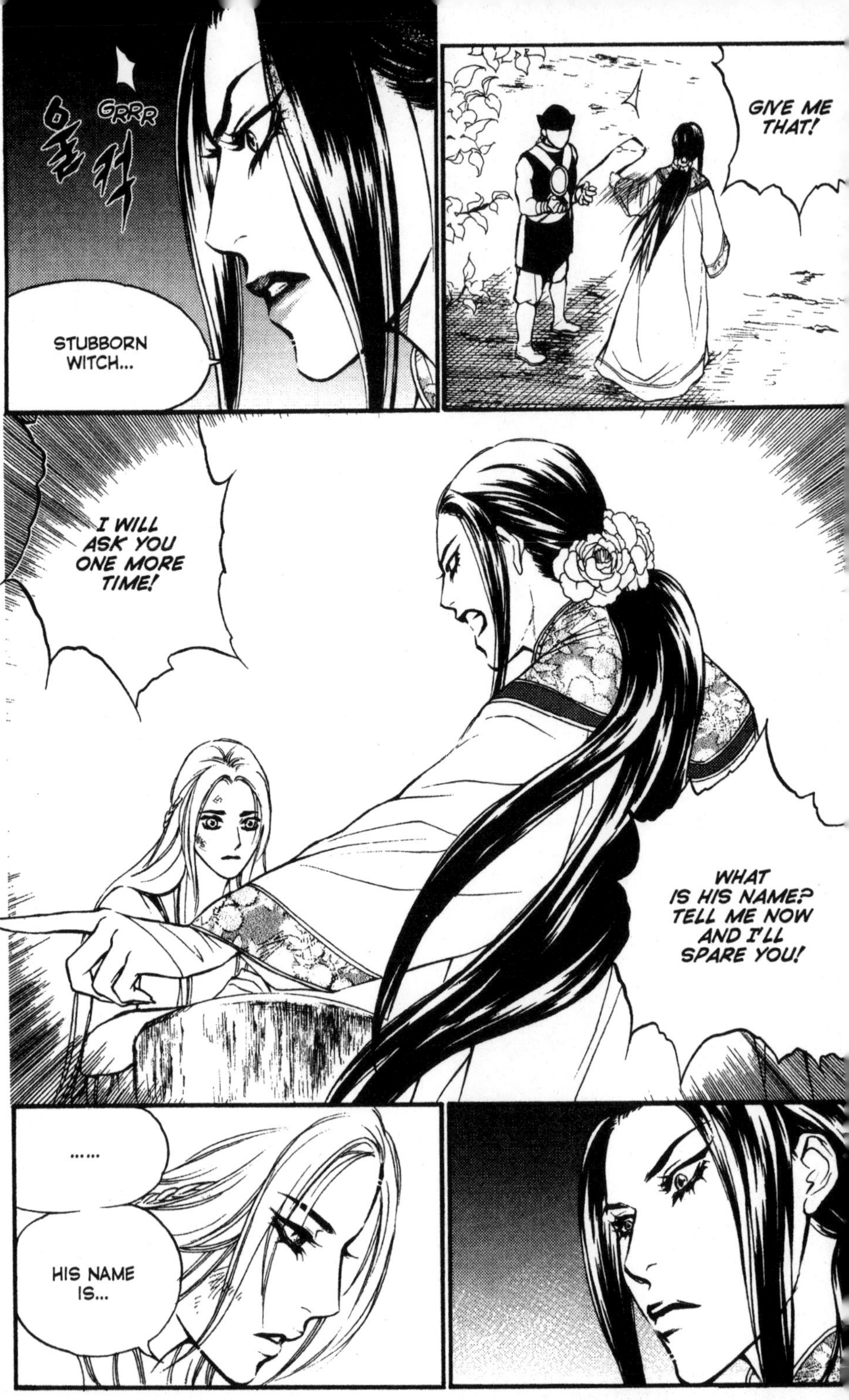
GRRR
울컥
STUBBORN WITCH...
GIVE ME THAT!
I WILL ASK YOU ONE MORE TIME!
WHAT IS HIS NAME? TELL ME NOW AND I'LL SPARE YOU!
......
HIS NAME IS...

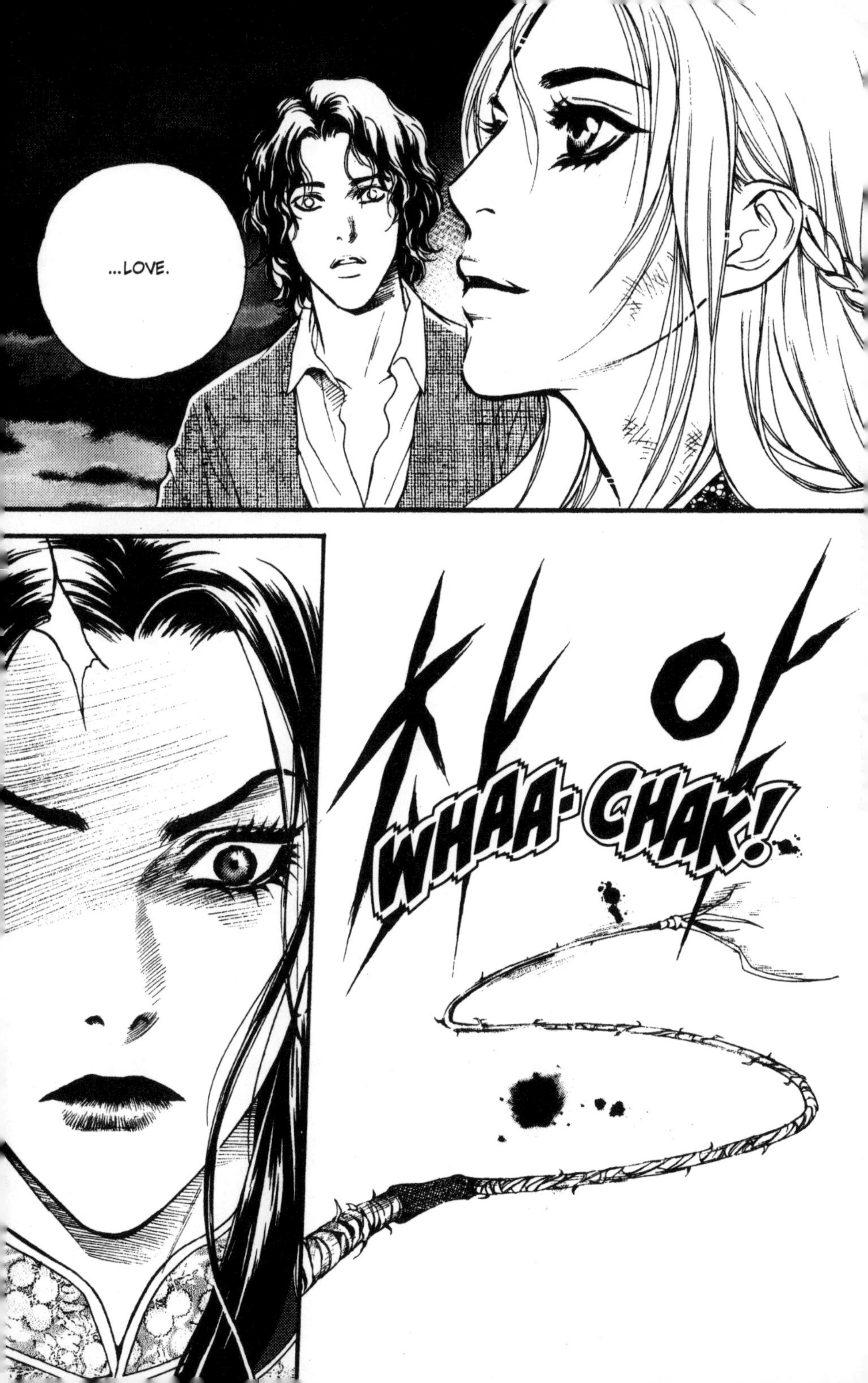
...LOVE.
WHAA-CHAK!

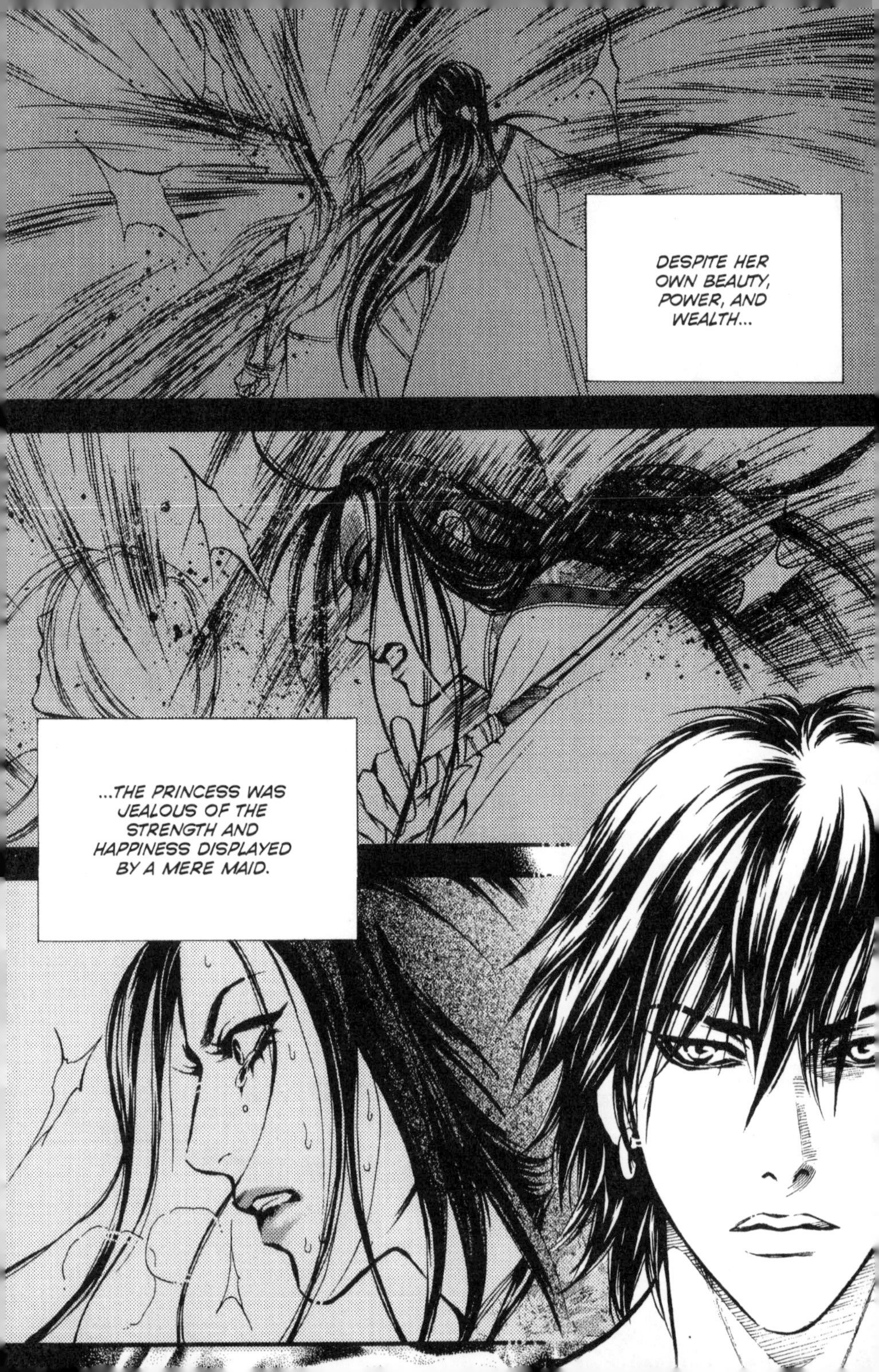
DESPITE HER OWN BEAUTY, POWER, AND WEALTH...
...THE PRINCESS WAS JEALOUS OF THE STRENGTH AND HAPPINESS DISPLAYED BY A MERE MAID.

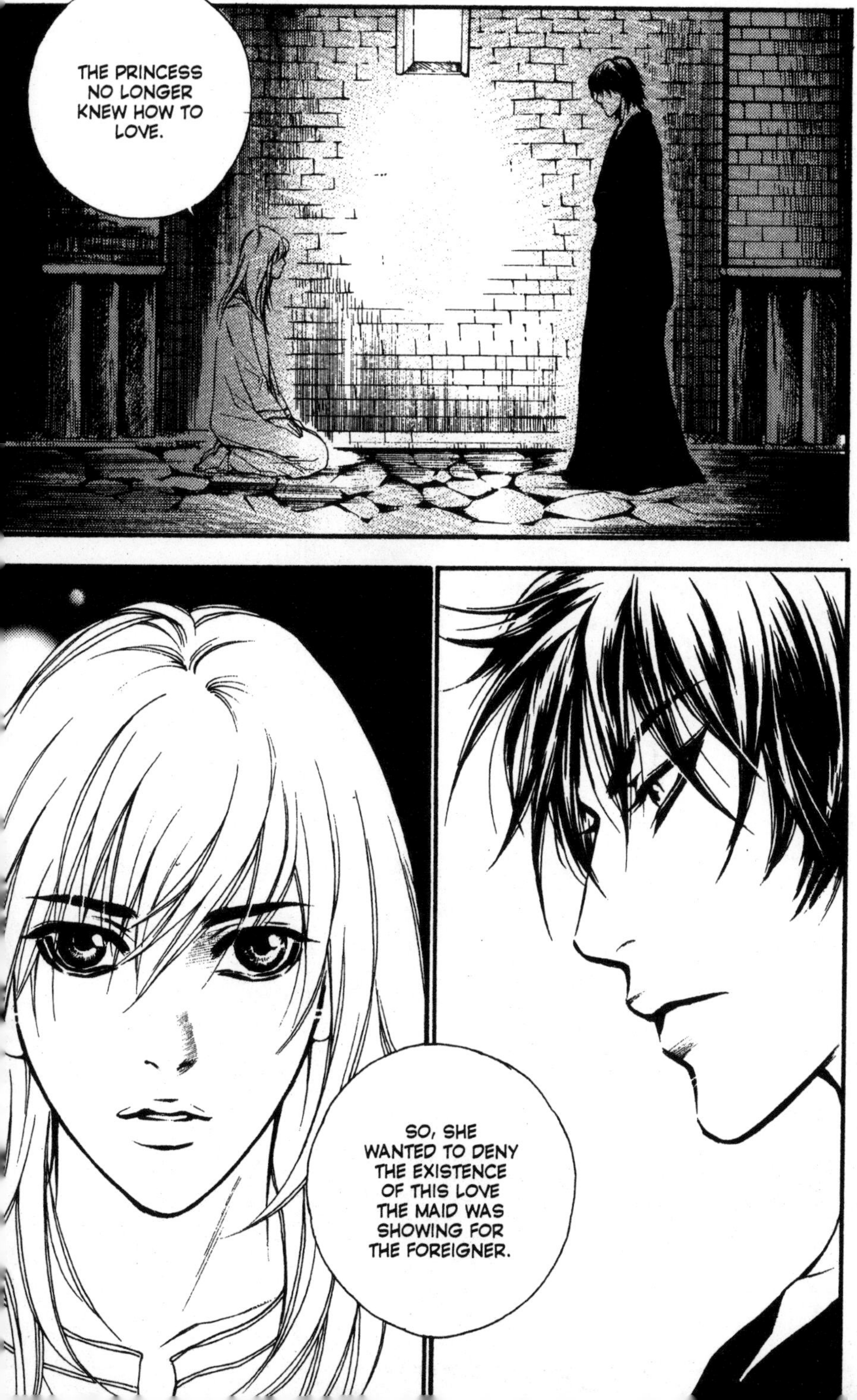
THE PRINCESS NO LONGER KNEW HOW TO LOVE.
SO, SHE WANTED TO DENY THE EXISTENCE OF THIS LOVE THE MAID WAS SHOWING FOR THE FOREIGNER.

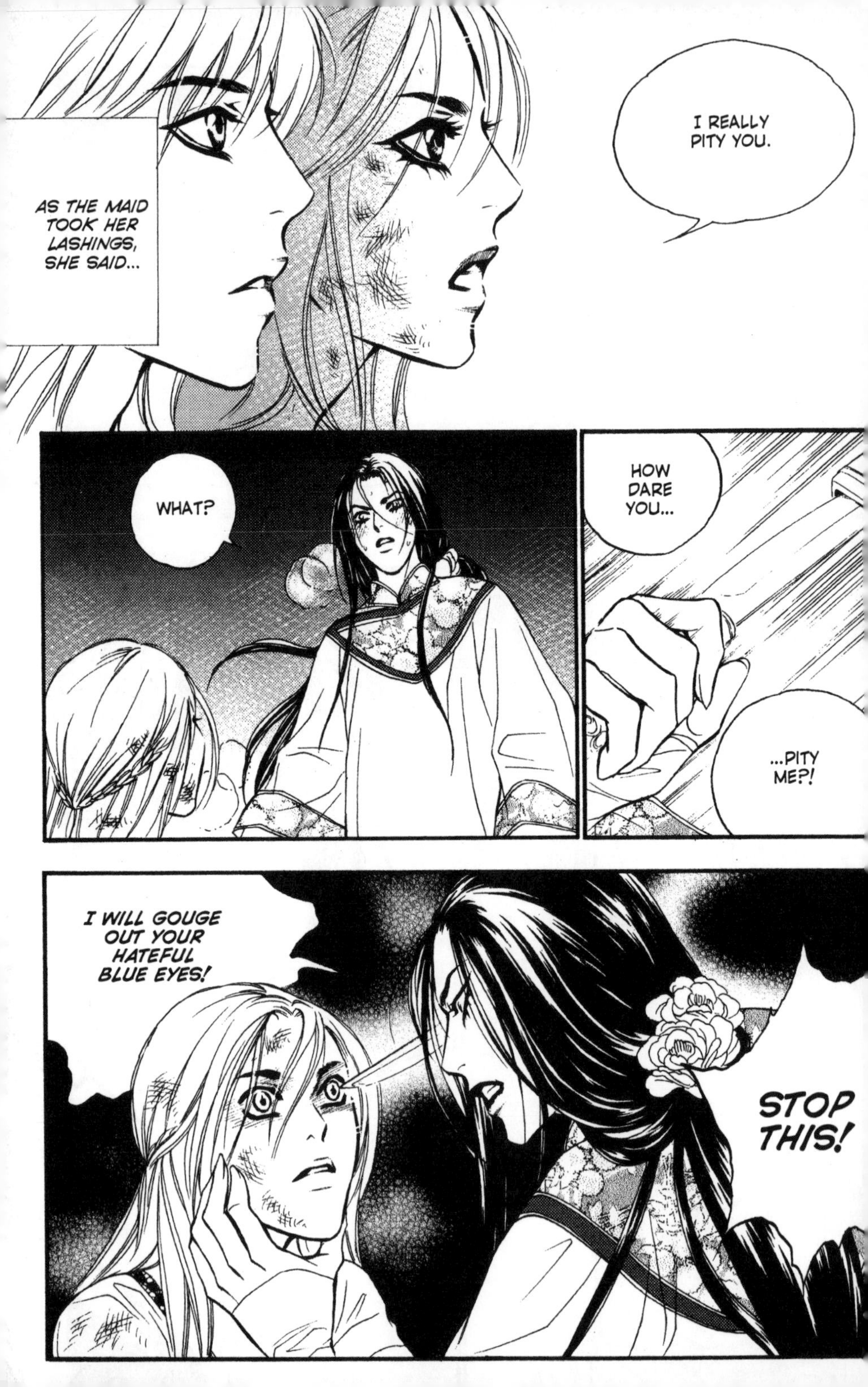
AS THE MAID TOOK HER LASHINGS, SHE SAID...
I REALLY PITY YOU.
WHAT?
HOW DARE YOU...
...PITY ME?!
I WILL GOUGE OUT YOUR HATEFUL BLUE EYES!
STOP THIS!

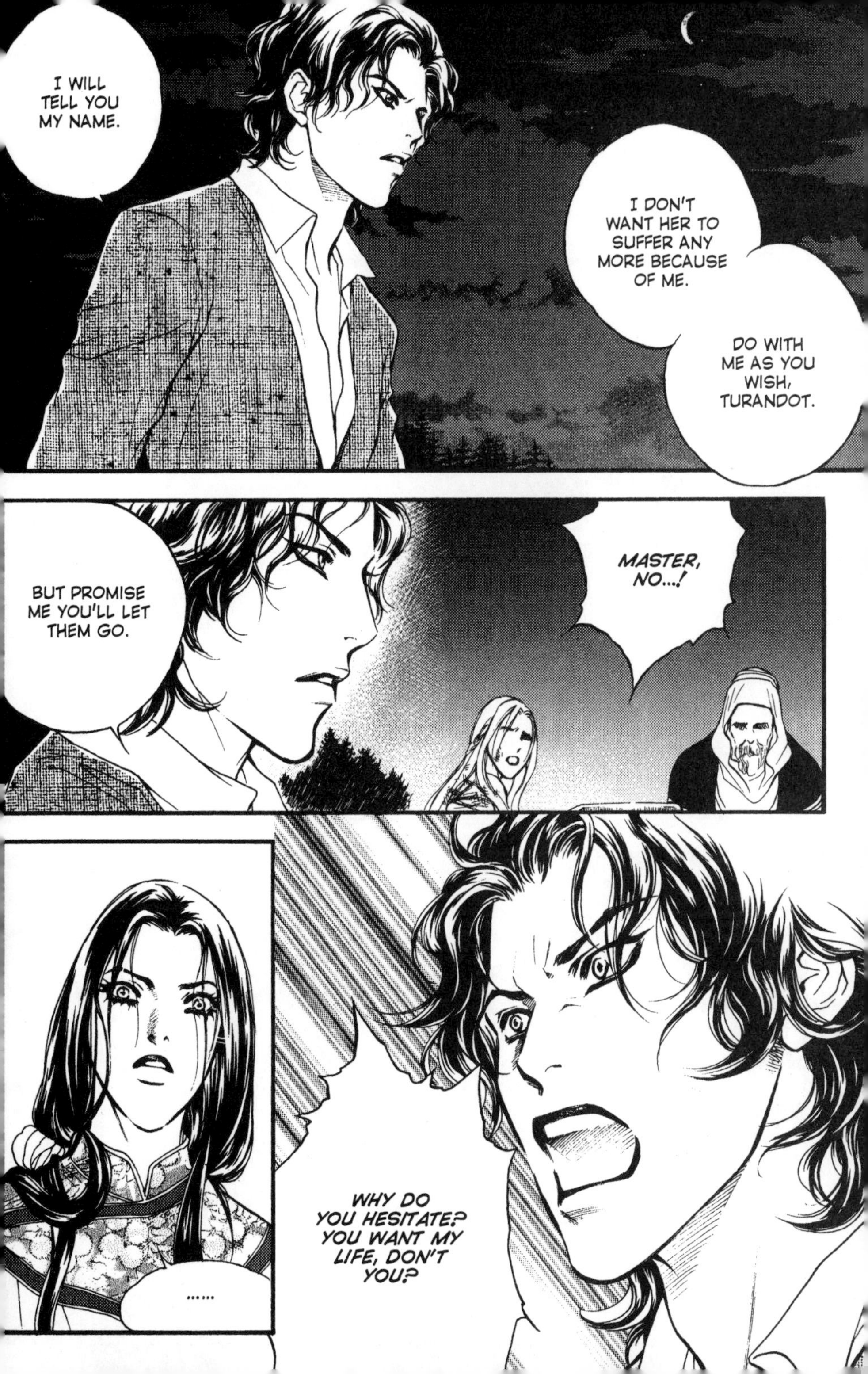
I WILL TELL YOU MY NAME.
I DON'T WANT HER TO SUFFER ANY MORE BECAUSE OF ME.
DO WITH ME AS YOU WISH, TURANDOT.
BUT PROMISE ME YOU'LL LET THEM GO.
MASTER, NO...!
......
WHY DO YOU HESITATE? YOU WANT MY LIFE, DON'T YOU?

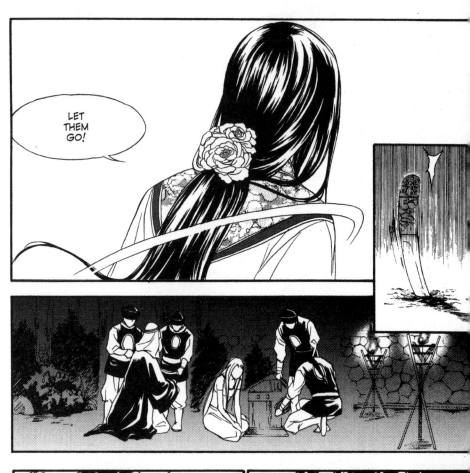

LET THEM GO!

TURANDOT...

THE NAME YOU HATE IS...

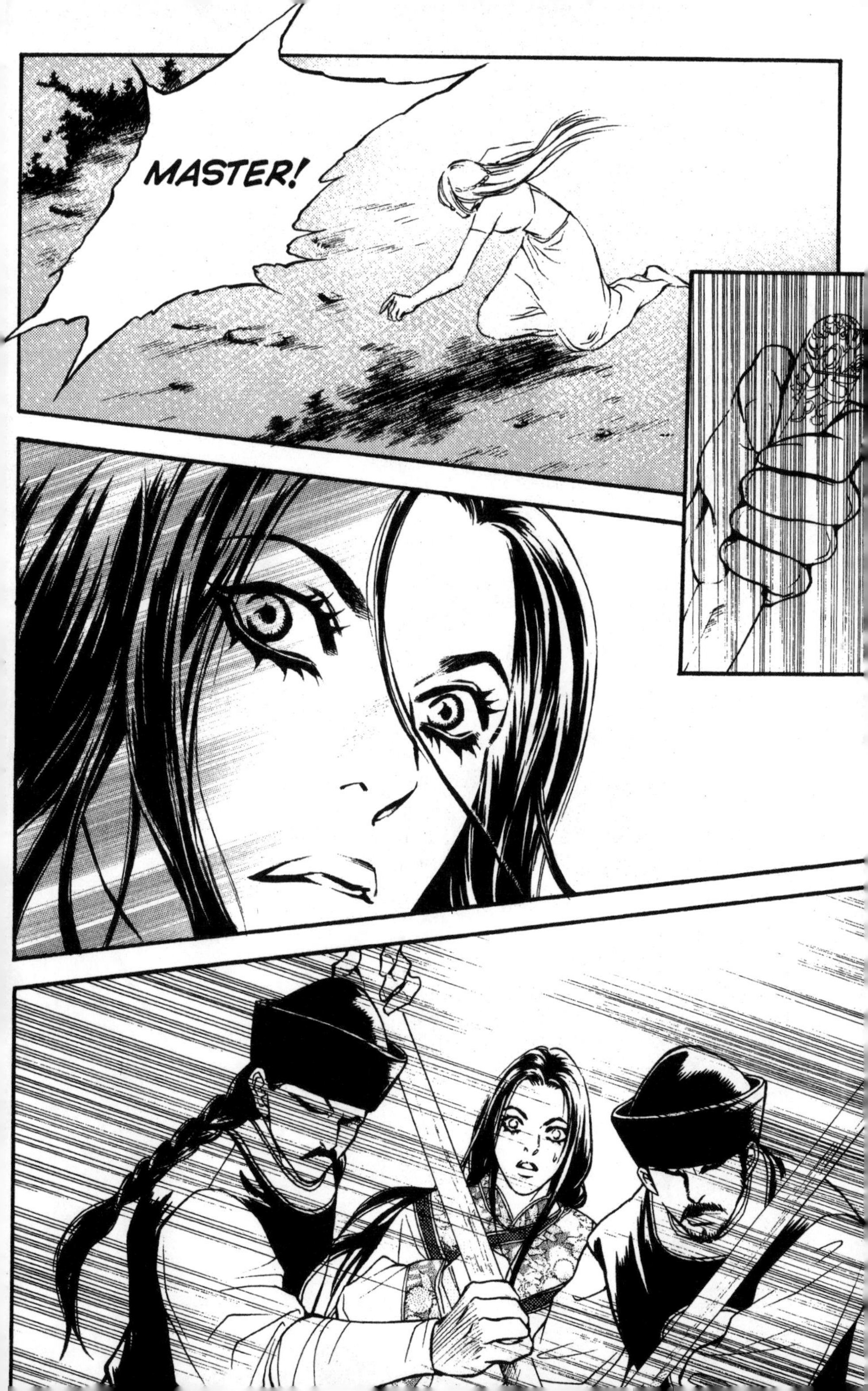
MASTER!

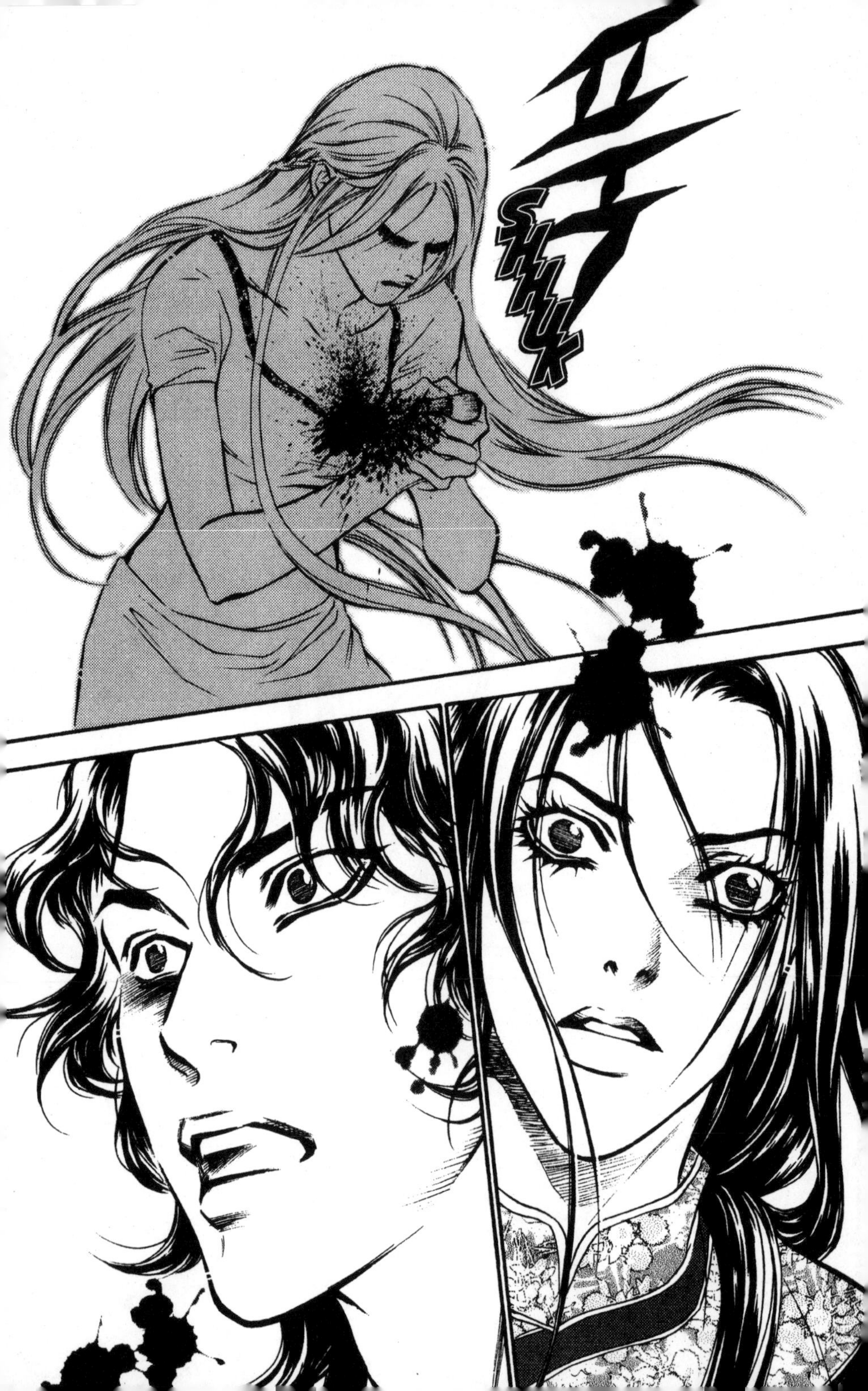
SHHUK

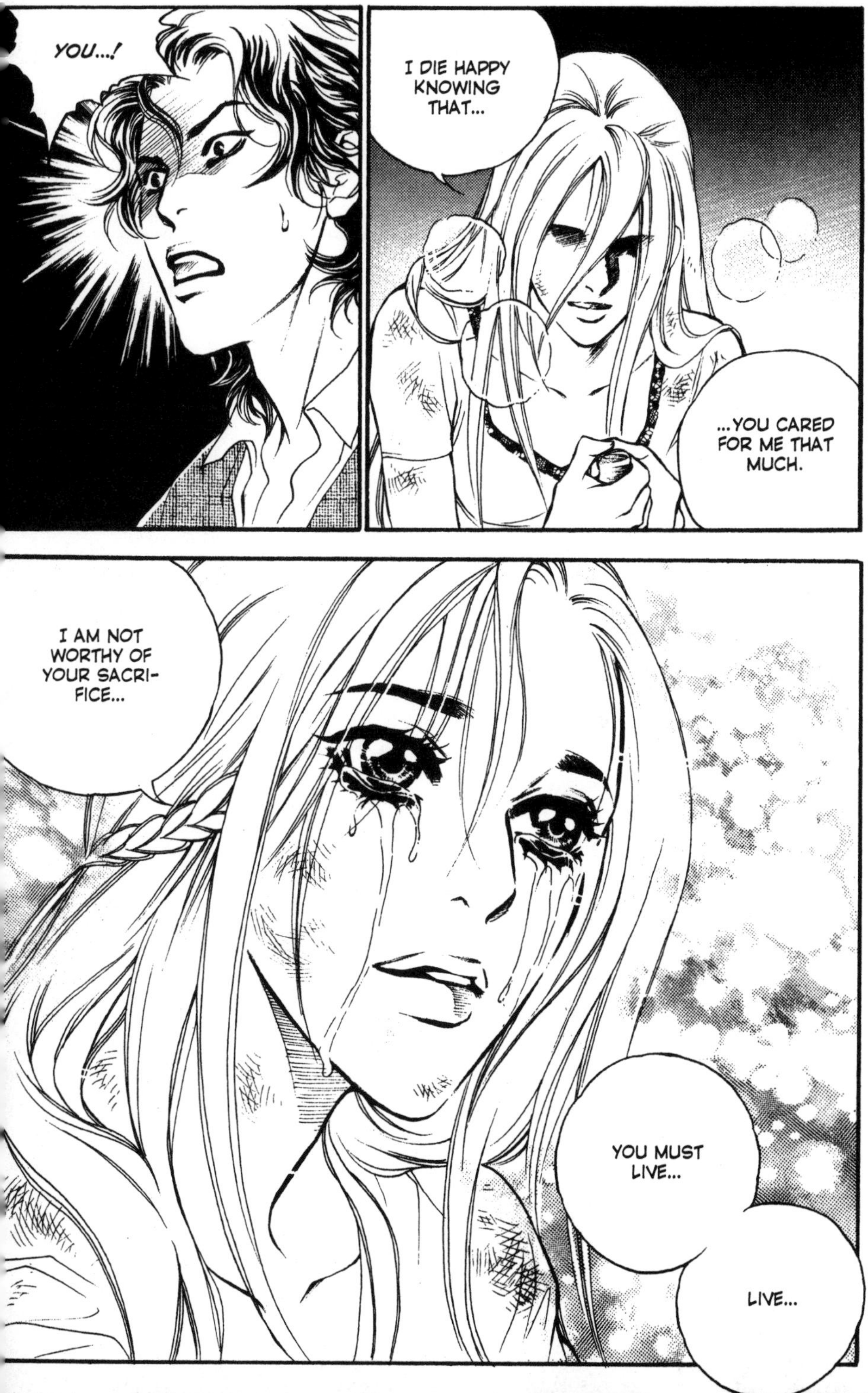
YOU...!
I DIE HAPPY KNOWING THAT...
...YOU CARED FOR ME THAT MUCH.
I AM NOT WORTHY OF YOUR SACRI-FICE...
YOU MUST LIVE...
LIVE...

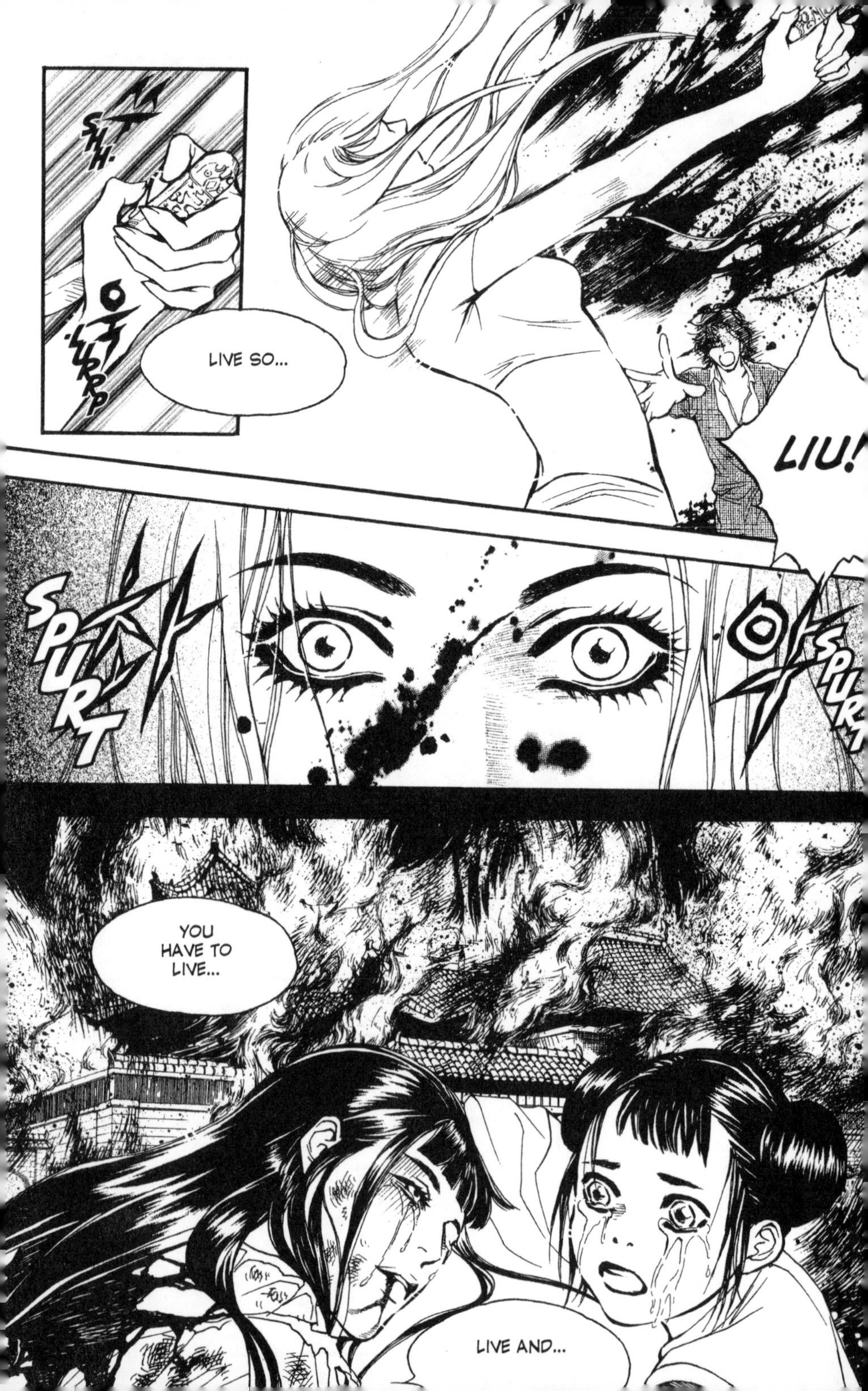
SHH.
SLURP
LIVE SO...
LIU!
SPURT
SPURT
YOU HAVE TO LIVE...
LIVE AND...

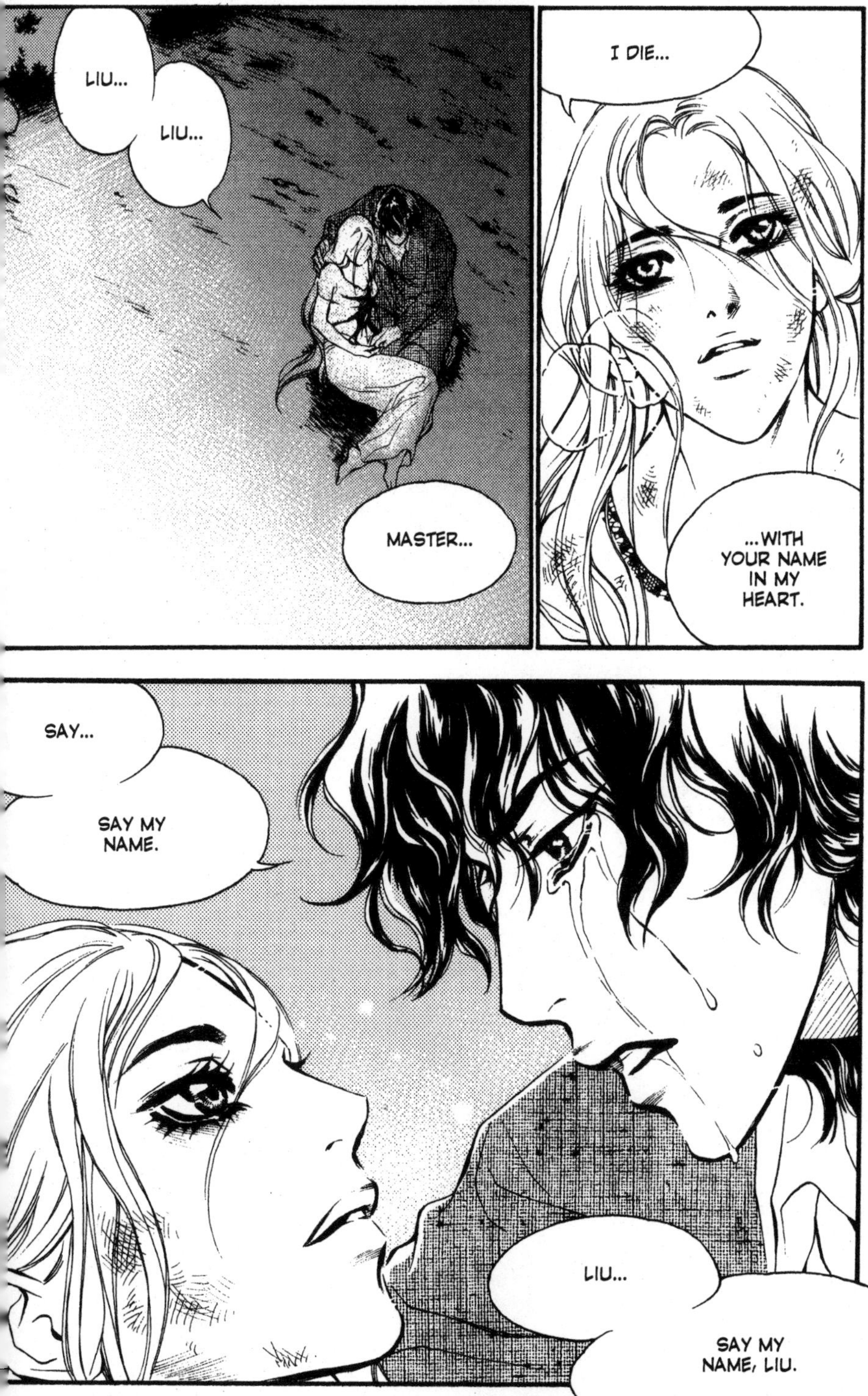
LIU...
LIU...
MASTER...
I DIE...
...WITH YOUR NAME IN MY HEART.
SAY...
SAY MY NAME.
LIU...
SAY MY NAME, LIU.

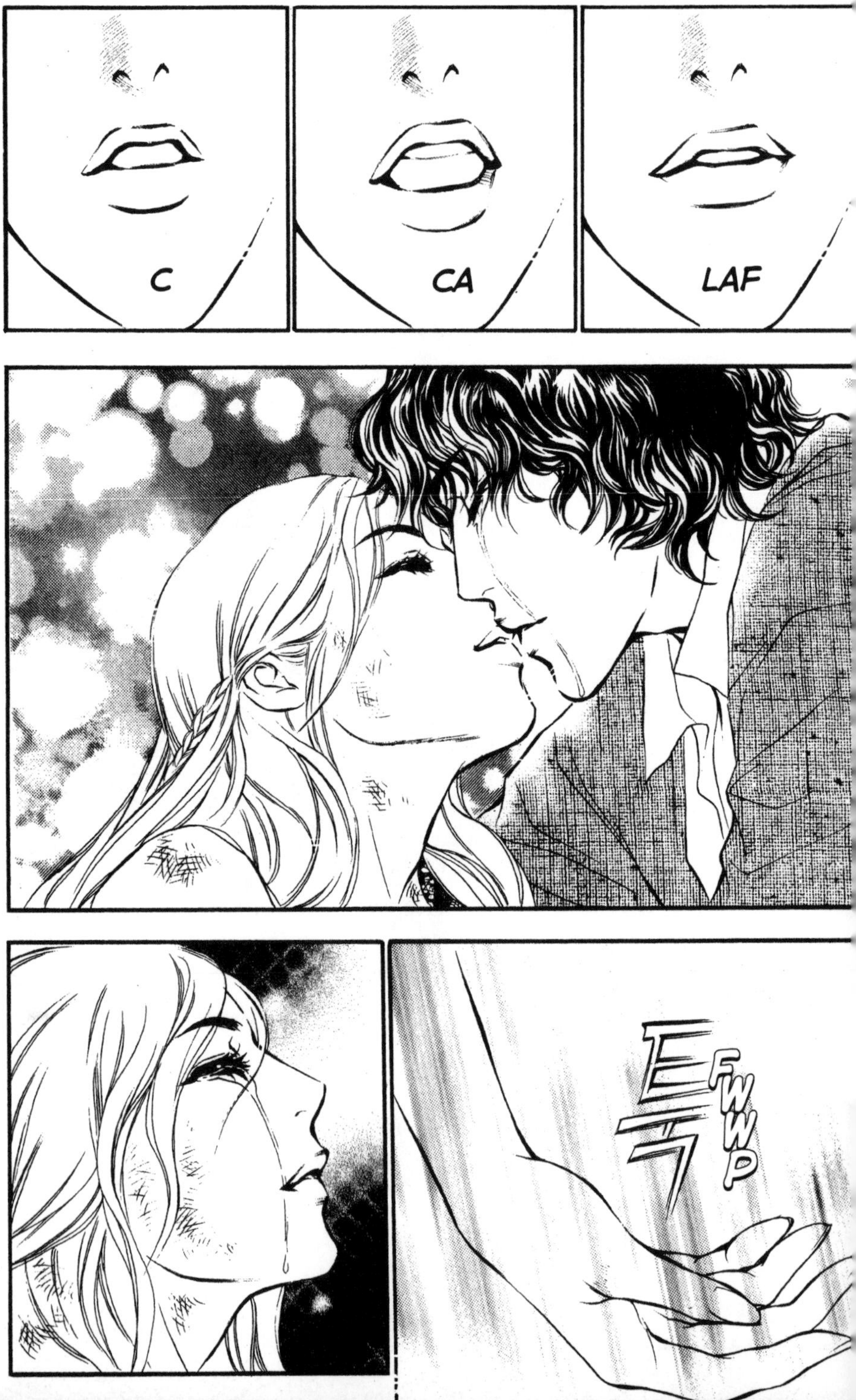
C
CA
LAF
FWWP

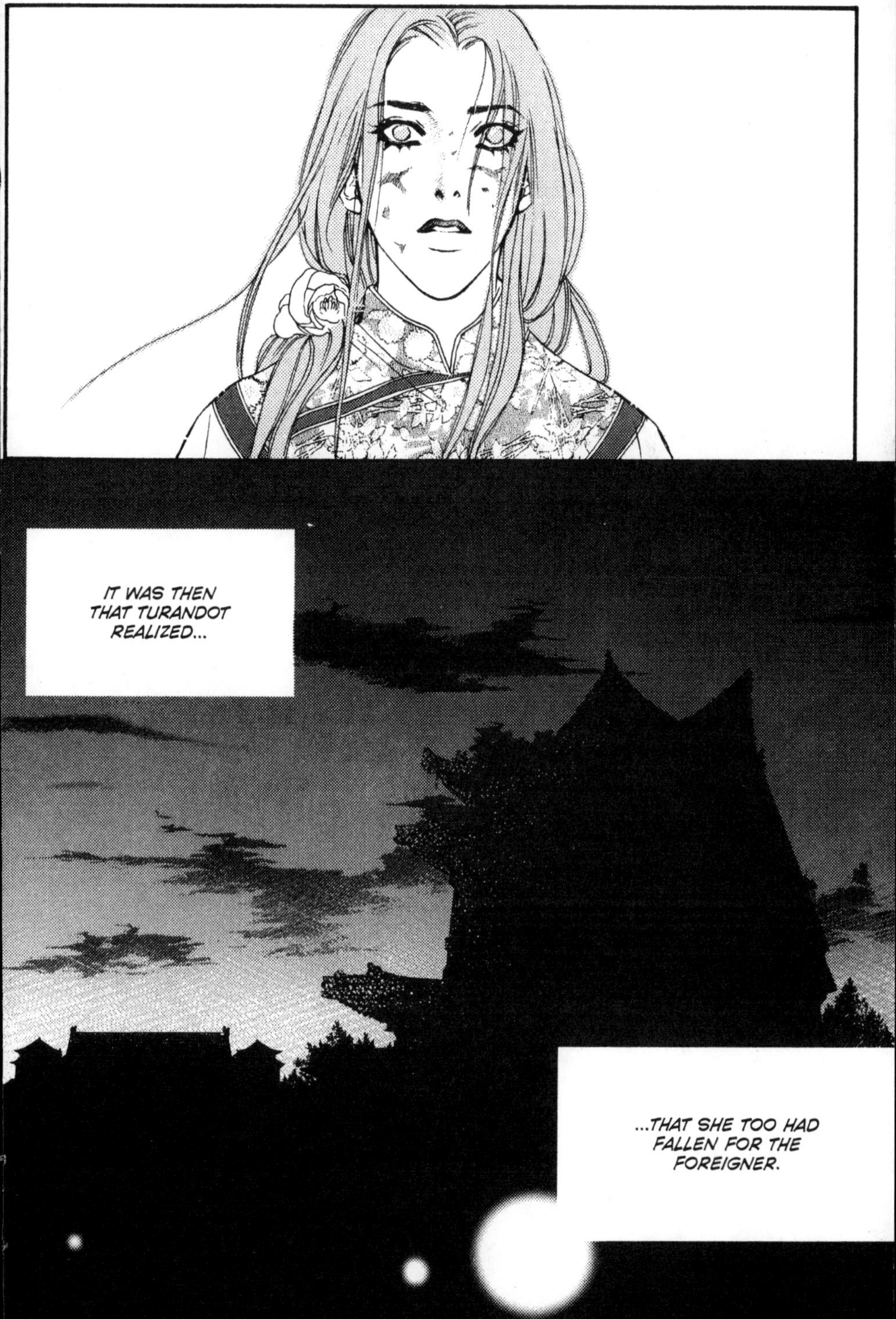
IT WAS THEN THAT TURANDOT REALIZED...
...THAT SHE TOO HAD FALLEN FOR THE FOREIGNER.

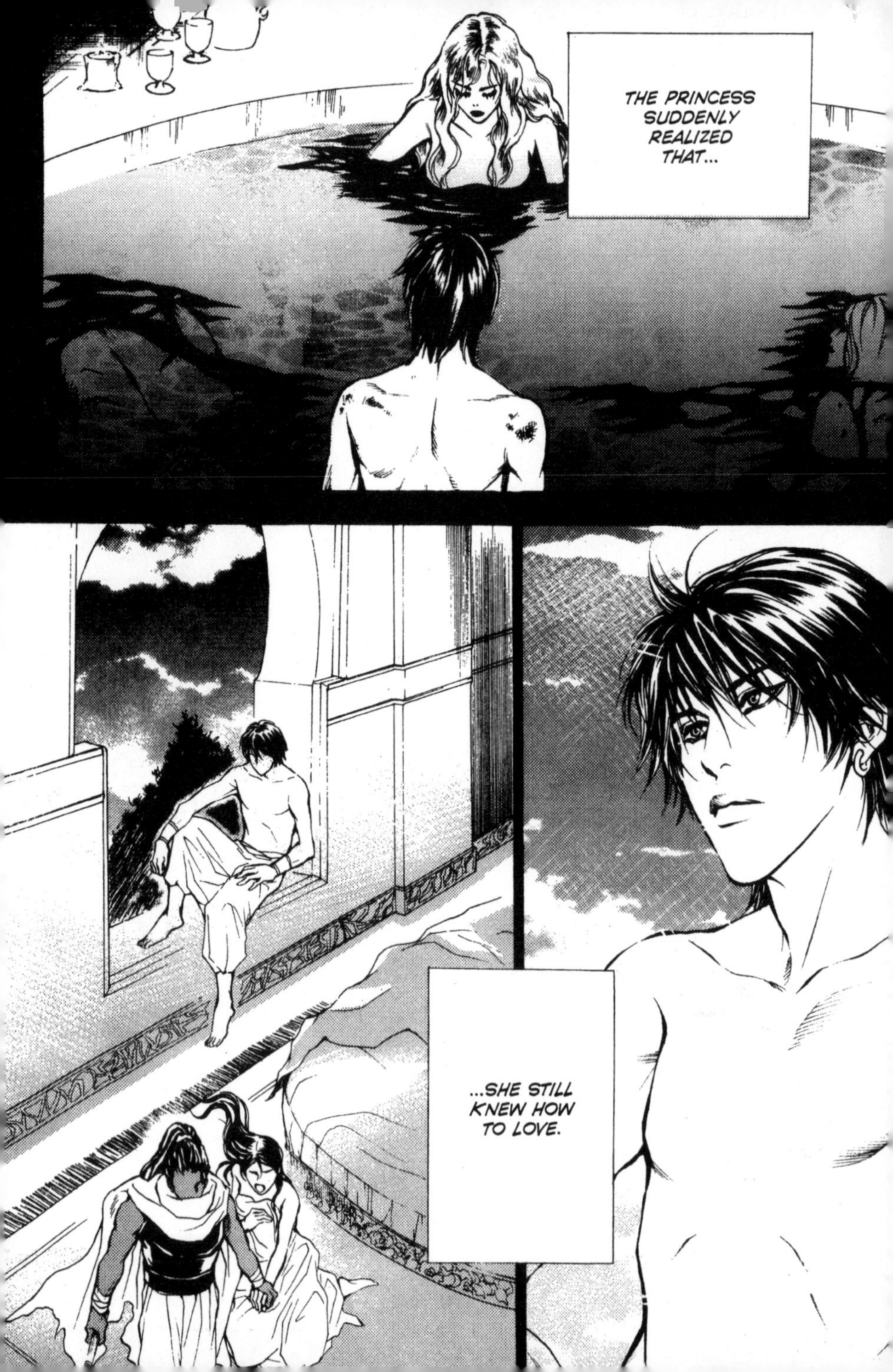
THE PRINCESS SUDDENLY REALIZED THAT...
...SHE STILL KNEW HOW TO LOVE.

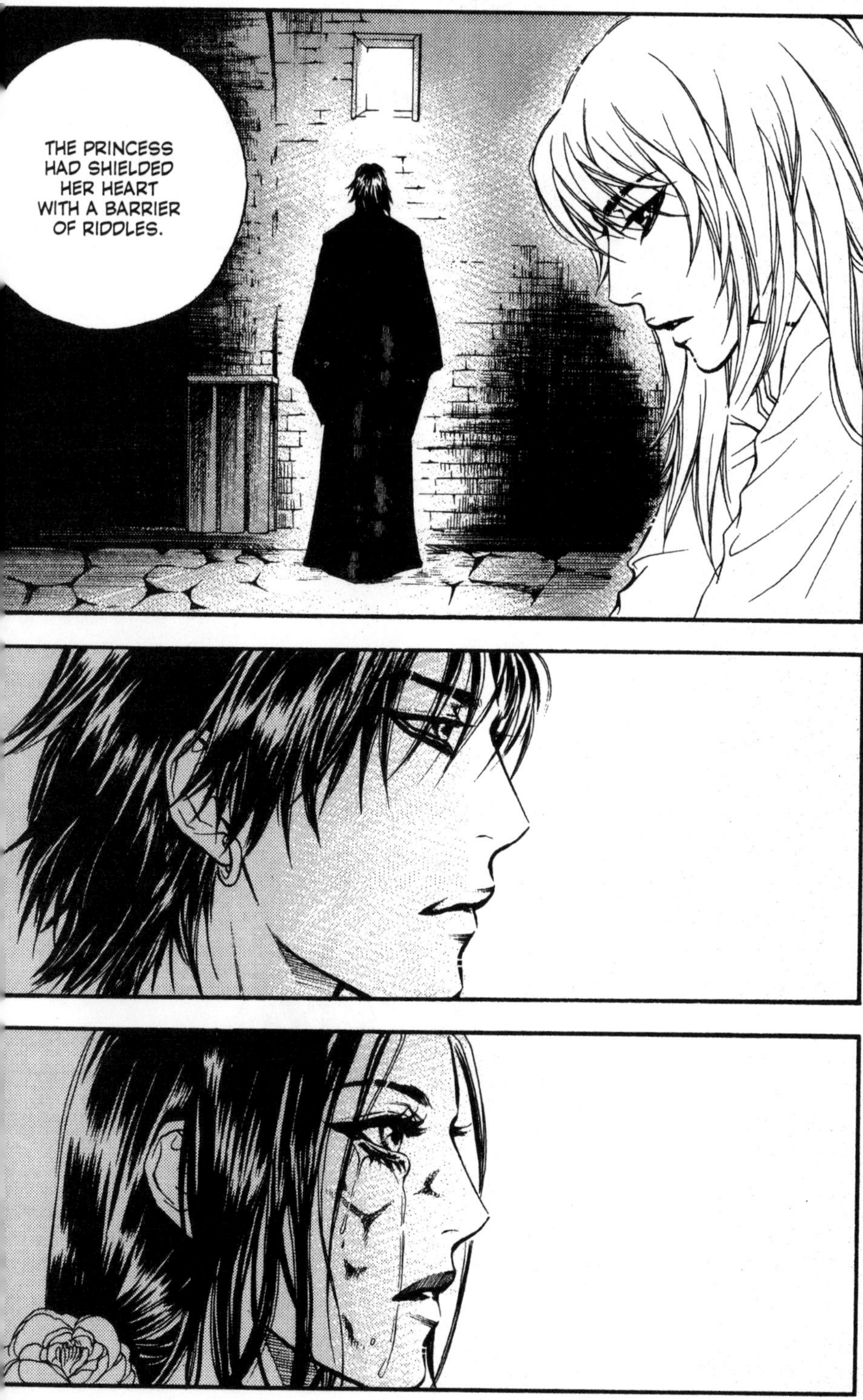
THE PRINCESS HAD SHIELDED HER HEART WITH A BARRIER OF RIDDLES.

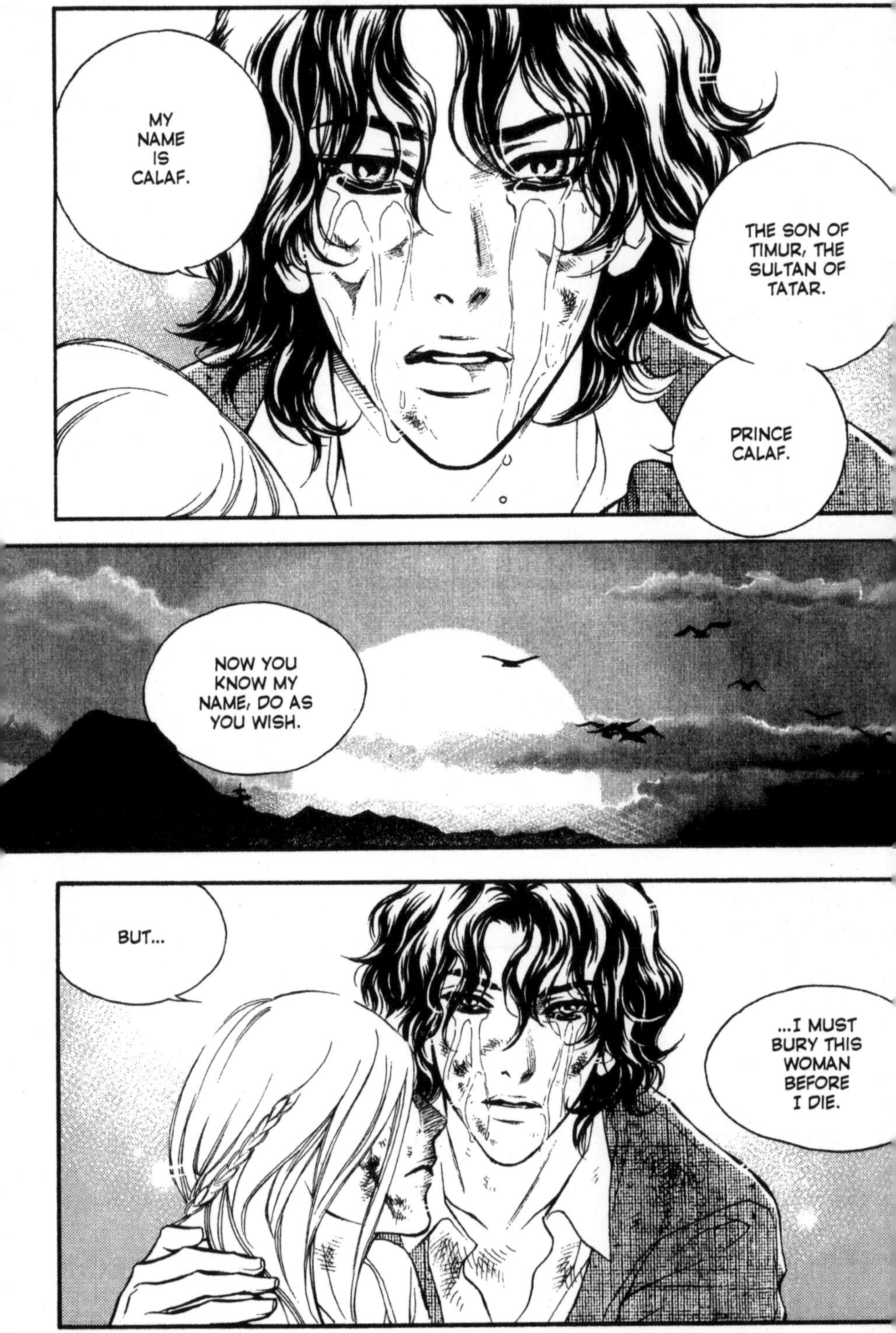
MY NAME IS CALAF.
THE SON OF TIMUR, THE SULTAN OF TATAR.
PRINCE CALAF.
NOW YOU KNOW MY NAME, DO AS YOU WISH.
BUT...
...I MUST BURY THIS WOMAN BEFORE I DIE.

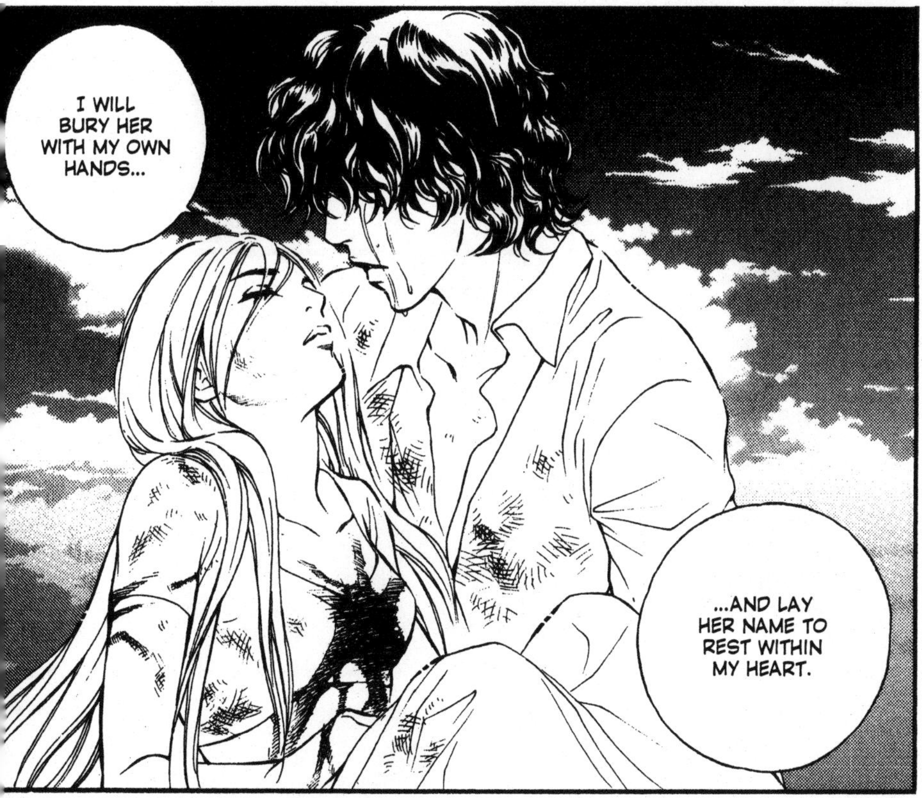
I WILL BURY HER WITH MY OWN HANDS...
...AND LAY HER NAME TO REST WITHIN MY HEART.

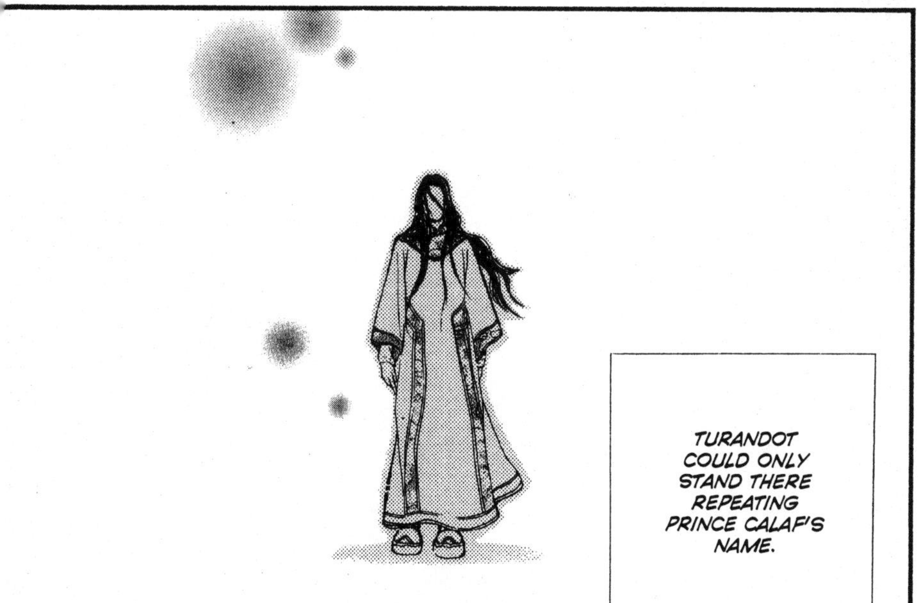
TURANDOT COULD ONLY STAND THERE REPEATING PRINCE CALAF'S NAME.

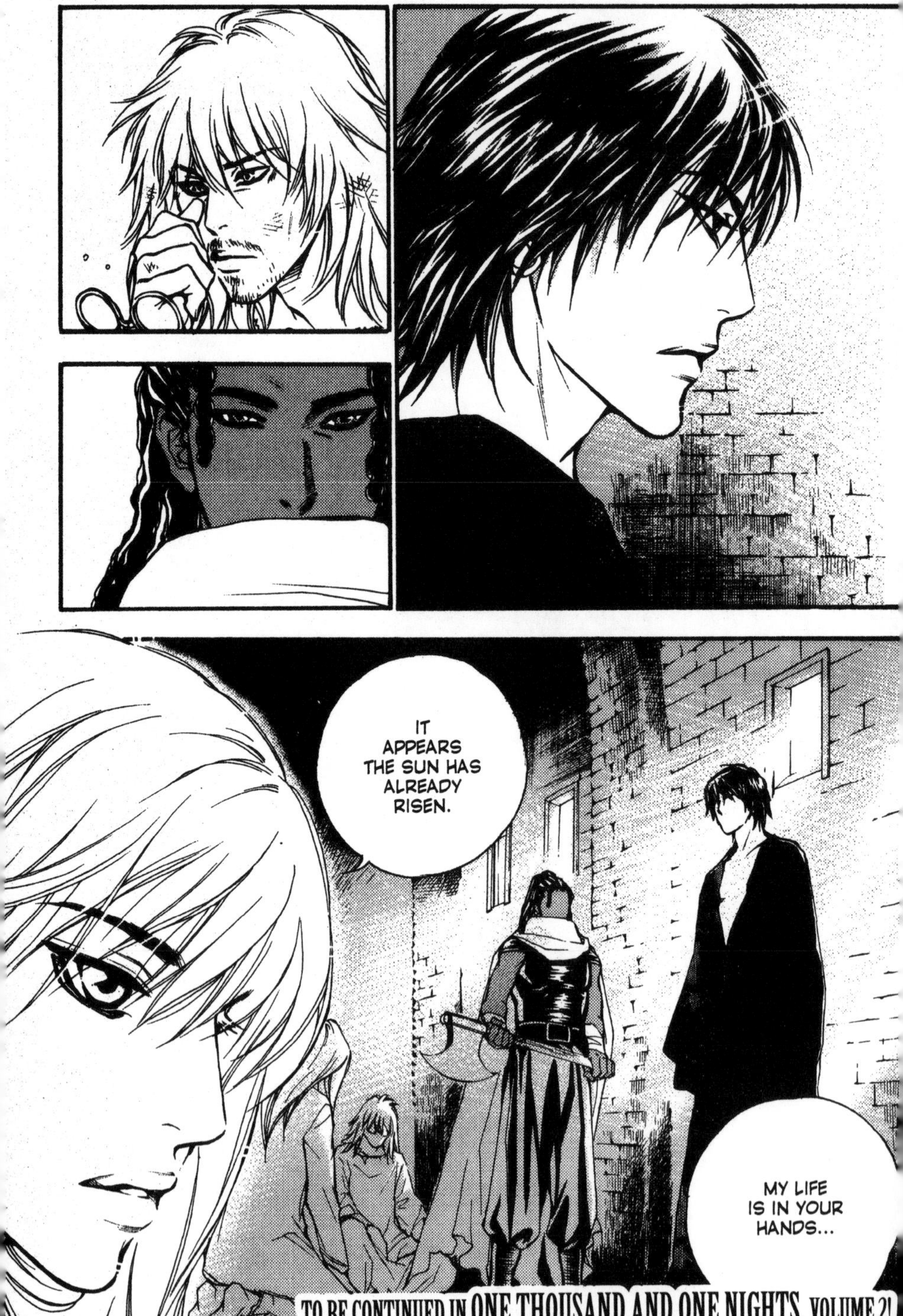
IT APPEARS THE SUN HAS ALREADY RISEN.
MY LIFE IS IN YOUR HANDS...
TO BE CONTINUED IN ONE THOUSAND AND ONE NIGHTS, VOLUME 2!

Appendix

About the Creator

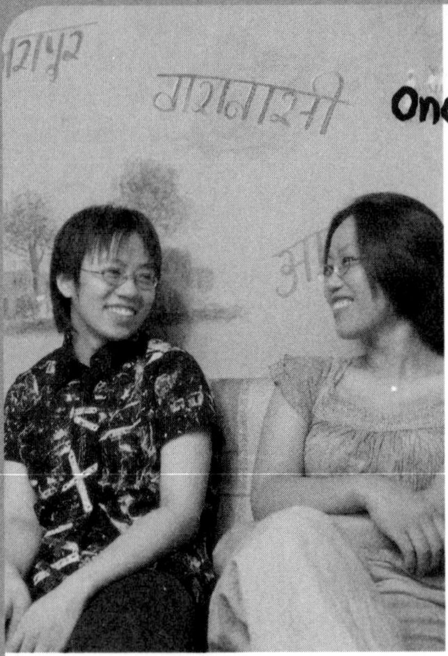

One thousand and one nights

Seung-Hee Han/ Jin-Seok Jeon

Artist : Seung-Hee Han

Birthday: June 19th (Lunar Calendar)

Blood Type: A

Since premiering in 1995 with <Kiki and Funny Joe>, Han has become one of the most popular contemporary shojo Manhwa artists. She is famous for her beautifully delicate characters and lush, gorgeous colors. <One Thousand and One Nights> is her first collaborated work.

Other major works

<Funky>, <Older Woman and Younger Man>, <Difin>, <Step>, <Vivika>, <Mong-Yoo>, <Welcome to Rio>

Writer : Jin-Seok Jeon

Birthday: July 27th

Blood Type: B

Jin-Seok Jeon launched his career in 1998 with <The Last Fantasy>, a shonen Manhwa sci-fi series. Jeon has also recently acquired a solid reputation for his skill as a meticulously subtle shojo style writer. Jeon once again successfully shifts into a shojo Manhwa style with <One Thousand and One Nights>.

Other major works

<Gun Beat>, <Last Fantasy>, <Combat Bible>, <Merlin's Magic School>

Character Introduction

One thousand and one nights

Seung-Hee Han/ Jin-Seok Jeon

A classic reborn!
Remember all the stories of the Arabian nights? The beautiful and wonderful worlds told throughout one thousand and one nights... now, this classic is born again in the totally different, even more charming story of 〈One thousand and one nights〉! Let's take a look at the characters who keep us up for one thousand and one nights enthralled with all their stories.

Sultan Shahryar

The prince who fell in love with his father's mistress, Fatima. After marrying Fatima, he gets his heart broken so severely, that he starts to summon and behead a girl every night. He was once a hero, but has become a mere tyrant, even imprisoning his best friend, Jafar.

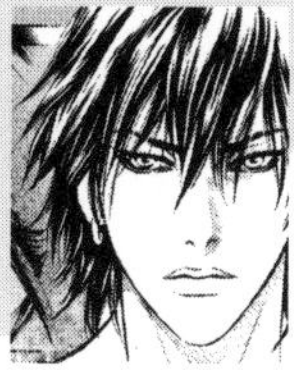

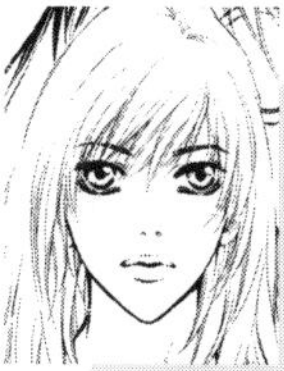

Sehara

Brother of Dunya. To save the life of his sister, he disguises himself as a girl and goes to meet the Sultan instead of his sister. He studies hard, and has translated many books as well. Due to this great knowledge he has, he starts telling amazing stories to the Sultan.

Fatima

One of the most beautiful girls of the country. She was once a mistress of Sultan's father, but after he passes away, becomes the wife of Sultan. But she betrays Sultan, for no apparent reason, at least not one she's willing to share.

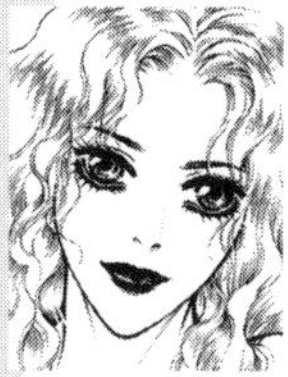

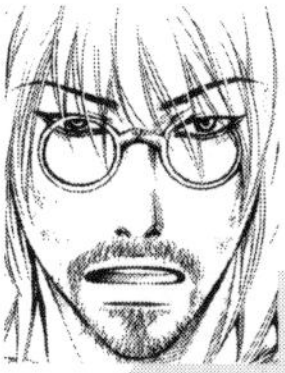

Jafar

Sultan's best friend. He is from a noble family, and was the only one who could stand up to the Sultan and tell him what's right and wrong. Due to his straightforward acts, he gets imprisoned by Sultan and meets Sehara there.

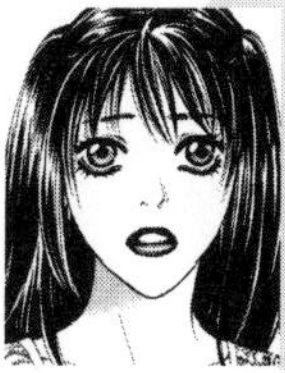

Dunya

Younger sister of Sehara. She is in love with Sehara, and asks him to marry her when she is summoned by the Sultan.

Getting Personal :
Interview with the Creators

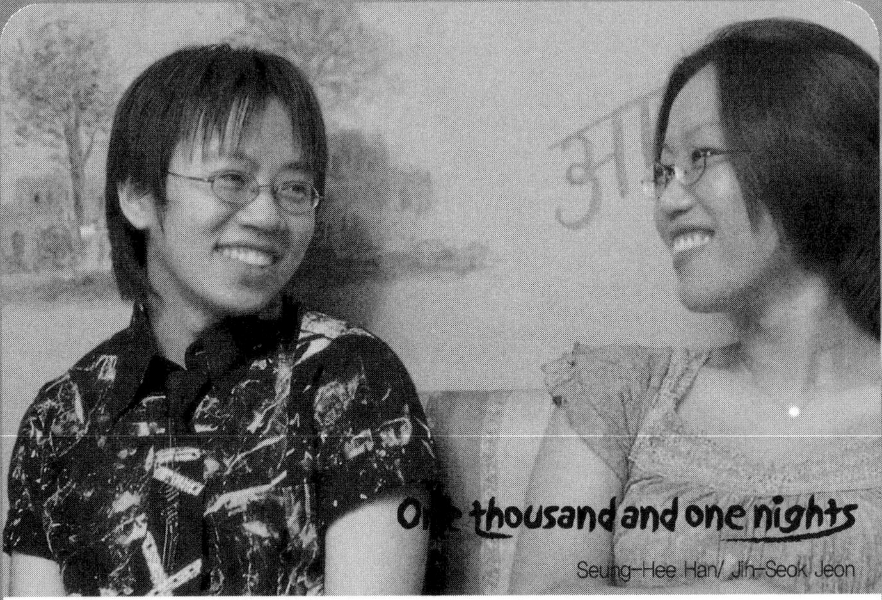

One thousand and one nights
Seung-Hee Han/ Jin-Seok Jeon

Who says blind dates don't work?
Meet Seung-Hee Han and Jin-Seok Jeon!

Most Korean manhwa are created by one person, especially the romances. And most collaborations are between people who are friends, which helps the symbiotic nature of a creative collaboration. However, the editors of Wink Magazine did something different with <One Thousand and One Nights>. They brought artist Seung-Hee Han and writer Jin-Seok Jeon together for a kind of comic creators "blind date." The two manhwa creators had never even met let alone collaborated before. This is the story of how they got together...

Wink: Hello! You guys look like a couple. How did you meet?

Seung-Hee Han: It's funny that the one who introduced us to each other is asking that question. Remember when you said you had a writer that you wanted me to work with?

Jin-Seok Jeon: Yeah! You told me that you wanted me to create a new version of "1001 Arabian Nights" without telling me who would draw it.

W: Yes, I did. And you guys said yes to the project right away. What did you think about doing this project?

Jeon: I was a Wink kid. I sent artwork to the magazine hoping to make a dream come true. When I got offered this project, I was like "Finally." This wasn't my first comic book but it made me want to be in a "new writer" frame of mind.

Han: I liked that this comic book would be exotic. I had never worked with another writer but I thought this project would be a positive experience.

W: Both of you agreed to this project without knowing each other but didn't you have any reservations?

Han: Even if I did, how am I supposed to say? (Laughs) I guess I thought he wouldn't be familiar with romantic manhwa because he worked on boys' comic books.

Jeon: When I found out that the artist was Seung-Hee Han, I cheered "Hooray." Even if I wasn't the best writer for this book, she was the best artist for ‹One Thousand and One Nights›.

W: Wink readers are not familiar with Jin-Seok Jeon because you did not work with us previously. So tell us about yourself.

Jeon: When I was a senior in high school, I got an offer to write a short story for Wink. That fell through and I thought that I'd never work as a writer. I didn't get another offer for a long time. (Laughs) So, I majored in engineering and led a normal life. While I was taking a break from school, a friend and I pitched a comic to "Anitech" magazine. And that's how I started my career. I told my parents and they supported me. I've been working on different comic books ever since and I sometimes work on children's books as well.

W: What were your thoughts about the original "Arabian Nights" before you worked on this project?

Han: I don't know how to say this... it was like a frame inside another frame... the storyline was quiet complicated. And I couldn't understand some of characters either. Anyway, I was attracted to the fact that ‹One Thousand and One Nights› could be interpreted differently from the original.

Jeon: Ha-ha-ha! She is totally right. The original stories were very conservative and there was no equality between men and women. I felt that they were just stories that a woman made up to survive. But there were some interesting stories for sure.

W: Wink readers love the twists in ‹One Thousand and One Nights›. What is the difference between the comic and the original stories? Many readers are curious about this.

Han: Some people say that every story's already been told, and if artists can't create new stories then they have no reason to exist. It's fun to create new characters. In my opinion, this is the real attraction of comic books.

Jeon: <One Thousand and One Nights> is not a comic book that just copies the original. It is like a new interpretation of the original. A story changes as time goes by. Our comic book will be very modern. We will talk about subjects people consider taboo such as a love between members of the same sex or extramarital affairs. But the point is that stories help to heal.

W: What stories will Sehara tell readers?

Jeon: There will be some well-known stories as well as some original stories. Stories won't be limited to the Arabian ones and they will be stories from all over the world. And the timeline will not

be limited as well.

W: The project is only beginning so you haven't worked together for long, but tell me how you feel about each other?

Han: Jin-Seok Jeon is energetic and enthusiastic. I am thankful that his energy makes me upbeat.

Jeon: Seung-Hee Han's art is so beautiful! Even before working with her, I was able to relate to her characters. I trust her because she has so much experience. I learn from her and I feel humbled in her presence.

W: You probably can't give too many details, but can you tell the readers a little bit about what's coming up in <One Thousand and One Nights>?

Jeon: Sehara can't die because he is a main character, right? The story develops further as the two main characters change. Sehara's mission will be to mend Shahryar's soul.

W: This is fantasy but the original stories already exist. It can't be easy to work on this project, so can you tell me what the most difficult or the best part of it all is?

Han: I have a hard time illustrating some parts. I first have to imagine the picture before drawing it. But it's not easy because the clothes, architecture, and accessories are ancient. One of my assistants cried because of the big scale and complexity of the backgrounds. I'm so sorry...

W: This is only the beginning of your working relationship. It might be too early to tell, but how satisfied are you with each other?

Han: I'm really satisfied, and I'm not just saying that. Jin-Seok Jeon is not too controlling as a writer. He always asks my opinion and tries to discuss details with me.

Jeon: I'm satisfied too. (Laughs) We've already gotten close, but I think our working relationship will be even better as we work together more. My final goal is to be welcome in her home anytime.

W: As the writer and the artist, I guess you have different characters you like. Who is your favorite character?

Han: Do you remember the Chinese merchant, Zhao? Didn't you find his face with that missing tooth attractive? It's hard to like the main characters when you're an artist. It's hard to draw main characters. They are more troublesome than they are fun to draw. I sometimes like the extra characters because I can draw them however I like.

Jeon: My favorite character is Zafar who is Shahryar's friend. Ha-ha. I am usually attracted to characters with glasses. I like supporting characters that also help the main character. I like their warm nature.

W: Any closing words to our readers?

Han: We will work hard to make a fun comic book so keep reading.

Jeon: I wish I had the ability to read female readers' minds like Mel Gibson in the movie "What Women Want." Please tell us what you think about our comic book.

Seung-Hee Han and Jin-Seok Jeon have similar interests and they are also both generous to other people. The relationship between a writer and an artist is similar to that of a married couple. Things will sometimes be sweet and sometimes bitter. But I believe that their honeymoon with the readers will last forever. Cheers!

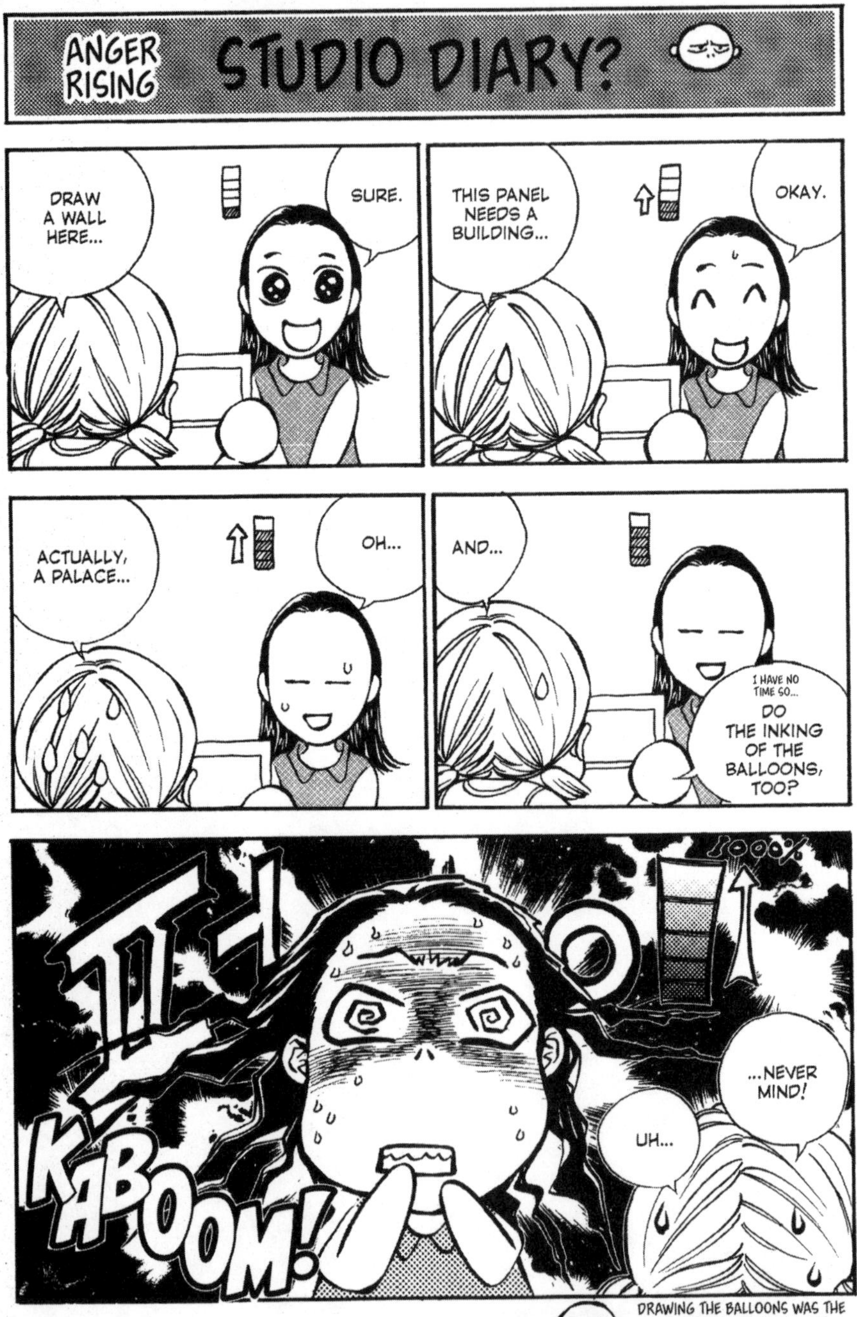
ANGER RISING
STUDIO DIARY?
DRAW A WALL HERE...
SURE.
THIS PANEL NEEDS A BUILDING...
OKAY.
ACTUALLY, A PALACE...
OH...
AND...
I HAVE NO TIME SO...
DO THE INKING OF THE BALLOONS, TOO?
KABOOM!
UH...
...NEVER MIND!
DRAWING THE BALLOONS WAS THE LAST STRAW FOR KYUNG-SUN.

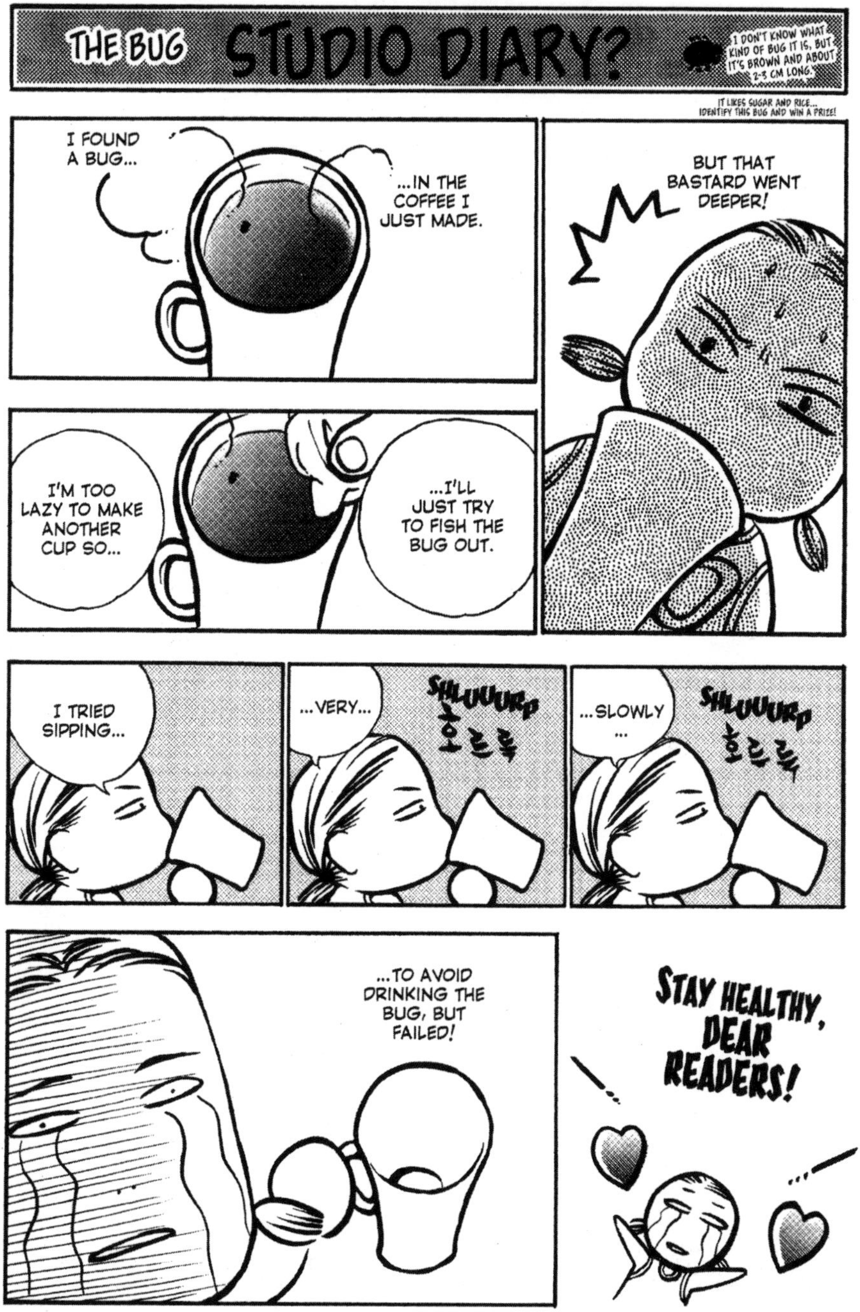
THE BUG
STUDIO DIARY?
I DON'T KNOW WHAT KIND OF BUG IT IS, BUT IT'S BROWN AND ABOUT 2-3 CM LONG.
IT LIKES SUGAR AND RICE... IDENTIFY THIS BUG AND WIN A PRIZE!
I FOUND A BUG...
...IN THE COFFEE I JUST MADE.
I'M TOO LAZY TO MAKE ANOTHER CUP SO...
...I'LL JUST TRY TO FISH THE BUG OUT.
BUT THAT BASTARD WENT DEEPER!
I TRIED SIPPING...
...VERY...
SHLUUURP
...SLOWLY...
SHLUUURP
...TO AVOID DRINKING THE BUG, BUT FAILED!
STAY HEALTHY, DEAR READERS!

Special **C**ommentary

from the writer
Jin -Seok Jeon

Baby face

Illustrated by Do—Chang

One   The Original Story and Changes

"One Thousand and One Night Stories" is also known as "1001 Arabian Nights". But did you know that these stories are not only Arabian in origin? The stories have been collected from a variety of places including India, China, Persia, and Egypt. Originally, there were only 1000 stories. The Persians were the first to collect the 1000 stories. The Arabs translated them into "One Thousand Stories" in Arabic. It then became "One Thousand and One Night Stories" when the French translated it into their language. It became "1001 Arabian Nights" with the English translation.

Why is there one more night? The answer is that a writer named A. Galland who translated the stories into French made some additions. Ironically, the most famous stories from the book are "Aladdin and the Magic Lamp" and "Alibaba and the Forty Thieves" which were both added by Galland. When I first found that out, I felt betrayed.

Stories were added and edited as time went on. Social and moral changes led to narrative changes. This editing occurred even more with oral storytelling. When I first started writing 〈One Thousand and One Nights〉 in the magazine, people said that I changed the stories too much. But no one really remembers the original stories written 1500 years ago. Readers will then decide if 〈One Thousand and One Nights〉 by yours truly and artist Seung—Hee Han will be remembered in the future.

Two   As finishing the Story about Turandot

"Turandot" is a great opera written by Puccini based on a story from "1001 Arabian Nights." "Turandot" was Puccini's last opera. Puccini did not want to merely portray Turandot as a cold and cruel woman. Instead, he wanted to depict her as a woman suffering much pain inside. Puccini also created Liu who was not in the original story and depicted her as the tragic heroine. Puccini died before completing the romantic duet which was supposed to be sung by Calaf and Turandot after Liu's death. Puccini usually composed tragedies and could not bring himself to write an ending for Calaf and Turandot's ending in marriage following Liu's death.

After Puccini's own death, one of his pupils completed the song and the premiere of the opera was conducted by Toscanini. During the premiere, Toscanini stopped the show after the scene in which Liu kills herself. Out of respect to Puccini, he told the audience: "Until this part is what the Maestro created." I would like to put my pen down and say "You were right, Puccini."

Behind the Scenes

Compare the thumbnails and completed pages of <One Thousand and One Nights>

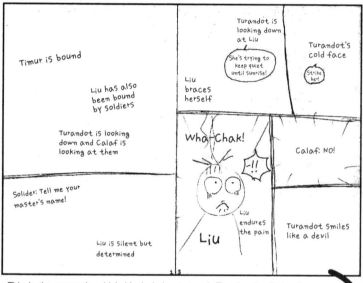

Timur is bound
Liu has also been bound by soldiers
Turandot is looking down and Calaf is looking at them
Solider: Tell me your master's name!
Liu is silent but determined
Turandot is looking down at Liu
She's trying to keep quiet until sunrise!
Liu braces herself
Turandot's cold face
Strike her!
Wha-Chak!
-!!
Liu
Liu endures the pain
Calaf: NO!
Turandot smiles like a devil

This is the scene in which Liu is being tortured. The thumbnail drawings are done by the writer, Jin-Seok. Some elements are added and others deleted by the artist so the final layout is not exactly the same as the thumbnails. It's the artist's job to flesh out the artwork from these thumbnails.

Compare the face of Liu!

-!!

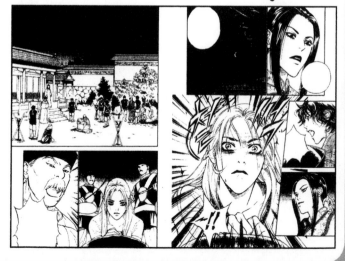

Congratulatory message from a colleague

Congratulations on the first issue of <One Thousand and One Nights>!
This comic book is gonna be a big hit!
Go for it, Seung-Hee Han and Jin-Seok Jeon!
- From Do-Chang

— 도짱

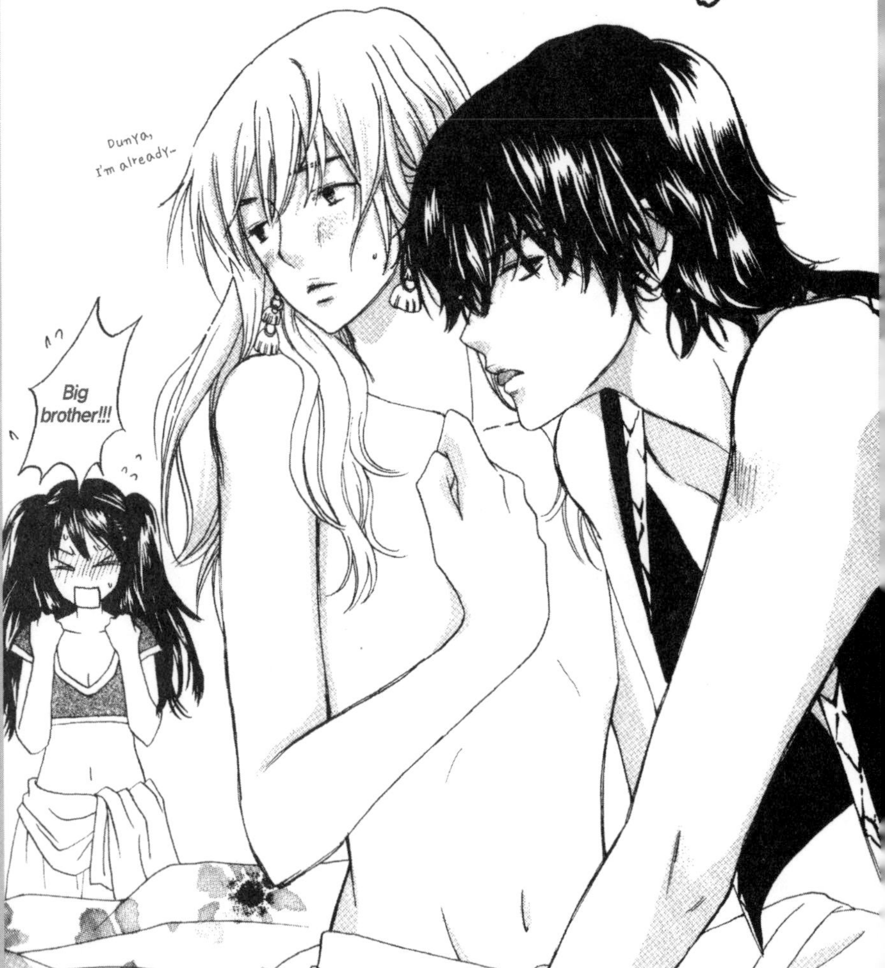

Dunya, I'm already...
Big brother!!!

Cynical Orange

vol.1

Yun JiUn

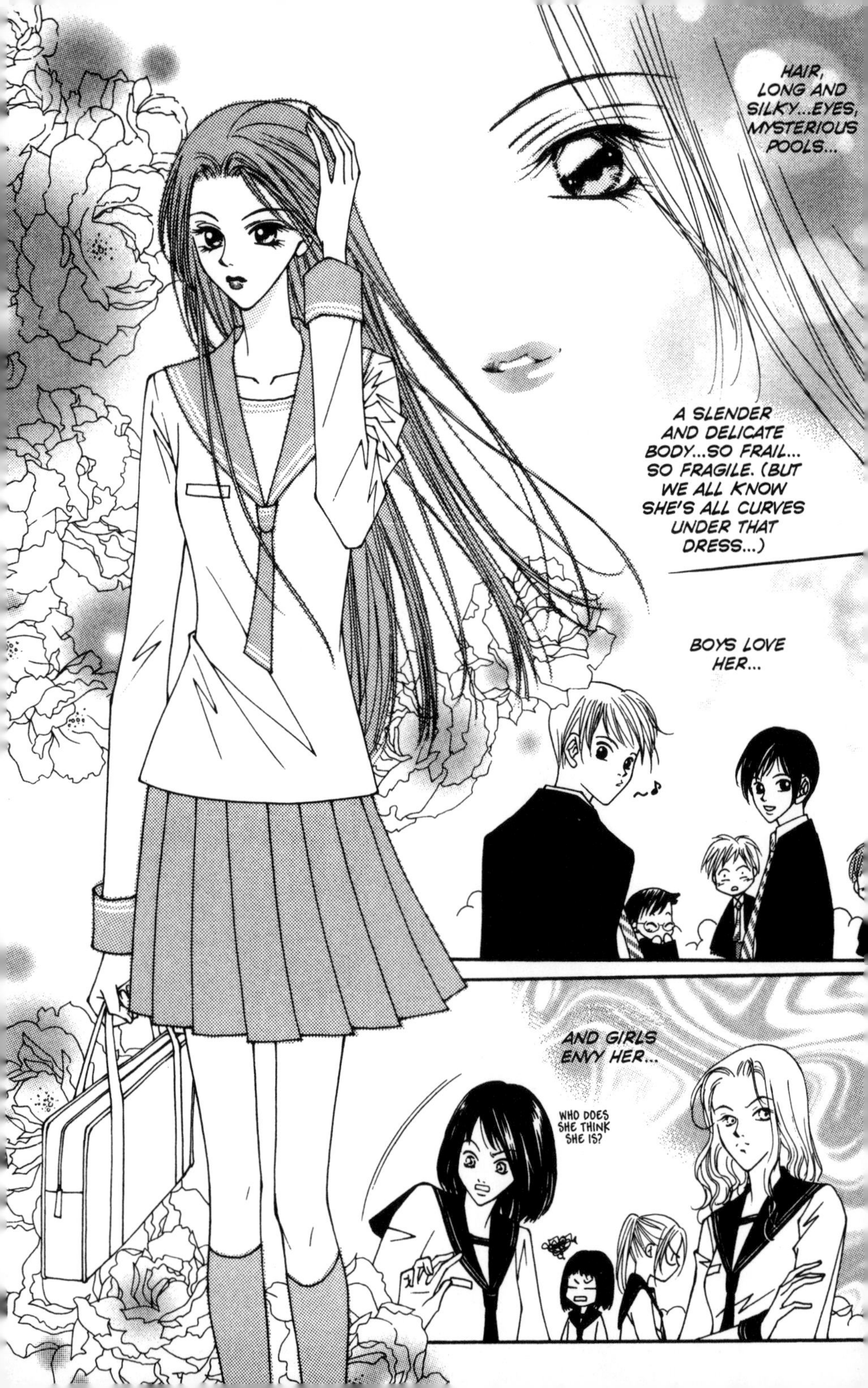
HAIR, LONG AND SILKY...EYES, MYSTERIOUS POOLS...
A SLENDER AND DELICATE BODY...SO FRAIL... SO FRAGILE. (BUT WE ALL KNOW SHE'S ALL CURVES UNDER THAT DRESS...)
BOYS LOVE HER...
AND GIRLS ENVY HER...
WHO DOES SHE THINK SHE IS?

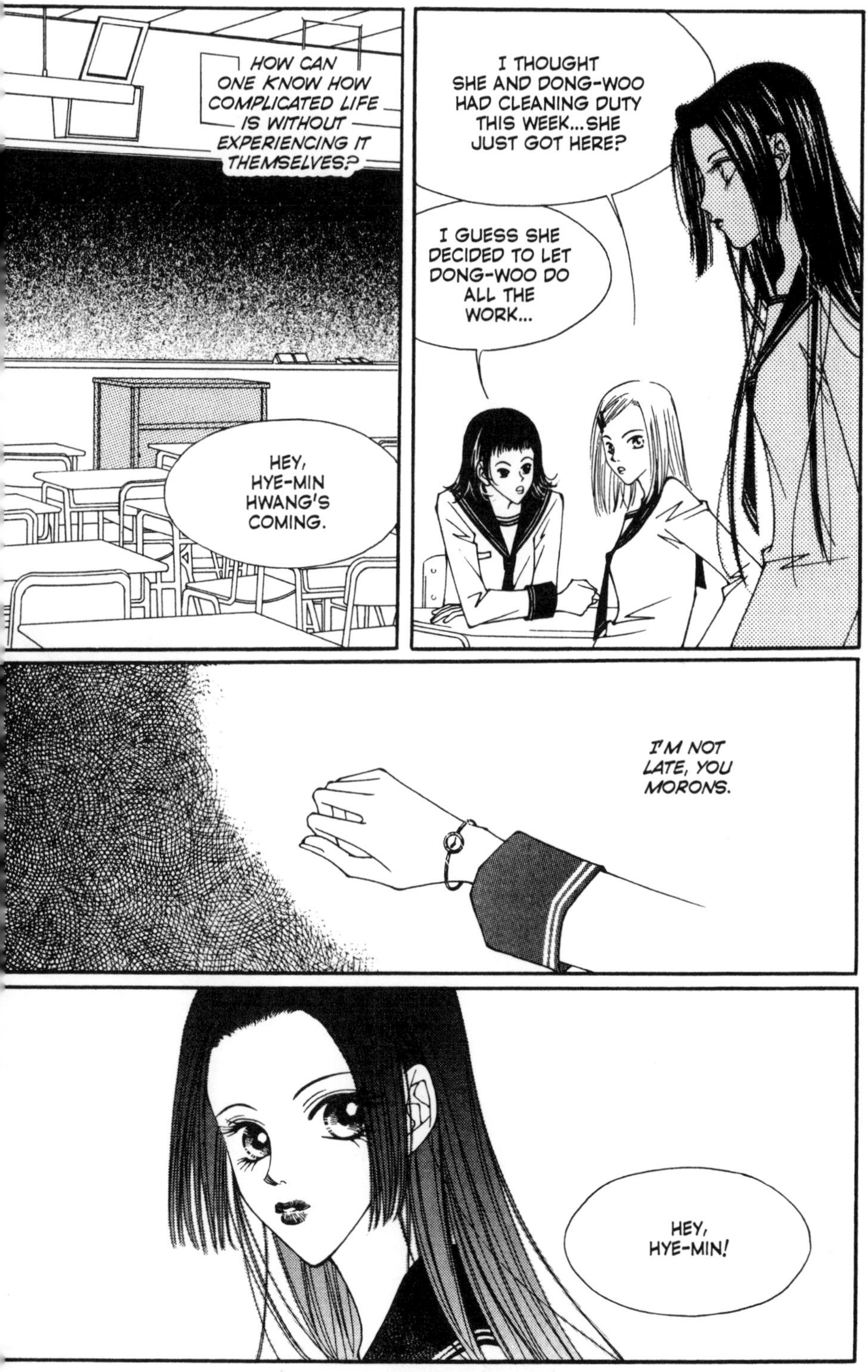
HOW CAN ONE KNOW HOW COMPLICATED LIFE IS WITHOUT EXPERIENCING IT THEMSELVES?
HEY, HYE-MIN HWANG'S COMING.
I THOUGHT SHE AND DONG-WOO HAD CLEANING DUTY THIS WEEK...SHE JUST GOT HERE?
I GUESS SHE DECIDED TO LET DONG-WOO DO ALL THE WORK...
I'M NOT LATE, YOU MORONS.
HEY, HYE-MIN!

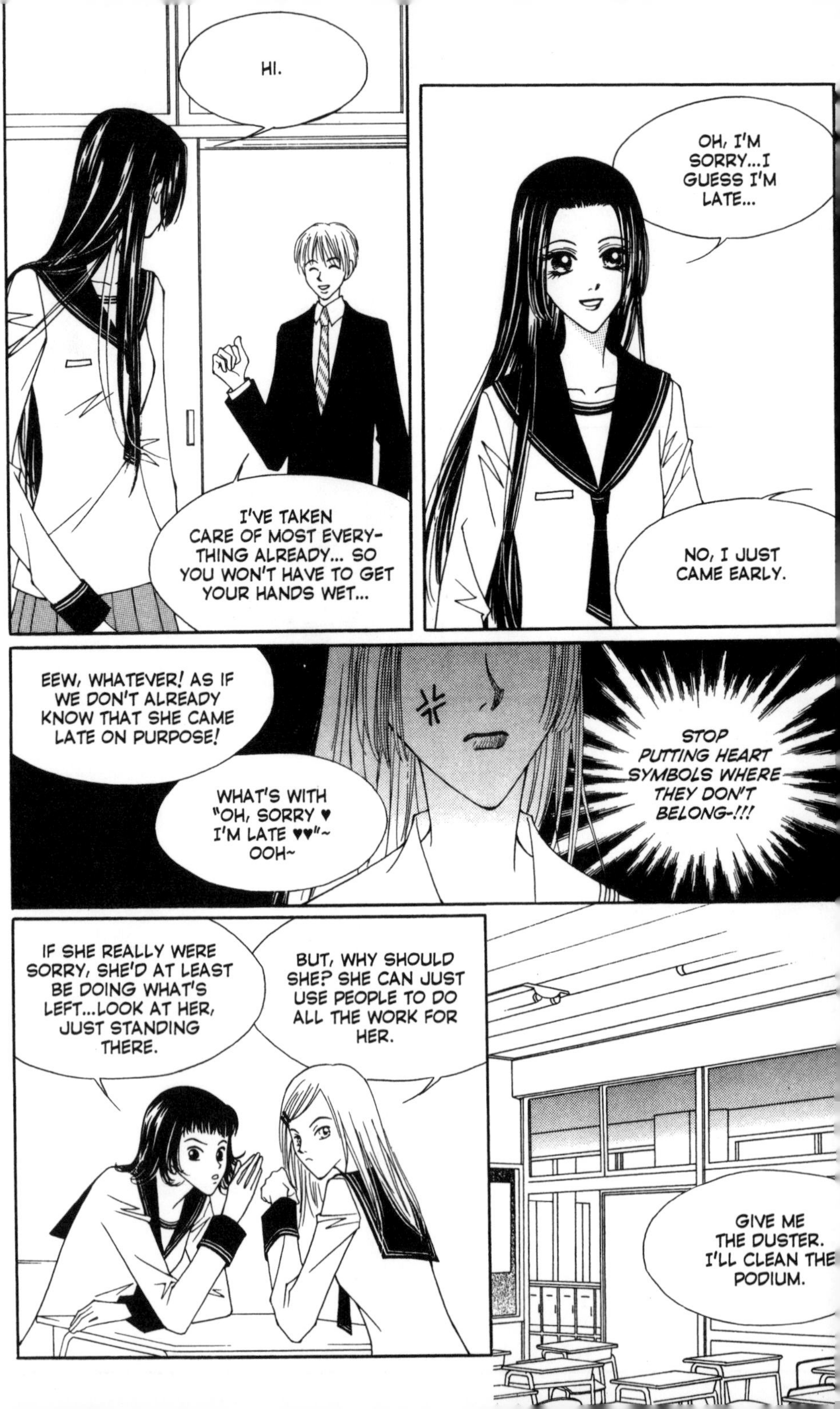
HI.
I'VE TAKEN CARE OF MOST EVERY-THING ALREADY... SO YOU WON'T HAVE TO GET YOUR HANDS WET...
OH, I'M SORRY...I GUESS I'M LATE...
NO, I JUST CAME EARLY.
EEW, WHATEVER! AS IF WE DON'T ALREADY KNOW THAT SHE CAME LATE ON PURPOSE!
WHAT'S WITH "OH, SORRY ♥ I'M LATE ♥♥"~ OOH~
STOP PUTTING HEART SYMBOLS WHERE THEY DON'T BELONG-!!!
IF SHE REALLY WERE SORRY, SHE'D AT LEAST BE DOING WHAT'S LEFT...LOOK AT HER, JUST STANDING THERE.
BUT, WHY SHOULD SHE? SHE CAN JUST USE PEOPLE TO DO ALL THE WORK FOR HER.
GIVE ME THE DUSTER. I'LL CLEAN THE PODIUM.

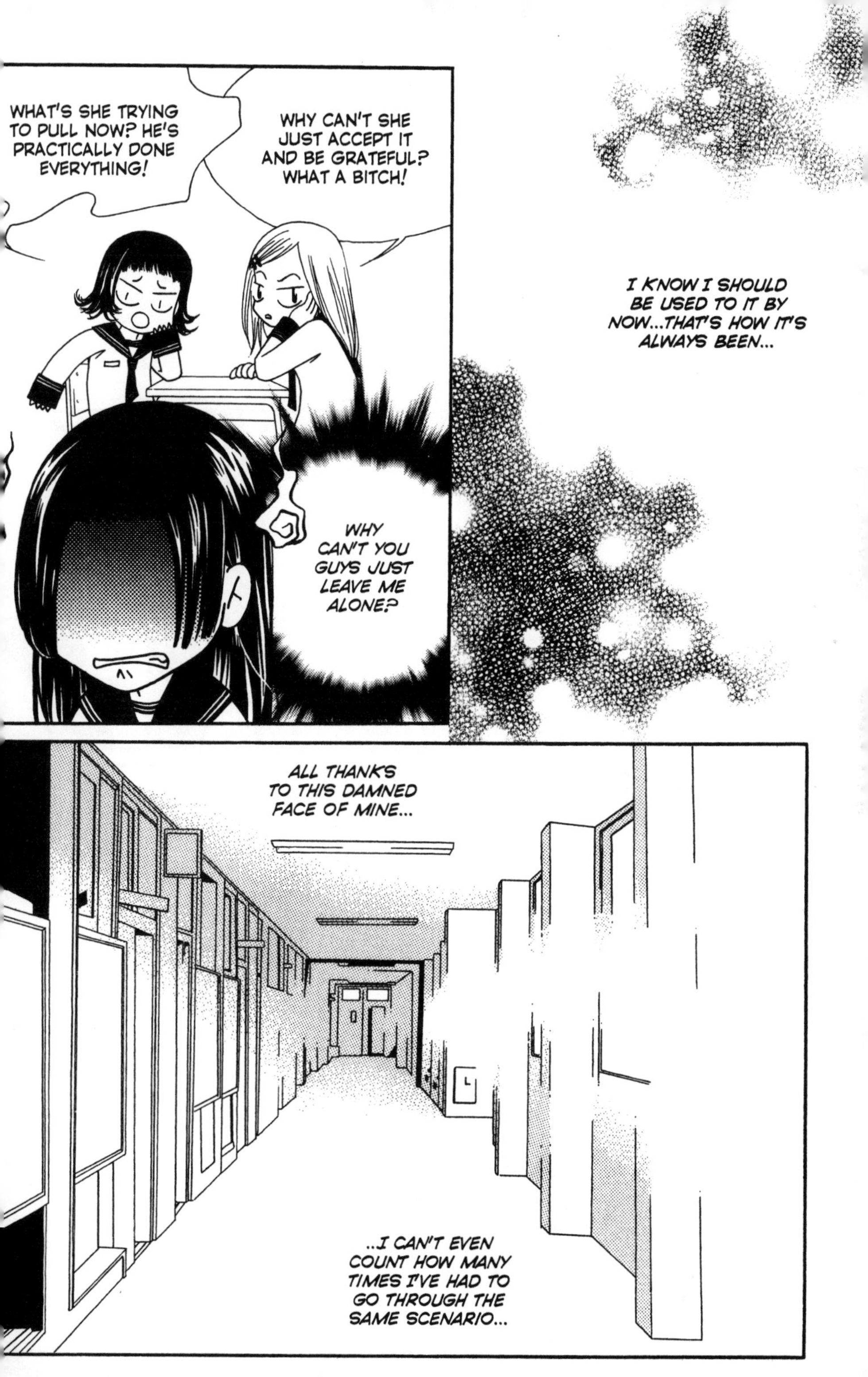
WHAT'S SHE TRYING TO PULL NOW? HE'S PRACTICALLY DONE EVERYTHING!
WHY CAN'T SHE JUST ACCEPT IT AND BE GRATEFUL? WHAT A BITCH!
WHY CAN'T YOU GUYS JUST LEAVE ME ALONE?
I KNOW I SHOULD BE USED TO IT BY NOW...THAT'S HOW IT'S ALWAYS BEEN...
ALL THANKS TO THIS DAMNED FACE OF MINE...
...I CAN'T EVEN COUNT HOW MANY TIMES I'VE HAD TO GO THROUGH THE SAME SCENARIO...

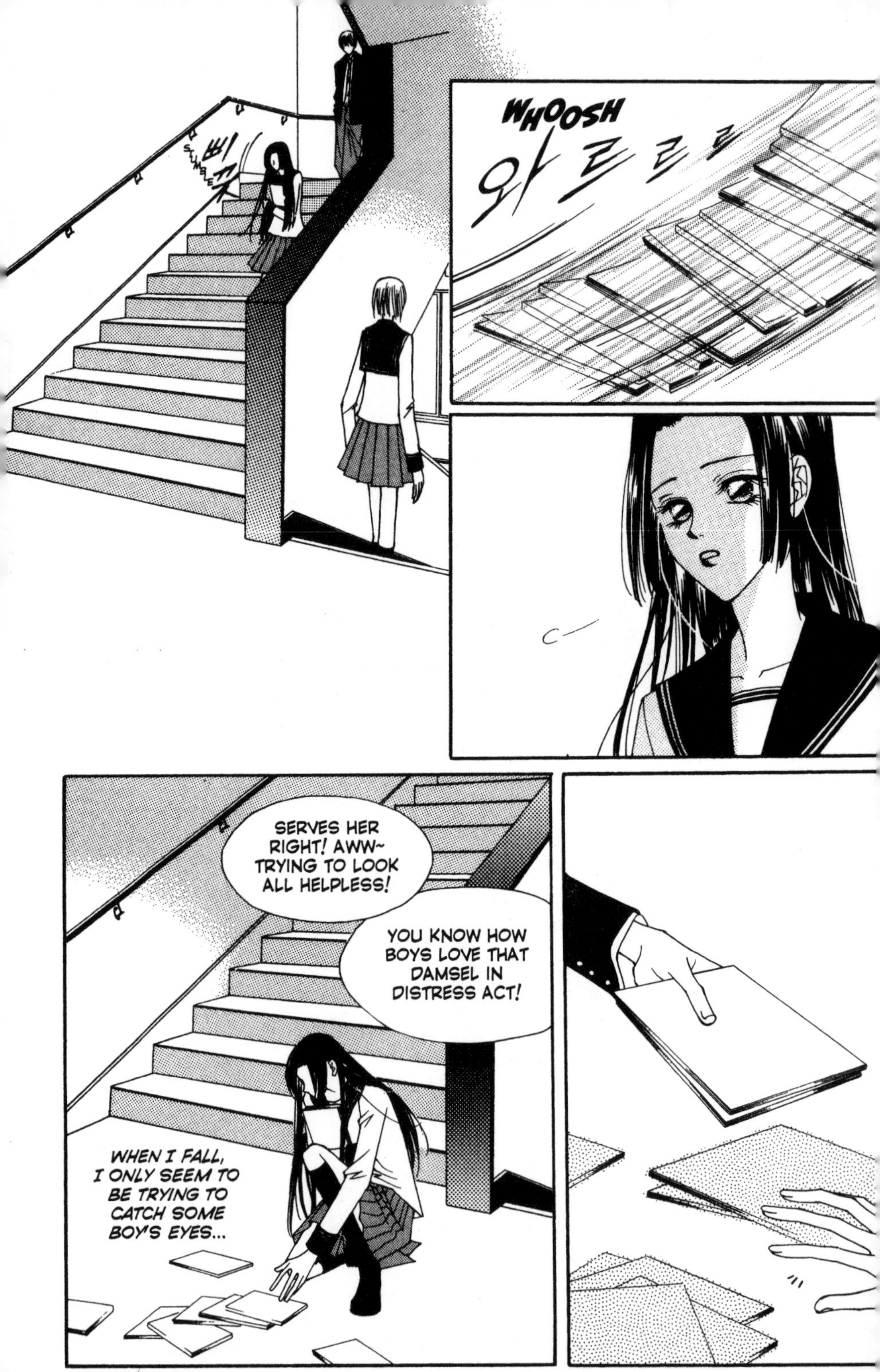
STUMBLE
WHOOSH
와르르
SERVES HER RIGHT! AWW~ TRYING TO LOOK ALL HELPLESS!
YOU KNOW HOW BOYS LOVE THAT DAMSEL IN DISTRESS ACT!
WHEN I FALL, I ONLY SEEM TO BE TRYING TO CATCH SOME BOY'S EYES...

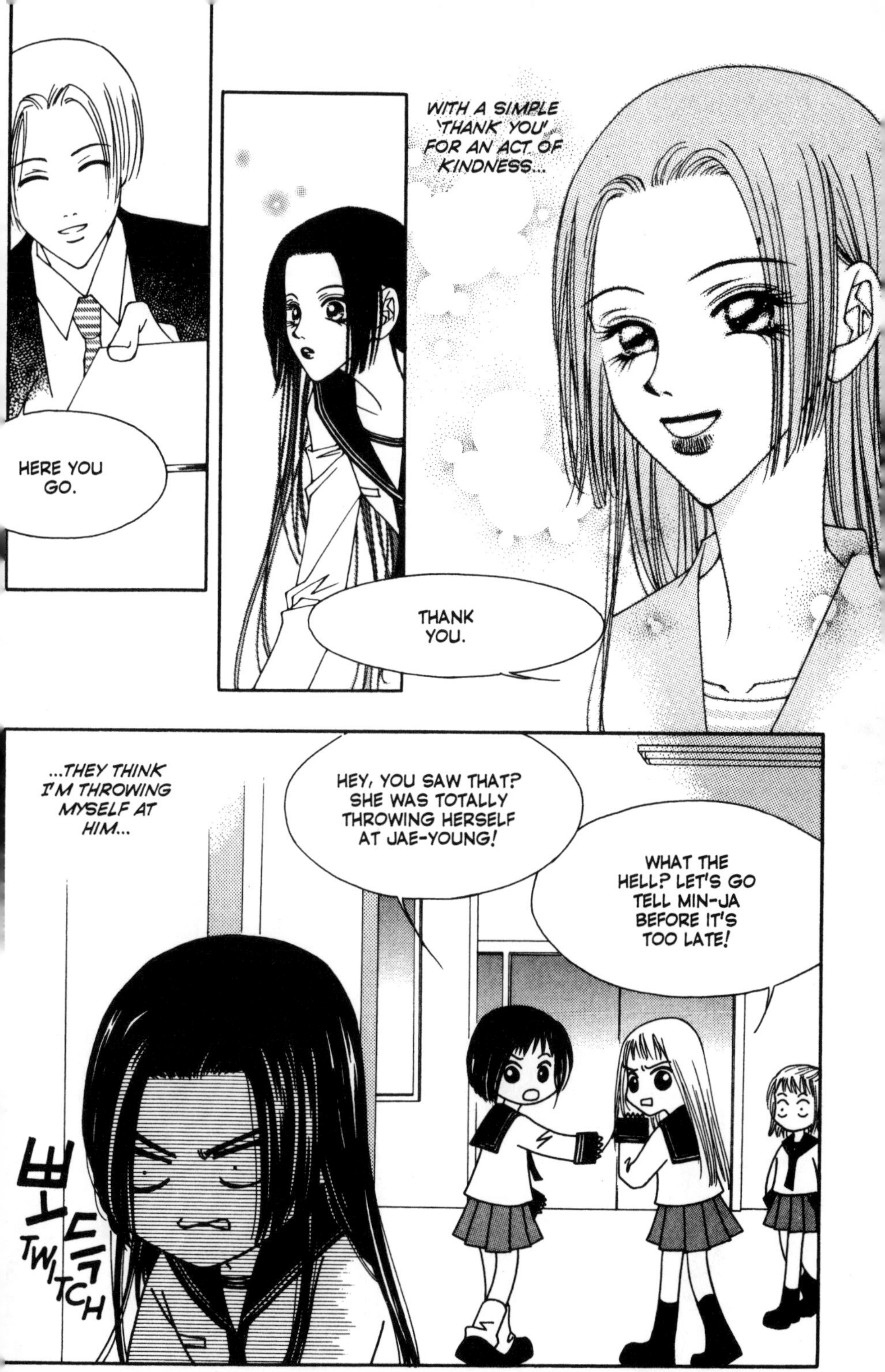
HERE YOU GO.
WITH A SIMPLE 'THANK YOU' FOR AN ACT OF KINDNESS...
THANK YOU.
...THEY THINK I'M THROWING MYSELF AT HIM...
HEY, YOU SAW THAT? SHE WAS TOTALLY THROWING HERSELF AT JAE-YOUNG!
WHAT THE HELL? LET'S GO TELL MIN-JA BEFORE IT'S TOO LATE!
빠드득
TWITCH

ALTHOUGH I RARELY SAY MORE THAN 10 WORDS IN SCHOOL,

MORE THAN 100 FOLLOW...

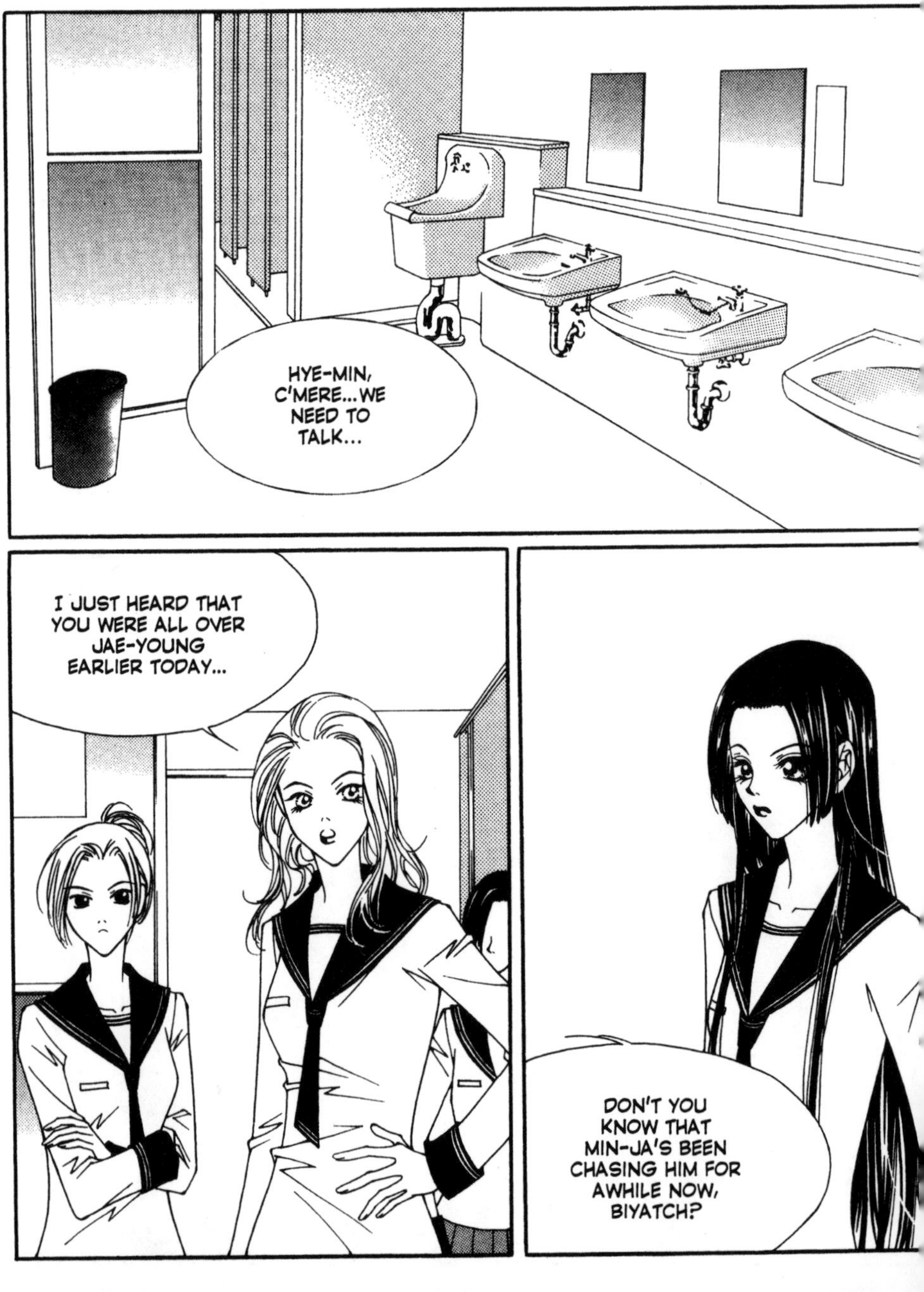
HYE-MIN, C'MERE...WE NEED TO TALK...
I JUST HEARD THAT YOU WERE ALL OVER JAE-YOUNG EARLIER TODAY...
DON'T YOU KNOW THAT MIN-JA'S BEEN CHASING HIM FOR AWHILE NOW, BIYATCH?

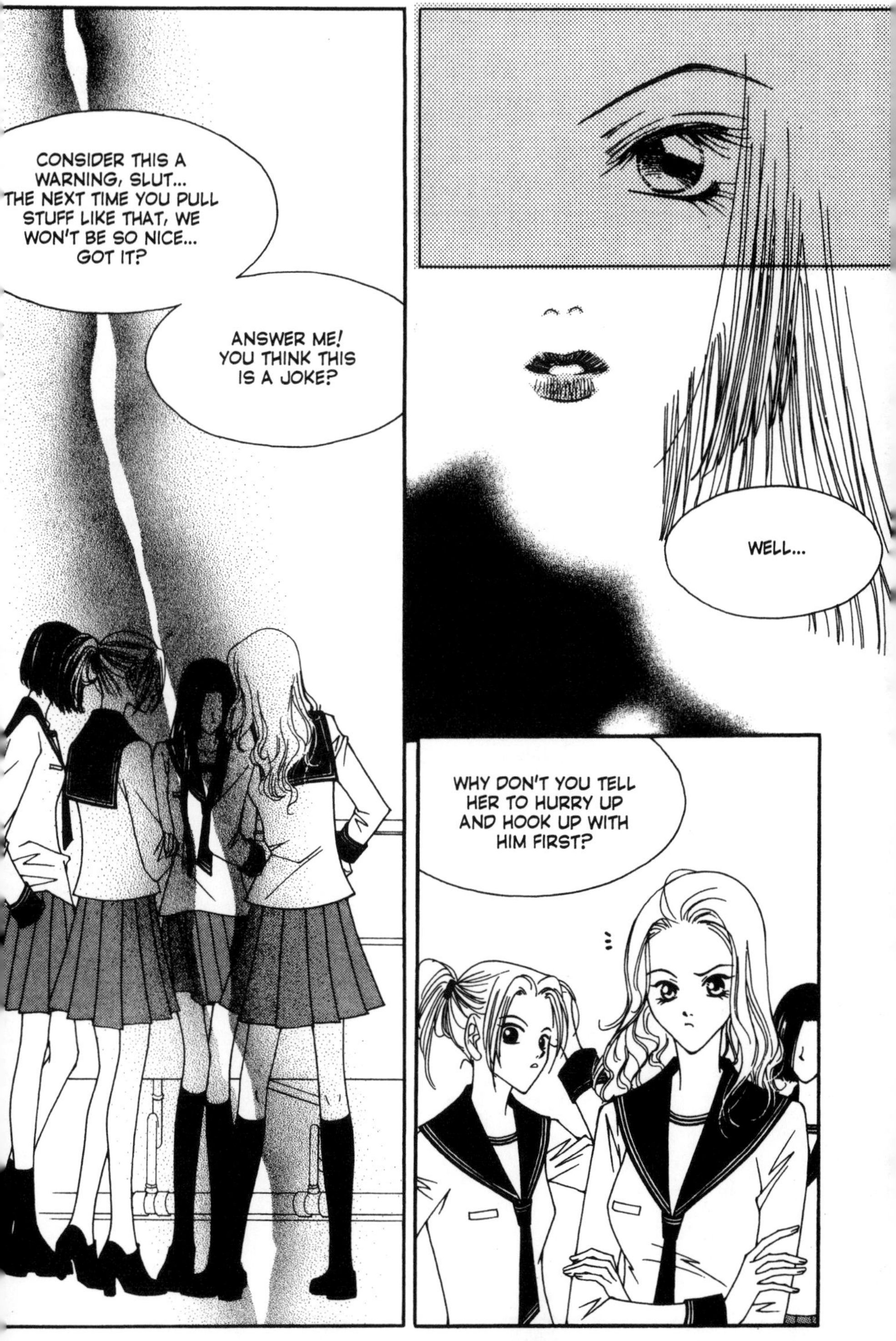
CONSIDER THIS A WARNING, SLUT... THE NEXT TIME YOU PULL STUFF LIKE THAT, WE WON'T BE SO NICE... GOT IT?
ANSWER ME! YOU THINK THIS IS A JOKE?
WELL...
WHY DON'T YOU TELL HER TO HURRY UP AND HOOK UP WITH HIM FIRST?

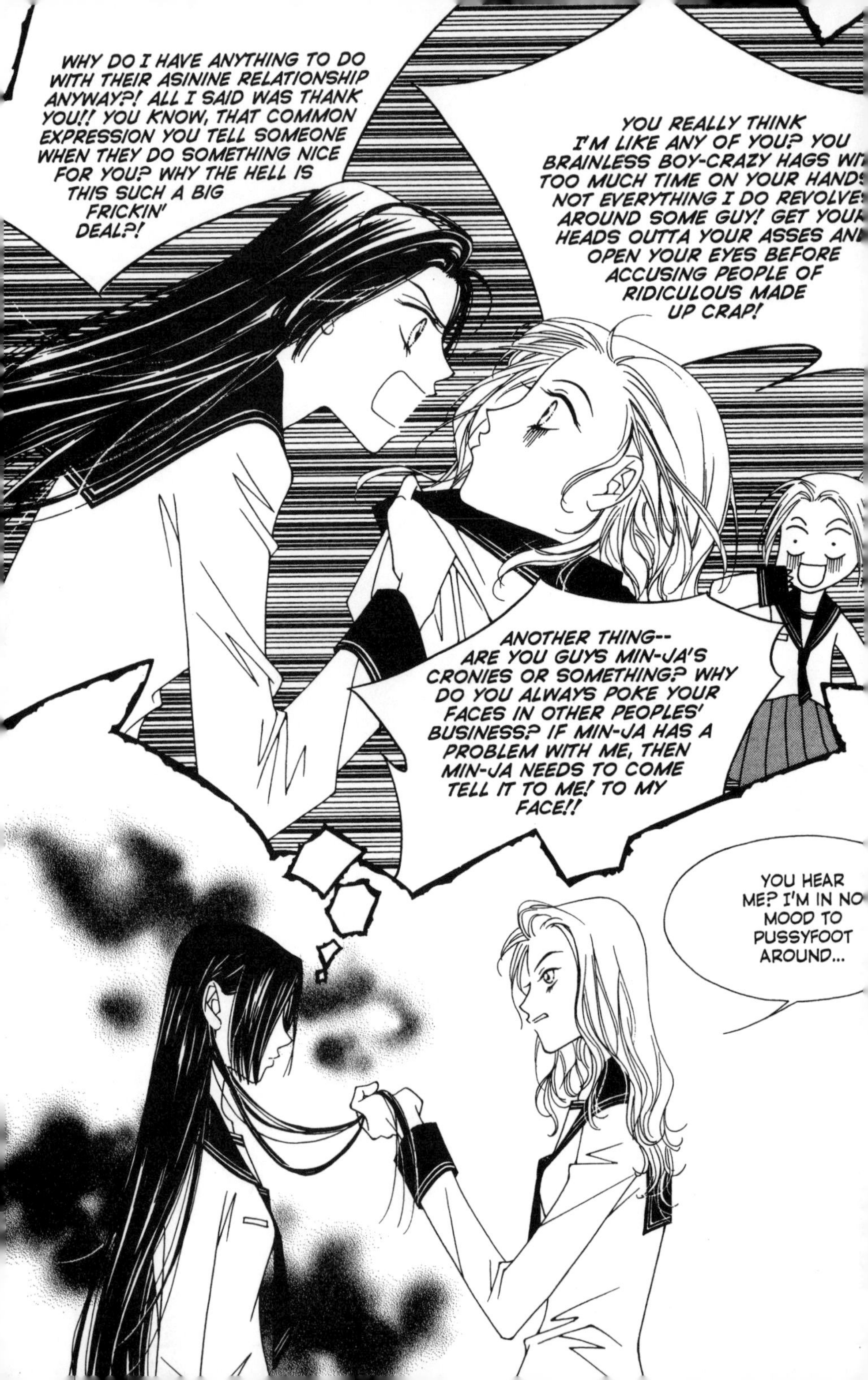
WHY DO I HAVE ANYTHING TO DO WITH THEIR ASININE RELATIONSHIP ANYWAY?! ALL I SAID WAS THANK YOU!! YOU KNOW, THAT COMMON EXPRESSION YOU TELL SOMEONE WHEN THEY DO SOMETHING NICE FOR YOU? WHY THE HELL IS THIS SUCH A BIG FRICKIN' DEAL?!
YOU REALLY THINK I'M LIKE ANY OF YOU? YOU BRAINLESS BOY-CRAZY HAGS WI TOO MUCH TIME ON YOUR HANDS NOT EVERYTHING I DO REVOLVES AROUND SOME GUY! GET YOUR HEADS OUTTA YOUR ASSES AN OPEN YOUR EYES BEFORE ACCUSING PEOPLE OF RIDICULOUS MADE UP CRAP!
ANOTHER THING-- ARE YOU GUYS MIN-JA'S CRONIES OR SOMETHING? WHY DO YOU ALWAYS POKE YOUR FACES IN OTHER PEOPLES' BUSINESS? IF MIN-JA HAS A PROBLEM WITH ME, THEN MIN-JA NEEDS TO COME TELL IT TO ME! TO MY FACE!!
YOU HEAR ME? I'M IN NO MOOD TO PUSSYFOOT AROUND...

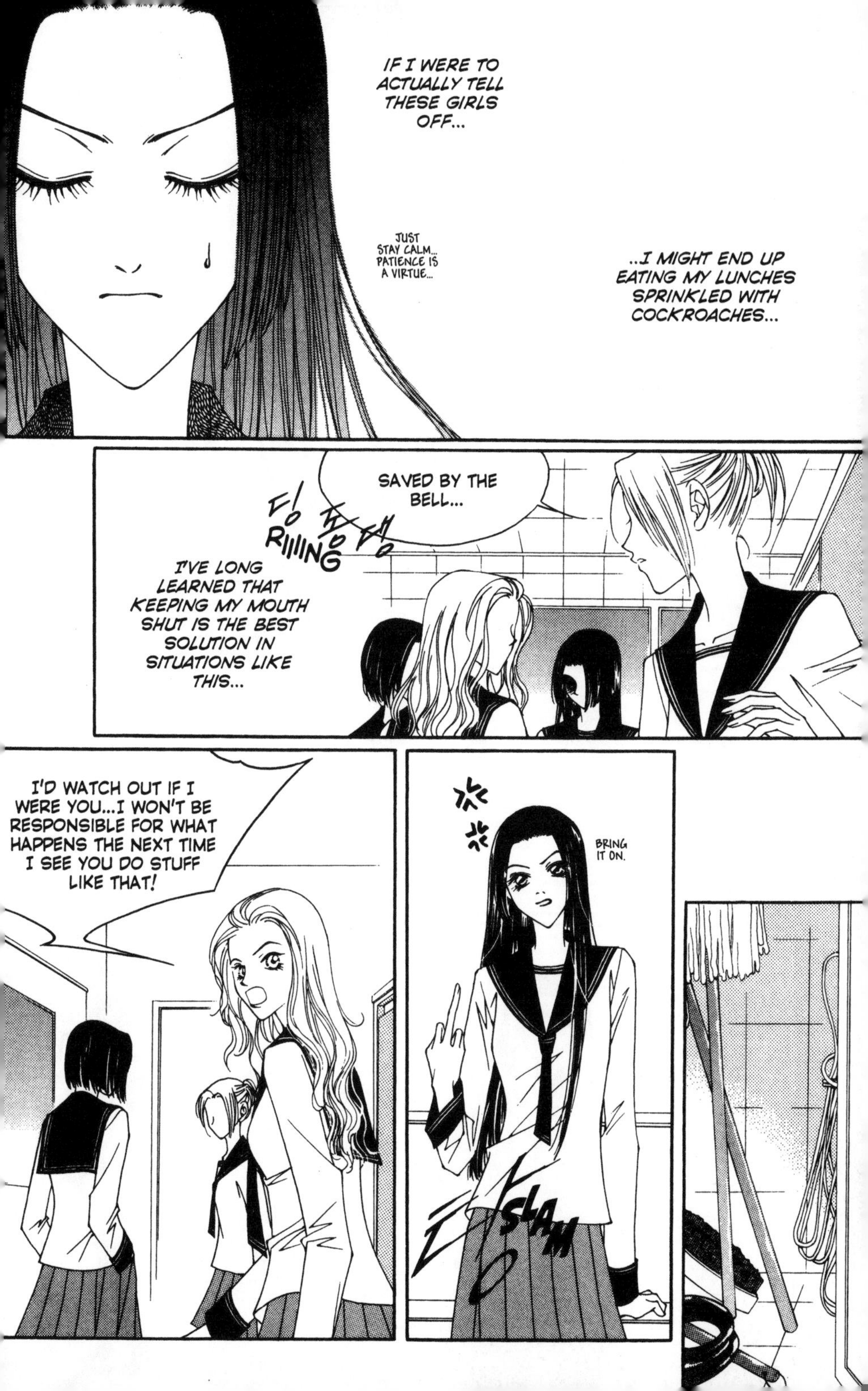
IF I WERE TO ACTUALLY TELL THESE GIRLS OFF...
JUST STAY CALM... PATIENCE IS A VIRTUE...
...I MIGHT END UP EATING MY LUNCHES SPRINKLED WITH COCKROACHES...
RIIIING
SAVED BY THE BELL...
I'VE LONG LEARNED THAT KEEPING MY MOUTH SHUT IS THE BEST SOLUTION IN SITUATIONS LIKE THIS...
I'D WATCH OUT IF I WERE YOU...I WON'T BE RESPONSIBLE FOR WHAT HAPPENS THE NEXT TIME I SEE YOU DO STUFF LIKE THAT!
BRING IT ON.
SLAM

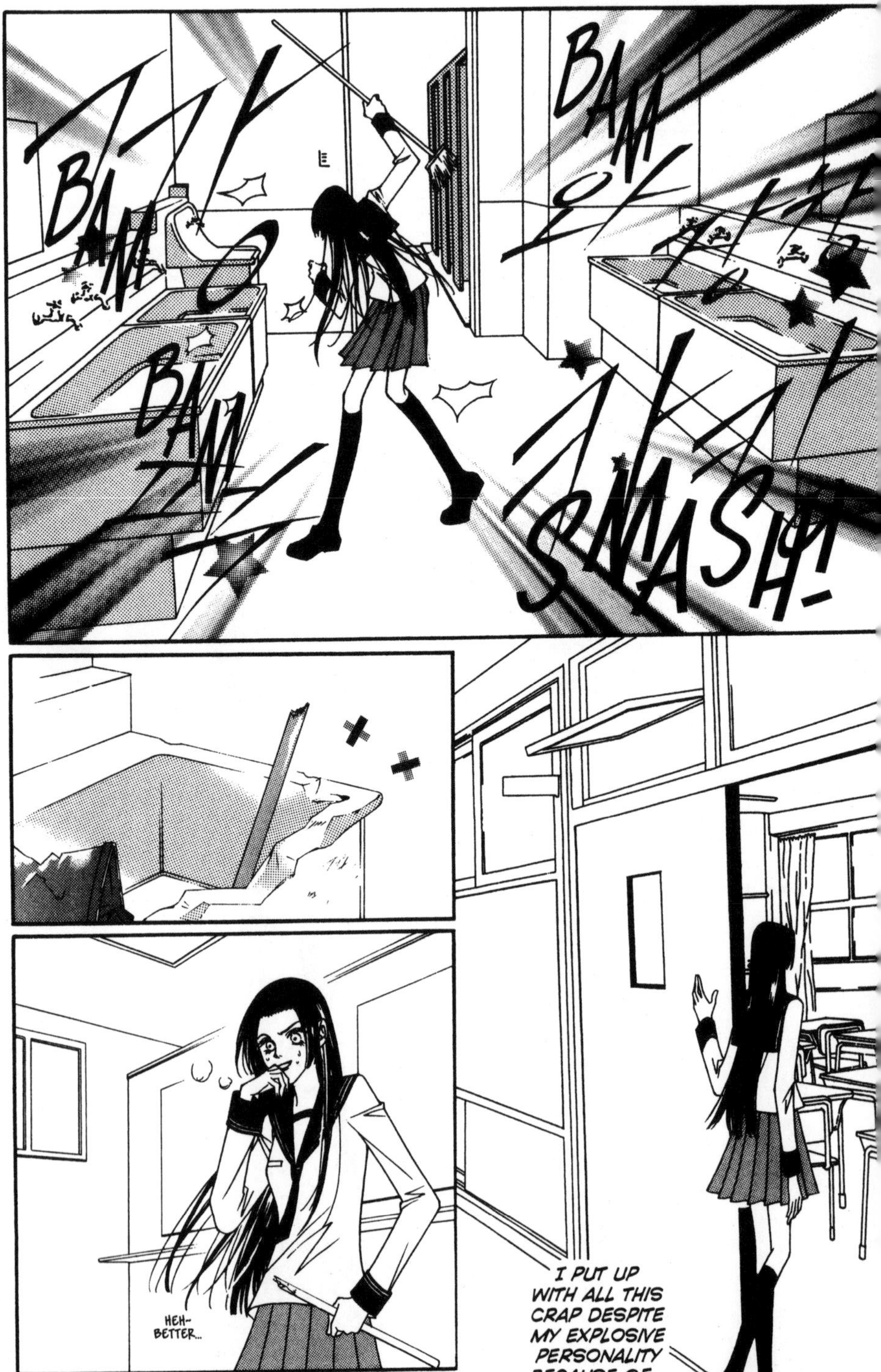
BAM
BAM
BAM
SMASH!
HEH-
BETTER...
I PUT UP WITH ALL THIS CRAP DESPITE MY EXPLOSIVE PERSONALITY BECAUSE OF...

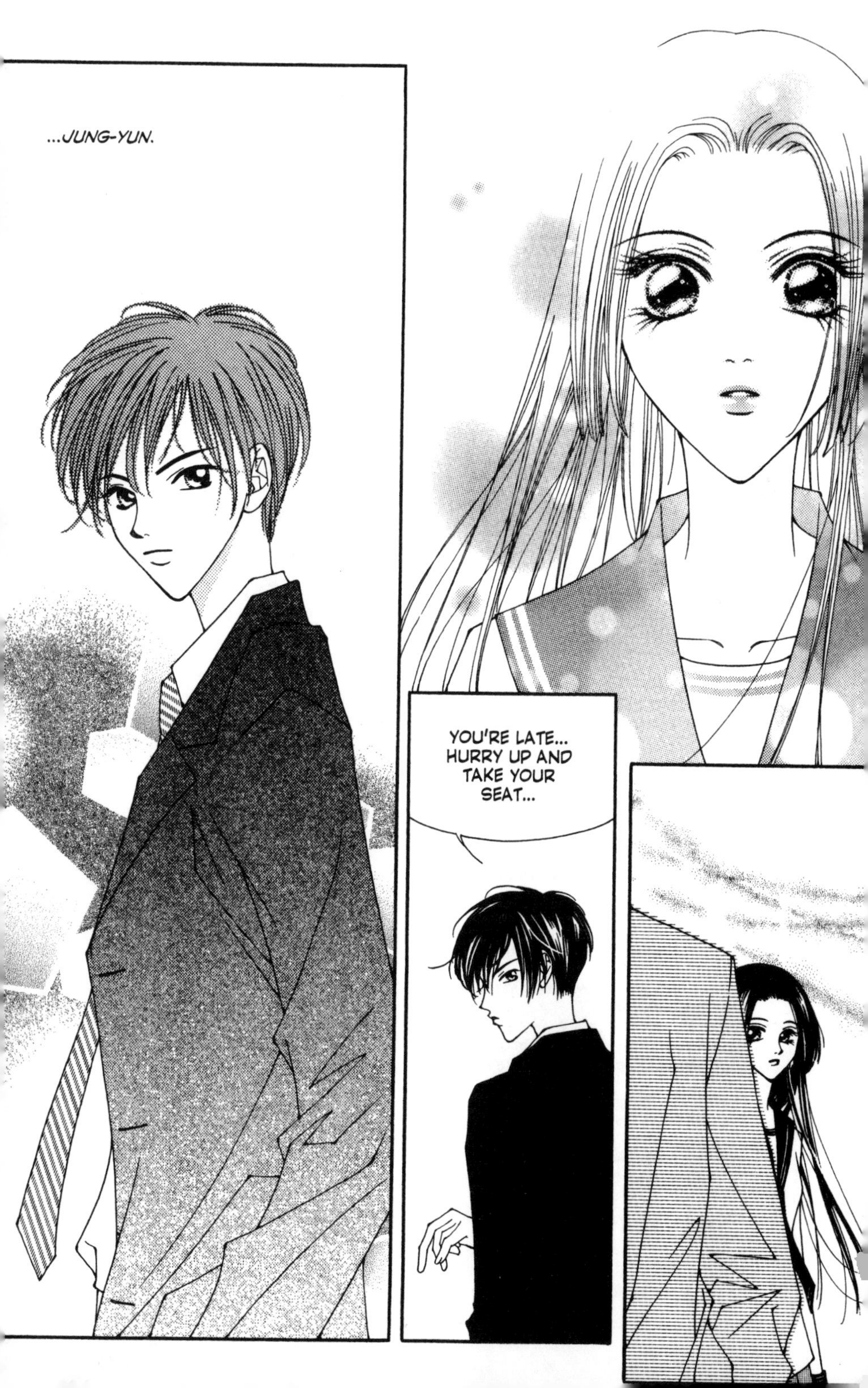
...JUNG-YUN.
YOU'RE LATE... HURRY UP AND TAKE YOUR SEAT...

One Thousand and One Nights vol. 1

Story by JinSeok Jeon
Art by SeungHee Han

Translation: HyeYoung Im · J. Torres
English Adaptation: J. Torres
Lettering: Marshall Dillon

One Thousand and One Nights, Vol. 1 © 2004 SeungHee Han · JinSeok Jeon. All rights reserved.
First published in Korea in 2004 by SEOUL CULTURAL PUBLISHERS, Inc. English translation rights
arranged by SEOUL CULTURAL PUBLISHERS, Inc.

Yen Press
Hachette Book Group USA
237 Park Avenue, New York, NY 10017

Visit our Web sites at www.HachetteBookGroupUSA.com and
www.YenPress.com.

Yen Press is an imprint of Hachette Book Group USA, Inc. The Yen Press name and logo are
trademarks of Hachette Book Group USA, Inc.

First English Printing: December 2005
First Yen Press Edition: May 2008

ISBN-10: 89-527-4470-5
ISBN-13: 978-89-527-4470-8

10 9 8 7 6 5 4 3 2

BVG

Printed in the United States of America